FROM LUCKER STREET
TO
WONGAWILLI

[A story of Australia]

Ian Patterson

GET Publishing

First Published in Great Britain in 2006
by GET Publishing, Bridgnorth, Shropshire WV15 5DG
info@getpublishing.co.uk

Copyright © James Ian Patterson 2006

The right of James Ian Patterson to be identified as author of this work has been asserted by him in accordance with the Copyright, Designs and Patents Act, 1988

ISBN 0-9548793-6-8

All rights reserved. No part of this publication may be reproduced in any form or by any means, graphic, electronic or mechanical, including photocopying, recording, taping or information storage and retrieval systems - without the prior written permission of the publisher.

Printed in the United Kingdom by
Direct Imaging Limited, 3 Prince Road, Kings Norton, Birmingham B30 3HB

Acknowledgements

The author would like to thank all our family members, whether in Australia or Britain, without whose help this book would never have seen the light of day. Special thanks to our son John for the sketches and granddaughter, Jessica for being a technical whiz. Lastly, and by no means least, thanks to my wife Patsy for her continued forbearance and support.

Introduction

Every story must have a beginning, and ours must start in a wretched London, back in 1784. It is half past three in the morning and, already, servants in the big houses near St. Paul's Cathedral are rising to greet the early summer light.

One such girl, a scullery maid, late as usual and her hair a mess, hurries to the coal cellar, intent on nothing except getting a blaze going in the kitchen, before the heavy-handed cook puts in an appearance.

At that cellar door three life times ago, my life like countless others, changed. The lass, now forgotten by history, had interrupted a burglary and whilst the shadowy figure outside continued to focus on removing an iron bar from the small fanlight, off she crept to raise the alarm.

"Gotcha!"

James Morrisby, a newly married man from Yorkshire, moonlighting as a night watchman from his job as a soldier stationed in the Tower of London, was arrested and charged with the theft of an iron bar worth ten pence.

On the 26th January, 1788 our James Morrisby landed with the First Fleet on the shores of the eighteenth century's equivalent of Mars: Australia! There was no return ticket, and he would never see his wife and child again.

As coincidence would have it another of our ancestors was one of his gaolers, a Marine by the name of James Angell.

The two Jameses went about populating the new colony with some vigour and, whereas I do not suppose for one minute the hard land ensnared the unwilling with its beauty and mystery, subsequent generations from our British family tree have been wooed by its intrigue, its love, its brazen seduction and, most of all, by its promise.

My wife, Patsy, and I, have been incredibly fortunate. Australia has welcomed us so many times now and enriched our lives with its haunting images, enigmatic vitality and sheer diversity. Yet, Australia has terrified us too. I suspect terror was one of our forebears' constant companions, whereas we only glimpse it occasionally, when the veneer of western civilization is stripped away by its unforgiving, raw power.

Our people may not have made historic, epic journeys through the continent's deserts, jungles or mountains, but they are real people who saw Australia lift herself from a starving handful of dispossessed to become a great nation.

In this book, we seek to discover the Spirit of Australia - and that of its people today, by travelling along the pathway left for us by the pioneering generations who fled the back alleys of Lucker Street for a new life in a new land.

Journey 1
Victoria

Werribee

It is ten in the morning, and we are getting our first view in five years of the 'Lucky Country.' Down there, Australia is a permanent living contradiction. We pass low over deserted, brilliant yellow crescent moons of sand, strung together as if some crazed creator had not been able to stop repeating perfection.

After the beaches; the trees: Endless trees: Million upon million, stretching for as far as the eye can see. A greenery denied by my generation of insular schooling. A desert continent should not be green...and then, to add insult to injury, the mountains, snow-capped and proud.

We land and are whisked away into 'the country', where the contradictions continue unabated. The trees, so green from above, display blackened and charred trunks beneath the canopy. A grass fire burns, yet no one bothers. The Fire Station is engulfed in smoke from a second blaze, but the fire risk indicator board out front says, 'Low Risk Today,' so the single engine sleeps on, oblivious to the billowing smoke, ash and fiery embers.

Eventide: Drink in hand, under the Acacia tree we risk the affections of the shy honey-eaters and boisterous parrots above. Earlier, I had watched a citizenship ceremony on the telly. An English song writer is now an Australian. He says, "I've always felt, always been, an Australian."

I know how he feels, for I too, feel at home here.

Werribee Park

A sip of rather nice chardonnay to help lunch go down; followed by a spot of local sightseeing to ease our way into ancestral doings.

With one jet-lagged eye more or less open I spot a sign: 'The Hulme - Howell Expedition camped here, 1824.' Now why would they wish to camp so close to the sewage farm? Fair do's! It is a very nice sewage farm, with barbecue tables, picnic areas, and trees probably planted by 1877, when the town was the stagecoach post between Geelong and Melbourne, and the Chirnside brothers were busily implanting a piece of England into Victoria.

Their creation, Werribee Park, is a sad place for me: Interesting, but sad. They tried so hard to remain English; the house could be straight out of Derbyshire or Devon - solid stone, with etched glass depicting familiarities: fox, red deer, heron.

I suppose it was the same misplaced nostalgia which affected other settlers who had some good ideas - like releasing English rabbits into the unsuspecting bush. The rabbits did what rabbits do best - so much so that they threatened to overrun the whole of Australia at one stage. To eat the rabbits, why not release English foxes, who did what they do best - and ate everything they could. Add in feral pigs, dogs, buffalo, camels, toads; the wild horses called brumbies and, worst of all, the humble domestic cat. No wonder the native Australian wildlife is under siege. Extinction awaits many.

And I have not even mentioned the plants: blackberry from England; cacti from America and lantana from South Africa. All of them like it here very much indeed, so much so, they are now classed as noxious, sprayed with any and everything imaginable. And still they gobble up the countryside.

Here, on their estate, the Chirnsides did their bit. Even in their garden today are the silver birch, weeping willow and roses of yesteryear, all vying with palms, gums and bottle brush. Blackbird song fills the air and, for a moment, it could be England. Then a brilliant blue wren breaks cover.

You cannot hide from Australia. It is over thirty degrees in the shade, and even the wealthy Chirnside agriculturists could not stay inside their illusion forever. No, this is not England, for England does not have the extremes of weather or the dangers of the garden; for, like Eden, it is flawed.

Mike, ex- R.A.A.F., his white hair belying a non-stop energy, tells me about Charlie Lash.

"This area is infested with Tiger Snakes," begins Mike.

"Poisonous?" I enquire, knowing the answer.

"Not deadly, but, unlike most other snakes, they come after you."

Enter Charlie.

Mike continues, "Charlie was the local snake catcher for years and paid by results. This one day I'm in the boss's office: "How many Tigers today, Charlie?" the Squadron Leader type says, smoothing his ridiculous moustache. "Thirty-one or thereabouts," replies Charlie. "You'll have to be more specific than that. I can't pay out on 'thereabouts.' " With that, Charlie heaves his writhing canvas bag onto this bloke's desk. "Wanna count 'em?"

Charlie got his money!

The Badlands of Ballarat

So what has brought us here to Victoria? - to this now bustling and prosperous Garden State, which was nothing but a lonely colony of sheep runs until gold was found, lying about all over the place, in 1851. That gold emptied Melbourne of all its able-bodied men within three years, all hoping to make their fortunes, just like the hordes of immigrants - British, European, Chinese - who joined them in the wild frontier lands around Ballarat and Bendigo. Now if this were an academic journal, no doubt we would have to discuss the effect that the lure of gold has had on the Australian psyche: But it is not, so one quick rejoinder will have to do; something for us to think about. Out here on the goldfields of this British Possession, all notions of the British class system ended. Out here, in the heat and dirt, members of the privileged elite worked alongside people who had nothing, and in some cases, were even employed by those who 'back home', they would not give the time of day to. Out here, all men were equal in two things: hope and freedom.

Our John Moresby, from Tasmania, was one of the sons of our First Fleeter. He never reached Ballarat. He died on the road to here, in the October of 1852, at the age of forty-seven years. His passing is not marked by any grave, nor, somewhat surprisingly, by any written records in the State archives in Melbourne. He left thirteen kids behind across the Bass Strait.

So he never got to take part in the Miners' Rising at the Eureka Stockade; nor did he get to see the wild frontier town of Ballarat, which is now our destination.

We have done our travelling the easy way. Walking through virgin country is replaced by a swift car ride on comfortable roads - with the air conditioning blasting away, of course. We defy the temperatures and the highway robbers - and I would like to be able to tell John that the town has preserved some nice old buildings from his time. They have erected a monument to the memory of the men who fought and died for their rights on the very rise where the stockade was; but, even more impressive, is Sovereign Hill, an authentic re-creation of 1850s life on the goldfields.

We were feeling good about ourselves. After all, we had ridden on a stage coach, emerged unscathed from a mine, panned for gold without a licence incurring the wrath of a stroppy copper. Yes! We could have done this; sought our fortune out here, amongst hard men and even harder women. No problems!

Then the temperature rose to forty-two degrees' centigrade and the kookaburras came.

Now kookaburras are possibly my favourite bird. It is all to do with their dishevelled look, hunched back, and that incredible hoo-hoo-hoo ha-ha-ha laughing call. The trouble is that they are by the barbecue where we're cooking up some grub, sitting on the tree branches only about three feet up, and taking a great interest in the ground cover about our feet.

Question: What do kookaburras eat?

Answer: Snakes! [Amongst other things:]

Now, whereas I am not too worried by 'other things,' I do worry about the 170 species of snake that presently populate Australia. I say presently, because new ones are being discovered occasionally. I do not know how many species are poisonous, how many are deadly, nor how many are benign. All I know is that seeing my favourite birds so close is a mixed blessing.

We watch them and they watch the ground, stubby beaks at the ready. Waiting patiently for grub and some action in the shrubbery, I cannot help but remember visiting a 'snake house' some twelve years ago. We passed exhibit after exhibit, each with an explanatory notice:

"This one is dangerous. A nasty bite:"

Next pit: "Need to get medical help in two hours."

Next: "You are dead in two minutes."

And again: "This one is more dangerous than the last one."

Aussie humour!

The kookaburras leave empty-beaked, and for the life of me I don't know whether to be relieved or disappointed.

Ararat - Havelock.

The township of Ararat snuggles beneath the mountains of the Grampian Range and is some two hundred kilometres west of Melbourne. It was founded in 1857, the same year as another of our families arrived here from the north east of England.

1857. That year, three thousand ounces of gold were just picked up off the ground - and 'sod's law' dictates that our John Reedhead, his wife Sophia Heslop, and their one-year old daughter, Sarah, did not see any of it, whilst others picked it up hither and thither. However, John had been blessed with his forebear's spirit - that of a certain notorious Scottish Border Reiver. You can see it in the twinkle of his eyes, staring out at you from behind a full, bushy beard. John had been a coal miner and an adventurous mariner, having jumped ship once before in Australia.

He must have liked it here, for he was back, taking his young family into the dense forest which covered the whole country. What is more, it was a dangerous place back then, with bush rangers, drunken miners and an astonished local wildlife. And there were John and Sophia, carrying all they owned on their backs, or maybe pushing a wheelbarra' to the 'easy' riches of Ararat.

Well, Sophia was some tough cookie; living in a bark shack, washing in the creek, cooking over an open fire, chopping wood with a great axe so big it looked as though it were swinging her, rather than the other way around. In her spare time a growing number of children were appearing on the scene; and, of course, hubby always needed a hand, shovelling about in the creeks.

After five years they gave it up as a bad job. Instead, they turned their hand to farming, staking out 275 acres about 90 miles to the east, around Havelock. Of course, the land we now see is cleared and the area and people look reasonably prosperous; but it was not like that when they first arrived. It is also fair to say that, despite having its own mini gold rush in 1858, the settlement has never been a centre for anything. By 1914, the population was only 265 souls, accompanied by a whole lot more sheep and cattle. Can't think things have changed that much.

It was here, in Havelock, that one of their sons was born - another John. This lad served the Empire in the trenches of a war-torn Europe, dying in the slaughterhouse that was the Somme in

1916. He has no grave; he merely ceased to exist.

So we felt.....reassured is probably the best word - to come across Milton, a survivor of war.

Milton's Welcome

Milton threw another piece of pear onto the open grassed area in front of the unspoiled nature reserve.

"We're really lucky to have all this in front of our verandas aren't we?" I said.

It had not taken much to break the ice with our neighbour, his loneliness being quite apparent to any but the casual observer.

"We sure are," agreed Milt. "Just watch now."

Another piece of fruit was despatched onto the lawn of the holiday units. We sat together, his life unveiling before me - and all the while I am bewitched by the antics of the regent bowerbirds. The radiant, royal-blue male dominated the scene - which just happened to include his dour brown mate, who turned up with the kids. He sure was making certain he got the pick of the fruit. The various, darting honey eaters and scarlet finches stood no chance. As we sat, it became a privilege to know Milton.

"With a name like yours I'd expect you to be an American," I joked.

"Nearest I've been to the States was in the war, when the Yanks gave us Aussies a lift back from North Africa: Took us to Timor, to fight the Japs. Weren't we lucky, though! Next ship in line to dock and the news came through that Timor had fallen. We skedaddled p.d.q., with two Jap submarines after us: Chased us all the way to bloody Cape Town. Was we lucky, or what? The old U.S.S. West Point was a fast 'un, and we zigzagged all the time. We eventually got to Adelaide via the Southern Ocean: Iceberg country. Jeez! It was cold, with seventy foot waves breaking over the bow. Jeez!"

"So did you get to fight the Japs?"

"Oh yes! They only gave us two weeks' leave and then we were sent to the islands."

"The islands?"

"The Philippines: Oh, we got around a bit."

"A good friend of ours lives in Melbourne," I said. "Her dad....."

"Hold on a sec.," he interrupted: "Watch!"

From under his chair he produced a bag of chicken leftovers and cheese which he emptied in a heap onto the grass.

I don't know how I hadn't seen it - day dreaming again, I suppose - but a huge goanna, scaly face streaked with blue, wandered out of the shade, tongue flickering, and walloped the lot, bones 'n all.

The goanna retreated majestically with its crocodile walk and I took up the story again.

"Anyway, her dad served at Tobruk and when the Japanese entered the war, he ended up fighting in Borneo. He was so appalled by the cruelty, beheadings and what have you; he wouldn't buy anything Japanese."

"What's the good of cutting your nose off to spite your face? Make bloody good cars," he replied.

"So what happened after the war?" I prodded.

"Me and the wife looked after a property: Owned by an English bloke. We ran the place 'cos he only came out to put the crop in, and again at harvest.....It was a grand time.....We did everything together."

A baby 'joanna', following in parents' footsteps, was ignored. Milton was now too involved in a life long gone. However, the kites were not ignored - even the bumptious male bowerbird and the noisy rainbow lorikeets, did a runner from the soaring, searching, hungry pair of very rare brahimy kites.

"That's where I picked up the skin cancer," said Milton, continuing his story unabated. "Now I've got to cover up all the time."

To be honest, I had wondered at the socks, long trousers, long-sleeved shirt and beaten-up old hat with the biggest brim ever. I also couldn't help reflecting on another difference between Britain and Australia. No matter how hot or long a British summer was; there is no way I'd be allowed to wear Milton's canary yellow shirt, multicoloured red and orange trews and sweaty Akubra hat. Such a colour scheme would be met by cries from my wife, "I'm NOT going out with you dressed like that. Get changed - NOW!" But not here: Maybe it's the sun that allows you to strut your stuff?

I could not ignore the big-little lizard any longer. Well, he was ten feet up the house wall and climbing fast.

"Looks for birds in the eaves," Milt remarked casually and carried on. "It's me heart that stops me getting about a lot. Tried bowls since my wife died, but some bloke didn't like the way I chucked it. Felt like smackin' 'im in the kissa. It's not for me.....I'm happy enough here though, with my little pals."

Under a blue sky, my new-found friend dozes the afternoon away, whilst I sit surrounded by flowering hibiscus, powder-puff grevillea, and the wonderful bottle brush, hypnotized by Milton's welcoming committee. I can see why he is as content as a lonely person can be.

PS: I found out later that the male, royal blue bowerbird was no such thing. It was a drongo.* [I kid you not.] The male bowerbird is a fabulous yellow and black - so much for my knowledge of the natural sciences.

*Drongo is also an Australianism for a person who is an awkward simpleton.

Bendigo

Bendigo was built on gold - tons of it - and whatever was dug out, the town spent. That inheritance can be seen today in the delightful parks and impressive public buildings – which, incidentally, were all designed by one of their own - a German miner called Vahland.

However, nothing on view would have led yours truly to the conclusion that Vahland's Vunderland used to be one of the richest towns in the whole of the British Empire. This impressive statistic [gleaned from the guide books] is especially impressive when you are as old as I am and can remember world atlases being predominantly pink to indicate the extent of British possessions.

And it was to this thriving township that one Sydney Palmer Bulford came, a quarter of a century after the initial gold rush. Now Syd was not endowed with the genes of a Rothschild or a Bill Gates. No: He managed to buy a Cornish tin mine for three thousand pounds and only months later sold it for five bob. Today we would call it 'negative equity'. In 1875 it was the grounds for doing a runner from Victorian Britain and an inhospitable debtors' prison.

So here he came, to this lovely old town and, as far as I know, here he stayed, getting by on a bit of this and a bit of that. But England was not done with him. One of his sons returned to Europe with the Australian Infantry Force during World War 1, only to spend years of near starvation in the infamous German P.O.W. Camp of Soltau.

Guess that squared the books, poor lad.

The weather has broken. The walk in the park has turned decidedly soggy and so, bathed in warm, scented rain, we call it a day.

*

I found out later it was called a mouse spider. It was as big as a mouse....and furry. Its eyes were as big as mine, and were fixed on ME as it ran up the wheelie bin. It was determined to show me who was boss of the rubbish, not that I had any doubts. I dropped the lid, then the rubbish - and ran.....

"Don't be silly," said my wife. "It only wanted to get out of the bin."

"Don't you be silly," I retorted. "Mighty Mouse is big enough to lift the lid all by himself."

She didn't believe me.

That evening, the national news ran an item on spiders.

"The dry weather," began the newscaster. "But it's only just stopped raining," I cry.

"The dry weather," continues the news reader, oblivious to my contribution, ".....has made the poisonous creepy-crawlies leave the bush for your laundry."

The old story about redbacks [or black widow spiders] biting your bum whilst you are on the loo, is trotted out. But it's not a laughing matter. Whereas my mouse spider and the redback can cause such inconsequentials like pain, nausea, breathing difficulties, dribbling and numbness, the infamous funnel web is potentially fatal.

Helpful advice is given:

1. Check your washing, clean or dirty; the spiders are not that fussy.
2. Check your shoes.
3. A spider in water is not necessarily dead. They live for up to three days submerged, using air trapped in the fine hairs covering their body. So check your swimming pool.
4. If you are bitten by a funnel web, make sure you are near a hospital. You need the anti-venom pretty damn quick.
5. If possible, catch the offender.

"You must be joking," we cry in unison. The T.V. researcher has obviously never come face-to-face with an Aussie spider.

For sure, the Flickman* will be doing good business on the 'morrow.

I haven't seen 'the mouse' since - but emptying the rubbish has become an exciting job for daylight hours only.

*Specialist Pest Control Firm.

Kerang

And so to Kerang on the Loddon River in the far north of the State: It is ideally situated for agriculture, sitting as it does near to the confluence of the Murray and Loddon River valleys: Beautiful, green, rolling country.

Yet if we wanted to sit in the car for another couple of hours or so, and head west, we would come to a different world. We would hit the start of the Mallee, a huge expanse of desert covered in scrub, with its fingers reaching out for Adelaide. The scrub is the Mallee Eucalypt, which seems to be the only thing to thrive in the hostile environment.

The story is told about one Mallee farmer. The place was so dry that no rain had fallen on his property for seven years, causing him to fall on real hard times. Then, one day, a single drop of rain fell out of a clear blue sky and hit him on the head. It was such a shock that he fainted.....It took three buckets of dust being thrown in his face to bring him around!

However, I have no appetite to brave the journey, especially the heat, to try and find an unconscious farmer, or the rare and endangered Mallee fowl, for which the area is famed. This notable bird likes to stick its head down holes in the sand. Why?* - Who cares, 'cos I'm not going.

I am quite content to rummage about this good country, once settled by our Stewarts and Mowatts, and it does not take a great leap of imagination to see them as the pioneer homesteaders, creaking and swaying on bullock carts, leaving civilization further and further behind over the other side of the Great Dividing Range. Imagine their excitement, their relief, at finding such fertile land on which they could realise their dreams.

I don't suppose it was like this when the first mob arrived, but now the land is neatly broken up into paddocks. Stands of Eucalyptus give welcome shade to the farm animals; cattle stand knee-deep in pools of water; the green pastures are covered with the white dots of sheep; and here and there are little communities - the centres of activity away from the properties with their corrugated iron roofs.....And to me, it is those rust-coated roofs which epitomize rural Australia.

As well as a number of rivers hereabouts, the area is dotted with lakes, which have evocative names like 'Lake Charm', or 'Kow Swamp' - so it comes as no surprise to be offered a fishing trip.

* During the egg-hatching process, the male Mallee fowl makes an incubator of rotting vegetation, and then, for eight weeks, keeps sticking his head into it, to ensure it does not get too hot for the developing offspring.

The Futile Fisher

"Do come," he said.

"Yes! Please do," said Little Tom.

Still we dithered. I came out in a cold sweat. Monster sharks, world record breakers, are caught regularly just off the beaches: Great Whites, tigers.....fishing? No! No! No!

"It's not out at sea," he urged, seeing the naked fear in my eyes. Surprising that, as it was revealing itself to me much further down my anatomy.

Phew! I relaxed a little and my mind somersaulted back five years: A balmy day on Lake MacQuarrie. Still water lapped the hull of the yacht: Wonderfully lazy. It was a pity we moved from the jetty. There were waves out there - and the thrashing boom nearly decapitated me several times. Fishing? No, I don't think so.

"It's on a river," he mocked.

"We'll be on the bank," helped Little Tom.

What could go wrong? What better than a day's relaxation under the shade of an old tree: A meandering river: Maybe a beer or two: A barbecue for lunch.

"Mmmmh." No boats involved. "O.K.", we agreed.

If life were so simple: We were rolled out of bed before first light. It took three hours to drive there. River after river disappeared astern to the cry, "I know a real beaut-bonza place."

The beaut-bonza place was at the end of a track, signposted variously, 'Private!' 'Go Back!' 'Road Impassable.' The river was also in full flood.

Of course, the 'best place' was on the other bank.

"We'll wade over," he said.

"Watch my lips," I replied.

"No chance," said my wife more politely, no doubt contemplating a number of factors dismissed as unimportant by our benefactor. She listed them for his benefit:
1. The five foot deep swirling water. The second finger rose impolitely:
2. The black snake doing breaststroke against the current; and
3. The idea of spending the rest of the day in wet undies.

Abandoning the finger exercises, she finished with: "I'll chuck my line in right here."

Not even the carrot of seeing a duck-billed platypus - who lived just around the bend - on the other side of course - could move the immovable.

She chucked, and sat.

Exasperated, he and Little Tom walked the wrong bank this way and that, casting a line here and a line there. The lines hardly had time to sink before: "Nothing here! Move up a bit" and: "We should be on the other side, you know."

"I've caught one dad."

"Don't be silly," he said, not looking.

"Can you untangle my line from the bushes please?" I ask pleasantly for the umpteenth time.

"But I have caught one," insisted a near-tearful Little Tom.

"Well done, Tommo," said my wife. "Err.....What is it?"

"It's a yabbie," replied Tom proudly.

The freshwater crayfish was too small to eat and, in any event, it was covered in eggs. Throw it back.

"Let's move up."

"I've caught one," cried Tom excitedly.

"Well done!"

The mind is a funny thing. I was back facing decapitation on that yacht. My young daughter caught 27 fish in an hour. My even younger son: 17. My wife, three: Me? Not a one! Zero! Zilch! Even when I pinched my daughter's spot, I still got nothing, whilst she pulled fish from my vacated place as though there was no tomorrow.

"I've got another one," said Little Tom, becoming cocky with it.

By this time, the score was seven, nil-nil-nil.

Fishing!

As the tiddlers and yabbies went home, one after the other, my dream of a lunch of a large, tasty trout over a charcoal fire was disappearing as quickly as snow off a dyke.

"What's for lunch?" I nearly shouted the question as my stomach rumbled yet again.

"The pub, I think," he replied, admitting defeat. He yanked at his line entwined about branches - on the other bank. "As soon as I get this....." [Edited, for the sake of decency and Little Tom, who might get to read this:]

"But the pub's an hour back up the track."

"It's O.K. It's a real beaut place.....Come to think of it - it's the only place."

Fishing!

Benalla – Glenrowan

It is a long drag across the northern end of Victoria, from Kerang to Benalla and its smaller, but more famous neighbour, Glenrowan. But it is an important area for us as we have two tales to tell.

Both townships are on the Hume Highway, the modern name given to the old inland road which linked Sydney with Melbourne. It was along this road that the nineteenth century bushrangers robbed rich and poor alike. Ned Kelly, the son of an Irish convict, showed a certain dash and daring in his misdeeds, even holding up whole towns. Undoubtedly, his letter of 1879 addressed to the Australian people, in which he extolled the virtues of Australianess and Irishness whilst decrying the rule of the British authorities, gained him a legendary status.

Our connection to Ned was through the gang's blacksmith, someone called Devlin. With a name like that, he was obviously also of Irish descent. The whisper is that he dropped Ned Kelly right in the mire.....In June 1880 Australia's most famous outlaw was cornered at Glenrowan, where he donned his suit of black iron. Unfortunately, some blacksmith forgot to make the leg plates and in the shoot-out - guess where the coppers aimed for? He was captured and "done to death," [hanged] in Melbourne Gaol, only five months later.

Just down the road, on the way back to Melbourne, lies the small town of Benalla, once home to a typical modern-day Aussie hero. Meet our Don Maclean who led rather an exciting and charmed life. He ran away to war whilst he was still too young to join up, enlisting in the 13th Light Horse, part of the Australian Expeditionary Force, which sailed for Europe early in 1915. His parents were looking for him, of course - and found him just in time to give him a wave bye-bye as the troop-ship left the dock. Anyway, off Don went to the trenches of France, but on the way made a side trip to a little-known place called Gallipoli. He emerged, unscathed, from the war and returned home, only to enlist again when round two kicked off in 1939. This time his prize was North Africa and the defence of Tobruk, before being recalled to the Southern Hemisphere to fight the Japanese: He emerged, sound of wind and limb, for a second time.

But today, Don has followed the blacksmith and the highway robber into history and there is nothing to hold us here but memories and imagination; so we are off to the more tangible delights of Victoria's capital city.

Melbourne

I reckon I do not have what it takes to be a trailblazer: to put a bag on my back and walk 'out there'. We have been floating around Victoria for a while now: good roads, nice people, a good country - but.....but I am so pleased to have arrived in a major city. Australia always has that effect on me. I don't mind poking and prodding at its innards - I just need to touch base now and then; get some reassurance from the familiar.

And whether we had a reason to visit or not, there is no way we would leave Victoria without visiting one of the foremost cities of the world. Great vision by Melbourne's forefathers' means that, today, the city is a pleasure to behold: plenty of parks and gardens; the arts; wonderful shopping at the multicultural markets and the visionary Diamaru Centre which encompasses the old, fifty metre high Coops Shot Tower.

Our guide is a good friend and budding author, Natalie Gretton. Just at this moment she is pointing at the gleaming yellow edifice of Flinders Street Railway Station and saying, "My great grandfather arrived by barge up the Yarra in 1824 and was deposited, with all he had in the world, on a piece of mud just there."

Melbourne is Australia in microcosm. It was built on immigration and hope. Gold provided both. Immigration continues unabated today, with hope being born out of political repression and trade rather than the lure of gold. The streets are filled with Asian faces; yet, at least on the surface, there does not appear to be an open friction between ethnic groupings. A beautiful, coloured schoolgirl hugs several white school friends in turn, before disappearing in the direction of Natalie's finger. There are no sniggers or wry comments behind her back. She is accepted. She is Australian.

Later, a Lebanese restaurateur greets us. "Ah! British! My grandfather was a prisoner of the British in Egypt." No resentment; just a huge smile and a belly laugh. "He made a fortune by collecting the tea they threw away, washing and drying it and selling it back to them. He died one of the richest men in Lebanon." We celebrate his good fortune with tea - to be recycled later.

A poem by Natalie:
'New neighbours move in
a family of non-European background.
Gossip suggests one should tie up the dog
Lock up the cat
or Dim Sims will follow.
There are three generations
Grandparents speak no English

> only four other languages
> and instruct and care for the children.
> Mother and father work shifts, work long hours.
> Appear to be pleasant.
> The children find the hole
> in the dividing fence.
> Once more the barrier trembles.
> Through the hole in the fence pokes a head
> followed by a small body.
> Soon shouted teenage
> instructions for Aussie Rules
> Force the barrier to tremble once more.

Poll after poll of Australian citizens continue to confirm what ordinary people want of their society: to be offered a chance of quality of life and to be a genuinely cosmopolitan country.

If any country in the world can allow love to overcome prejudice, it will be Australia.

The Twister:

The middle-aged man looked down his long, patrician nose at me, as though I was something unpleasant the cat had dragged in. Although we were about the same age, all similarity ended right there. He was resplendent in his fitted jacket and tie, groomed to within an inch of his life: And me? There I was, standing in the lobby of 'his' mega five-star hotel, dressed in dirty shorts, a sloppy cardigan that had not seen a washing machine in three weeks and a pair of boots that revealed my socks through a hole in the uppers [though only the right one, the left boot being near perfect in condition: Shame the socks weren't a perfect match though.] I don't think the trail of sticky-seedy crud on his carpet endeared me to him either.

I shook him, though. "Can I upgrade our room, please?"

My fantasy of a couple of nights of luxury - a shave with hot water; hot, deep, non-sulphurous baths, without the aid of nature's own thermal heating system - evaporated in an instant.

"I'm afraid that won't be possible.....Sir." A lot of unpleasantness went into the afterthought. To add insult, he smiled wanly. "We're full for the bank holiday weekend."

'Fair enough,' I thought to myself. I should have thought ahead, not acted on a whim: "Just our room then, please."

"Name!" he snapped as a sigh of exasperation escaped from his lips. He was acting as though he was doing us a favour - and that always kind of rankles with me - especially when the room is pre-booked and paid for.

Yet, in a way, this Caesar look-alike did prove another of my worldly theories: reflected privilege. You know the sort of thing: A butler in an aristocratic household would look down on the cook; the cook would look down on the domestics - and the domestics would look down on the most unfortunate of girls; the upstairs maids. I just did not expect this sort of snobbery in a cosmopolitan city so far from the United Kingdom, where we still make a virtue of the sin of privilege.

George: that's what his name tag says - unless he's grabbed someone else's jacket: [A moment of reflection: No, it is George. He would never wear anyone else's clothes - and he would probably wash his entire wardrobe if anyone got to within five yards of his personal gear.] George pounded the keyboard of his computer, his pale face growing paler, but developing little spots of rouge high up on his sullen cheeks.

His antics gave me time to check out the reception: knee-deep luxury, with real leather seats, polished brass and a few framed photographs adorning the expensive, yet fake, 19th century, fabric wallpaper. I take a closer look: The photographs are of 'Employee of the Week;' the Quarter; the Year. The fourth frame, small and high up in a corner, held a certificate which read, "Thank you for your services to Kill-a-Pest." I could not get my head around that 'award;' but it came as no surprise to see that George was not amongst the glorious triumvirate of employees hanging on the wall. However, he did draw my attention back his way when he raised his voice to an invisible person in the rear office: "Excuse me, Charlotte."

A moment later, I was rewarded by the sight of a young, nubile Charlie - as her name tag announced. The nickname was an obvious source of distress to Georgie. He leaves her - and us - without a word, shuffling paper into a blizzard as he goes.

"Now, let me see," she began; her big, round, brown eyes sparkling with life. "Mister Patterson. Ah, yes.....!" Now, I'm sure George would have said something subtle; lied through his teeth to preserve the good name of the hotel. But young Charlie had no such hang-ups. "..... Oops! You seem to be lost in the system....."

"Just so long as my money hasn't disappeared as well....."

Of course there was no trouble. We were never 'found.' But an hour later I'm in a deep, hot, upgraded bath - one of two in our suite on the 26th Floor, with panoramic views over the cityscape. As I lie there, letting the stresses and strains ease away, I reflect on the nice people in this life, adding Charlie to the list of ordinary folk who have gone out of their way to make sure we have always had a bed for the night.

I had thought about asking George to come up and see us - indulge in a bit of nose rubbing - but I couldn't think of a single thing we needed from a concierge – not up here in our penthouse. I lie back, smiling, content with the world.

Then, the tornado hit.

Within seconds, the marble-sized hailstones battering the roof above my head make me flee the bathroom. The blue sky of a few seconds ago was black and the hailstones were beginning a reign of terror down there on the street. Car panels are dented; people are fleeing streets being blanketed in icy white. Tree branches fly; advertising signs wave crazily; a rubbish bin and its contents scud along a road, already flooding. There is thunder. And lightning. Then the twister spirals across the sky.

As the lights begin to go out, grid by city grid, the little devil in me raises its head. No electricity means no lifts - and I can't help but wonder if George is still in reception.....

Dark Digs.

I got talking with this guy quite by accident, following a quick side-step around his trim, athletic figure. He had stopped in mid-stride, with an "I'm lost!" But I wasn't and so we chatted about this and that. It did not take long to establish that the be-suited African-American businessman was well-travelled and well-heeled – and, from his outgoing personality, well-liked.

The conversation turned to hotels - well we had just rolled out of a particularly pleasant one, The Regent in Collins Square, which has a million dollar opal in the basement and a view from the toilets, 35 stories up, where the floor-to-ceiling glass outside wall forces you to grab at the non-vertico-inducing partitions.

"Nah! They're the same the world over," he stated.

Mind you, after last night's queen-sized everything, cossetted in harmonized shades of grey, I shouldn't feel like contradicting him.....

He continued. "Some psychologist dreams 'em up you know.....The colours. It's to relax the executive types.....No kidding!"

He thought he had seen my scepticism. He was right, of course, but he would have had to have been exceptionally clever to read my mind, as I was away visiting the Hotel Atlantique in a small oasis town in North Africa. I know it was decades ago, but it did make a lasting impression. Perhaps it was that experience which makes me forsake life's hardships. Perhaps tranquil harmonization has overtaken the Atlantique by now, but I doubt it. It was colour-coordinated all right, even back then. Everything was pitch-black! We had arrived after dark, courtesy of a de-saddled, green-slavering camel [indicative of gonorrhoea] to find the town had exhausted its daily two-hour supply of electricity. It was as black as black can be and the flickering light, cast by the hand-held candles, only made things worse. And.....!

He interrupted my panic attack. Sweat beads had started forming on my forehead; rivers were running down my arms....."Am I the only person who needs a degree in applied physics to get water out of a shower head? Hell!"

Shower! Bath! Get real! The Atlanteek had only a hand basin, complete with one tap, out of which came groans and farts and nothing else. Our nine-year-old lad put it to good use by peeing in it around midnight - and I, for one, didn't blame him. Would you, if a trip to the toilet involved rolling up your trouser legs, before advancing by candlelight through communal unmentionables towards an overflowing bowl?

With its potted palms and bed bugs; window shutters which rattled incessantly with every whiff of passing camel dung - and, from 4 a.m., - an unrelenting Muezzin, we were welcomed to the world of travel.

"Anyway, take care. Perhaps I'll see you later in the pool?" With that he left, one of us still believing that hotels are the same the world over.

Melbourne Cup Day

No matter where you are in Australia, everything stops for Melbourne Cup Day. From Outback pubs to city wine bars, the bets are on, the excitement grows. Hundreds of millions of dollars are punted on the runners of the famous race at Flemington.

And it is raining. Pouring!

Three thousand, two hundred rain- soaked yards await them, with well over a million bucks, or a bucket of oats, for the winners. Runners from Britain, Ireland, Hong Kong and New Zealand are amongst the starters for the nation's premier sporting event. At least the European entries will feel right at home in this land of sunshine.

Television sets blare across the nation. It is 10 a.m. The race does not start until just after three, so we calculate that we have time for a quick walk. A totally-lost seagull shows what it thinks of me and my shirt.....

"That's lucky," says my wife. "Get a bet on quick."

But who? We are not into gee-gee's, but a top English jockey is riding.

"He's not here for nothing!" Knowing winks: We agree. We're on him.

The rain is merely torrential as the jockeys are introduced, one by one. All appear to weigh seven stones soaking wet through. And they are. Their skimpy racing silks quickly become see-through; anything to entertain the growing T.V. audience.

Then a singer tries to get the huge crowd to sing Waltzing Matilda, rain cascading off the brim of his hat. Good try mate, but you were onto a loser there.

At last it is time for the off. Our horse is mentioned. It's last out of the gate.

Another mention: Still last.

We console ourselves with the thought that he is playing it cute. After all, he has the experience; that's what counts.

Another mention: Still last.

Still last and only eight hundred to go: He's leaving it late.

No hope. The finish comes and goes to the drumming of hooves. It was kind of the commentator to mention the horse again. Second last: I can hear the groans of punters all across the continent, the tearing of tickets from Tasmania to Townsville.

Two things about racing I have learned today. First, the driver needs a Porsche, not a Nissan Micra; and secondly, do not bet on English riders who are obviously on an all-expenses-paid jaunt to surf and play beach volley ball.

Disappointment reigns for all of, oh - three seconds. Then laughter, as a rather portly sports commentator trots out onto the racecourse on a nineteen hand tall shire. He is not into gee-gee's either, but he's a professional. As nervous as a kitten, he manfully tries to ignore the stair-rodding rain - and his old war horse sniffing the rear end of the winner. He sticks a microphone under the nose of the emotional and breathless rider.

"How do you feel?"

Don't know about the jockey, but the shire and mare are getting randy.

Totally ridiculous: But great fun.

The Novice

Beneath the fluttering National flag, the greens are swarming with clucking vestal virgins. Retired, ageing, redundant, over-weight, slightly tarnished nympholets, to be sure; but still all are immaculately dressed from head-to-toe in starched, regulation whites.

A bowls match. Worse! A women's bowls match: Bowling, at whatever level, in Australia is taken as seriously as a Liverpool – Everton; or Rangers – Celtic soccer match back in the U.K.

Etiquette is all, or so it appears, as the rotund ladies, tape measures in hand, bustle about the rinks in their double slips and tights, ignoring the thirty-plus temperatures and perspiration. 'We will be demure,' is the order of the day - any day for that matter. The undercurrent of noise is relentless and broken frequently by cries of "Be up, Joan." "Grass is cheap, love." "Don't cross the head." "Drop one in there, Marge." "Kill it!"

[Somebody getting nasty under a bit of pressure:]

Not being a party to the bewildering catechism, I want to ask Bill the price of grass, but have to wait. No-one is allowed on the hallowed ground beyond the plinth without a certificate of competence to bowl - which needs six hours of tuition and supervision. And that is why we are here, feeling totally out of place and self conscious.

Bill, the professional coach, is always here - if he's not off beach fishing - and he's as easy as an old boot. His sunburnt figure makes his assured way across to us, his big smile protruding from beneath his big hat. We are easy to spot, dressed as we are in multicoloured shirts and shorts - even our wide-brimmed hats are not white. The uninitiated are exempt from becoming virginous. For that, we need a clean bill of health. [Excuse the pun.]

We learn quickly from the old master, including how to genuflect on bended knee before smoothly releasing the wood. It's harder than it looks and I elevate the old lady, bowling with the aid of a walking stick, to sainthood. Obviously we are in need of divine help, or practise. Even better - both!

Bill puts a hand over his eyes. A call goes up from the startled starched bottoms several rinks away. "Who does THAT bowl belong to?" A chorus of "Drinks all round," greets this red-faced idiot, who cannot even sort out left from right.

Let me tell you, it is a long and uncomfortable walk to retrieve your bowl from the midst of such formidable maidens.

The 'Barbee'

The 'barbee,' Australia style, is really quite similar to the barbecue in Britain – only here there are more of them; more a way of life, rather than a special treat snatched between scurrying rain clouds. And there are no pretensions to grandeur here. No striped marquees on manicured lawns, just in case the weather changes; or the Joneses look over the fence. The whole experience is more relaxed, more down-to-earth, where etiquette amounts to finding the biggest glass available and sticking to it, no matter what the booze on offer.

Ordinary people are the same the world over. They joke and laugh - and talk of hopes and plans; of family and sport – and, very occasionally, of their fears. I am sure the elderly are no different to their European cousins, but I have never heard the sad phrase: "I'm too old to live and too frightened to die," in Australia. It is more likely to be:

"I'm ninety-two-and-a-half. How old are you?"

"Eh!"

"How old?"

"I'm ninety-one and seven months."

Another tinny is drained, followed by a polite burp.

"Eeh! That means I'm nearly a year older than you."

"Eh!"

It is funny how months become as important to the elderly as they are to children.

But only in Australia can the gregarious chatter be drowned out by the cacophonous kookaburras perched overhead.

Food and drink appear from a dozen houses. A huge fish, a ton of steak, chops and snags lie in ambush. Smoke rises from the charcoal, enveloping the perspiring, aspiring-bronchial cook.

"Take over mate. I need another shower."

Laid back? If the host gets any more relaxed, he'll fall over.

More salads arrive. Wine and beer flow. The children and elderly noisily compete with the rattling of the invisible cicadas and the still-battling kookaburras.

A small terrier, also ninety-one-and-a-half in doggy years, already full of peanuts and crisps, sees its chance. It retreats, tail-a-wagging, jaw full of lamb chop. I could swear it's grinning.

A sudden shower: Food, plates, dishes, cushions disappear - leaving the cook to get wet.

Just like home!

One or two Australian words for the dictionary:

Snaggs are sausages; a beer is a tinny and cicadas are large insects which beat their wings furiously to cool off.

One of our favourite family recipes:

Sandra's Salad for Six:

Take and mix together:

1 cup of cooked rice, 1 chopped green pepper, 1 tablespoon of chopped parsley, 1 chopped red-skinned apple, one large onion, [uncooked], 1 teaspoon curry powder, 1 teaspoon of sugar, 3 tablespoons of sultanas and 1 cup of cooked red kidney beans which have been washed.

Next, take and mix together:

Half a cup of Olive Oil, one third of a cup of white wine vinegar, 1 clove of crushed garlic and salt and pepper to taste.

Final Stage:

Chuck the dressing over the other stuff. Simple and delicious!

High Noon on Rink Seven

Do not equate Australia Day, commemorating the start of European life on this continent [albeit not the cause for universal celebration], with St. George's Day, St. Andrew's Day or even St. David's Day. Australia Day is a serious business - a public holiday - and that means a Sunday service for the public transport, which in turn means no 'buses at all around here. Australia Day - when local and national figures vie for a plethora of Australian of the Year Awards, test matches begin and patriotic music and verse invade the airways. Even on television there is no escape. Flags wave and pictures of people from every corner of the world, swelling with pride, are taking their Oath of Allegiance.

We celebrate our life in Australia practising on the bowling green, whilst the President of the Ladies Section gnashes her teeth and wails, her fingers constantly wringing the life out of her tape measure cum rosary.

The women have just lost a grudge match against their local rivals. Heads will roll. Excuses have to be snatched from the ether and clung to: White Leghorns* scatter to safety of car and home as the last bowl comes to rest. Each walks passed six rinks packed with novices honing their skills - and speak only to those on rink seven - us! We think people are getting to know us and we're secretly pleased. Fools! It is not friendly recognition, but sympathy. They are out of the firing line and commiserating with the unsuspecting.

The formidable figure of President Vera bore down upon us. The Aborigines around here would call her 'Bundala,' a name given to anyone with the height and weight advantage of a heavyweight boxer. Poised at her heel, reminiscent of a beady-eyed chihuahua, was a diminutive, silent lady, overly concerned with polishing her badge - 'The Secretary.'

"We've got dress rules for roll-ups and you are in breach of them." Vera's opening broadside.

Standing there with her hands on her ample hips, I would swear her forearms were as thick as my thighs: If she hit anyone.....

"Oh dear!" replied my wife looking down at her lilac coloured cycle shorts. "I didn't know."

"Can't have it!" President Vera continued, huffing and puffing a bit by now.

Then I had it. No boxing champ this, but rather a caricature of a British Army Colonel, circa 1890, India. The only difference was the moustache - hers didn't bristle quite as much as Colonel Blimp's – what with bristling being impossible under the layers of face powder which surely had been applied with a trowel.

"No, we can't have it. Bending down in cycle pants puts my girls off."

It would appear Patsy - or more precisely - Patsy's bum, has cost the ladies their match. That's my girl!

"Shorts below the knees only:"

"I don't have any shorts below the knee," countered my beloved.

That warmed Vera up a bit and she was really getting going when good old Bill, thankfully spared by the ocean for another day, hurried across. He knew Vera of old and had guessed at what was going on.

"Madam President," he interrupted her in full flow about the lengths of hemlines and the necessity of double slips to protect a woman's modesty. She had not quite got round to the lechery of men, but it was next on her check-list. "I'd like you to present these Certificates of Competence to Patsy and Ian here. They are now qualified to bowl through life. I've signed them, as their coach."

Vera would have sooner knocked us down and put the boot in, but instead went redder and redder and looked totally flustered. "Congratulations," she just about spluttered. There seemed to be something wrong with her throat.

"Ooooh! Thank you," said Patsy, genuinely pleased.

"Ooooh!" says I: "A bollocking and a certificate - and all on Australia Day too."

A stony, fixed smile and she was gone, taking the Shadow with her.

A big smile and a wink from Bill: He secretly likes lilac cycle shorts, but for all that, he deserved his pint. We all did!

* White Leghorns is the derogatory term given to lady bowlers by the more laid back men. It dates from the time when the rules insisted that the women wore white stockings, which reminded the uncharitable fella's of white Leghorn chickens.

Bottles, Buses and Bickering

Australia does have social problems; no-one can deny that. Homelessness; corruption; crime; environmental issues; and those with 'alternative life-styles' coming into conflict with authority. Sound familiar?

Yet, Australia liberates your spirit. I am sure it has something to do with its vastness - as if those great distances somehow flood into your mind and put space between everyday problems. Problems do not seem to press in upon you somehow. Here they seem so low key, more laughable than frightening.

Take, for instance, our bus journey back from shopping today. The bus was late – again. It was oppressively hot and sticky and everyone was feeling it. Being the last bus for two hours, thirty-three fidgeters waited nervously for the thirty-five seater coach. Would we all get on?

There were four potential passengers who didn't care. They stood out - and would in any crowd: Three men and a woman. It was not so much the layered dirt and the tattoos which covered every inch of exposed skin, but the love beads and matching rings through their noses were a nice touch: Frustrated Hells Angels, unable to afford throbbing Harleys, swallowing their shame at a bus stop. Anyway, there they were, four of them, sharing a bottle or two or three, content to be last aboard.

They took their disparate seats toward the rear. No trouble to anyone, except for the unpleasant smell of the great unwashed and the normal loudness of drunks.

Third stop - and two of the men prepared to leave us, staggering and making heavy weather of the walk towards the front. They gave a good impression of walking the deck of a small ship with a large ocean swell running. "See ya' later," they shouted, as they disembarked.

"Yeah: See ya'," came the shouted reply, accompanied by much banging on the windows. "Make Jimbo come later," added the woman in a voice that went straight through you.

"Why don't you shut up! You're not allowed to drink on the bus." And this from a young woman sitting six seats away, looking as though butter wouldn't melt in her mouth. Up until then she had been invisible.

Every head swivelled to look at her in amazement. It can't have been.....

It was.

"Shut up! Always shooting up on heroin," continued the young woman. "You cow!"

Oooh! Fifteen luv!

"You can talk," said lady Hells Angel, entering the fray. "How come you're so high and mighty when your dad's in gaol for selling the stuff?"

Fifteen all!

"I don't use it," said Miss Innocent.

"Neither do we," replied she with the bull's rings. No-one believed her.

"Huh! You're nothing but a cat stealer," continued Miss Demure.

A charge of rustling: Could this be the ultimate in Aussie insults?

"And you're nothing but a ***** who leaves her ***** kids all day with a ***** stranger." [There were lots of 'ings in the word-endings during that 'pleasant' exchange.]

"Where did you pick that heap of sh*t up?" the 'nice' girl asked.

We were in no doubt that she meant Mr Angel.

"Eh! Who me?" He woke up with a sharp elbow in his ribs, all bleary-eyed and befuddled by beer [or worse.]

"None of your ***** business," replied his escort.

"Uh!" he said, totally bemused.

Mrs H. Angel hadn't finished with Miss Innocent. "Anyway, who fathered your kid? Don't know, do you?" She stood up, getting well into it by now.

The bus driver didn't know whether to continue driving or stop and watch. His eyes flickered uncontrollably between road, pantomime and back again. Passenger heads were going back and forth as quickly as a good rally at a tennis match.

Bull-nose pin-balled her way from seat to seat toward real trouble: Now that morning my stars had said, "Keep calm and those around you will also." I admit I was enjoying myself, but I swear it was an accident.

It would appear the ageing Angel - she looked a well-worn forty – did not see my foot in the aisle and went sprawling across the back of the seat in front, hit her head on the window and did sort of a backward roll onto the laps of two elderly ladies studiously looking at nothing outside.

Embarrassment all round. By the time the drunk had collected her smouldering reefer from under one of the old dears, her hat [twice], chiffon scarf and ear-ring from under the seat, little Miss Innocent had gone, grinning like a Cheshire cat.

We left the near-empty bus soon after, the tattoos and rings in a clinch which would put Michael Douglases Fatal Attraction in the shade. Trouble was, ours was the last-stop-but-one and in another half a mile they would be on their way back to the terminus.

I had a feeling no-one was going to tell them.

A Filthy Night in Melbourne Town:

The storm system has not let us out of its grip yet and the locals are pleased. Pleased! They are deliriously happy. [Well, most of them.] The dams, up country, were only forty percent full after eighteen months of scarce rains and there is 'already' a hose-pipe ban in force: Now the traffic crawls along at twenty, the windscreen wipers unable to deal with the deluge. The tyres whoosh along waterlogged roads; the grass on the central reservations turn into a quagmire; the gutters pool and overflow. Rain!

The petrol station attendant is happy to talk footy [not to be confused with soccer hereabouts] and give directions to this lost soul, who had been half expecting to wander suburbia for ever more. And why shouldn't he be happy to spend some time, as no other customers could possibly be expected on such a dark and filthy night.

Our warm and cosy haven is blasted with cold air as the outer door is forced open. An unshaven man, dressed in a dark anorak with the hood up, is blown in. He disappears down an aisle full of choccy biscuits. For a moment I can't help but think "robbery" - he doesn't look a biccy eater; but I soon relax as he approaches the cash register with a bottle of Coke rather than a 'sawn-off.'

"Be with you soon, sir," says the cashier, gleefully: Two people to talk to. He was in seventh heaven. "Now where were we," he continues, his eyes dropping once more to the map covering half the counter. [Melbourne's a big place.] "I think the beach road is better. You see….."

There followed a lengthy discourse on traffic lights and cameras, during the course of which our 'robber' began to cuss like a trooper before storming out into the night, ditching the bottle amongst the bread on the way. The storm burst in as he went, only to slowly subside as the heavy door returned to its appointed place.

I looked at the cashier; he looked at me. Then, after a momentary pause, he shrugged philosophically….. "Now, where were we? Oh yes! Mind you, Beach Road has loads of traffic cops….."

The cashier wasn't the only one glad of company.

The restaurateur was young and huge and filled the room with his twenty-odd stone. However, tonight his normal, cheery countenance was overlaid by a frown as he watched Melbourne's melancholy commuters pass by, bowed into the wind. By the hundred they crowd about the light-operated pedestrian crossing outside his premises, almost huddling together against the rain which patterned the street, before breaking forth in a human wave toward tram and train. All have one thing in mind tonight. Home!

Home thoughts meant the restaurant would have been empty had it not been for a morose birthday party of six celebrating the life of an eighty year old. Their bill and our two teas weren't going to cover many expenses.

Perhaps it was this sobering fact that made our host look so miserable. But, no! We know it's his diet. All his good intentions were likely to go out of the window tonight, when faced with his dilemma: to bin the mountain of left-overs - or eat them himself?

Rain!

Devlin's Devil:

'Do something before you get old and boring.'

It is an appeal to the young; appearing on the sides and windows of buses, trains and trams all over Melbourne, courtesy of the local Education Board. To what end, I'm not sure, but it is enough to get me motivated in an effort to stave off the inevitable for a while.

So, two ambitions fulfilled in one day. A return to Melbourne's old bluestone gaol on Russell Street and an Aussie Rules footy game, under lights, at the world famous Melbourne Cricket Ground.

The historic gaol, where Ned Kelly and others met their end, has certainly improved its presentation to visitors over the intervening years since our last visit - so it is with some excitement that I enter, hoping for insights into the recent research done on the phenomenon of the Kelly Gang.

Our Devlin connection to the Gang is not there - although it is now proven that the outlaws' blacksmith [our Devlin], was not a professional smithy at all. He was, in all probability, a supporter of theirs; a small farmer who changed plough shares into suits of armour. [Devlin obviously was not a Biblical scholar.]

Today's researchers know this because of forensic tests on Ned's armour, which determined it was worked at a relatively low heat, probably at a place called Devil's Basin. Is it just me, or could Devlin's and Devil's be one and the same?

Two things struck me about today's visit. Firstly, the 'system' cared little for its victims. 'It' hung whites and blacks, Chinese and Indians, men and women, the sane and the crazy, with equal alacrity.

Melbourne Gaol, built in 1841, saw 135 executions up to 1967. Amongst the first [on 21st January, 1842] were Bob Smalley and Jack Tummunperway - Aboriginal men, hung in public to teach the indigenous population a lesson. Jack took a long, long time to take his leave of this life. Seemingly, along with three women, they had taken their revenge on a couple of white blokes, whalers at Cape Patterson, killing them after having identified one as 'Yankee,' a man who had murdered Aborigines in Tasmania sometime before 1839.

The second thing to strike me, whilst browsing through the stories of the lives of real people incarcerated in this tragic, tomb-like structure, was that 'they' - the Government, the authorities, those with the power - always win.

Ned Kelly, Australian folk hero extraordinaire, is proof enough, hung for his challenge to the British rulers as much as for his misdeeds.

Strangely, this feeling of the little guy getting it put to him by the big guy pervaded the Hawthorn – Carlton footy match that evening.

The stadium was fantastic and the atmosphere good for a thirty thousand crowd watching a match that did not mean a great deal. It is a long time since 1969, when the Blues of Carlton put two hundred points past the Hawthorn Hawks - the first time the two hundred point barrier had been broken in A.F.L. history.

Now Carlton is bottom of the table - and played like it. Despite battling all the way, they were well and truly battered into submission by the big guys. However, it wasn't the match that grabbed my attention, but the performance of a player wearing the gold and brown of the Hawks. He had been identified to me by a cousin of mine who'd relocated to Melbourne and become a fanatical supporter. Anyway, the player in question was not just playing for his place in the team. No, sir! It had come down from on high that he was playing for his career: two matches to prove his worth or he was out - at twenty eight, to be released to join the scrapheap of the old and boring.

It's clear what his team-mates felt. They patted his back and shook his hand every time he touched the ball. They even encouraged him with a passing word as they ran about for two hours like demented chooks.

For me, he was a battler. His mates stood shoulder-to-shoulder with him, determined to do the right thing as they saw it.

Just like Jack, Bob and Ned from yesteryear. We know their fate - unlike that of the footy player. I just hope he makes it.

A Winter's Day.

There is nothing like a leaden sky and a gusting wind threatening to turn the umbrella inside out; to deaden the spirits - especially when you are on a beach. Somehow your mood sinks toward oblivion as the rain spatters across the cold, crusted sand at your feet. Be brave! Lift your eyes and see the wind scudding crazy patterns over the sullen face of a monstrous, uncaring ocean.

Dreams unfulfilled, put to one side for another, distant day.

Damp. Deserted; no dog walkers; no joggers. No fleets of cyclists racing along the Promenade: No-one and nothing to disturb winter's grip on the city:

We burrow down into the padded jackets and scarves scrounged from understanding relatives as the chill wind hurtles and blasts about the sighing eaves of the garish beach huts which adorn the expensive piece of real estate that is beach-front Brighton. The huts are painted in vibrant, multi-coloured hues and, set against the impressive cityscape of a not-so-distant Melbourne they should be the heralds of spring; of activity and excitement - and especially of the hope of relief from the grey skies and even greyer sea.

But they don't. Instead, they emphasize the chill, greyness of spirit - and so it is with considerable relief on my part that all thoughts of the 'how' are dismissed. ['How long before summer?' 'How can people afford a hundred thousand bucks for a wooden beach hut?' 'How can Melbourne continue to expand its towering skyline, as evidenced by the forest of cranes, in the face of economic realities?'] I dismiss all such thoughts in favour of the welcoming Cappuccino culture offered everywhere throughout Never-Never Land.

The hours pass easily in the art-deco coffee shop. Our haven is warmed by a spitting log fire, before which we are content to read and watch the huddled and wrapped world pass us by.

The 'how' returns: Not the how and why of world-changing events given pride of place in the newspaper; more the mundane. For one thing, how do the owners of this café make a living here? A thought stimulated by an ageing hippy type who is stretched out and fitfully sleeping across two chairs in the café's outside pavement area. It is not as uncomfortable as it sounds; the canvas awning and the six foot high, barbeque-type heaters that resemble street lights, do afford some protection from the day.

The hippy is wearing only a vest [in need of a washing machine]; jeans [in need of a seamstress]; and a single sandal. The other, naked, foot is blackened from the grime of the street or the detritus of a winter's beach.

There has to be a story - but I'm too afraid to ask.

He is soon joined by an elderly 'English' couple. I have no idea if they are English or not, they just look that way; he with jacket and tie, she with blue rinse hair, a warm tweed two-piece and the, no doubt, obligatory, pearls. They would surely be shocked, should someone inform them of Queen Victoria's demise. They pull their chairs close to one of the enormous heaters and take out a host of sandwiches – wrapped in greaseproof paper, of course.

The laconic cafe proprietor seems not to care. Denied of economic activity, he has left his invisible kitchen in favour of incessantly fingering his tight, curly hair, a tall bar stool and the morning's paper. Tall enough to have once been a basketball player, he touches and eases and fondles each wayward strand, before taking whatever he finds and examining it closely. Nonchalantly, each louse is squashed in turn between forefinger and thumbnail.

An involuntary shiver runs the length of my spine; the driving rain suddenly a thing to be embraced.

Wilson's Promontory:

"A Place of Many Moods:" [According to the brochure.]

"I'll just nip and get a photo down there."

"You will not!" ordered my wife, her voice carrying a good deal of force.

"It's only fifty feet or so. And those striations on that boulder will look stunning with the waves rolling over them."

"No! You're stupid! I'm having nothing to do with you."

Stupid I might be - I was told that often enough at school - but I know my wife well enough to back-track a little. "We'll sit here for a while, then. Get our breath back."

She still wasn't talking, but we needed a break anyway as we had been walking on fine, brilliant white sand for an hour, before climbing the steep headland that separates Squeaky Beach from Norman Bay and its encampment at Tidal River.

The area is called Wilson's Promontory, a National Park named after Tommy Wilson, a London friend of the explorer, Mathew Flinders, who had explored hereabouts in 1798 -99. Flinders that is - not Tommy, who preferred the delights of London.

What Flinders found - is what we found: A strange, wild, ugly-beautiful, remote place; a place of fantastic beaches, cool fern gullies, swamps, and above all, spectacular rock formations.

We sit in an uneasy silence - I hadn't been forgiven yet - and look at the cracked and broken boulders, strewn about with reckless abandon at the place where Australia stops. Here, plates of granite have broken away from the continent and, like tiny, house-sized marbles; lie in a jumble one hundred and fifty feet below.

The surging, ultra-marine, Pacific Ocean nibbles and bites at the landmass. Unrelenting, long swells grind into the cliff face, each wave boiling momentarily: then they are gone.

"And you want to go down there? You're nuts!"

My resolve is weakening, but I dare not say so – not yet.

The wind is incessant, courtesy of a storm centre over Tasmania; the fury to come but a premonition carried to us in the flecks of rain in the biting air. People would die that night; roads would be blocked and trains delayed. Whole cities would be left without electricity….. But we were not to know.

I turn away from the boiling ocean, now indifferent to the lines of dark blue, infant waves, which would grow into giants within seconds and smash the coast again and again. Instead, I begin to study the headland behind us. The soil is thin and the sparse scrub is being given a helping hand by the park wardens who have everywhere staked and tied and planted their favourite plant – the austere, grey – green banksias. Yet, even now, in late winter, there is the occasional glimpse of a scribbly red flower.

In a gully, just before it widens, filled with boulders and sprawling invitingly down to 'my' photo, there is enough shade and protection from the wind to support a host of ferns and mosses. Yellow sprays of mimosa are everywhere, filling the air with a heavy scent. Spring is surely just around the corner, but not yet. I pull my coat tighter about me.

The 'Prom,' as it is affectionately known to Victorians, is the southern-most tip of the Australian mainland and has been a reserve since 1898. We have only spotted a minute number of the seven hundred native plant species - and none of the thirty mammals [except one distant, grazing kangaroo,] - but the wonderful, blue and red parrots, their immense black cousins and the fat, cheeky finches, wagtails and robins, entertain us royally; as did a run of Pacific salmon just off the beach.

"It says……" Patsy awakens me from my thoughts. "That we shouldn't be without ambulance service cover – in case anything happens." She lays the open park guide across her lap. "Forget that photo!"

It is a command, but I'm still unconvinced. I stand up, ready to press on before the rain gets any heavier. In doing so, I uncover a memorial - a small, engraved plate dating from the 13th April, 1998. It speaks of twenty year old Joe Proksik, and a nineteen year old, Jesse Nguyen, swept to their deaths by a freak wave. They too had probably been tempted by the striations of the boulder. The memorial finishes with a comment: 'Stay on the path!'

"It says here," continues my wife, oblivious to the pallor which had engulfed my face. "The rocky areas are extremely treacherous. Ocean swells can crash up and along the rocks for long distances and freak waves are common. See!" She hands the booklet over.

"You're right, love," I reply. "It was a stupid idea."

And she beams with pleasure as we make our way from one perfect beach to the next.

The Bellarine Peninsula

The newspaper headlines shrieked, "33.5 Degrees! Hottest day since 1873:"
White winter bodies were ignoring the skin cancer campaign yet again - and so, we decide it is a good time to include Melbourne's beaches and spectacular coastline in our itinerary.

On the morrow we rise to find the sun has gone, but, bolstered by the local adage "If you don't like the weather in Victoria, just wait an hour," off we go. Now then, these words of wisdom may well be quite correct - Melbourne can have four seasons in a day; a bit like blighty. But today is winter - and winter it remained. Not a freezing British January with a north wind; my disappointment just makes it feel that way. However, there are no flabby bodies baking in oil - just a plethora of anoraks and jumpers. Still, it's not cold enough for me to abandon my shorts; and nothing is going to stop a flake-and-chip lunch on a deserted headland overlooking the tumultuous sea.

There is a great sense of satisfaction in eating flake - shark to you and me: Something of a sense of justice in it. I wonder if we taste as good to them as they do to us.

Because of the eating habits of one of nature's 'nightmares', the narrow passage into Port Phillip Bay from the Bass Strait is best viewed from the safety of the old-fashioned resort of Queenscliffe. The rip tide, between here on the Bellarine Peninsula and Point Nepean across the bay, makes this one of the most treacherous stretches of water in the world.

Not only have hundreds of ships come to grief hereabouts, with the subsequent loss of life, but did you know that even an Australian Prime Minister has disappeared beneath those swirling waters? That was Harold Holt, just before the Christmas of 1967. For some reason he decided to have a dip and did not come back.

Did a flake get him? Did the rip? No! Most Aussies I have spoken to, if they remember that unremarkable leader at all, prefer to believe that their womanising chief was taken away by a Russian sub.

And why not: I'll go along with that flakey idea, as no-one in their right mind would want to swim here.

And that is probably why the Surf Championships are regularly held - just - down - there!

The Bass Strait and Phillip Island

Australia's eight million square miles are surrounded by something like three oceans, four seas and twenty thousand kilometres of coastline. Of them all, none is as dangerous as the Bass Strait. Out there, the waters are stormy and dotted with half-submerged mountain peaks, against which the great seas smash. The oceans are funnelled into a narrows, piling up waves one upon another, until they tower above the mast heads of the old sailing ships, turning to liquid the bowels of even the most hardened sailor.

In the days of sail, ship captains were always confronted by the choice: to go through the Strait and brave the Shipwreck Coast - perhaps forty hours of extreme danger - or put an extra month on the journey by going around Tasmania. Most took the chance - after all, time is money. Many did not make it.

One of those who failed to make it was our Commander Fairfax Moresby, R.N., to whom we lay claim by common descent over several centuries - even though he was from the monied branch who had nothing to do with our direct line; the poor lot, who included in their number the transported convict. Fairfax was the skipper of H.M.S. Sappho, which was lost here in 1858. It was last seen entering the Bass Strait, but no-one knows what happened to her.

However, a letter back to Yorkshire from another of our emigrant families called Birkby, whom we will meet later, describes what happened to them on 12th October, 1834, at the entrance to the Strait. Perhaps something similar accounted for the Commander:

".....the sea was dead calm as we entered the Straits but on our nearing the land at about ten at night there was a heavy swell running with small breakers and a heavy sea.....the ship rolled till the main yards touched the water.....The Captain called out but it was too late and but for the will of Almighty God who caused the wind to blow an instant from the land few of us would have lived to tell the tale.....The passage through is at all times dangerous and without a fair wind, impossible."

And so to Phillip Island which juts out into this great waterway, ever so thankful that no boat is involved.

*

The wind came straight from Antartica and went through me without stopping: A lazy wind. I would not have cared, but I was wearing practically everything I had brought with me: two shirts, two jumpers, one cagoule. It made no difference. A few weeks ago I had looked with disdain at the woman with six suitcases at Gatwick Airport. How could anyone need so much stuff for a short holiday in a warm climate? Now I knew where she was going: Phillip Island. Next stop the Ice Cap!

The fairy penguins [Eudyptna Minor for the scientifically minded], were playing with us - frolicking in the icy waters, out of sight and surely laughing in penguin-speak at the stupid homosapiens sitting on concrete benches in the ferocious cold. And paying for the privilege!

As the twilight grew, so the cold increased. It took an act of faith to stay; but the brochures said the penguins arrive each night at 'about' dusk.

I must take a quick time-out here. Who decided to call these eighteen-inch-tall hardmen - who perform heroics in the unforgiving sea and then embark on a mountain climb to get home with supper for the kids – "Fairies?"

'About' dusk turned to blackness - and that's when they came. Each tiny Hector in waiter's uniform waddling across the sand, many so bloated with fish that they fell forward frequently. Others, dive-bombed by seagulls, fled back to the sea - and then tried again. Their arrival dispelled the cold - temporarily - as we were held enthralled by one of nature's showstoppers.

We wish them well, and succumb to the lure of a hot shower and a comfy bed.

Journey 2
Western Australia

The Fair Maids of Perth

"This is your Captain speaking. As you will know by the changed pitch of the engines, we are slowing for the approach to Perth. We've some seventy five miles to go and it's a beautiful day down there. Perth is standing out on the horizon and Rottnest Island is clearly visible: A truly wonderful sight." Pause for effect. "Unfortunately we are making a head-on approach - so you won't see any of it."

Click! Pregnant pause, followed by stunned silence. That was it. Our introduction to what is reputed to be the world's most remote city. I couldn't help but wonder if the captain's mood had anything to do with the exceptional bottle of wine our steward had earlier managed to filch from first class. So impressed was he by my enthusiasm for the demon drink, he had left the bottle. Perhaps Captain Moody had his eye on it?

"Shonky bastard!" someone whispered from six rows back.

I admit to 'shonky' being a new one on me, but it seemed to neatly encapsulate my feelings.

We are approaching Perth, on the trail of three families now living 'way out west,' drawn here for the want of better jobs within the telecommunications business or in the glass factory. And the closer I get, the more unsure I become: How do you conduct yourself with someone you have never met - yet from whom you need information. Not hard, in the normal course of events; be yourself and take your time seems to work. The problem this time is that one of the guys was terribly tortured after the fall of Singapore. It might be over a half a lifetime ago, but he lives with it every day.....

I decide not to think about it - and so look out of my little piece of Perspex, surveying the burnt flatness disappearing into endless tracts of brown. And there it is again - Enigmatic Australia! Western Australia - well the northern bit - only a thousand or so miles away, is sinking under floods. Not here. This bit is baking.

After the now expected, "Is this all your luggage, Sir?" [Much more of this and I'm going to start feeling pretty disadvantaged], we make it to the taxi.

"It is twenty eight degrees today and it's a nice breeze we've got. Set fair for the next few weeks I reckon.....Mind you, that's bush fire weather."

That was the only conversation we got out of the sun-cancered driver: He spent our entire fare on mobile phone charges; constantly speaking into the piece of hand-held plastic, which responded uncertainly to his admonitions to collect the 'three ugly sisters' from the Returned Servicemen's Leagues' Club after a lunch-time session. No-one wanted to collect the old maids, despite reassurances that they were all over eighty - and that one of them was "O.K. really." They are probably still at the 'pokies', pint in one hand and fag in the other. Good on 'em!

Later, much later, we got a room. More plastic technology showed a reluctance to cough up our booking, despite, or possibly because of, the hammering fingers of an increasingly embarrassed receptionist. She was not embarrassed by the technology on display – more, because of my wife's presentation of the case for pens, paper and filing cabinets.

Later still: The telly shows our taxi driver to be a prophet in his own town. The screen is full of cinders and smoke.

Perfect Perth

I have read just about everything there is to read about Perth - and a bit more besides. Not actually everything - just what is easily available to the tourist. We are told the Swan River was not colonized until 1829, just in time to beat the French here - and the place did not take convicts to help out the struggling free settlers until 1850. I know already that Western Australians are justly proud of their achievements since then.

I like these 'Do you know?' snippets of useless information. For instance, do you know that Western Australia is larger than a whole heap of places put together - like France and Texas? Or that five-sixths of the State's population lives in and around Perth?

I throw down the magazine. What the writer is trying to say is that the place is big and, to those of us used to 'civilization', empty. Mrs Aeneas Gunn would not have agreed. Back in 1908 she wrote a book called 'We of the Never Never.' In it, she cries "Back blocks! There ain't no back blocks left: Can't travel a hundred miles without running into somebody." I wish I had known her. I know I would have liked her immensely as, without exception, all the Western Australians we have met are great; very friendly, happy and outwardly content.

I have read the descriptions of this place, as I am sure you have: Mediterranean climate; Californian life-style; and as we cruise along the Swan River to Fremantle passing yacht clubs, rows of millionaires' houses, white sandy beaches, the Iron-man training camps, bronzed bodies on jet skis, para sails, etc. etc., I come to the conclusion it is all true.

The place is beautiful and stunning; wonderful and just absolutely perfect. True to form, I find that just a teeny bit irritating. We have not seen a fly or a bird in the city. Even the several zillion jellyfish churning about in our bow waves are docile and harmless. There is no litter - unlike Britain where we have festivals of the stuff: [We even make art forms out of it to decorate our traffic islands.] But not here! It is as if there has been an air-burst of D.D.T. all over the city. It is just so sterile. Even the sky isn't allowed a cloud.

Don't think I'm a whinger: Far from it. I do not want the places to which I travel to remind me of home. I can live with sun and cloudless skies - and I don't care if I never see another cockroach. It is just this feeling I can't shake off, that anything not perfect has been banned - ordered out of existence.

And surrounded by the beautiful people I had better shape up, get a tan and become sylphlike - or I'll be banned too.

St. Paddy's Day

St. Patrick's Day runs Australia Day a close second in its intensity. And so it should, with forty percent of the population boasting an Irish heritage. It is a proud past, born of dissension, civil unrest and transportation - with or without trial. The first Irish exiled to this sunny Siberia came in the early 1790s. These 'normal' felons were soon joined by a flood of political dissidents exiled following the 1798 rebellion. All the Irish were branded by Governor Hunter as "turbulent and worthless creatures" and were subjected to unusually harsh punishments.

From the exiles' perspective, they were being oppressed in their homeland, oppressed in Australia and felt they were being punished for being Irish rather than for any crime. This keenly-shared sense of injustice forged an identity which grew as Australia evolved into a modern nation - and has undoubtedly influenced the character of the Australian identity and attitudes in both the political and social spheres.

Today, it is somewhat sad that we are reduced to having a dwarf [or should it be height-impaired person in these politically correct days?] dressed as a Leprechaun, serenading lunchtime shoppers.

The joviality is not all forced; impossible, as the Irish coffees and the Guinness have been flowing down willing throats since the pubs opened at 6a.m. It seems that every Tom, Dick, Mario and Imran are Irish for a day.

We are included. With family surnames like Ryan, Keating, Fitzgerald and Devlin, we would be accepted as honorary Irishmen anywhere. In fact, one of the wife's mob** died in Dublin Gaol in the June of 1798, after being shot in the leg and captured. He was a protestant - a leading light in a rebel organization - the forerunners of the I.R.A. - and I suppose he would have been transported along with the rest, if someone had a clean bandage handy. Can you keep that to yourselves though; with a son serving seventeen years in the British army and me twenty five years in the cops - it's not something we broadcast too loudly, even to kith and kin: Until we get to know them.

I am meeting with that ex-Army rello* I told you about - the one with the horrific wartime experiences. Disfigured - and presumed dead - his wife was shocked to see him walk through the door. Well, she would be – she was due to marry someone else that coming Saturday. But that was long ago. However, by the size of the beer paunch, he may be seeking solace in the local grog. He breaks off from singing along to an indistinguishable jig as I approach, easing his wobbling bulk from the protesting door frame of the pub: A cheery wave and a shout. "It's good to see yer wearin' the green."

It's only my socks - but what the hell. I'm not a real drinker, but raise a smile and a glass 'o' the black stuff.'

We get on famously - but I couldn't decide. "Are you from Irish stock?" I ask.

"Sometimes," he replies.

Still none the wiser, I try again. "Go on then, tell 'us what St. Pat did?"

"Well," he said seriously, draining another pint and licking his frothy lips. "He chased all the snakes out of Ireland.....They came to Australia, you know."

My eyebrows ask the question "Did they?"

"Surely: Unfortunately they all turned into politicians."

Wonderful thing, history!

*Rellos: Relatives.

** A convoluted line of descent involving illegitimacy.

The Duke of Perth

"Arrangda ungda. Eh! Eh!"

The whisky fumes wafted over my Aussie meat pie, just as I raised it to lunch-starved lips. The fumes entrenched themselves in my nostrils as the owner lowered his head to mine - just close enough to allow the head lice to pop over for some grub too.

"Arrang de summa," he said.

I didn't understand a word. The whiskered jowls and straggly hair sticking out at all angles from beneath a woollen bobble hat had obviously decided I was an idiot, or worse.

Ignoring me, he leaned over, reaching out for my wife, and said, "Arranga....." [You know the rest.] The more she inched away along the wooden bench, the more he leaned over, spluttering saliva with his, "Eh-Eh's!" By the time Patsy's bum was hanging in space, the drunk was angled so impossibly, there could surely be no way back to the vertical.

"Don't worry about Duke, mate," said the jolly Aussie on the next bench, coming to the rescue. "He's our local celebrity. He'll piss off if you give him yer pie."

The jolly chappy had a grin like a Cheshire cat with all the cream. I would be grinning like that too, if 'whisky whiskers' had fancied his crisps rather than my pie, or my wife, or both - in any order of preference.

Immune to the forces of nature as drunks so often are, he raised himself, obviously distracted by the interruption.

Now I have read somewhere that when abroad and feeling threatened, an Englishman should always resort to his Englishness. Being pure bred English - except for a Welsh bare-knuckle fighter, itinerant Irish pit-sinkers, Scottish reivers, wandering gypsies and thieving Vikings - I take the book's advice. "Sorry, Duke. Must eat, I'm starved." I bit into the scalding meat pie and fixed him with a smile when I really wanted to scream, " ****! That's hot!"

"No worries," he replied, and waddled off toward the next pie-on-the-hoof emerging from the deli'.

Now this would not normally have seemed so remarkable had it not taken place in front of two of Western Australia's finest. Two uniformed Bobbies - guns and all - were literally only five yards away. 'To protect and serve' was not on their priority list. They were both actively and volubly selling raffle tickets to passers-by. First prize: A thirty thousand dollar car. Things have certainly changed since I was the new boy at the police station and getting lumbered selling lottery tickets for the 'Grand Christmas Draw.' When the first prize is a bottle of sherry, scrounged from a local publican, it isn't much fun I can tell you.

The officers stood in the centre of the mall. The sun belted down: 35 degrees and warming up. No worries! "Get your ticko's here!" Or some such catchy phrase. Only the very desperate gambler or loonies were out in that heat. The shoppers and sitters and Duke had more sense. We were all in the shade, hugging the awnings and enjoying the blasts of air conditioning escaping from the shop doorways along the length of the precinct.

Two things made my day. Firstly, the coppers both wore kilts in a fetching blue and had positioned themselves outside a shop dedicated to the sale of Damart thermolactyl clothing - you know, the stuff "As worn by Arctic explorers."

Secondly, and perhaps strangest of all, I am quite relieved to see Perth has its warts. Well, hardly warts, but certainly at least one royal pimple on its perfect persona.

A Defining Day:

I am at the small seaside town of Cottesloe and sitting on a rocky promontory which thrusts out, like an accusing finger, into a benign sea. The sun is slowly, slowly sinking toward the blue millpond and I am more than looking forward to my first ever sunset over the Indian Ocean. Ten minutes yet, so I have time to reflect on a most memorable day.

We have said goodbye to Perth. In time its pimples have developed into a full-blown case of measles: Drunks down town; dope in the bogs and a bureaucratic, bungling, balls-up at the bank. Now I am irritated by Perth's sullied virginity. There's no pleasing some people.

The sun is getting lower and two fishermen appear with rod and line, eager for the night's hunt. Now this is exciting - photographs with character. I re-check the camera for the umpteenth time.

But it has been a memorable day. One of those defining days in your life which I am sure everyone has, even if they fail to notice their passing. I will try to explain by way of example.

My first such day happened about forty years or so ago. I was watching a television documentary on whales. It included a sequence when the whalers sliced open the belly of one of those persecuted creatures. The whole deck flooded in an avalanche of milk. That meant an infant was going to slowly starve to death out there in the ocean - alone. I have never liked whalers: nor the consumers of whale, since: A defining moment.

Today it was a white, gypsum skull cap on display at Perth's marvellous Museum of Western Australia - a skull cap made and worn when a human being mourns the death of a loved one: In this case, an Aboriginal human being.

I confess to knowing and laughing at the yarns told by white Australians in pubs and clubs and in each other's homes. Stories like 'How to get rid of your anti-social Aboriginal neighbours?' Answer: spread some caustic soda on their lawn, so that when the soles of their feet burn, they leave, believing that evil spirits have inhabited their home. Or the one a landlord of a pub told me. He 'taught' one particular "black fella' " a lesson. "This one bloke used to pee up against me shed every night, see. So it's a galvanized iron job. Just run an electric current through it and when he takes a leak, he don't half jump: Hasn't done it since!" I am assured they are true stories.

Now, looking at the exhibits, Aboriginal culture comes to life. The displays palpably reach out to you. The anguish, the tears shed by the wearer of the cap; leap the centuries. In that moment, the culture of others is no longer negative - something to be derided - but rather, something deserving of admiration. This person, with so little, has loved another, grieved for another - and survived in an unforgiving land.

Next to the grieving cap is a statement of Aboriginal Spirituality - their theology, if you like. With conception comes your spirit - that scientifically unprovable thing which makes you, YOU: A Hitler or a Mother Theresa. During the stages of your life - initiation [equating with our Christening or circumcision], marriage, parenthood, old age - your spirit, [or soul,] develops and on your death, returns whence it came.

I spent three years of my life at university searching for an 'ology' to help me find my path and these people have known it from within for thirty thousand years or so: Somewhat humbling.

Some folks have said I shouldn't write about 'it': About 'them.' I would ruffle feathers on both sides of the negative divide. But I thought, why not? No book on Australia can surely ignore the original inhabitants and the subsequent clash of cultures and self interest. I don't know where this Defining Moment – this new knowledge – will take me; how it will affect me as a person, but at the moment I feel like an Eater of Whale.

The sunset is marvellous imparting the whole ocean with an ethereal quality.

Unabashed: I run off a whole reel off film.

Dee-Dee's Day Out:

The bus driver is called Eddie. He's big in every way, from his drooping Mexican moustache to his exuberant bulk. In fact he looks every bit the policeman he had been for seventeen years, until the loneliness and boredom of diplomatic protection drove him to find another outlet for his outgoing personality. Strangely, he found it driving: first taxis; now a bus. A bus driver who genuinely likes his passengers and a chat - one who goes out of his way to drop the less able off at their front doors. Consequently, published timetables are more a guide than a reality.

"You! Big Fella'! "

I nearly answered automatically, but managed to suck in my stomach and bite my tongue as I looked up to a see a woman, as wide as she was tall, clambering and heaving herself up the steps onto our bus. The task was made even harder, as she used both of her hands to clutch a huge handbag to her ample chest. She was talking to Eddie, their eyes meeting on a level, but she was standing and Eddie was still sitting, his beer belly pressed hard against the steering wheel.

"How are we today, Dee-Dee," he beamed?

"How much you dink and then you dive," demanded Dee-Dee, ignoring the pleasantry?

It was obvious to everyone in the first three rows that Dee-Dee had managed to have a couple of quiet ones whilst waiting for the bus. Well, in fact she was as full as the Warragamba Dam.

"Not the one-and-a-half bottles of red that politician says he gets down his neck before he drives home Dee-Dee," said Eddie referring to an item on last night's television news.

"You dink a bottle and then a half a bottle of red. I not get on your bus."

The queue shuffled nervously as she swayed alarmingly, her brain trying to order her body to turn around. No contest; the brain failed.

"No, Dee-Dee. I said....." Eddie realized he was onto a loser. "It doesn't matter. Three dollars to get home is it?"

More swaying. The handbag was searched with flamboyance. "Dinking and diving is bad," she said seriously.

"Yes, I know. It's three dollars. That's only sixty cents," Eddie said, as he moved the small coins around in the palm of his hand with a podgy finger.

Dee-Dee disappeared into the bag once more. "You see that advert?" came a muffled voice from within. "The government says you divers should cut down. No more than a dozen bottles a night."

"Is that so? Nearly there: That's two dollars thirty now."

The queue behind Dee-Dee was becoming restless in the searing heat. The seated passengers were becoming restless as they slowly cooked. No air conditioning, so the bus is only cool when it moves.

"You dink that much, Eddie?"

"Not when I'm diving, I mean driving, Dee. If you can't find any more, give me the rest next time."

"You're a lovely man." I winced when she smacked his cheek, supposedly gently and with affection. In effect, she left the imprint of her fingers. She put her nose three inches from his. "I'll tell you a secret," she whispered to the whole bus. "I can't dink what the telly says I can."

A Sledging we will go

Today is a red letter day. We give ourselves a day off in our little unit at Cottesloe; catch up with the washing and ironing; have a beer and a little sun. Bliss:

The weatherman is a hoot. He tells us "Thirty five degrees isn't so bad: It's not real hot," before going on to say that 'we' Western Australians are a hardy bunch. 'We' can take it apparently.

As the beautiful people, joggers and roller bladers, cyclists, and marathon, bum-wriggling walkers all pass us by, I cannot help but notice they are all hatless and sunscreenless. The U.V. rating is extreme - but then who wants to be a wimp 'out west', where people can take it? ME!

I burn my feet on the concrete yard as I take in the washing - and my better half, Patsy, is covered in a three-inch layer of sun-block, just to do the ironing. It is 3 p.m. and she hasn't been out yet - but she might. She's going to take a Masters' Degree in how to avoid the Australian sun.

Everyone tells us how lucky we are to have missed the sledging last week. I must have looked as bemused as General Custer at the Little Big Horn - especially when last week was forty-two degrees - all week. It would appear 'sledging' is not hurtling down icy slopes, precariously perched atop a piece of wood or plastic, but a euphemism for feeling beaten up by heat.

There is a cold snap moving in. It will be down to twenty-eight by the weekend. Can't wait to get the sledge out!

Another wonderful sunset over the ocean, watched from beneath a stand of Macquarie Pine filled with thousands of screeching parrots preparing to bed down.

Snapper n' chips, and all is well with the world.

Muscle Bound

Bums! A whole beach full: The burning white sand is a multicoloured confusion of tents and boats and bronzed muscle power. And bums: White ones on public display amongst the frenzied activity.

"Posers!" My wife put on her disgusted face.

"Nah! They've got to have bare buttocks so they can stick to the seat of their boat," I explained.

"It's enough to make anyone blush," continued my wife with no sign of redness and a strange twinkle in her eye.

Well, so as to save any blushes belatedly putting in an appearance, the starter got the next race under way. It seems as though life-saving craft from every bit of Australia are here and taking things very seriously indeed.

More crews limber up along the beach.

"I can't look," she lied.

Meanwhile, the guys with muscles on their eyebrows heave and grunt into the oars. The boats rear up over the breakers before catapulting forward, away in the direction of the not-so-distant shark nets.

Now, it is only a few days ago, the newspaper told me, three sharks - big 'uns with all their own teeth - had been snared in those self-same nets. The iron-men can have 'em; it'll take a bloody good fish to get me, Mister Intrepid, the ankle-deep photographer.

The strange thing is, for all the thousands on the beach, no-one is cheering or urging the competitors on. Above the usual background noise, the 'ugh's' of exertion are plainly heard.

Then it was the sun-bronzed, lightly-clad ladies' turn to race.

I wasn't given the chance to overcome any embarrassment.

Fremantle

We like Freo. It's got birds and bugs and flies and Aussie meat pies - and we like it a lot.

Now Fremantle cannot be described as a big place. No high-rise buildings here. Big is off the agenda - even the dress shops we visit [repeatedly] have no size 14s. I draw my wife's attention to a dress identical to one wholly responsible for what led to the birth of our daughter three decades ago - but for some reason she refuses to buy it.

We like Freo. We like its intimacy and compactness, where its venerable old colonial buildings preside over atmospheric pavement cafes, piazzas shaded by palm trees and the on-going street theatre that its heritage has spawned.

We also liked Brenda. Forty-ish and size sixteen-ish, she entertained us as we meandered through Old Fremantle Gaol. Four years ago she had visited her rellos in our adopted home town in England and found its narrow streets and black and white Tudor buildings, 'quaint.' Now quaint I can live with. I like quaint - it has overtones of eccentricity; but when she added "The people didn't seem to have much initiative over there," I felt I had to delve deeper.

"Put it like this," she explained. "In this cafe I asked for a toasted ham and cheese sandwich. Not much to ask for at the end of the twentieth century. But no! I could have ham OR cheese, not both."

Ah well! I gave my mouth a rest and, for a couple of cell blocks, pondered on what, if anything, had happened to good old Anglo-Saxon inventiveness and desire which drove Britain to its past glories. Surely we still have it - and with plenty to spare. As a country, we have sold off every asset to pay out welfare. We have taxed British companies out of existence - only to give huge grants to foreign ones to create the self-same jobs. We still have millions out of work, or on long-term sick, while those with a job are having to do the work of two or more. Nah! I decided Brenda was just unlucky in her choice of sarnie.

There was certainly nothing wrong with convict initiative way back in the 1800s, when British prisoners made life difficult for their warders in oh so many different ways. How about the guys who were put in charge of the prison aviary as part of their rehabilitation? All the scraps of fruit and veg. were assiduously collected from the prison kitchen for the delight of the parrots and cockatoos - who saw nothing of this daily feast, as it all went into an underground still. Some idiot spoiled the plot by taking pity on the birds - and fed them with the sediment. They promptly fell over dead drunk at the feet of a warder. Or how about a rope made out of single sheets of toilet paper? Brilliant! No initiative, indeed!

Yes, we like Fremantle. We think it is quaint, which is probably why we feel so comfortable here. Any place where the locals carry jumpers and wear woolly hats in thirty degree temperatures is worthy of our esteem.

With evening comes a 'sausage sizzle' and a game of lawn bowls. A wonderful evening; surrounded by galahs, laughing kookaburras - and a host of new friends in pullovers.

Rottnest Island:

A Nip of Bad Spirits:

"The land over the sea," the Aborigines call it. They are not too keen to visit the place either, believing that the Spirits of the Dead are blown over the ocean to Rottnest Island.

It must also be the place where the ghosts of worn out 'express' ferries - like this one - go, given the reluctance ours is showing in moving forward toward "The holiday experience of a lifetime." The overloaded boat rolls with the ocean swell. I see the sea. Count one....., two....., three....., I see the sky. Count four....., five.....six....., and then the ocean is back.

The ancient ferry plunges this way and that. Apparently any-which-way except forward to Perth's very own island resort - Rottnest. The island got its name from some Dutch sailor who landed here and didn't know his miniature kangaroos from his large rats. Excuse me a second.....

Sky, one.....two..... Water, one.....two..... Sky, one.....two..... It would not be so bad if the waves were hitting the boat in a regular rhythm. Then the youngsters amongst us join in. Sky; one..... two....."Ooooh!" Sea; three.....four..... "Ahhh!"

A lady, size twenty plus and wearing a dress made by Khan brothers, Tent Makers to Royalty, slides into some 'Oooher's' who become 'Agher's' in a trice.

I suppose it was only coincidence that we were having one of those days when nothing goes right. Nothing to do with bad spirits, but I cannot stop thinking about that John Wayne movie - the one where he wanders into a Red Indian graveyard to escape some bad guys. Not a good move.....

Maybe today was not a good move, as it had started to go pear-shaped at the bus stop early this morning. The local asylum must have let some of the inmates out for the day. The bus was late, very late in fact, and the boys and girls must have been starved of outside company for some time because we have become the centre of attention. Throw in a couple of drunks who start to fight just as Michael is telling me for the thirty-third time: "M.y....n.name,....i.i.i.is....Mmmmmmlkel"

We escape in the transport, to be dropped at the ferry terminal. It was obvious from the noisy turmoil of the rugby scrum involving thousands that the entire asylum was out.

The ferry was late: Very, very late.

And now! Sea.....Sky.....Ooooh! Someone throws up. Sky.....Sea.....Agggh! Regurgitated breakfast rolls across the foot-wells: All the way to the island of spirits and rats' nests.

We arrive - and instantly the journey is relegated to history. The place is actually, impossibly beautiful. A photographer's delight:

However, hundreds of us mere mortals had but one thing in mind - to pee! No one had fancied the onboard conveniences and so we make for the single loo, arriving in time for merely a long wait.

But now things are on the up: A snorkelling trip around a couple of shipwrecks. We are not novices - but that was before today: Before Rottnest.

"That's one way of doing it," said the young man on the rescue launch as he hauled me in like a bloated walrus. I didn't care how I got into the bouncing rubber thing. The bruises and grazes will heal. I was just sick of sucking in salt water. No way could I snorkel with a six-foot swell breaking over me. Now snorkelling involves putting your head in the water and breathing through a twelve-inch tube. That means every few seconds I was five feet under water. The others managed, but I couldn't get the knack of sucking in time with the waves. Not me: Not today.

The spirits continue to haunt. My wife, Patsy, changes out of wet swimsuit in the only place of privacy on board - the swimming platform in the stern. Half naked, and becoming more so by the millisecond, twelve heads bob to the surface two yards away:
"H.h.h.Ello. M.m.m..my.....n..name is MmmmmIkel."

We leave the boat. "Thank you, Sir." "Thank you, Madam."

Sir! Madam! Could that be us? I look around and suddenly realise we are the only people over twenty-five on this 'experience' - and we're over fifty! I'm reduced from a would-be ageing adventurer to a boring old fart by a single word: 'Sir!'

Things are on the up again. A nice cuppa tea and a Quokka turns up unexpectedly. These kanga-rat things are not supposed to be found so close to the touristy bits of the island, so naturally I begin to think that we have been forgiven by the Spirit World.

My certainty grows as the return ferry shows no deference to the angry sea. We power our way to the mainland, the heavy swell breaking and boiling white over our decks and windows. Most exciting!

The bus back is late and overcrowded - with youngsters of course - and my old boss's favourite saying now has more than a ring of truth: "There's nowt wrong with the younger generation - except I'm not one of them."

Fair enough. I kept that thought firmly in my head as we endured the antics of the drunks on the train back home.

That was nothing to do with the world of Spirits though. Was it?

Not the Pinnacles

"What's the best way to the Pinnacles then, Ron?"

Ron had become our neighbour overnight. Sitting on the adjacent veranda, with a cool breeze whispering in from the ocean, he took a long drag on his cigarette before answering.

"You don't want to go there," he said, exhaling slowly. "It's nicer here."

But all the brochures and guide books had said we must go; we must see for ourselves one of the world's strangest sights.

I try again. "We'd like a look."

"Nah! I live up there.....well, a hundred and forty k's inland. Believe me. All there is are bits of limestone sticking up out of the ground.....Forty plus temperatures and stuff all else." He paused for another drag and again spoke as he exhaled. "I know 'cos it's been over forty since last November."

"But IF we wanted to go: Which way?"

I didn't get a chance to find out. He flicked his fag end over the balcony and lit another. "Only two places worth visiting in this State.....Albany and Geraldton."

"But those are over eight hundred kilometres away: And in different directions." I was genuinely appalled.

"So?" He was genuinely puzzled.

"We can't possibly go there.....They're......they're so far away," I said lamely.

"No. A long way is Melbourne and back," he explained: "Just delivered a ram over there. Wanna see a piccy?"

He removed a wayward strand of tobacco from his lips, and produced one saliva-stained picture of identical sheep after another. But I was too astute to fall for that one. I kept my mouth well and truly shut.

"This is me best bloke.....And this one is King.....And this one is Rameses.....And this one..........

And he obviously knew his rams from his sheep. Mind you, at sixty thousand bucks apiece I'd know all about them too.

He also proved he was an expert on artificial insemination. As he spoke about the various mechanics of sperm collection from behind billowing clouds of cigarette smoke and falling fag ash, the lure of Fremantle markets suddenly became stronger and stronger. Question! Do I want to drive for six hours in forty degree temperatures to reach the Pinnacles, or do the eight hundred k's to either of those other two places? For a day out! Answer. Nope! Let's go the four kilometres down to Freo.

I will never be able to reconcile the Australian concept of distance with that of the British. To travel the highways and bye-ways of old England the journey is planned, mulled over, thought about. Possibly for weeks! Tyres are checked, petrol tank filled and a flask prepared. 'Leeds you say? Oh! That's three hours away. Don't hit the M6 motorway after 7.45 in the morning around Manchester. That means leaving here about 6.30ish. Could be icy at that time of the morning - and there could be fog over the moors. That's the M62 you know - and the traffic! Terrible! Best to stay overnight! Make it a two or three day trip. Where to stay? I've got a bed and breakfast book you can borrow.'

Not so in Oz. You want to go - you go. That's it! Distance is a part of the way of life and yet the distances are real. A helicopter can take six hours to reach an emergency and a three hour trip each way to the doctor or dentist is a mere irrelevance.

Yet to me, the urge to gobble up vast distances is still-born: The four k's to see the markets win hands down.

"There's me Missus. Gee! She's got the cases. All right luv!" He beamed down from the balcony looking at her in just the same way as he had looked at his best fella'.

The lady's reply from the courtyard was lost by an angrily crashing car boot as the heavy suitcases were safely stowed. She was as mad as a politician in a one pub town - just like the one they were returning to.

Ron was oblivious. "Did I ask you if you wanted a photo?"

Blank stare: Surely he didn't mean one of his long-suffering other half?

"One of me rams, mate?"

I huffed and puffed a bit.

"She's back with the other cases." He flicked away half an inch of cigarette, this time in his wife's direction. It did not improve her demeanour: "Must shove off."

And so to Fremantle markets: We are not disappointed. The teeming old wool sheds are a shopper's dream and a husband's nightmare. Everything is for sale – from jewels, which we didn't buy, to paw-paws, which we did. The markets may not be unique, but they are excellent.

Barramundi and chips on the jetty under the riggings of the fishing fleet bring to a close our perfect day in this western paradise.

Yanchep

We were quite right not to go as far north as the Pinnacles. We have gone north but only to Yanchep National Park. It is less than a two-hour drive from our relative's home and down-town Perth, but it is HOT! Incredibly so: Like standing in front of an oven.

By noon, even the raucous, yellow-tailed black parrots had fallen silent, leaving the park symphony to be orchestrated by a billion, wing-flapping cicadas.

We had driven to this marvellous, wild place near the ocean, passing through mile after mile of expanding suburbia, which had gradually given way to garden centres, industrial estates and vacant lots, until we found Perth's missing millions.

Correct! This is where the flies go on holiday. They were everywhere - on legs, arms, raised tea cups. They were in everything - eyes, mouth, car boot, sandwiches. Best of all they liked the tea, preferably with milk and sugar. They were into the cup before you were.

Still, no complaints: No grouching. An early morning walk around a lake, trying to avoid the neatly signposted, 'Tiger Snake colony', and all the while bewitched by droning dragon flies, cheeky wildfowl and, of course, the argumentative, intoxicating parrots. All conspired to make everything worthwhile.

A short side trip to the small township of Yanchep itself, to view the breathtaking coral beach - and then on again to the yachts of Two Rocks - both places predestined to bloom into suburbia as Perth blossoms still further.

Scarborough Beach

I'm up to the armpits in warm water. The next wave, unmolested since its inception somewhere out there near South Africa, breaks over my head and knocks my feet from under me. I don't care. I am not trying to breathe under water today and my feet can find the sand again in an instant. Anyway, there are two muscular life-guards over there.

Life is good. Up to the armpits in luxury and surrounded by dozens of kids on surfboards. I feel an affinity with them, an unspoken agreement - albeit one-sided, as they don't see me. I do not exist in their delight. I prefer to think that they accept me as an icon. Well, who was it who once remarked that Australians are the only people in the world who consider a beer belly to be a status symbol?

In return, I do not mention their spearing surfboards just happen to be in a prohibited area: 'Swimmers Only' in this part of the ocean. After Rottnest, I suppose I should be excluded too. The kids show a healthy disregard to the shouts and gesticulations of shore-bound supervisors encouraging them to leave.

Disregard of authority is not a new phenomenon. The Premier of some state or other gave an award to a 'new' Australian for saving the life of a Police Constable who was getting worsted by a maniac with a knife. He acted to help the policeman - the symbol of authority - whilst a crowd of 'old' Aussies - people whose forefathers had helped settle the land - stood around and cheered on the madman. The Premier said, "You're a fair dinkum Aussie now," as he handed over the plaque and cheque.

Nothing could be further from the truth.

However, generations of such nose-thumbing at authority can have a down side. No generalizations, so we'll look at Pete's Place. It doesn't sound too grand - and it's not: A shuttered, concrete shack by the beach where Pete dispenses such essentials as Coca Cola and ice cream.

Pete sat smoking on his bacteria friendly counter, trying to regain some sort of equilibrium after a hard night partying. His thirty-five years looked to have been very long and very, very wearing.

A request for two teas elicited a response. "Ohhh!" A rub of the forehead: "I ain't put the water on yet."

A plea for us to go away, no doubt, but we waited and chatted. Pete had been down-sized by the bank he worked for in earlier [and better] days. Now, his only interest was surfing - and how to live on the dole. Unfortunately he had been a "bit slow," as he put it; and the Commonwealth Employment Services [the Job Centre to you and me] had got him tied into this concrete prison within sight of his ocean and freedom. A discussion of what the future held elicited a shrug of the shoulders.

Now meet a 'new' Aussie: Liam from Dublin. I couldn't help but compare the two. Liam had felt constrained by home-town small-mindedness, so he sells all and moves to Perth. Now running his own car hire business with zest and efficiency, he has one hundred cars earning him and his family a place by their pool in the sun. He has plans, and ideas, and a future here. He is now an Australian citizen - even bought a pullover - but he leaves me with a question about where the true spirit of Australia lies.

Maybe Australia needs immigration to remain viable and prosperous; needs new blood to keep its vitality in the face of unrelenting hedonism. The sun and surf - and the life-style they offer, can surely drain away the work ethic.

In truth, we know plenty of hard working Aussies whose families came here generations ago, so I suppose it is not worth looking for that quintessential essence of what makes an Australian. Best just to accept every individual for who they are and enjoy them.

Come to think of it, maybe that is the Australian way.

York

It was a musty, cell-sized room. A small, rectangular window high up near the ceiling allowed a little light to catch the spiralling dust plume. The gloom was not lifted by the green paint on the walls and the dark brown of the woodwork - a colour scheme lifted straight out of some Civil Service handbook.

But nothing could spoil my delight. I was no longer 'up country'; no longer in the sunburnt York of the Avon Valley, a fertile place over the Darling Ranges to which the early settlers were drawn. Instead I was miles away in space and aeons away in time, as I looked at the plug-in switchboard of yesteryear made by the A1 Telephone Company of London.

Why the Old Court House and Gaol Museum had 'my' switchboard displayed in all its glory behind heavy ropes and 'Keep Off' notices, was a mystery. But I didn't care.

I was back in another small room painted by government money and administered by colour-blind functionaries. It was 1963 and I was in a police station in Yorkshire, somewhere near the industrial city of Leeds. The office was complete with a tiny hatchway through which conversations with 'the public' took place, a coal fire and a smell all of its own. The smell is impossible to define: A combination of years of soot, cigarette smoke, polish, excreta and fear. Amongst it all stood the A1, its rows of matching pairs of plugs with extendable leads nestled, just waiting for a home amongst the myriad of tiny holes marking the extensions and telephone lines. It was a daunting obstacle for any young probationary constable intending to make his way 'in the job.'

On the job was Constable Godfrey - a large man with a hooked nose that wandered across his plump face at will. He had a nose Caesar would have killed for. At six feet three inches tall he should have been a formidable guy, but he had two problems. One, he was frightened of the dark - which made night shifts a bit difficult. And two, whatever the weather, rivers of sweat ran down his face and disconcertingly dripped off the end of his nose: A magnet for every pair of eyes.

But it was the A1 that did for him.

Now, Inspector Masterton WAS a formidable man. He was the most ferocious I have ever met.....Well, almost - but that's another story. Small, dapper, authoritarian, you could cut your finger on his pressed uniform; shave in the shine on his black Oxfords. Rules one to infinity - DO NOT CROSS HIM - EVER!

Fair go, the Inspector had waited quietly, if not patiently, for his telephone connection to be made. Quite a long time in fact, for in those days, contacting the Chief Constable was not an everyday occurrence. At last!

"Good morning, Sir."

"Is that you Masters?" The Chief was not good with names.

"Ye....." B.u.z.z.z.z. Line as dead as a Tassy tiger.

Masterton went white. Never a good sign that. He went looking for blood. I know, because I was there when he cowed the office with his icy stare. His pebble glasses moved up and down on his nose as his temples twitched. I shrank deeper into a large, leather-bound ledger marked 'General Occurrence Book.'

Silence reigned - except for the strident telephone bells. The A1 had decided to do its Christmas tree illumination act.

In the presence of greatness, Constable Godfrey leapt to his feet and, with six jerking, homeless leads in his right hand, saluted with the other and sprayed a mixture of tears, sweat and saliva at the world with a despairing, "It's no me! It's the atmospherics!"

We didn't see him again.

But York is brilliant. Its old, historic buildings and courtyards conjure up pictures of the mid-1800s, when constables and troopers enforced law and order with leg shackles and beatings. Close your eyes and you can see a patrol returning from a ten-day expedition to uphold peace in the wilderness. It is so unchanged.

It reminded us of our past in oh so many ways: Shop assistants who know the names of their customers and have time for us outsiders: A main street devoid of traffic - and a Co-op store I remember from my mining village back home, circa 1950. It is here in a time warp. Each large window abutting the sidewalk given over to a department within: garden equipment in one; children's clothes in another: Then curtains and women's fashions. Not a museum, just unchanging: A constant factor in the life of the people of the town since 1912. I suspect it will still be the same for the generation as yet unborn.

I bet they even have penny liquorice roots, real strawy ones, in a glass jar inside.

Margaret River

Margaret was from Margaret River. We met during the Reel of the Royal Scots at a dance in Perth, some three hundred kilometres away from her home. She had just popped up for the dance - an evening out - and within minutes we were invited to stay. At that time I was not looking my best, out of breath and soaking in sweat [you try a reel in thirty degree evening temperatures] so the invitation was a pure act of kindness.

No matter where you go in the world, Scottish Country Dancing seems to attract a similar type of person. Whether in a church hall on a housing estate at Perth, Scotland, or in a school gym in the suburbs of Perth, Western Australia, people dress the same [in pullovers], wear the kilt, dance the same dances and extend a warm welcome to new friends. There is also no chance of being called 'Sir'.

We never did meet Margaret again, but we did find her river - a pleasant enough spot, surrounded by wineries and manicured greenery.

It was a long way for her to go a-dancin' - and just as far for us to retrieve the credit cards our bank had helpfully sent here.

Bunbury:

It rained today. The first time for six months, so I'm told. Only a few drops, but the pungent smell of the eucalypt forests exploded into the car. Wonderful!

4p.m: A quick visit to Koombana beach. And why not! After all it is the reason we came. Nothing doing!

*

The next day dawns and things do not look too good. The rain has worsened overnight; the clouds are low and scudding, the ocean grey, sullen, uninviting.

I ignore the spider's web, two feet above my head and try to concentrate on what the young Japanese student of marine biology was saying.

"They've come these last three mornings: Each time at eight."

It is 7.15 a.m. We've been up since six. More intrepid folk arrive, dressed in shorts and raincoats. Some people will do anything to feed their obsession.

"We've had as many as forty-two here at any one time."

7.50 a.m. Expectancy mounts.

"Sharky usually comes first. We treated the shark bites to his face and fins and he has never forgotten the kindness."

I do not know how the itinerant help knows so much, but it helps the waiting.

8.00 a.m. The rain bleaches mockingly into the faces of the huddled few. Nothing!

"They usually come straight in toward us."

8.05. Nothing.

"They don't always come."

In desperation, even a fishing buoy causes momentary excitement.

The rain continues unabated, pounding noisily on the roof and sides of the disused cargo container which is now our uncomfortable shelter at Koombana.

Koombana Beach: "Better than Monkey Mia for dolphins," say those in the know. Question: Are those in the 'know' here?

I do not know much about dolphins; still less about wild ones which come and go as they please - but I do know they exert a positive influence on me. Unkindness to dolphins is unthinkable - unless you're a shark or a tuna trawler man. It would be like bashing old folk.

Dolphins obviously have the same effect on others. Why else would we all be up at the crack of a dismal dawn in an unremarkable Bunbury and on a pretty ordinary beach surrounded by oil and grain and wood chip storage tanks breathing air tainted by diesel fumes?

8.40 a.m. Sharky and his mates have done a no-show.

And so to Cape Naturaliste: A wild and fascinating coastline, great walks over heath and dune, fantastic views every-which-way out over the haunt of whales and dolphins and other such leviathans.

And guess what?

*

Next day dawns and at 7.43 a.m. we're back at Bunbury's Koombana having quickly rewritten the travel script.

Optimism is overwhelming. Same faces, but today the cagoules have gone, replaced by a clear blue sky and warming sun. The ocean is still; not a wave laps the sand: Today for sure.

8.00 a.m. Excitement peaks.

8.30 a.m. Excitement begins to fade. We settle in for a long wait.

9.45 a.m. Dare we go for a pee and/or a tea? If we do, I just know there will be hundreds of them here doing double back flips. People will be in the water swimming with them. We'll return to be faced with an empty bay once more and, "Did you see .....;" this or that or the other. We will miss the show of the century. I cross my legs. Patsy has had hers crossed for ages.

10.30 a.m. The would-be wild dolphin watchers are reduced to taking photo's of each other in the water where we will the creatures to be.

11.00 a.m. We pass the time chatting with people from all over the world, and begin to apply wads of sunscreen.

11.31 a.m. Two dolphins are sighted, frolicking one hundred and fifty yards offshore. The Sea World display lasts all of, oh..., five seconds.

12 noon. Sun scarred, we admit defeat. The dolphins are happy with each other's company today and we have to be on the road again, gobble a few miles before dark.

Disappointed? Yes! But happy that Sharky and his mates are free to dispense their affection and charm at will.

Journey 3
South Australia

Doing yer time

"Is that all the baggage, Sir?"

Now I am definitely starting to get a complex: This old and deprived spirit subjecting himself to enduring yet another day in the tender loving care of another airline.

Rain had cancelled the 'let's-mooch-around-the-pool' idea and so we people-watch at the airport, something I never tire of. People embarking on journeys stir the imagination. Are they commuting? Back at five with a "Hi honey, I'm home!" Or is it a long journey, perhaps one which will irrevocably reshape their lives. Perhaps it is a goodbye forever.

Some wear their hearts for all to see: Parting lovers, anger, disappointment, regret, resignation. It is all there.

Today's offering was a young husband with two small kids meeting his wife returning home with yet another toddler.

First welcoming little one to the returnee: "I've got measles!"

Second welcoming littlee: "Don't tell him. It's a surprise."

The humour did nothing to still the nerves. I will admit to being a bit nervous, even though travel writers don't usually admit to things - like fear! But I have seen our plane arrive - you haven't! It's small: Can't have more than a gross of seats. I remember listening to an interview once, when the inventor [or some such] of jumbo jets was asked why he only travelled in a plane with four engines. Reply: "Because we haven't got any with five."

To take my mind off impending diarrhoea, I cast my eyes about, only to re-discover the phenomenon of the plane spotter, a sort of up-market anorak type who used to hang about the sooty railway stations of the Swinging Sixties, waiting for the appearance of the Flying Scotsman or The Mallard. Today, they have gone international. Row upon row of elderly obsessives are strung out in front of us, hogging all the seats in front of the large plate glass windows of the airport terminal building. And, before you ask — yes, they are wearing anoraks, despite the temperature controls being set in favour of the decorative palms. These guys [and here is another fact: no women are ever seen] have certainly joined the technological age. Gone are the 'I-Spy' books and a chewed stump of a pencil. Instead they reach interminably for binoculars, zoom lenses and flasks of tea...And biscuits. [The eagle-eyed observer soon notes the preference for digestive.]

One gentleman sits alone and as he bends an ear over his crackling radio set, the curls of grey, unkempt hair fall over his bushy, white eyebrows.

"Come to taxi-way two-a left-a Alpha India Hotel Nine-a eight-a."

He brushes his hair away impatiently, as his hand records another entry in the voluminous papers spread out all over the table in front of him. I cannot believe that anybody, anywhere, or at any time will ever need to know that vital piece of information...But! But if they did, he'd make a fortune. He sighs, looks down at his offending hand and begins to pick at a fingernail.

I begin to wonder. Why has the tower stopped talking to Alpha India What's-it? Why do they need zoom lenses? Are there still train spotters, or are stations now deserted? Why.....But there is no time for wonderment. Things are happening all around. An "Agh!" from over there and a "Yes-Yes!" from over here demands attention. Be-camera'd and binoculared watchdogs are producing reference books, veritable tomes. An aeroplane trundles toward us. At least it looks like an aeroplane to me…..two wings, two engines and moving things…but no! People are drooling, or jabbering, or both, speaking at a hundred-to-the-minute over each other. The noise grows; the conversation incomprehensible to us mere mortals.

They all write the plane's identification number down. I write it down…..you know - just in case - but alas it was on a piece of paper washed in my jeans. Anyway, this historic craft was built by Boeing, in Seattle in 1793 using the rolling stone and chisel technique. Did you know that the two bolts which hold the tail on have only four twists on them - and they need to stand up to one thousand and one cubic inches of kinetic energy per polar-insulated thrust? [Or some such technical guff:] No! Well, you know now to get one of those strange books these chaps have for Christmas next year. Or, did you know that the front tyre was made from rubber taken from tree A1043? It's in the third section, just up on the left as you walk through the plantation outside of Kuala Lumpur. Of course if you cannot wait until Christmas you could always fix a flask, don an anorak and sit next to a dedicated digestive biscuit eater.

Here comes another plane. I wonder if they would lend me a pencil stump.

Admittedly the airline itself was good. When my attention span faded from the anoraks, it arranged for a couple of propeller-driven things to taxi around outside - and then, once inside our tiny tot, the in-flight video showed pictures of canvas and string biplanes: All to make me feel much better.

It is nice to arrive somewhere by plane and not be jet lagged. Mind you, on arrival at our Adelaide hotel, I looked at the lift buttons to find they were marked 'U' and 'D' - and couldn't figure out what they meant.

Adelaide

Our modern hotel overlooking park land and impressive cityscape posted this statement at the entrance to the swimming pool:

'Central Board of Health
Regulation under Health Act 1935 - 76
Part X11 Swimming Pools
12th Schedule
NOTICE
No person shall enter the swimming pool unless the body is clean.
No person shall spit, spout water, blow nose or urinate in the pool.
No person shall permit any animal to enter the pool.'

Adelaide is a city of statements: Slightly archaic, like the notice nailed to the door of the pool maybe, but a very fine city because of it. The streets make a statement with their width, straightness and cleanliness. The main thoroughfare is King William Street, but as the City Fathers did not want to upset a distant royalty, they renamed every street which touches upon it: Magnificently over-the-top. Parks encircle the city and the continuous green belt is but a mere canon ball's shot away from Woolworth's and Myers. Was that the way nineteenth century surveyors worked? "Fire!" "That's O.K. lads, start planting the trees here." The parks and garden squares are a great idea; they allow the city to breathe, give rest under the shade of old trees to those weary in the sun, and add an air of tranquillity. Yet they are as nothing when compared with the world class botanical gardens.

The historic churches and public buildings are bold and stylish and yet Adelaide is not afraid of the modern. The environs of the Festival Theatre brandish modern art at the city's past, yet the vibrant statement is somehow in keeping with the whole. Like it or not, it is the most ingenious method of concealing air ducts that I have seen.

And of course we must mention the glistening River Torrens which acts as a foil for Adelaide's perfection. The place has an atmosphere, a pride in itself, its people anxious to please. What more could anyone ask from a city.

Well, since you mention it - and if it doesn't sound too churlish - road signs would be nice. There are none. Anywhere! I'm sitting five storeys up on the balcony of our room, overlooking a busy road junction: Twenty-eight lanes of traffic going in ten different directions - and not one blessed road sign. The locals obviously do not need them and in any event they would just spoil the views.

And what views!

Adelaide, you are a beaut!

The Strange Case of the Two Thompson's:

So why South Australia: I could give a politician's reply, talk forever and say nothing in an effort to justify our trip here. I could tell you about an uncle of the Bulford Ilk who came here back in 1875 after he failed to find gold in South Africa - but no one knows what happened to him. And there is a full cousin here somewhere. But the truth of the matter is we just wanted to come.

And we are pleased we did, for truth is often stranger than fiction. One night we take our dancing feet to the Scottish Society dance at the foot of Mount Lofty and get talking to this bloke who arrived at the tea pot at the same time as us.

Coincidence one was that we were both researching our family history: Nothing unusual in that; millions are doing it world wide. But we're both looking for a William Thompson. O.K., that could be just another coincidence; but both our Williams were born in 1817 in the village of Meldon near Morpeth, in Northumberland, England. Whereas Thompson might be a common name, two guys with identical details in a village with a population less than the hotel we're staying in, becomes a might suspicious.

My Tommo went missing from England – well, we can't find him. His Thompson arrived in Tasmania on a prison ship, whether voluntarily or not we don't know. This was sometime after 1839. Anyway, his William arrived in Adelaide on 1st November, 1849 from Tassy, married a local lass, sired a daughter – Sarah - and then disappeared forever: A century-and-a-half later Sarah's line is slurping tea next to me. Did Tommo return to his wife in Northumberland and father my great grandfather four times removed?

Who knows if my new found friend is indeed a 'cousin,' but we are here and, however bemused we get, intend to enjoy it.

Adelaide

Now and Then

"No-you-can't-have-your-dinner," said the security guard, muscles bulging, eyes as cold as a shark.

I am appalled: "Why not?"

"Your shorts are not suitable." The gnarled hand stroked the butt of the gun carried low, like a gunslinger's.

I cannot believe this. I'm arguing with someone toting a gun! "But they cost eighty bucks. My wife's were only ten.....and they're tartan - and horrible."

Maybe I am arguing, insanely now, but I can see my three dollar Casino dinner disappearing fast.

The guard regarded me with contempt and delivered the coup-de-what's-it. "Your wife's dolphin tee-shirt is not allowed either."

"She can take it off!" I shouted, arms waving wildly.

"Out!"

I could feel the female sentinel of nineteenth century virtue burning her smile into my retreating back. The branding only added insult to injury, as I now add 'scruffy' to my personal portfolio, which already designates me as old and disadvantaged.

We return, hungry, to the twenty-eight degrees beyond the icy air conditioning of the Adelaide casino. The atmosphere was as cold outside as it had been moments earlier.

"I thought you liked my shorts," said my wife unforgivingly. The chill lasted until we found a pretty ordinary sarnie bar down the street.

Mind you, it was nice to experience a little discomfort today of all days.

The name, 'Grace Darling,' had made us pause for an instant - an instant which turned magically into hours as we became lost in the Adelaide of yesteryear brought to life by the Migration Museum. I'm still not sure what Grace Darling, the heroine of Northumberland [and a very distant relation by marriage], had to do with the Destitute Asylum for Children which had borne her name back in 1867. What a place this must have been back then for those excluded from the booming Adelaide society: One hundred unwanted, filthy urchins, five to a bed and covered in sores [the 'Itch'], falling victim to measles, gangrene and much more besides. Twenty-eight died - their parents, even if alive, were not informed of the passing of their children.

The unwanted and dispossessed, adult and child alike, were kept well out of sight as more and more ships arrived, bringing thousands of free settlers to the new Promised Land.

Dinnerless - and the sarnie repeating on me unmercifully - we spend a couple of hours at the Mortlock Library, part of the State Library on beautiful North Terrace. I belch my way through passenger lists of ships arriving in South Australia: Ships with such stirring names as 'Agincourt' [1850] and British Lion [1866].

The people they discharged had left poverty in Midlothian and Kilkenny for a new, strange, beautiful land. Many couldn't afford the twenty pounds' disembarkation tax in Melbourne and so left their transport to the Victorian goldfields here - and walked. The people of the records had one thing in common – youth - so I guess they had nothing to lose and everything to gain. But death is no respecter of age. Numerous names on the manifests are pencilled through: 'Dead!'

Yet many prospered, and now Adelaide, the city they created, is a truly fabulous place. Its citizens are amongst the most privileged in the world. As Joseph Orchard of Adelaide said in a letter dated 1848 to his folk back home: "I bless God that I came here."

He will get no argument from us.

Glenelg

I was ready for Miss Muscles. I was dressed to kill in the Aussie green and gold - albeit gold socks and green underpants. Today we would get our three dollar tucker in the casino for sure.

But we didn't. It was Glenelg's fault, helped in no uncertain terms by the Italian patisserie just off the promenade.

We had travelled from the city to Adelaide's seaside suburb on a 1929, bull-nosed tram, not intending to make a day of it. The tram was great - all polished wood panelling, its sash windows the sort British Railways used to have in the days of steam and the saying of long goodbyes at smoky stations. And the clippy shouted "Tickets please:" A blue uniform with an old ticket machine strapped about the chest with shiny leather. Nostalgia! Great!

For twenty-five minutes the tram hurtles its way over street junctions with alarm bells clanking, rolling and swaying, and with so much noise that conversation becomes impossible.

We arrive, conversation starved, at Glenelg terminus. Old Victorian buildings, including the Town Hall, surround the shady square where the tram now sits, out of breath, girding itself for the return. Pavement cafes abound. A limestone church; its rendering about arched windows and doorways are painted cream, brown and pink. Yes, pink! But it sure looks good.

We paddle in the unpolluted, tranquil waters which silently lap the burning white sand - which in turn barbecues the immobile forms catching the rays before 'winter' sets in.

We are at the end of the season, but there is sufficient activity on the beach and in the attractive little shops to make you wonder what it would be like in high season. I will hazard a guess and say it will be just like today - only more kids looking for MY sea shells.

If all that weren't enough, this tiny cafe popped into view. The pasta - ricotta and spinach - was good but stopped short of heavenly. The cakes didn't. They took the lift through heavenly and divine, and stopped at the floor marked 'god-like'.

I would like to be objective here and describe these.....these.....creations; fifty or more along the counter. But I can't. Mine was rum. They hadn't skimped on the alcohol, which was disconcerting, not least because I had just popped a pain killer: rum - surrounded by a tiny amount of flour, milk and butter, and large amounts of dark chocolate with milk chocolate floral arrangements on top. Bite into fatso-paradise and the white chocolate, hidden until now, becomes supreme.

After pasta and pastries, the casino will have to keep its 'roast of the day.'

The Beach Bum

Do you remember Walt Disney's classic, Lady and the Tramp? It is certainly hard to forget - and for me, Tramp is the star: scruffy, lovable, one ear up and one down, head quizzically to one side: Nobody's dog but his own.

He is here, alive and well, and reincarnated as a beach bum on this fine beach. He's on his own, playing in the surf and rolling in the sand. He scavenges for leftovers [from the Italian patisserie owners, if he has any sense] - and for company, adopts anyone walking the golden miles.

Now it's our turn. We are adopted - which is all well and good until he does something anti-social or mischievous, and then you look around frantically, wanting to cry out to anyone giving you the evil eye "He's no mine!"

You can see the thoughts doing the rounds before burning out through the eyes of passers-by:
"A likely story." "You must think we are stupid." "Where's the cops."

I just thank God there are no uniforms around with their on-the-spot fines.

Yet you can't blame people for thinking those thoughts, as Tramp bounces about your feet, all the while keeping pace with you, oblivious to all as he looks adoringly into your face.

Then he's gone. Back to cool off in the surf. Hopefully he will adopt one of the glares back down the beach and let them have a go at the, 'But he's no mine' routine with the beach patrol.

Me Best Bloke!

Adelaide is even lovelier by night. Tree lights sparkle along the leafy boulevard that is the historic North Terrace, stretching all the way from the Botanic Gardens to way down past the railway station. The old buildings and churches are illuminated: St. Peter's Cathedral is a picture, standing beyond the River Torrens. People throng the streets; the pavement cafes are doing great business; live bands perform in the pubs, their music spilling out onto the sidewalks like little oases in the warm, sultry darkness.

Adelaide is undoubtedly a lovely, lovely city.

And tonight we become part of that city's history. We are at the Adelaide Oval for the first ever home match of the Mighty Rams. To the uninitiated [I include my wife amongst this group - and she was there] it was a rugby league match.

There is plenty of hype - fireworks and prancing dancers. Unfortunately, there are few fireworks on the field of play, so I too am reduced to watching women. No! Not like that. These women are the poor lost souls, sent for the beers by their men folk and who now wander aimlessly about the crowd with absolutely no idea where they left them.

The alternative was to watch the stilted antics of the home team mascot, 'Super Ram.' Some poor guy is so in need of a dollar that he has been willing to don a giant ram's head and a wool coat to run about like a demented Jumbuck. A sixty thousand dollar Jumbuck, whose time had come to manfully prove once again he was 'me best bloke.'

Baa!

Mount Lofty

We've done it again!

We are in an Adelaide suburb. The beautiful city of churches and gardens awaits: There are shopping malls with air conditioning. There are speciality shops - and supermarkets with 'the sales' on just around the corner. The market is a good 'un, and there are three world class bowling clubs just up the road: So many ways to spend a civilized afternoon.

What do we do?

"Let's go to the Botanic Gardens on Mount Lofty."

Why not? It's only a thirty minute drive.

In half an hour, knuckles now white, I was a mental wreck. The road went up - I expect that - you know; to go up to a place called Lofty. What I had not expected were the miles of hairpin bends requiring double backward loops [with pike] - the sort that Olympic divers would have been proud of.

At last we are there: Weak smiles for the camera in lovely gardens with wide, concrete paths. Cared-for signs point to exotic locations like 'The Rose Garden,' or 'The Lake.'

What do we do?

"Let's do the Nature Trail."

Why not? After all, the sign says "800 metres. Allow one hour." That timing must be a bit out: An hour for half a mile?

All went well until Wattle Swamp. We had meandered along a trail which got narrower and narrower until we were fighting our way through head-high bracken and blackberry, and heaven knows what.

It was almost a relief to fall into Fern Swamp with its local inhabitants. Not human, I'm afraid. The signs had long gone - and the birds in the tree canopy merely emphasized our growing predicament. They were singing and happy and free. We were sweating and tired and worrying - and under attack from all sorts of flying things with sharp teeth.

Each rustle in the undergrowth and overgrowth makes your heart jump and your bum twitch. "Only a skink"....."Only a skink:" Then the spider took guard in the centre of the tiny path. It was only little, but it looked mean. It was also quick and could jump. We try to edge around it - it jumps towards us. We try again; same thing. To hell with this! We resort to stone throwing and as it ducks, we run for it.

Our hearts had not returned to normal when it was the ants' turn. Ants! These guys were on steroids. Hearing our heavy footfalls, designed to let the pygmy copperhead and the red-bellied snakes [poisonous of course] know we were in town, these inch-long Tarzans ran AT us. For no reason! Believe me, if you had seen the ant bites on the legs of a lady at last night's dance, you would be sprinting with Patsy and me too.

Relief! We're out! Out of the jungle and into wide open spaces; cut grass and ordered borders with recognizable plants. Unfortunately, we had parked the car at the top of Mount Lofty – and, in the excitement of the chase, I had failed to notice we were now at the bottom.

It was a long way back up.

Several hours later, showered and fed, and now lying in bed drinking Queen Adelaide chardonnay, the day doesn't seem so bad after all.

Does it?

Port Adelaide

Port Adelaide is unique. I do not use the word lightly. Unique!

Why? Because at last we have found a place in Australia which we can truly say is a dump. One or two old buildings have been renovated, but by and large the place is pitiful. Saturday afternoon and the main street is near deserted; graffiti sprawls over boarded-up shops, litter blows. Even the pubs are empty.

The only sign of life revolves around a couple of supermarkets on the edge of town. Here, an 'out-of-town' development really has hurt the original little shops that once must have thrived in the dead centre. Planners! I would bet that the person responsible for this was a 'consultant' out from Britain on a jolly.

Not only is Port Adelaide dismal in the extreme, but the people catch the mood of their environment perfectly. For instance, we ask directions from a wane, pimply youth who turns out to have an attitude. Can't say that I blame him, but he is the perfect example of someone a friend would describe as "a gutless wonder who couldn't pull a greasy stick out of a dog's arse."

Throughout Australia we have always found people to be especially friendly and helpful to us strangers. Not here. This is the land of horn honkers where the rush-and-push attitude of self interest rules supreme.

Somehow, the good life in the 'Lucky Country' has passed these people by - and I'm left wondering whether they know it or not.

The Fleurieu Peninsula

Yankalilla

It was a wooden hut. It might be a very nice hut. It may even be the 'De-luxe Motel-Type Accommodation,' as per the weathered sign nailed to the old tree up the road a-ways. But hut it was - and forever will remain: A veritable cockroach paradise.

We're here at Yankalilla on the Fleurieu Peninsula for yet more dancin'. Tonight it's on in the Masonic Hall, just opposite the church that.....well, more of that in a minute.

Cocky-land was not enhanced by a spider dropping out of my swimming trunks. Unfortunately, I was half in them at the time and so a frantic, one-legged war dance began around the tiny, linoleum-covered floor space.

You will want to know if it was a poisonous one, but alas I cannot tell, as it is now very flat and in many parts.

I was beginning to wish I was back in my four-star Adelaide hotel when my wife runs across the car park of the pub next door: Nothing unusual in that, except she doesn't run much any more - and never in her knickers. She is obviously getting into the spirit of small-town Australia in a big way. The lonely hut behind the pub, with its holes in the fly screen and a gap under the door big enough for a king brown to slide through, suddenly becomes much more attractive.

I had asked the barmaid-cum-motelier two things: First for a non-smoking room.
"Don't have one - but they've been empty for a week."
Secondly, "Is there anything to do around here for the afternoon?"
"Well," the studied reply came, "There's the church. The plaster is coming off the wall and looks like the Virgin Mary and Child. People come from miles around to see it."
I'll bet they do!
The wind began to howl. I felt like joining it.

McClaren Vale

I'm punch drunk; nigh overwhelmed by the impressions of the day. I cannot order my thoughts, even should I wish to. Trees are full of various parrots and galahs, which disappear in an instant as the curtains are drawn back to reveal another perfect dawn. An Australian dawn chorus is something very hard to ignore.

The beach at Normanville has sand as white as the polar ice cap and stretching nearly as far. The school kids' rush from the clear ocean, awkward, knees lifted high, shrieking at the appearance of an eel.

Images! Images to last a lifetime:

Wineries: The list is a long one. Some world-class and familiar, such as Hardy's, Chapel Hill, Seaview: others not so. The established families have splendid premises - converted churches, stained glass, deep cellars, huge carved barrels, picturesque gardens with roses and palm trees.

A road up Wilunga Hill: 'Hill' does not do justice to the one kilometre climb with hairpin bends and unprotected drops. At the summit, thousands of feet above a distant ocean, are secluded and tranquil lakes covered with water lilies and dragon flies: A very special place.

And all our experiences are set against an unexpected backdrop of hills and plains painted yellow and brown and gold by the heat. The whole tapestry is occasionally relieved by a splash of green, where the all-powerful vine commandeers the available water.

Exhausted by afternoon temperatures in the high thirties, we retreat to air conditioning and, would you believe, a heated swimming pool?

Tea by the pool: I lie watching the line of ants queuing patiently for their grain of sugar from the bowl on the tray. They make me realise I've had nothing but a pineapple since breakfast. Time: me-thinks; to visit the local bowling club for the aptly named 'Scrounger's Night.'

Goolwa

"To reach this point, the river has travelled two-and-a-half thousand miles."

It was obvious by now that Bruce was a great talker. He sat opposite us aboard the slightly worn [or should that be 'historic'] Motor Vessel Arooma, silent wife by his side, and talked steadily through half a chicken, green salad, vegetable salad, pasta salad, bread, sticky puddin' and copious quantities of tea.

"See them fishermen there?"

We nodded in unison, only half listening now, as the sight of the Southern Ocean bursting and pounding over the sandbars at the entrance to the Murray River was indeed an incredible, ferocious sight: White breakers boiling every which way: Breathtaking.

It had made the tedium of our slow boat from Goolwa, broken only by bouts of frostbite, multifarious, unrecognisable sea birds - and Bruce of course - all worthwhile.

Bruce - sixtyish, wrinkled, grey haired, but with long, grotesque sideburns straight out of the 'Teddy Boy' era - munched and pointed.

"See them fishermen there?" he repeated. "They're right at the mouth: Travelled seventy k's in those four-wheel drive efforts from Policeman's Point. They cross at low tide when the water is ankle deep, drive like crazy over the sand dunes and fish for the Mullaway. Then they've got to get out before the tide changes."

"Mullaway?" I asked.

"Fish as big as a bloke and weigh up to, oh.....seventy five kilo's.   Stupid bastards! Fish stopped running last week."

I was not sure how Bruce knew all this, but I wasn't going to ask that of this hard case from the interior who had earned his living by breaking wild horses, called brumbies, and working sixteen hour days. The only tractor on the property was needed to pump bore water during the day, so he had worked the evenings and nights and early mornings all his life. That was before his life changed - when he parted company, prematurely, with an almond tree and broke his back.

I told you he was a talker.

Anyway, his family were so far 'out-back', I would not have been surprised to find out that it was his mob who, when completing a census form, had written under the heading 'Length of residence in Australia': "Twenty seven feet three inches - with veranda on three sides."

I was brought back from day dreaming.

"The mouth of the Murray is impressive, isn't it?" I wasn't given a chance to murmur my agreement. "It changes you know. In the last hundred years it's moved three kilometres up and down the coast here. April last year the river dropped twenty feet of sand in thirty minutes.....Just there!"

He pointed at an indistinguishable patch of tormented water.

"It's an incredible place," he said, with a look of admiration bordering on love.

He would get no argument on that score from us.

The journey back was a long one for a non-sailor. The monotony was relieved by sail boarders doing dolphin-like things around the bow wave. And Bruce!

Naturally enough the conversation turned to youth – or, should I say, lack of it. Between the four of us around the chook bones, we had put more years in than Australia had existed - and had more ailments than a government with too many long years in power.

And after three hours of non-stop Bruce I am feeling a lot older.

My elderly mother-in-law [God bless her cotton socks] used to visit her even older sister in the nursing home. In a child-like huddle under the bedclothes, with hurried glances for vigilant staff, they used to swap their medication.

"Little green ones: I've never tried those."

"Well, I'll swap you two of them for one of those big purple horse pills. They're good!"

My wife and I used to be appalled by this. Now, I give Bruce two of my little yellow back pills.....

Strathalbyn

The earthquake hit Strath at 11 a.m.

It was only a mark two, "What-the-*-was-that," type of earthquake, and certainly not enough to stop the preparations for the Lawn Bowling Pairs Invitational Championships scheduled for that afternoon.

At 11.45 a.m. we hit Strathalbyn, a pretty little town first settled by Scottish people back in 1839, who even named their river 'Angas', just to remind them of home.

By six that evening the locals were saying: "Who-the-*-was-that?"

We did not win the bowls. In fact, we were cleaned out on this Australia's National Clean-up Day. Slaughtered is more the term I am looking for - beaten 24 to 5 by a millionaire builder and his wife who bowled like pro's [they were lucky]; and 14 - 10 by a nice old couple with bad eyes, bad arms and bad legs, who apologized for winning by buying the beer.

Victor Harbour and Port Elliot

A decent crowd had gathered in the middle of the afternoon. The fans whirred, their clack-clack-clacking eventually being drowned out by a series of country and western warblers leaking from a portable hi-fi.

"Buttermilk! Buttermilk!" The young, thin, dance teacher screeched once more, her voice enough to put the fear of God into your very soul: "Side-together-side:" "Montana-kick-kick." "Vine left, vine right."

There is no way you are going to refuse orders - even when the sweat starts to run. Armpit patches appear, then widen. But we don't care - this is good for us.

You can tell the regulars - they are the ones near the wide open door of the church hall and under a fan.

"Strut! One-two-three-four: Reggae! Reggae! Vine left, scuff!"

A flock of rainbow-coloured parrots, attracted by Patsy Cline from 1959, invade the car park and start gobbling the gravel. Some of this country and western stuff makes you want to do that. The birds destroy what little concentration I have left.

"Twinkle! Twinkle! Vine left, vine right."

Tee-shirts develop other sweat rashes.

"Twinkle! Stop.....Stop.....STOP!"

It's me - wrong again. My left foot is always where the right should be. I can get away with that in the melee, but when you are the only one heading north when everyone else in the line is fleeing south.....

She smiled pitifully at my ignorance. "This is a twinkle.....This is left."

And me thinking she was saying 'tinkle.'

The dull day on the south coast has not forced us indoors - more a lack of enthusiasm for the adjoining towns of Victor Harbour and Port Elliot. We had travelled the few miles from nice, old Goolwa to South Australia's equivalent of Blackpool, to find the area "a convenient base for touring the places of interest:" Gobble-de-speak for 'nothing much doing hereabouts.'

My heart had sunk more than a bit as I studied the huge sign erected for the entertainment of expectant tourists. You know - the really big brown or blue ones covered in symbols explaining what there is to do, where to go, what to see, out of season or not.

BBQ: Nope! Not at ten in the morning.

Crossed knives and forks: Nope! - Just eaten cereal and fruit.

Petrol: Could do with some, but it's hardly the day's highlight.

Adventure Playground: Why would two, fifty-something-year-olds, need a swing?

Steam Train: That's good. We'll go for that. Oh.....It runs on Sundays only. Just six days to wait.

Hotels: Got one.

Beaches: Better: But not today, not with the low cloud and gale-force wind. [Did anyone else ever have those family holidays at the British seaside? - Windswept, with sand in everything, even when you try and hide behind a portable windbreak: Puts you off for life.]

Parking: Why?

'I' 300 yards: Information bay. Plastic-covered map with a 'You are here' sticker.

I have a strong feeling I am on familiar turf, because the same sign-writer bloke works in Britain. I want, NEED, more information: Information like where to go to experience something worth coming twelve thousand miles for.

"Buttermilk!" "Buttermilk!"

Cape Jervis

Up until about half-an-hour ago this story was going to have a completely different slant. I was going to centre it round the chance meeting with a Norwegian couple who had traded in their computer careers for a twelve-month odyssey round Australia. They looked at us disbelievingly at first, and then with great pity in their eyes as our statement - that our grandchildren had to switch the word processor on for us - sank in.

Computers notwithstanding, we do have something in common with them: there's no way that we will get across Backstairs Passage today. Those torrid, deep straits that separate us from our goal of Kangaroo Island, home to sea lions, penguins and other such hardy species hiding in vast caves or on remote beaches, are going to be spared our attentions. The waves are just too big.

Anyway, we met our Norwegians hiding behind the lighthouse at Cape Jervis, the coldest place in all of this, vast continent. Conditions are so bad that the local T.V. station has a helicopter down here doing a weather story. I am not sure of the temperature, but I shouldn't have been in shorts. It doesn't take a computer genius to work that out as the rain, like icy darts, was being driven by an Antarctic gale right into numbed flesh.

On the up-side, the wind has whipped the Southern Ocean into a frenzy; raising huge breakers allowing us to glimpse this rugged coastline at its brilliant, wildest; exhilarating best. Our nineteenth-century seafarers might not agree with their landlubber descendants, but there it is. Out there looks great from up here.

The place is truly awesome: Precipitous cliffs: Clear, clear water. Rocks, some orange and some black, give the beaches an eerie feel. And the singing, groaning, all-engulfing wind which helps numb the senses ensures that the usually raucous gulls remain fixed to the sand with their backs hunched into the icy blast.

I would like to say more about the Norwegians, but their English wasn't too good, and my Norwegian is limited to raising a glass and shouting "Skol". So, instead of Kangaroo Island, an alternative is presented to us by my better half. "I don't think you gave Victor a fair going over yesterday."

I don't know what nuance our new-found friends placed on that statement, but they promptly disappeared, leaving us to return to our disappointments of yesterday.

But this time we found Granite Island, which is connected to Victor Harbour by a narrow bridge frequented by pedestrians, fairy penguins and a horse ignominiously fitted with a dung bag. This allows the penguins to walk only in their own eco-friendly poo, while the poor horse hauls tram-load after tram-load of continent visitors to over-priced tea rooms and toilets.

Granite Island is situated in Encounter Bay - itself once famed for its slaughter of whales - and is actually a wonderful place. The huge, weather-worn boulders, granite at a guess, would have been here perched high above the white capped ocean back in 1802, when the bay was first discovered. Majestic: Timeless.

All of a sudden the place has become memorable.

Well done Victor - but shouldn't you mention this, your treasure, on that road sign?
PS: We found out later that the temperature was 16 degrees Celsius - a veritable summer's day in England.

The Murray Lands

It had been a pleasant day - sun shining and open roads. God is in His Heaven and all is well with the world. A day following the course of the meandering, but mighty, Murray River, as it wanders at will, seeking its way to the waiting ocean.

Our road marked 'Droving animals' sometimes ran across the flood plain within touching distance of the sluggish, brown watercourse. Here the fields are green - a first for our South Australian adventure; the cattle are fat and looking well polished. The ibis and egrets feed lazily among the idling hooves: Undisturbed beauty.

Occasionally the road detours, following the contour of a rolling hill; and here, still within sight of the river and green pastures and prosperity, were the yellows and browns of parched grass: A place of scrawny beasts and rusting machinery: A place of dying dreams.

I cannot say the day started to go wrong at Murray Bridge - better to say this unremarkable outpost of civilization supplied a foretaste of a strangeness to come. Imagine this. Take an attractive park set alongside one of the great rivers of the world. You know the sort of thing - old trees overhanging a lazy river; the air full of perfume and expectancy of what must be to come. Now - take a tipper lorry full of rock and dump it over a concrete, air-raid-shelter type of building. This is now called a grotto, where, for twenty cents a go, you can listen to the mythical Bunyip Monster roar its lungs out. The 'roar' sounds more like the 'Laughing Policeman' so beloved of the British seaside pier, but the local council get the real last laugh. Their monument to bad taste allows them to bank four hundred bucks a week. On my maths, that is something like two thousand people being attracted to this Monster Monstrosity. Is it just me - my mental state - or does this have something so say about people's gullibility?

Thankful to leave Murray Bridge behind, we continue sedately on our random trek through the world's second largest river basin. At Wellington we turn our back on the winch ferry and the willow-lined banks, and start to climb toward the hinterland. It was here that the day really did become spectacularly weird: Mile after mile of desolate plateau. No trees, no birds, no livestock, no nothing except for pinky - white salt pans, stinking of sulphur and death. The bleached bones of a horse and a bloated, putrefying, legs-in-the-air kangaroo, bore witness to this eerie place - silent testimony to a desperation for water which can drive the living to a certain death.

Then from nowhere, a brown, ugly finger of Lake Alexandrina reached out for our tiny car on our tiny, empty road. Miles from anywhere, the place suddenly becomes unnerving, threatening. I still don't understand Australia. Its mysteries keep on unveiling themselves and I'm left incapable of interpreting them. How on earth the lake is here at all is beyond me. We have surely been climbing steadily from the river up onto the plateau. Here's the lake on the plateau. So far so good - but the river feeds the lake. Weird!

And now the muddy water laps at our wheels. In the distance the water seems to rise above the level of the car, gathering itself to sweep us away: All optical illusions? The lake is fresh water - then why are the salt pans at the lake's edge? No doubt everything can be scientifically rationalized, but it is unnerving nonetheless.

Australia! A land of such violent contrasts - and even today, at the beginning of the twenty-first century, little of it seems to have any relevance to the order we would like to impose upon it.

Nothing Doing

A, 'nothing doin' day' on the Fleurieu peninsula: That is, if you can call parrots, cockatoos, our first ever naked spa bath, wineries galore and yet another dance, nothing!

And oh! Mustn't forget to mention McDonald's Café: Not THE McDonald's who are threatening to take over the world, but Donald McDonald's tea rooms, all done out in tartan, with big windows overlooking the main street of this tiny place where the 'town' crier, dressed straight out of Ye Olde England, struts his stuff.

But really, I am pleased for a nothin' day; it gives us plenty of time to sit and sip what's on offer and watch the world go by. It also gives me this chance to talk about something which I find fascinating the world over: - street names.

Should you need directions in Britain, the conversation will probably go along the lines of: "Melville Terrace.....Yes, that's not a problem. Go to the traffic lights and turn left into Wilson Street, left again onto Gladstone Way. Then at the roundabout, go right onto George Road, right again on Wellington Avenue and it's just there."

So much better if there are a couple of pubs on the route so that The Red Lion or The Star and Garter can be thrown into the equation: I suppose the more theologically minded would recommend a way via St. Mary's or St. Chad's churches, but more likely it will be by way of the 'cathedrals' of today - Sainsbury's or Tesco's Supermarkets.

We have not travelled too extensively in the United States. When we have, it has always been "Right onto First, left onto Fifth, left again on Seventh," or whatever. Now I'm sure America harbours addresses to fire the imagination. Something like; number 23, Turkey Track Hollow; or number one Apache Gulch – it is just that I have never seen them.

But Australia displays an appetite second to none in the literal interpretation of its history and place in the world. A conversation about directions here can be illuminating, certainly different. [The names are true.]

"Cameron of Wild Dog Road: Mmmmh! Well, I reckon you need to go up James's Track along Back Valley to Sandy Springs. When you get to the fence line, you go left about two hundred kilometres to Willow Creek. You can't miss it - there's a tree there. Straight up the track to Tonto Ridge. The Cameron property is up there off to the right a couple of clicks."

On many occasions, journeys are undertaken without the reassuring sights of telephone boxes or other cars. No tarmac roads, no supermarkets, no people to ask or give help if things go awry.

But tonight's directions are simple, big Donald McDonald assures us. "Willunga, right to Myponga, through Wattle Flat - and if you see Wirrana Cove, you've gone too far."

Simple!

Warrawong

As a kid, I was told by a fey great aunt that if you can remember your dream when you wake up, it'll come true.

In my dream last night I was playing rugby again: This time as lock-forward, not in the second row where I used to play. Each person I tackled turned into a seven foot tall centipede with hard, crunchy shell and a million kicking legs. I had been allowed to go and play with the boys again, instead of shopping as per usual, as my wife was a bit busy with a flame thrower and a rolled-up newspaper, discouraging an army of one inch long, orange and black hopper ants from entering our sanctuary for the night. I'm not anxious about Patsy. She can handle herself, especially as the hopper is a proper Aussie - it gives you a fair go. The first bite is on the house - it's harmless. The second bite puts you in hospital with breathing difficulties. Anyone would find breathing difficult when your throat and lips puff up alarmingly.

Yet there was some justification for my dream, as for the 2 a.m. loo patrol you needed a pair of wellies and Patsy's rolled-up newspaper to clear the wildlife out of the way. That, and nerves of steel! And it's an inside toilet! We had the choice earlier that day: mud brick house [3,640 bricks] or a tent. We chose the wrong option and took the house.

Now, Australia at its best, which makes the rest pale into insignificance.

We are here at Warrawong, a sanctuary for native fauna and flora from which all feral animals have been eliminated in an effort to reverse the decimation of true Australian mammals, principally by the voracious domestic cat. To give a lead, the eccentric visionary who started this project, which is now expanding throughout Australia, wears a Davy Crocket type hat made of dead cats. As a cat lover, I feel it is a great shame that they were ever introduced into the continent. But they were, and are now an absolute menace to the nation's ecosystem. I could not wear the hat, but applaud the idealistic stand.

We had started the day fairly early, drinking tea on a veranda overlooking a forested area where a heavenly multitude of rainbow lorikeets and honey eaters vie for attention. In amongst the tropical display struts 'Henny-Penny' - a single, white domestic chook who scrats in the debris and leaves an egg each morning for "Ron in the kitchen," with whom she is in love. Ron must be a strange guy, with a hormonal imbalance or some such, as the female black swan is also in love with him.

The afternoon heat reveals how sensible the locals have become after two hundred million years of evolution. They are in the deep shade of the forest, leaving the sanctuary seemingly devoid of life. Only stupid homo-sapiens are out and about, exploring and examining despite the crippling sun.

Undeterred, and now restored by much tea and a two-hour kip for sun stroke, we are back at sunset, to be held enthralled once again by Mother Nature. Never mind the feeding kangaroos, wallabies, and a host of their miniature cousins with strange-sounding names like pademelons, potoroos, bettongs and the like. Forget the possums and the bandikoots - we saw our first platypus swimming wild.

We'd had a leg-tiring wait as the night drew ever darker about us. As we waited in silence, watched by the eyes of a cast of thousands, no-show dolphins kept rising like spectres in my mind. That thought played tag with how things appear at will for David Attenborough, no matter whether he's in Antarctica, Alaska or Chipping Snodsbury. Maybe they would appear if we had a television crew and satellite dishes with us, instead of a pocket instamatic.

Then all thoughts are put aside. Tonight, we are all David Attenborough's. A platypus appears, not once but twice, making the journey, the discomfort, the later dreams - and a ten-year-old Ross who kept reminding us to look out for spiders and snakes - all worthwhile.

We leave the lake and river system, and beneath the dazzling Milky Way, complete with shooting stars and infinity, we make our way home.

Hahndorf

Hahndorf reminds me a great deal of Broadway in Worcestershire. Both have wide, tree-lined main streets which sport autumnal colours, and which, during the summer, serve to mellow and clothe the old stone cottages with an air of elegance, grace and mystery with their regal branches. The whole spectacle is enhanced by climbing roses and wisteria. Both villages represent the ideal to strive for; the essence of people's dreams. The sweet smell of success and flowers mingle and fill the air.

Except, of course, they are all but undone by their own beauty: Every tourist, day tripper and would-be adventurer wants to experience the charm of yesteryear that the advertising executives and tour companies work so hard to sell us.

So today in Hahndorf [and I'm sure in Broadway] is like yesterday was and tomorrow will be. Traffic clogs the streets and coaches disembark Japanese tourists festooned with eight cameras each, who then proceed to pursue one another from photograph to photograph.

The villages wilt under the ceaseless pressure and become suspect as living entities in their own right. The inhabitants become commuters and the number of second home's mount: Supermarkets and petrol stations are not good for the packaging of dreams - and in any event, there's more money in antiques and ice cream.

Yet to say the villages die would be too easy. It is always easier to describe something in absolutes:

'the village is dead;' far harder to paint the shades of grey which is reality. Amidst the pressures of the modern world, church bells ring on Sunday mornings before the coaches arrive and the car parks fill.

Hahndorf reminds me so much of home because it is so unlike Australia. It is a little piece of Northern Europe transplanted into the rolling Adelaide Hills, and has been ever since 1838, when Captain Hahn, of the good ship Zebra, impressed by his passengers' fortitude, found land for them to settle on. In gratitude, Hahn-dorf was born.

The British were not grateful at all and promptly re-named the place Ambleside. So, in effect, we had a Germanic people in a British village in Australia.

However, tourism was born and Hahndorf returns. After all - it's so much easier to sell dreams in black and white.

*

I do not like visiting stately homes and that is a fact. To witness the myriad of treasures hoarded by a privileged few and bought with the sweat of others offends my conscience. Brought up in a Christian - Socialist family, I well remember the farewell from my grandmother as I left home, full of confidence, at the ripe old age of sixteen. Not "Be careful," "Write soon," or "Always wear a condom." [Not that 'Mam' would acknowledge the existence of such things.] No! Her final words were "Promise me you'll never vote Tory."

But today I did visit a stately home - stately in my eyes that is - all bought and paid for by the genius that lay in the hands and eyes and perception of Hans Heysen, Australia's foremost landscape artist.

The house would never meet the British definition of 'stately.' No great dining halls nor book-lined studies; no ballrooms with crystal chandeliers; no mile-long drives to arrive at the front door. Yet this house, The Cedars just outside Hahndorf, with its leaking, rusty, galvanized iron roof, has more to offer than a palace. It was the home of Heysen and his beloved wife for over fifty years, and now oozes love from every nook and water-stained cranny.

The wooden furniture and scatter rugs are not out of one of those 'home and garden' type magazines; but the exquisite Australian light, filtering through verandas and shades, gives Heysen's pictures a translucence and depth which is immortal.

The garden, too, is a special place. A little piece of 'England,' created by roses and more roses - all with a heady, all-pervading perfume. Set against, and surrounded by, a backdrop of gum and cedar, the place is truly magical.

The house is a gem, the artist's studio and garden affording an intimacy to the most casual of visitor. Surely this is something truly unique? I had never even heard of Hans Heysen before today; - now I feel I've known him all my life.

The Barossa Valley

Impressive!

The first touch of autumn has laid its hand over the Barossa: A perceptible tinge to the morning air; a speckling of dew on the bougainvillaea. The first blush of yellows and reds are appearing on the leaves of the vines which dominate the landscape.

The villages and towns have changed too. No longer unreal places full of tourist hype, these are working towns, with their industry based on the grape, first planted way back in 1847 by German Lutheran settlers. Visitors are of secondary importance to the valley and the towns are all the better for it. Night and day, heavy container lorries pound the highways and dirt roads, loaded with wine in the making. Grape harvesters are working at a frenzied pace in the fields. Impressive!

Impressive, however, was not the adjective to describe my own particular Mecca. Jacob's Creek

- the name of a very quaffable wine at a good price, and which almost single-handedly propelled Aussie wines onto the world stage - is no more than a near-dried-up river bed, overhung with willow, its edges eaten away by unrecognizable grasses as tall as bamboo.

Mengler's Point looks down over the Barossa's patchwork quilt of vineyards. It should have been a special place as the sun sunk slowly and the shadows lengthened across the valley floor. But it wasn't.

The day was ruined by three larakins in a white Volkswagen camper van who turned up at that isolated and lonely spot. It is a fair observation to say that they weren't into sunsets! It is the only time in Australia that I have ever felt threatened by our fellow man. Snakes - yes! Spiders - most definitely. Bush fires and all the rest of nature's foibles - yes! But never by our own kind: Not until Mengler's Point.

Come to think of it, if something untoward was going to happen to us, it would have to be here, in this place, with a name synonymous with the utmost evil that man can do.

Nonchalantly, we rushed our money, credit cards, airline tickets, passports and US from the stupendous view, just as the camera should have been clicking wildly.

Undeterred, and feeling safe once more, I leave the security blanket the car has become to try and conjure a sunset out of very little raw material. A car draws alongside. Palpitations - but I needn't have worried.

"Need a lift mate?"

Faith in human nature restored, we call it a day.

Cockatoo Valley

"Well, I think it is incredible," I said.

"That's the way of it," replied Stanislav. "You have to be hard to go look for the gold."

You could cut his heavily accented English with a knife. It didn't detract from his wealth of knowledge about gold, but I spent most of my time trying to work out [a] what he was saying; and [b] where he was from.

I had once read in a travel book that a true explorer never turns down a meal, so it came as no surprise that after his eight-hour drive to see us again, Stan tucked into the cheese and tomato sarnies, beer, wine and whatever else was lying around with some gusto. He was remarkably dexterous for someone missing all four fingers of his right hand: Something to do with a grape harvester.

We sat in the dappled shade cast by an ancient and spreading walnut tree, which creaked alarmingly for no reason in the still air. The feeling of vulnerability was increased by the rocking of our equally-ancient wooden chairs, whose weary legs protested our weight. It was early evening, warm and balmy, and the beer and wine flowed - mostly in Stan's direction. Beautifully relaxing except for the blasted mossies! I had clouds of them, whilst there were none anywhere else in the courtyard garden. I suppose I was the more appetizing proposition - tastier than the tough, gnarled, seen-it-all, done-it-all, leathery-skinned Stanislav.

He continued. "I remember a story 'bout an old gold prospector out west. Hurt in a fall he was, this old guy. So his mate pushes him three hundred and twenty kilometres in a wheelbarra' to get some medical help: Hard men eh!"

Another glass of red disappeared in a twinkling. I knew then for certain we had not bought enough grog.

The conversation about gold had been prompted by yesterday's news that gold - lots of it - had been re-discovered amongst a hundred-year-old spoil heap left by the original gold rush miners. - That, and the fact that the talk always turned to gold when Stan was around.

With the news of a fortune just waiting to be picked up off the ground [where have I heard that before] Patsy and I had eagerly headed for the hills above the Barossa. We returned after a long, hard day. The scenery was just amazing. Just the way I like it - burnt brown, but.....! But the heat had been enough to fry the proverbial egg, and all we'd seen for our trouble was a hole in the ground, half-filled with water. Mind you, the hole was big enough to float the entire British Navy. No ships being available, the old workings were now a dam.

Tired, hot, and irritable at my lost chance of finding a fortune - probably feeling a lot like John and Sophia Reedhead had every day of their prospecting years down in Victoria - I was to be tested even further. Stan 'One Finger' was still managing to eat three sandwiches to my one, which I found most irritating.

"Can't understand it myself," I challenged testily. "Why can't they find gold somewhere accessible? Somewhere close to.....something! Like the beach!" I was getting fair wound up now. "It's always the same. Remember George's gold mine over in New South Wales? Where is it? About a million miles up a mountain in thick forest: Not even a proper road there even now."

Stan was immune to my moods. He's known me too long. "And remember that trip to Ballarat," he urged. "Can't fail to find the stuff down Victoria can you: Got handcuffed to a horse rail once round there for panning without a licence: What a laugh!"

Good try, Stan. But I was on my hobby horse now [O.K. - one of them], and there was no way I was climbing off that easily: "And today! Cockatoo Valley: The nearest place for miles is called One Tree Hill: Ten thousand blokes up there sweating away once upon a time. Can't imagine there was much attraction in walking over to One Tree Hill on your day off. Why did they keep at it? - For years!"

More beer disappears in answer to my eloquency. Stan studied the bottom of the can, belched so loud that the tree shook, and then chucked the crumpled container in the general direction of an over-full trash can.

"Greed: Adventure." He reached for a bottle of red. "A good mate of mine had a great grandfather." He poured as he talked. "He owned some real good land near the sea in New South Wales. Nice it was; lush grass, fresh water, cool breezes off the ocean. He swapped the lot for a horse and cart so he could go to the goldfields. Land's worth a fortune now of course - it's called Sydney Harbour. True! I swear it!"

[Our family never seems to have much luck when it comes to making money. In America, one relative sold some swampy, good-for-nothing ground for a handful of beads, only to find the city of Houston being built on it. Another one said "No thanks" to the franchise for the Ford Motor Company - cars would never catch on.]

"So did the guy from Sydney harbour find his pot o' gold?"

"Nah! I've found more than 'im - and I've only got half an ounce in twenty years."

"They must have had to put up with some things back then: Makes me feel like a wimp."

"Yeah!"

[He could have disagreed with me.]

"It was different then," he added. "They had determination and endurance all right. Every shovel you took could be the one - so they kept at it. Plenty lived in tents and caves. One German fella' called Herbig, he became a farmer out here: Started off with his wife and two kids living in the hollow stump of a gum tree."

He yawned. My cheese sarnies, five beers and two bottles of red had disappeared. "I'm off." He nodded toward something behind me. "Here's Herman the German comin'. Only bloke I know who can scoop a glass full of fat off whatever he cooks. He wants me to put fifty grand into Bulgaria, but he'll have to be quicker than that. See ya' later."

59

I enjoyed the company, my single glass of Rosemount cabernet - and the security I had in the knowledge that I didn't have fifty grand to lend Herman the German or Bulgaria.

Elizabeth

We have forsaken the beautiful Barossa and its lovely towns of Tanunda, Gawler, Angaston and Nuriootpa. We've left behind the grapes, and a cousin who makes his way through life singing Northumbrian Pit Songs in Australian clubs and Australian Folk Songs in British ones.

We are on our way to the township of Elizabeth, or Little London as it's known to the locals. We are always sorry to leave behind a place we could call home, and the Barossa qualifies; yet we are not sorry to leave behind the tap water slurped out of the Murray River and discharged brown and smelly from bathroom or kitchen taps. In fact I would swear it lies there looking at you, daring you to touch it. Even the flagons of rain water which concerned hosts provide you with come complete with twigs and green algae. It's O.K. though - the water company assures us it is all safe to drink. That's good to know. Hands up those who believe them:

Not that the water of Adelaide is supposed to be much better. We are nearing the end of our South Australian odyssey and have only just discovered that South Australia is one of the only two spots in the world where ocean-going ships refuse to take on 'fresh' water. We've not been buying the bottled spring stuff like everyone else – no-one has mentioned it until now.

*

1956. Elizabeth: Fly-ridden sheep and dusty fields [not my description]; selected as a place of settlement for the influx of English migrants.

Forty odd years later, Elizabeth is a city with everything one needs. Things like supermarkets, shopping malls and four-lane highways to speed you around the place. Now! About these roads......There I was, minding my own business in the slow lane of the west-bound carriageway, when this lorry appeared and was not too happy to see me. You could tell that quite easily by the flashing headlights and the blasting air horn. It appears I'm heading east in the fast lane - not west in the slow.

Don't ask! I blame my age!

One guess as to why we are in Elizabeth? Correct! There's a Scottish dance in Little London. One fact about this dancing lark: No matter where you go, there are nearly always insufficient men to go around as partners. Logic dictates that women therefore have to dance the men's parts. The outcome is that when you are the only man amongst the many, you kind-a get mixed up as to who the other guys are - a fact only important to dancers and me.

A spinster in her late middle age - small but with an ample chest - begins to prance about in front of me. I'm momentarily confused. "Are you a man?" I ask.

She went every shade of red, looked at her own heaving bosom, then, giving me a sheepish, Diana look said "No, I'm all woman."

Two boobs in one night!

The Cappuccino Bushman:

I saw a postcard in the window of a little shop the other day: One of the little islands in the bay at sunset; every shade of orange and red, and very beautiful. Not for the first time, I am envious of the photographer. I want to be able to take a photo like that! The good news is that I know exactly where it was taken from. I spotted the location on the way to the fish market the other day.

We have had a perfect day. A bit of walking through the bush, the flowers as sweet-smelling as incense, before ending up on a near perfect beach with turquoise water lapping at its edge. Wading birds of every description had become annoyed at our intrusion, some putting on that damaged wing act to keep us away from their nesting sites. And in the evening: THE spot.

The sun falls and falls and blazes its last. Perfection puts its arm around the bay, as if to comfort it before the approaching blackness of a southern sky.

Drooling, I switch on the camera. Nothing! No whine of a shutter opening; no sound of a lens zooming. The batteries in my point-and-shoot are dead - and I've no spare. Still, we have the memory, not only of the bay at sunset, but also of the incredible, humbling display that only a southern night sky can anoint you with.

And there is always tomorrow.

*

We have had a perfect day. A different day, but perfect all the same, consisting of a much needed rest from all pretensions of becoming intrepid bushmen. Instead, a shopping trip interspersed with regular cappuccino breaks, followed by a sumptuous meal of meaty blue nose. It may be a strange-looking fish, lying there filleted on the ice-covered slab, but I'm not eating the weird head - just the very tasty flesh.

Evening comes on and the camera is fixed: A walk along the sand, holding hands like the couple of school-kid lovers that we once were. The shadows lengthen, turning the sand black and sending the hosts of orange butterflies, the size of your hand, scurrying for home.

We're hurrying too; back to the far side of the bay - to that vantage point, for that photograph. Relief: We make it with time to spare. Location; camera: both checked and okay. All I have to do is be patient.

Then the unexpected: cloud. There has not been a blemish to the clear blue sky all day; but now, at the critical moment, from nowhere, cloud. The colour of the sea turns, not red, but black, with a streak of brilliant white sufficiently bright to hurt the eyes and confuse the lens. The little island becomes momentarily silhouetted, but black against the brooding, black mountains beyond. Then it too is gone: lost, like the intrepid bushman I wish was within me.

Achmed's Angst

"Too much luggage, Sir......Have another bag, courtesy of Qantas."

At least I am no longer classed among the disadvantaged, even though it's only a pair of old trainers which have caused the minor crisis at the airport check-in. I suppose the grimace on the clerk's face came from the expense of the plastic bag he was handing over - or the horrendous smell permeating the air around the stained footwear swinging from the rucksack strap. Ah well!

In fact we are privileged beyond belief, for last night we returned to the centre of Adelaide for a final farewell. A wonderful, warm evening: The symphony orchestra was putting on a free concert in the park by the river, and so the wide thoroughfares were thronged once more. But it is a different crowd in nature to the invasion of the followers of rugby league. This mob must have followed us down from Port Adelaide. Sharp elbows are called for.

But the hurrying masses could not spoil the delight in store. No! - Not the concert. Silly you! We fought our way against the torrent of humanity out for a free-bee to reach our goal - the ultimate high in the life of this spectacular city: a pie floater at The Pie Cart outside the railway station. This is a road-side food stall with class. The blokes serving have mixed with the stars - even served the irreverent Billy Connolly - and a twenty-stone copper who holds the record of eating five floaters in one go.

We settle for a single meat pie floating in an ocean of mushy peas. They say that Australia was built on meat pies and galvanized iron. Well, I don't know about the galvanized iron, but the pie floater is food fit for the gods.

That was last night. This morning, hovering between the airport lounge and toilets, I remember a childhood ditty which goes something along the lines:

> Dah.de.dah.....
> "Next day dawns
> As next days will
> To find poor Ian
> Proper ill....."
> Da-de something else.....
> "He cried out loud
> 'Come 'ere quick, mum.
> I've got an awful pain
> in me tum'..... "

It is either the peas or the sight of the small 'plane - but I'll spare you my cowardice.

Later, the stewardess asked, "Can I get you something?"

She was not in the least amused at my reply, as I looked wistfully at lunch - a single ham sandwich. "A three course dinner and a four-engined plane please."

I suppose this is a link which I cannot ignore: 'plane journeys and a couple of the characters we've come across.

We will start with a bloke whom we'll call Achmed, a confused son of Pakistan. It was evident right off that he was not a seasoned traveller, and, to give him his due, it was a long flight. It was going to get a lot longer. After twelve hours of mind-numbing boredom, accompanied by the re-assuring drone of the never faltering engines, he decided to take refuge in the demon-drink. He didn't understand much English, but in the interests of Darwinian solidarity, he resolved to do what everyone else was doing to survive. He started pointing at the little bottles on the service trolley. We took a little bottle of water; he took gin. The little Scottish lady in the next seat took water; he took vodka. Her partner took a small orange; Achmed took a gin and orange - a double this time.

The glass mountain grew in front of him....somehow in proportion to his smart three-piece suit disintegrating and his whole body being slowly swallowed by the seat. If he wasn't a seasoned traveller, then for certain he was not a hardened drinker. To be fair though, it did take him a couple of hours of constant self-abuse before he finally became comatose.

And that is fine too; perfectly acceptable in the secular Occident. It was when he came round that the problems began. It was immediately obvious he was distressed. Communication by hand signs began which involved a lot of grunting and pointing: Bad head? Point: Bad eyes? Point: Bad throat...Bad back, kidneys..? Point.....Point.....and yet more point! Point to chest: Bad heart? Bad move! That final wandering finger signalled immediate confrontation. He didn't want to get off the plane; the English crew didn't want anyone with a bad heart on it; the heavy-handed Singaporean aircraft guard wanted everyone off; the Irish guy doing plane protection duties wanted to pull his gun and see some action; the demure Scottish lady wanted Achmed to remove his "Grubby little hands," which accidentally kept striking her bosom. All great fun: Eventually we ended up in a crowd scene involving six air stewards, their supervisor, an armed Chinese policeman, the pilot, two baggage handlers, a doctor with an E.C.G. machine, the Irish guy with the short fuse, several trapped by-sitters and someone trying to sell glass beads through the open cabin door.

A clambering, gesticulating, disunity of nations: Compromise was reached. Achmed was taken away by the Chinese guard, the baggage handlers removed his luggage, the supervisor supervised, the passengers waited impatiently - whilst the doctor re-inserted Achmed through a different door back into the cabin, the bags re-appeared as if by magic, and the street vendor was booted down the ramp. Compromise and honour satisfied.

Yet the result was unfortunate. Our plane missed its scheduled spot within the invisible air traffic corridors, leading to endless, sweltering delays on the ground and an apparently aimless circling over a desert landscape somewhere near an invisible airport - which should have been Sydney.

Whereas I feel a bit sorry for a misunderstood and penitential Achmed, my thoughts are turning less charitable when I recall another incident. See what you think......

And there he was, slap-bang in the middle of the departure lounge of Las Vegas Airport. He was nothing to look at - normal height and weight; normal features - but he would stand out in any crowd because of his anger. He bristled with animosity, bile and high dudgeon. It oozed from every pore in his body. It was the very core of his being.

"That's him," whispered my wife, as several bystanders gave his swinging golf club a wide berth. "Last night I dreamt he was on our flight again."

Again! Our first encounter was enough to give anyone the eebee-jeebees. He had boarded our flight three days earlier, elbowing his way to the front of the line. As he walked down the central aisle of the plane he had carelessly thrown his suit into an overhead locker [number 20], his case into another [28], and then sat in my seat, 40c.

"Excuse me, but I think you've got my seat:" English politeness at its best.

"So what!"

The flight attendant, a nice girl about the size of a Sumo Wrestler, decided in favour of the British.

And now here he was again. We beat him to our seats, 40a and b. The plane filled to capacity, leaving Bristles to swagger up the aisle. No suit. No case. Ungenerously, I hoped Las Vegas had relieved him of the lot. The golf club [a putter for the record] was a new addition, but still got itself thrown into locker number twenty.

And guess where he plonked himself. Yep! 40c! Two hundred and eighty seats and we got Mr Nice Guy. It was a long, long forty-five minutes. If there had been any service at all on the flight I may well have joined Achmed in making glass mountains. Our American friend glared at crying babies, picked his nose, dissected and tasted the contents and made things difficult for the nice stewardess, most certainly of the Non-Sumo, non-scary variety.

I would like to report that he got his comeuppance - but no. He left us, barging his way toward the exit as I suspect he still barges his way through life.

But we return to the present. Sydney is waiting, so come on.....

Journey 4
New South Wales

Sydney and the Blue Mountains
Sydney

Sydney is big, brash, buxom and beautiful.

People hurry, are impatient. People are on the go, on the make. Hustle! Hurry - hurry - hurry. So much to do: So much to see. The place is so similar to home in very many ways and yet the fish stalls offer blue eyes, leather jackets and John Dory's; fruit shops, custard apples, sour sops: So very different.

If we find it so different, so exciting, how must the first colonists have felt? And this is not idle speculation as far as we are concerned. There were two family members on the historic First Fleet which landed in the mid-summer heat of 1788 right here in Sydney Cove - or Circular Quay, as we all know it now: One prisoner, one guard. Both had been sent to the eighteenth century equivalent of Mars.

The first was James Moresby, a Yorkshire lad who had joined the army, was posted to London, and from there managed to find his way to the Old Bailey for a bit of liftin' and shiftin'. He got an iron bar worth ten pence, a dishonourable discharge from the Guards in the Tower and seven years in gaol. He became familiar with the insides of the infamous Newgate Prison, with iron bars on the doors the thickness of a man's arm, and the prison hulks moored in the middle of the River Thames at Woolwich. There he languished for two-and-a-half years, shackled in leg irons to deter swimming exercises, and managing to avoid the miasmas of epidemic proportions as well as the quelling of prisoner revolts. His reward for staying alive, even though he looked "pale, ragged, lousy and as thin as a wading bird," was a place on board the former slaving ship, Scarborough, due to leave English shores in the May of 1787.

On 26th January, 1788, the fleet dropped anchor in Sydney Cove and James began his seven year stretch.

The following morning, a party of a hundred convicts from the Scarborough were set ashore to begin clearing the land of the paperbark scrub and grey-green eucalyptus - obviously to make room for the Aboriginal didgeridoo buskers and the busy ferry terminal of today.

James never returned to England. There was no return ticket; no way back to his wife and child in London - and God knows what happened to them. James consoled himself in his new land by fathering thirteen children to two women, which has certainly helped to make New South Wales our most travelled-in State.

The guard was called James Angell, a Private in the 26th Company of Marines out of Portsmouth. He was a single man and actually volunteered for the job. Once in Australia, he divided his time between soldierly duties, working for the officers on their extensive land grants, and trying his hand at becoming a settler - farmer himself. Something he wasn't too good at, as he had to join up again.

In 1803 he was due to be sent back to England on leave, but he was having such a good time, he deserted instead. We don't yet know much else about James Angell - but his descendants still populate the southern parts of the State.

I cannot help but wonder if one or both of our James's were in that first group to go ashore on that summer's morn.....I like to think so.

They would not recognize the place now, of course, their virgin bush having been replaced by a world-class city where horns toot and sirens wail. Where the canyons betwixt and between the skyscrapers vibrate with noise and energy and excitement; where parks and gardens abound, but can offer only temporary respite from a city on the go.

The Excitement City

Sydney: The Excitement City. Dragon Boat races on the exquisite Cockle Cove [Darling Harbour] under a sky blue enough to make you want to cry. The place is filled with the Battle Flags of the competitors and the relentless pounding of the prow-head drums.

Sydney: The Excitement City. A short walk toward the beckoning shade of the canyon-like metropolis, passing world-class gardens and shopping complexes, and you are caught up in all the joy and exuberance of the Easter Parade: Marching bands, dancing troupes, prancing animals, gaudy, delicious floats, revered veterans, flower be-decked children. The 'country' has come to town for the day: Wonderful street theatre reverberating beneath the concrete canopy.

Sydney: The Excitement City. And as evening comes on, the sun sets over the most beautiful harbour in the world: The neon show grows apace, making it hard to drag yourself away from one of the harbour's open-air wine bars on the balmiest of evenings. But needs must: World class rock n' roll stars are in town and we're off 'a-scalping.' O.K., I know.....touting should be frowned on - but it is nice to know all those naughty genes haven't gone to waste.

Where else in this wonderful world can offer so much in a single day?

Sydney entices you, seduces you, excites you and will forever hold you in its spell.

Bennelong Point

There are not enough superlatives to describe one of the modern wonders of the world standing on Bennelong Point. I could drool at length about the history of the place, the stories of the people it spawned and the unique concept of the building which has come to symbolize Australia to the world. But I won't. There is no need, for the Opera House is simply exquisite - inside and out. It sparkles like a diamond, the triumphant jewel in Sydney's magnificent crown.

Yet even here, Australia's enigma continues unabated: Such beauty and passion for life, sullied by the sight of disposal bins for the needles of drug abusers. Sadly, the performing arts, no matter how brilliant, no matter how much they enable and free and enlighten the human spirit, for some it is not enough.

Sydney Opera House is also the place of my private pilgrimage: Many years ago now my mother died at the foot of its steps, still spellbound by the wonder of a performance of Swan Lake. Was she thinking of Act Four, the Dying Swan, when her own spirit was forever liberated in an instant? - A terrible, symbolic duality which would have graced any Wagnerian tragedy.

Today, there is a lone piper in full Scottish regalia wailing a lament unwittingly at my ultimate destination: A piper and a lament in the shadow of the Tyne Bridge look-a-like. Here am I, alone - yet amongst bus loads of milling Nikons, Yashicas and Canons, and I know with a certainty that his presence is meant: A tribute to mum at our special place, and a reminder of a home to which she can never return. I feel we are both content nonetheless.

You shop. I'll drop.

The Sydney shopping experience can vary between the sublime and the ridiculous. I am not sure which of these best sums up the imposing edifice of the Queen Victoria Building on George Street, variously described as "The best shopping in the world," or "A cathedral in the world of shopping." With its domes, stained glass and sumptuous detail, 'cathedral' sounds good. The four galleries of stone and marble host an array of small shops and boutiques unashamedly intent on separating the tourists from their bucks. It is a place to visit if for only one reason: to take a look at the Victorian loos dating back to 1898 when the place was built. The gents urinals are fountains to bad taste, but the mosaic floors would do credit to a Roman Emperor's palace.

By the time we emerge unscathed from the ridiculously expensive, the promised rain has arrived. Laughably, to all except the Water Board, it evaporates almost as soon as it hits the pavement.
We settle for a little, Australian-Jewish-lettuce-sandwich-eating jeweller elsewhere, thankful for personal service, even if it means coping with fingers still sticky from an interrupted lunch. "Give me a week and I'll make you anything."

Luck plays a part in all shopping, and shopping in Sydney is particularly confusing aimed as it is solely at the sightseers. All the traders, large and small, vie for the same passing trade. No empty shop frontages here. There is money about and plenty of it. Consequently, without local knowledge, the visitor is going to pay handsomely for their pleasure in the city centre.

So, without compassion for the 'poor' duty-free proprietors, on to Paddy's, an indoor market just across the road from Chinatown where I am assured value for money rules, O.K!

Beneath a sign announcing that "Between the four oceans, all men are brothers," I continued to survey the rather large Chinese lady with some trepidation.

Did I say rather large? Her hips are best described as 'child bearing,' her biceps are the size of rock melons, and with shoulders like that she could play prop forward. Perhaps she had, as her face wasn't pretty either, her appearance not helped by the austere bun her stringy black hair had been forced into. I found her nurse's starched white uniform uninspiring and certainly not reassuring.

She was looking at me from within a small circle of similarly dressed, slim, Chinese men and women, acknowledging me with her piggy eyes as a brother within the four oceans. I just knew she was going to be my Waterloo, my therapeutic masseur.

My sciatic nerve was trapped yet again and I needed help. My wife and sister-in-law had deposited me, clutching twenty bucks, amongst the acupuncturists, herbalists and masseurs in the Chinese Quarter of Paddy's Market. I was told to get well soon and off they fled, unencumbered by whinge, into the innumerable alleyways betwixt endless stalls selling everything from yukky tack to exquisite, handcrafted goods.

I could not help wondering ate the Fates as I stood there alone exchanging glances with Tiger Lil. I had spent a pleasant hour with a young Chinese doctor who had successfully diagnosed, from my pulse and tongue, that I had slightly raised blood pressure, was recovering from a viral infection and was occasionally constipated. To cure this I needed to eat fried lettuce and take fifteen black pills, the size of ball bearings, three times a day. It will purge my system. I just wished he was a massage expert and Godzilla over there dispensed the pills.

At this point I ought to say I am not taking the Mick out of Chinese Medicine. They have had thousands of years to get it right – and, like many other westerners, I have become disenchanted by our medical system in which common sense and good practices have gone out of the window in favour of the twin gods of science and administrators. I am tempted to put in here a few of the more noteworthy blunders which appear almost daily in the press, both in the United Kingdom and in Australia. But I won't - it only makes my blood pressure go up - and that means some horrible tasting brown pills: [Only twelve a day.]

I knew it! The massive girl waddles over to me and indicates the couch. "Lie down, please." "Nose through that hole:" "Don't move!"

For anyone with a bad back and pain there from, you will know the intrinsic God-like quality of opposites: of exquisite pain and sublime relief. In my case, relief came from those thumbs, as thick as sausages, which manipulated the strangled nerve.

Soon, too soon, it was over and I settled in for the long wait. I had just composed a terse announcement for the market's Tannoy system: "Will the two Mrs. Patterson's please return to where they left their husband," when they turned up, all apologetic and feigning embarrassment. Got lost indeed!

So, back out into the sunshine of Sydney's hustle and I'm off exploring an old railway siding, especially built beside the Central Railway Station at the top of George Street. Here, once upon a time, the dead of Sydney were segregated from the living, heaped up and then loaded onto trains to take them to the cemeteries out in the suburbs. The public relations men were apparently hard at work, even back in the nineteenth century.

The girls wait patiently for me in the shade. Sitting on the narrow window sill of a shop they chatted away as girls do, oblivious to the rubber penises and multifarious sex aids on display behind them.

Enlightenment did not seem at all necessary.

A Tale of Everyday folk

A quiet day on the veranda is enlivened by the radio news: Just an ordinary tale of Sydney folk. A true story.....

This lady gets into her car to go shopping at the local mall. Her head is filled with ordinary thoughts: shopping lists; shoes for the kids; an approaching birthday. She automatically straps herself into her old Holden; clunk - click every trip, and off she goes. Nothing strange thus far, except it took an age to get the belt to engage correctly.

On the journey her mind raced, structuring the day's chores whilst at the same time grappling with the rush-hour traffic. Her seat belt slips a little. She flips it back onto her shoulder without a thought. It's an old car, and in any event her mind has no spare capacity to dwell on this particular phenomenon.

The mall comes into view. She manages to find a parking space she can drive into without reversing, and it is a particularly good spot as no-one can block her in. She has no time for those irritations today.

However, she is quite decidedly irritated at the difficulty she encounters in untangling her seat belt. It will just not come out..... She struggles in the heat and humidity, her temper in free fall - and then, with the strength of Tarzan's Jane, she wrenches it free.

Although no comment was forthcoming, we can assume the five-foot long, poisonous brown snake, was none too happy either.

Australia!!!

Happy Hullabaloo Everyone

The change in the weather was as dramatic as it was unexpected. A cold front rushed in from the south east, its bad-tempered rain squalls driving the thirty degree night temperatures back into the desert interior. The rain squalls were sufficient to clatter the roof tiles and wake the dead. Well, it woke me and forced an activity at three in the morning I could well have done without. Fasten banging shutters, fight a cockroach for sole possession of the single blanket.....I settle down again, blissfully unaware that sleep had gone for the night. The storm passed, the cooler temperatures left behind encouraged me to snuggle down and embrace Morpheus once more, but then the cicadas and crickets, momentarily stunned by the force of the tempest, resumed their deafening dual.

No sleep, but at least I got to see the sun wearily poke through the remaining wispy cloud. The insect life went to bed - just as the dawn chorus began. We might be in the middle of Sydney's suburbia but the birdies and beasties have adapted wonderfully from virgin bush to, well - a bush.

And it's not the melodious song of a benign, temperate Britain. No! This cacophony is born of the harsh land that is Australia. The pied currawong's loud and ringing 'Curra-wong, Curra-Wong,' followed by a whistle and a kwak, provokes the minor birds into retaliation, 'Oh-kick-oh-kick-oh'. Add in the incessant and monotonous 'pip-pip-pip' of the cheeky, yellow eastern robin - a call that I swear must destroy your brain cells - and it is time to get up and make a brew.

Later, these two tired Sydney shoppers have their souls saved by some gospel-shouting blokes inaptly called "The Dumb Preachers." They competed manfully against a busking bagpiper from Braemar and two Sally Army brass bands. Unfortunately, all three were playing different tunes and hymns - and all within an area I could chuck a cricket ball across. [Thirty yards on a good day, downhill and with a following wind.]

Time for home and a well-deserved afternoon kip - a respite from the noise of the day before our barbecue party gets stoked up. Heads touch pillows, eyes close. Thank you Lord - but could you please send a bolt of lightning next door to shut the two kids up who've just started screaming. And why have they started screaming? I'll tell you! Bagpipes! Yes, bagpipes! From the Lebanon - where else! They have started to wail from the Lebanese Christian Maronite Church next door and the kids wail in harmony.

We lie and curse, silently, as we don't want to cause a nuisance to anyone, and the letter box rattles. A leaflet: "We apologise in advance for the noise we are likely to make at the church celebrations tonight." That's something to look forward to.

The morning light spreads over the sky. The bagpiper and the horn-tooters and the party-goers have all gone home, following the example of the flying foxes. This leaves a clear field for the morning chorus. Different birdies today. The brown honey eater squeaks appallingly from the single grevillea bush; the fighting eastern rosella parrots go 'Kwink-Kwink-Kwink-SCREAM-kwink'; 'Cookey-Cook' goes the wattle bird up in the bottle brush tree and the magpies start a punch-up over whose territory we dare try and sleep in.

Doin' Six Bodies a Week:

We have been coming to Australia for nigh on two decades now and I suppose I should not be surprised by the changes: better roads; better housing; whatever. The world moves on apace everywhere and here is no exception.

However, there has been one change, so subtle that until now it has not been apparent to me. The wake-up call hit me straight between the eyes when I saw a sign outside an ordinary little supermarket: 'Croatian, Arabic, Spanish, Vietnamese, Japanese, Cantonese and English spoken here.'

So I opened my eyes and started to look, really look, at the main street afresh. Our sign is to be found in the Sydney suburb of Burwood where we can often be found going walkies and shoppies. It certainly serves as a good example of the subtle change we referred to; a change reflected in practically every other metropolitan suburb.

The change is that of the growth of the Chinese influence within Australia. It is literally staggering the way in which the high street has changed, now truly representing that community - after all, the Chinese have been in Australia in large numbers since the gold rushes of the mid-nineteenth century. And yet it has taken until now for them to become......well......visible.

Once upon a time the Italian immigrants held the virtual monopoly on delicatessens and pavement cafes. Not now! How about the Kwok Can Do Cake Shop: the cream and chocolate arrangements looking wonderful, but suspiciously like the merchandise in various other emporia up and down the street. The Italians may be as mad as cut snakes at losing their stranglehold on a lucrative market, but they aren't the only ones: Financial loans, bread shops, chemists - all owned by Chinese Aussies. Even the Salvation Army has a Chinese corps opposite the new mammoth shopping centre.

Back in history, the only butcher's shop in Burwood was run by a Mrs MacNamarra, a tall woman of reputed strength who could wield her cleaver like a plastic toy and boasted she could "Do six bodies a week." Now there are butchers a-plenty, all fulfilling the Aussie desire for meat. Each person will devour 17 beef cattle and 92 sheep in a lifetime, but I still think some solid marketing is required to convince yours truly to buy his pork chops on a hot day from the 'Good Luck Butcher' - especially when he has a flashing blue light revolving over the 'Specials': Or how about your good self buying any meat at all from someone trading as 'Dong Poo?' Thought not!

I know I have touched on this theme elsewhere, so I will try not to bore you too much. Incontestably, Australia is built on immigrants: initially white European, but now perhaps every nation on earth is represented here. And that is good. The size of this vast, near-empty continent and its small population allows for tolerance; allows people to grow and become assimilated; to become Australians.

In Britain we are far less tolerant of immigrants, who now [officially] account for about eight percent of the population. Perhaps it is because of the smallness of our island, which ensures that we have to share each square mile with about six hundred others, which has made us suspicious: dare I say small-minded? We certainly have confrontation, fear, the ghetto and a seedy undercurrent of violent, radical politics.

The Old World struggles to accommodate the refugee - even the most worthy. To the outsider, like me, the New World appears to be succeeding - and at the risk of repeating myself - if multiculturism is going to be made to work, then this huge land offers it the best chance of success.

Freddy

I had this love - hate relationship with Freddy,

I used to love his big, doleful eyes - and he was always so pleased to see you.

That's the love part over with. Now for the rest!

Imagine it is six in the morning. The house is silent. People are still sleeping, not yet ready for the hurly-burly of the day. The curtains are drawn tight. Peace reigns. Desperate for a cuppa tea, you slip on a short, nylon robe to cover your nakedness, and ever, ever so quietly, you creep to the kitchen. Assemble a breakfast tray, and still as quiet as a church mouse, not a floorboard creaking, hands full of wobbly tea n' stuff, you edge toward the bedroom door. Thirty feet to go....., twenty....., seventeen..... Then, just then, every morning, it happens: A big, wet, juicy tongue all around your unsuspecting crotch.

You stifle a yell: A right leg kick at the sneaky little blighter. Tail wagging, little front basset legs bouncing off the floor with delight it gets around your ankles. Lick to crotch. Kick. Lick to crotch. Kick: Line dancing with animals. Try and open bedroom door. Tea slops, milk slops. Toast on carpet. Final push of the foot to stupid, slobbering face and you're in. Safe! Heart hammering and needing that tea more than ever, you wonder what to do about the saliva dripping from your 'bits'.

Time for work: The garden is small and fenced. Freddy has food, water, shelter from the elements, balls to play with, bedding; an outhouse full of stuff to wreck. What else could he want except a female Fred - and he's not getting one.

So, pat on head: "Bye-bye, Freddy." Pat - pat. "Be a good doggy." Pat - pat. "You gonna' miss me?"

He wags his tail weakly and I think the eyes are saying "Have a day off: Stay with me. Don't go. Please don't go."

"Bye, Freddy."

Home again: Excited waggings and pissings, slobberings and lickings: All from the dog: An excited charge around the garden, then the house and garden. Finally, knackered, we all curl up for the evening ritual of zapping telly channels.

Sadly, Freddy is no more. Allergies sent him to a home well out of the city. But shortly after....:

Butcher's shop:

"Good morning. How's that dog of yours?"

Puzzled look on face. "How do you know Freddy?"

"He was in here every morning at ten past nine on the dot. Always gave him a bit of something. Not seen him for a while."

"Oh! No, well....."

Fishmongers:

"Hello there. How's that basset of yours?"

Puzzled look: "How do you know....."

"He used to be here every morning around 9.20: Used to fix him up with a few scraps. - Great little friend he was."

"Oh!"

Newsagents:

"G'day. How's....."

[Got the idea?]

Puzzled look is turning to frowns by now. The newsagents' was across two lines of traffic. "How do you.....?"

"Ten thirty on the dot. Came and had tea with me regular he did."

"Tea! He never drank tea."

He did in here. Milk: Two sugars!"

"Oh!"

The Pub:

"Hi! How's that basset doin'?"

Worried by now - the pub's across a four lane highway. "How.....?"

"He was always in here for the lunchtime session: Always had a half o' beer with me."

"He didn't!"

"He did! What's your poison?"

"Oh!.....I'll have a half as well please."

By now I knew the unpalatable truth. First, the blasted dog had more friends than me; and secondly, he wasn't pleading with me to stay home.

"Dine not wisely, but too well."

American style, 'Eat-all-you-can' diners have hit Sydney. Pay over your dollars on the way in and pig-out. Eat all you want and then some. And people do. The patrons of such establishments are not yet of the elephantine proportions of their American cousins who have frequented these obscene establishments for a generation; but give the Aussies a chance – they are quick learners.

Now, have you noticed how thin people seem to be able to eat what they want, when they want - and stay thin? To someone who had been overweight [i.e. read fat] since the age of six, I should be used to this unfairness in life. But.....!

Today, for instance, we were lunched by the rello's at one of these novelties. It was surprisingly good. Excellent food, well presented in pleasant surroundings - with good company thrown in. I had a bit of this and a bit of that - one plateful. Well - and a bit of fruit.

Now, on the next table was an elderly, little lady - everybody's idea of good old Aunty Ethel. She devoured a couple of plates of savoury dishes, but by the fourth helping of various puddings, she was becoming the object of amazement. Bets were being laid. Bread and butter pudding - and tea: Cheese cake - and tea: Ice cream - and tea: Heaps of everything - all washed down by gallons of Earl Grey. Eventually, all seven-and-a-half stone of her rose from the table and stretched to her full four feet ten inches. She paused. The bookies held tightly onto the money. Would she? Surely not! She sat again, eyes fixed on the sweet counter. But we knew she was beat and the money gone forever as she popped out her teeth, examined them carefully and then washed them in the cup of cold tea at her elbow. Washing finished, the task was completed with a good polish with a paper napkin.

With one last, lingering glance over her shoulder at a newly arrived pavlova, she was gone. Tomorrow she would still be thin, whilst the bathroom scales and I will studiously avoid one another for another day.

"For the times they are a-changin'."

How times change. It's hot, I'm sitting under the welcome shade of a giant Moreton Bay Fig surrounded by hungry white ibis, and I have been put into a reflective mood.

Just to my right, set at the entrance to the park and exposed to the full glare of the noon sun, stands the brilliant white Memorial Arch upon which row upon row of the war dead are etched in black. The names; Taylor, Scott, Henderson, Foster, Ryan, Turnbull, and those too numerous to mention, are alike. All are of Anglo-Saxon heritage - yesterday's legacy to this nation.

And by the arch, today's Aussies are playing chess - on a giant chequer board with giant figures - and playing it with gusto: Two Italians in pork-pie hats and a Ukrainian smoking a black cheroot, are playing a confident, black-haired chap from somewhere in Eastern Europe. He's the one with the fag stuck in the side of his mouth and we decide his name must be Sid. [Why else would he be wearing a peaked baseball cap emblazoned 'Sydney?'] Each move is accompanied by much arm waving and shouting.

"No-no-no-a! Not-a there-a. Take-a the rook. The rook!"

"Noo! Yoo moost leet heem play 'ees own game," said Sid chewing hard on the ciggy before spitting out the filter: The filter caused turmoil amongst the ibis, who thought grub was up. The players remained oblivious to the battle raging about their feet. He lit another cigarette, his confidence oozing. "Poon to King's Bishop two." It was obvious he was going to win.

Pretty fiery stuff and once or twice it looked like coming to blows. It didn't - and the game continued with unabated gesticulations. Then it struck me. They were all speaking English, apart from the occasional, violent interjections which I took to be native oaths. All were communicating; different races at home in a new land. Gratifying to see, and perhaps in another war, at sometime in our uncertain future, the names on the War Memorial will reflect today's Australians. But not yet!

My reflective optimism turned sour only moments later. We had walked on, drawn deeper into the park by the dappled shade and came, by pure chance, upon three elderly Japanese practising T'ai chi chu'an. They moved slowly with a practised grace, lending their shadowy grotto a certain charm and ethereal quality.

Maybe it is just me, or this particular mood I'm in. Maybe I'm being less than charitable. Maybe I am of yesterday, not of today, nor of tomorrow. But the name 'Sandakan' jumped at me from the memorial in that shady corner of T'ai chi. Sandakan! My heart still bleeds for the two and a half thousand Australian and British men of the 8th Division who were tortured and died of ill-treatment at the hands of their Japanese captors in northern Borneo during 1944 and 1945. The local men are listed here: Anderson, Robinson, Kelly, Locke, Harris.....Name after name. Would the six survivors from that particular hell feel like I feel just now? Is this right? Could the practitioners of T'ai chi not have chosen to display somewhere else? Right or not, it is not tasteful. Or would the survivors be annoyed with me? Had they found forgiveness in themselves, even if they couldn't forget? I will never know.

Nothing is ever straight forward, is it? Never black and white…..No matter how much you want it that way - just damnable shades of grey. Here was I, feeling good about the sacrifices of yesterday's Australians for this, God's own country; happy about its future in the hands of the new citizens being welcomed in increasing numbers - but a welcome for only some of them? I don't feel good about myself any more.

In an effort to reclaim my spirit, I return to the chess game. The blokes are still huffing and puffing at each other - enjoyable street theatre - but I can't stop thinking...

But at last I get things in perspective with this thought. We are soon to be off on our travels again. We will be travelling in a comfortable, Japanese car which boasts more computer technology than the ill-fated Apollo 13 space mission had.....More technology than it took to land men on the moon.

How times change - and us with it!

Misunderstandings on the 436

I love Sydney. Despite its pollution, thick enough to sting the throat; despite the humidity, I truly marvel at its brash vibrancy, which I feel owes a lot to the ethnic mix of the city. We ride the buses - a cheap way of watching life's pantomime unfurl. Somehow I just cannot imagine Shrewsbury's Park and Ride bus being so exhilarating. Mind you, ethnology has its draw backs. Take today's tale for example: misunderstandings on the 436.

10a.m. and the temperature was already in the thirties. We were packed on the bus like sardines, our faces turned to the open windows gulping for non-existent air. It was hard to breathe when the bus was held up in traffic. No air flow meant a slow death by heat exhaustion. When we moved we got air. Unfortunately, when we moved, we moved fast, swinging wildly across lanes of like-minded crazies, screeching brakes, blaring horns. Sudden death was an imminent possibility.

Sitting across the aisle and one seat in front of us was a Chinese lady. I guessed she was Chinese because she was reading a book written in Chinese characters. In her early twenties, she was no Asian temptress, being respectably dressed in a demure, high-necked, cover-all, white dress. She sat next to the aisle, the window slot being taken by a city slicker.

Two elderly gentlemen - unknown to one another, but whom fate would unite for all time - ended up standing in close proximity to the reader of books.

The bus continued its erratic way toward Sydney Cove. Ninety miles an hour, swerve, stop. [Always suddenly:]

The first old guy, an Aussie with bad legs, two fingers missing from one hand and the other arm in a sling, gripped the seat backs fore and aft of Miss China, and hung on for all he was worth.

It was uncomfortable for the female book reader; I mean - having a complete stranger, male to boot, peering down at your tightly-bound chest with his crotch at ear level, would be disconcerting. But fair-do's, it was uncomfortable for everyone.

On we go. Ninety - air: swerve - pray: Stop! - Hang on and then gasp.

The second elderly gentleman was a friendly Italian - Australian bloke who smiled at everyone and made facial expressions to fit the rhythm of the bus.

Brake! Brake! Brake! Might as well try and reduce our speed at the point of impact. Missed! A close encounter, greeted in a broad, Italian accent "They're-a gonna' kill-a me: These-a bump-a's no good for my heart-a."

I smiled. Reason enough for him to tell me all about his heart by-pass operation - which, to be honest, did make me feel guilty for sitting still. But there again, bus seats are always at a premium - and when in Sydney.....

At this point, the city slicker decided the chances of getting killed were less if he walked to work and so he departed, first having to climb over the immovable book. The reader kept on page turning, ignoring the feeble efforts of Old Aussie to crawl over her into the vacated window seat. He made it before slumping forward with his forehead resting on the back of the seat in front. He was gasping for breath and did look poorly.

You would be forgiven for thinking that two blokes climbing over your white pinafore might cause an eyebrow to lift or the book to slip. Not a bit of it!

Finally, the Italian got lucky. Before his heart by-pass needed further repair, a seat became vacant just across the aisle from the young woman. He plonked down on the seat with an over loud "Phew!" and beamed a broad smile to all sitting nearby. His 'Phew' hadn't evaporated into the ether before the Chinese gal jumped up, shouted something unintelligible in a very loud voice, whilst at the same time grabbing him by the shirt collar and hurling him into her recently vacated seat by Old Aussie.

She took his place - and out came the book.

The Italian - Australian looked somewhat bemused. We were all somewhat nonplussed by the turn of events. All, that is, except Old-Ozzie; he continued to gasp and clutch at his throat.

"She's-a tryin-a kill-a me," cried the Italian.

Being the helpful type, I said "I don't think she liked the man next to you-a."

He smiled. The penny had dropped. Radiant in his ignorance, he prodded the bookworm. "Miss-a."

Prod. Prod.

"Miss!" He smiled and winked at me as he slowly undid his shirt buttons to expose his chest scars.

She wasn't to know - and certainly was not impressed. She looked at the prodding finger, the stupid grin and the steadily growing expanse of skin. It improved her English no end. With a screaming "Fuck you," she hit the friendly smile with enough force to knock his hat three seats away.

Still bewildered, and now concussed, he started to scream "She tried-a kill-a me. Stop-a the bus-a! Stop-a the bus-a!"

It was a shame we had to get off-a.

Now the next day you wouldn't believe.....

Sydney Buses

Yesterday this ditty would have been very different, for yesterday my view of Sydney's bus drivers was one of unmitigated dread. The explosive Latino temperament has been brought to bear with typical gusto to the negotiation of crowded city streets: Accelerator, brake, swerve, swear. Accelerate again. Repeat ad infinitum.

Passengers are a nuisance. They need things - like being able to get off and on. Perhaps some change from the proffered fare. A seat occasionally might be nice.

"No! No! No-a! You're notta-atta-the-right-stoppa."

She was only five yards away but, with a dismissive wave of the fist and an accelerating swerve, the unfortunate woman was left at the kerb.

Those passengers lucky enough to be admitted better hang on - tight. And they are the few with seats. They'll escape with minor bruising and claustrophobia: For the multitude standing.....

Accelerate and swerve, swerve and brake, brake harder.

There must be a bonus in it for the maniacs at the wheel. Maybe it's on a sliding scale - say ten dollars for a passenger with a broken bone and two bucks per complaint.

It is so totally unlike the small town buses [do they really share the same planet?], where the drivers know everyone, are happy to talk and even happier to oblige by forgetting the occasional fare or dropping you off "a bit nearer the door with all that shopping." One driver we saw even helped carry the bags!

But today my faith in humanity has been renewed - and all because of a Sydney bus driver with a sense of humour. Still braking and swerving, he shouts to the current sardine crop: "Too many people standing.....Some of you will have to lie-a-down-a."

First Footing

Another day, another barbecue:

Jim and Sue came into the shaded courtyard garden over-hung by wood smoke, mosquitoes and the smell of frying steak and onions. They were obviously well-heeled; a cut above the crumpled shorts and shirt brigade standing about with half-filled glasses. Anyway, we got chatting. In their former existence they had been 'something in the City' [of London], where Jim would have been James and worn his old school tie, and Sue would have been 'Suzzeee-Darling.' They had made obscene amounts of money speculating on the future price of coconuts, or something similar, and were now excited and eager to start a new life on the other side of the world.

London had given them a going away present. Every single thing they owned had been loaded into a van for freighting - and someone had nicked the lot. Nothing was recovered, not even the old family photographs.

We were sympathetic, at least in the beginning, until their superiority began to rankle, and we looked for a way of shifting the burden onto someone else. Yet I couldn't put the thought away that it was an appropriate way to start a whole new life and a new year. It momentarily allowed them a tenuous connection with previous generations of settlers who, unlike them, had nothing to start with, yet sought a better life under the sun.

Suzzee-Darling had two appointments on Monday morning: first with the bank, to be followed in short order by a visit to "A sweet coiffeur" she'd already found: So much for being in touch with the past.

The year ends just like the day had started for us - in a rush. It is 11.57 p.m. before we know it. This morning was a scramble for a train; now it's a scramble to open the champagne before a chorus of "Happy New Years" bursts about us like the explosions from the huge firework display over Sydney Harbour.

The champagne was Australian and very good, but it wasn't French - something which did not please the arrivals from London, if the nose wrinkling was anything to go by. - And they hadn't even taken a gulp yet. I guess they will find their feet in time. Hope so - for their sakes!

We were dismayed to find no First Foot entering the house at midnight carrying a lump of coal to bring good luck for the coming year. But British ingenuity is not dead, for whom now cometh through the living room with greasy barbie briquettes crying "It'll be right, mate."

And you know - I'm sure it will.

Quick Family Recipe for the Barbecue:
Potatoes with Parmesan and Herbs: [Serves 4]
Take 500 grams of old spuds, peel and slice quite thick. Cook on hot plate.
Take half a cup of grated Parmesan cheese, one tablespoon of parsley and one of chives. Add half a teaspoon of paprika. Mix 'em up and chuck it on the cooked spuds.

The Rocks

New Year's Day and the city centre looks and feels like 'the morning after the night before.' The city has a hang over. Everything is closed now, whereas a few short hours ago a million people partied the night away on these very streets. Incredibly, one - seventeenth of the entire population of the nation was here. Now, litter and broken glass and closed shops greet the eager shoppers looking in vain for the January Sales.

Still, the harbour is as fabulous as ever, and the lack of tourists gives us a chance to explore the historic Rocks in peace. Once the site of the original European settlement, it is the best place to see a concentration of restored buildings, to examine the chisel marks on the rock walls made by convict hands, and to wander at will through the cuts, alleys and hidden squares.

As we wander I feel our convict, James, is here beside us. We walk in his footsteps along the passageways and shuts that he undoubtedly helped fashion, and touch the stonework of buildings he may well have frequented as he made merry with the rum and his common law wife, Lavender Annie.

The drunkenness and whoring of yesteryear are gone from the Rocks - moved to a less high profile place up town - but the area is left with a wonderful, tangible atmosphere which makes us feel a lot closer to our roots.

Sydney's Fish Market

Glistening silver: Bright reds: Brilliant white and stunning orange: Burnished bronze, startling greens. The noise and colours assail the senses. Wonderful life theatre; as the throngs of Sydneysiders join forces with the hordes of tourists to ogle at the zillion fantastic fish, with exotic names to match their exotic colours. Names to conjure with: Moreton Bay bugs; tarmines; the three feet long, red throated emperors; or the equally large jewfish. The yellow-fin tuna stretches out on its mortuary slab, all five feet of it, waiting for the knife and delicate artistry of the Sushi chef.

The Fish Market on Pyrmont Bridge Road, only a short walk or even shorter tram ride from Darling Harbour, is a must. For the new arrival to this land, it epitomizes Australia as much as the Opera House or the Harbour Bridge.

Just rum and plain, bad luck.

We take the morning ferry down the Parramatta River, heading for the city. The sun is shining from a clear spring sky; the blue water of the river is speckled with yachts and motor boats on this, one of Sydney's oldest highways.

As the engines growl away, speeding us from jetty to jetty to collect waiting commuters, it is hard to believe just how far Australia has come in the last couple of centuries or so.

It is totally impossible to try and conjure up a black night in the September of 1790, when five escaping convicts from the Second Fleet silently poled a stolen skiff down a darkened river, passing this very spot on their way to their Tahitian dream. There was no happy ending to their particular story. Without a compass, and only a week's supply of food, they did not make it.

And there were a lot of people who didn't 'make it' in Parramatta: rebellious Irish sharecroppers;

and the unfortunate inmates of the Female Factory who were too ugly, too mad, too old or too pregnant to be selected for the booming marriage market, to name but two.

Yet it was to these rich, flat lands of the Parramatta basin, being quickly cleared of bush and scrub that our Birkby family came in 1834. They had been gardeners on a Yorkshire estate, and sought a way out of poverty when their employer could no longer afford his extravagant lifestyle and his estate. The staff had to go - so, Australia. And the Birkbys did have plenty of agricultural experience to give to the new colony. Yet even they didn't 'make it:' - Just like the father of Australian agriculture, James Ruse, the first person to make his one- acre land grant pay its way. It took him twenty-eight years to accumulate two hundred acres - then lost it all to "Rum and bad luck."

We pass hundreds of thousands of homes, each headland weighed down by the Australian dream of house and pool and more besides. Each headland is propped up by yachts, white painted jetties and tiny, picnic beaches. The dream is being lived in the here and now, a dream unimaginable to the city's founders.

I just hope and pray the current generation, prisoners of mortgages, stress and all the rest, don't lose their dreams to rum - or just plain bad luck.

A Stiff Neck on the 9.13:

The woman flopped down in the seat across the aisle from us with a "You've no idea what a strain it's been to catch this train."

Now this would have been okay if she had been speaking to a companion, albeit in an overly loud voice - but the only people in the carriage were my wife and me - and we didn't know her from Adam. [Or should that be Eve?] Our eyebrows raised in unison toward her.

"Hair spray," she said from inside a small box of chocolates. "Just couldn't find it, and it's something I just can't get through the day without. Can you?"

My wife, who never uses the stuff, being a wash-and-go type of gal, manages a grimace in place of a knowing smile.

Further conversation is interrupted as the Rattler moves out of the station with a hefty jolt - a jolt which propels several young ladies into the carriage. They seem to be with the lady under strain, as they silently plop down behind her in an orderly fashion - but with bad grace.

We smile at Hairspray Lady as she selects a sweetie from the box. That was a costly error on our part, as she took no second bidding. "I'm self employed," she began, slipping out of her cardigan and settling back for the journey. In doing so, she managed to expose the ample and fleshy upper parts of her body to the sunshine pouring through the grimy windows. The sides of her green top touched but briefly at the waist - the rest needed little imagination, especially when she began to hunt for a speck of chocolate lost amid her cleavage. "I go around all the shows you know," she continued unabashed.

I force myself to stare out of the window on the other side of the carriage.

"Cosmetics: That's the game. I put on demo's….."

Good manners insisted I turn back to face her as she spoke.

"I feel I'm real good at what I do."

I nod and look away quickly, convinced she would be pretty good at whatever it was she did. And I did not believe it was cosmetics. She may have been a well preserved forty year old with layers of make-up, powder, eye shadow and what have you, but there was something erotic – uninhibited - about the way she dealt with her missing chocolate. I kept looking out of my window, but she was talking at me again.

"I've a ten year old son. One's enough don't you think? Anyway, my man - he's so considerate.

We've been together now for eight years. We're two individuals. He lets me do whatever I want. He's so cute. My man, I mean.......So's my son."

I continue to seek refuge out the window, wondering if she will ever shut up. A cricket match zooms by - and I half wish we were stopped by a red light so I could concentrate on that. It would be so much easier to stop the eyes wanting to wander.

"I had an accident in the car you know? You couldn't tell now, could you?"

My neck was in a creak so I turned to look at her again. She was examining a chocolate minutely, nibbled at the edge and then began to use her tongue fettishly.

"Two months I spent at the physio and no good. First visit to a chiropractor and as good as new."

Her arms went aloft just as the choccy disappeared. Her fleshy bits went walk-about and my eyes dashed for cover.

"I went for my first jog this morning," she carried on.

My thoughts were revolving around the suspicion that she was touting for business: But surely not? – Not with the wife present: Surely no-one could be so oblivious of their actions. My lines of thought were soon overtaken by visions of her six-foot frame jogging through the streets of Sydney's suburbs, her clothing straining to confine the effects of the constant chocolate popping she was proving so adept at.

My attention wandered to the girls in the seat behind her. They were twelve to fourteen, going on nineteen, and full of themselves. They had donned wigs - bright red ones with devil's horns - and were making faces at their leader's back.

I couldn't grasp the relationship there...... Still haven't.

"Pitt Street Mall!" She was still talking. "That's the best place for shopping in Sydney..... I used to be a dancer you know....." [Logic didn't seem to be a part of this lady's make-up.....]

"I know it was only in a nightclub," she continued, without the need for breath: "Dancing in one of those cages for the fellas: Sweeties they were."

My eyes close. I know it's rude, but I couldn't help it: The soothing clump, clump of the train; her soporific voice. More importantly, by closing my eyes I might be able to save a stiff neck later brought about by the constant search for cricket matches.

Anyway, after thirty minutes in her company I reckon I could have written a five-thousand word essay on cleavage sunspots, freckles and suntan lines. And I certainly cannot cope with any more excitement for the rest of the day.

Heads up:

You know how it is. Some days you wish..... Well, today I had two, wishes that is. One, - that I didn't look like a tourist in sunscreen and shorts, believing the sky to be blue and the sun to be hot, whilst the Sydneysiders were in jumpers and jackets. Secondly, I wish..... I wish I were an ornithologist. I do not know what the birds were, but they were hunters circling with intent above the distant skyline of the city. Pure white killer snowballs who took skinks and mice from the headland heath at will.

We had taken one of the dozens of ferries plying the harbour and beached at Watson's Bay by Sydney Heads, home to Doyle's-on-the-Beach, the world famous fish restaurant. The restaurant itself is expensive, but the take-away around the side serves cheap, tasty tucker.

Full of fish and chips we take a short walk - and there are Sydney Heads: Huge weather-battered cliffs protecting the magnificent harbour from the South Pacific. Sydney Heads: Accidentally saved from the ravages of the developers by the Defence Ministry for many years, now parts of both headlands have been given over to parkland and opened to the public.

The water of the bay was alive with a billion drops of light necklacing the city as if in diamonds. The yachts are out from the Double Bay Yacht Club, their sails painting patterns across perfection. There are spectacular views every which way, rivalled only by the aerial displays of the real owners of this mind-blowing place.

Manly

The first time we saw the boy he stood out. Even without his shock of white hair he would have been singled out amongst the crowd of his school contemporaries. He was standing alone in the corner of one of the beach volleyball squares, whilst the others threw themselves this way and that, shouting and swearing; full of youth. The ball never went his way. He would be always the last one to be picked for any team sport. Never wanted, merely tolerated by his peers: Always alone.

It was incongruous that he should have been there at all - at a beach called Manly. Once known as Cabbage Tree Beach, Manly is one of the twenty beaches on offer to the people of Sydney. The cabbage trees have long gone; they beat a hasty retreat in the face of airborne sewage pollution. But Manly is still the home of the Iron Man, the citadel of life-saving excellence, as it has been since 1898 when daylight bathing became legal. It is also home to the world-famous Life Saving Carnival, where bronzed gods perform amazing feats of endurance and bravery in the shark-infested waters. They carry the tradition well, for at the start of colonization Governor Phillip visited here and found the Aboriginal inhabitants 'of manly behaviour.'

So Manly it became - and even though now it is heavily commercialized, the pull of sand, sea and sun still make it a place for lovers to love in, sun worshippers to reveal all in and athletes to sweat in. All are happy to be admired by the un-godlike tourist masses.

We left before the boy. He was standing alone at the water's edge, careful to avoid the incoming tide. Still no one talked to him. The rest splashed and played in the waves outside the shark nets and away from the Schwarzeneggerian beach patrols who would be there in a flash if things went wrong.

Something strangely allegorical about the whole incident: The carefree kids are the embodiment of Australia: daring, full of confidence, living life with a 'frontier' spirit which has served its people well, carved out a living from the hostile land and forged a place for this country in the world. Visibly the boy did not fit. There was no place for him or for his sensibilities today.

I was left wondering if there ever would be in this harsh, uncompromising, wonderful land.

The Blue Mountains

Don Patterson, the pilot of a Lancaster Bomber, was shot down and killed over Germany on Christmas Eve, 1944. His was one of six aircraft out of the 338 tasked to attack the Lohausen aerodrome near Dusseldorf which failed to return.

Don died, never to see his farming home in the Blue Mountains again, but we can pay a visit, if only in silent tribute to his memory.

The Blue Mountains are incredibly beautiful and yet lie only forty miles from Sydney. They get their name because of the countless millions of trees giving off droplets of eucalyptus oil, which shimmer in the atmosphere and so cause a blue haze to overhang the mountain range.

Back in the time of our two James's, it was thought these mountains - part of the two-thousand-mile-long chain of the Great Dividing Range - were impossible to cross and that China lay beyond them. The four-thousand-foot-high peaks, sheer cliffs and spectacular waterfalls disappearing into deep gorges, formed an impenetrable barrier until 1813 - and even today, standing so close to the easily accessible Three Sisters feature, you cannot help but marvel at how the first explorers found their way over them. They did it eventually - by keeping to the ridges. More remarkable is the effort of the convict labourers, and the motivation required, to drive an ox road up the mountains and force it through to the waiting interior.

Our expedition then, no doubt based on the false premise that whatever Blaxland, Lawson and Wentworth can do.....

Bushwalking:

"It's only a leech."

"Get it off! Get it off! Ugghhh!"

Several 'uggghhh's' later the offender was despatched to eternity. It was but a temporary respite as my brother and I continued to turn and watch incredulously every five yards as the female members of our expedition stopped and inspected their footwear.....and their legs.....and then each other's footwear.....each other's legs. It was going to be a long walk.

"Don't tell them," laughed Alan. "But they drop down from the branches as well."

At that point he stood on an invisible Red Bellied Snake which had been minding its own business devouring a cicada for lunch. It hissed and left slowly. We raised our eyes to the heavens, hurried along the track and called back to the girls who were still concerned about tiny leeches: "Come on. Hurry up. There's more to worry about than them."

In all seriousness, bush walking is an interesting and worthwhile experience. But! And it is a big but.....Care must be taken. The terrain, weather and wildlife can all be fatal so it's sensible to never walk alone and always take bottled water with you. It is probably best to stick to the visitor trails most National Parks have, or for the more adventurous, pay to go with a professional guide.

There are three places in the Blue Mountains deserving of an extended stay:

The Jenolan Caves:

"It's a time warp." I couldn't believe the Victorian guest house: Ancient waitresses dressed in black with white pinnies totter about. Tables are set with linen and silver: No self service here. The plumbing is even more ancient – and more or less worked when it wanted to. It was like being part of a stage set for an Agatha Christie mystery set in Malvern, Worcestershire circa 1920.

Yet the setting is surely unique. The road seems to end abruptly. A moment's hesitation and then you see the way through the jaws of the towering mountain and into the cone of an extinct volcano – and the waiting guest house.

The massive cave system that it services are well presented and worthy of a leisurely visit.

Katoomba:

Katoomba is the capital of the Blue Mountains. There're plenty of popular walks and the Three Sisters rock formation is unmissable. The Skyway Cable Car, on which the 'driver' reassures you with the words, "We're so high, if the cable breaks, it'll take thirty seconds to hit the ground below," is exhilarating.

The 'ground below' is Jamieson Valley which can be reached by the steepest tourist railway in the world.

The Wombeyan Caves:

These caves should not be attempted by the faint hearted. Dirt roads and precipitous drops welcome the traveller coming from the direction of Kangaroo Valley. However, the scenery is fantastic, the caves themselves make the trip worth the effort – and of course – there's always the adrenalin rush of the journey back to look forward to.

A Colonial Lass:

In the small, rhododendron-filled town of Blackheath, high in the Blue Mountains, lies a nondescript Catholic church - nondescript, but important to our extended family in one respect; it holds a memorial to a Margaret Devlin who died in 1917.

I feel sure someone could write a novel about Margaret's life; fill out the bare bones of what we are certain.

She was born in Ireland, christened Margaret McGuiness, a daughter of a world-famous brewing family and destined for life as a nun. She was just a novice when she met a young man, Joe Devlin, the local horse and trap driver - something akin to the local taxi today.

We guess a relationship of sorts must have developed, sufficient for her family to pack her off to Holy Orders in England - Newcastle upon Tyne to be precise. Unfortunately for her monied family, and happily for our mob, Joe took his job very seriously and, instead of driving her to the ferry, accompanied her all the way to England. They arrived in Geordie land, only the convent wasn't too happy about taking on a pregnant nun.

Within a short time, Margaret's mother got word to her that all was forgiven, so she and Joe returned to Ireland in time for the birth of their second child, Jack Guinness Devlin.

The reasons why Joe and Margaret settled in New South Wales have been lost in time, although Joe was never liked, nor forgiven, by the Guinness dynasty. So that's probably the reason - they thought they were best out of it. All we do know is that another eleven children duly arrived to the couple and that in order to satisfy her mother's whim "that she shouldn't have a Colony baby," Margaret returned to Ireland on a number of occasions to birth her children. I guess, whilst the old Irish matriarch lived, she still held sway, even from the other side of the world.

Margaret's Irish connections did not survive the passing of her mother and, in 1917 she too died, disinherited, but having sown the seeds of her own large, Colonial family.

Doogie saves the day.

I knew we had made a mistake, just as soon as the two tour coaches started to debus their elderly cargo.

Until that point the sun had shone, and the old steam train, 'The City of Lithgow,' had idled away at the station, filling the air with smoky nostalgia.

I had been torn between another mind-boggling, Blue Mountain bush walk or a trip on the world-renowned 'Great Lithgow Zigzag;' the first legend of Australian engineering. It might only be a kilometre from Clarence Station, where the locomotive was doing its 'Thomas the Tank Engine' impression, to Bottom Points via [wait for it] Top Points, but the return trip was a scheduled one-and-a-half hours, with five engine changes.

The history of the line had always intrigued me - well, at least since Great Railway Journeys of the World hit the telly screens in the late seventies or early eighties. In the 1830's it had taken a great effort of will and human ingenuity to get the railway line up to the summit of Mount Victoria from the coastal plain. Once up the 1600 metres, the problem was to get down again. Not an easy task, when faced with the sheer cliffs on the western side of the mountain ranges. In the 1860s the railway line made it. It was brought down in three tremendous swoops, the Lithgow Zigzag, and so opened up the way out west.

One of the wonders of the nineteenth century has now been restored by volunteers, the rolling stock being lovingly tended in the sidings. And I thought I'd make a day of it.....

But on the arrival of the buses I knew we had drawn the short straw, as 110 excited oldsters elbowed their way toward a day out.

Our dog-box - the old Australian name for a carriage fitted with long, wooden benches - filled up steadily but slowly. And each arthritic passenger brought us a present - along with an up-to-the-minute medical report on each condition they were suffering from - an open door with accompanying blowfly.

Doogie was the first one to catch my eye. His face looked like it had been hit by a truck, the old trilby and lopsided grin marking him out as a character.

"All a-board!" warbled the fat girl on the platform with the white flag.

And Doogie got off; video camera running.

He was rounded up by a big bloke in an official looking blue shirt and tie, and helped back on.

The door slams.

The whistle blows.

Departure is imminent: you can feel the steam locomotive girding itself for the kilometre-long fall to the valley floor below.

Doogie opens the door, but is pulled back in by an elderly female companion with moustache, so he contents himself by sticking his head and shoulders out of the sash window - the window directly beneath a sign: 'Don't.... or you'll get your head taken off.'

But it is we who are off, hootin' and a hollerin,' the old folks jabbering away excitedly.

My eyes leave Doogie - breathing in black smoke funnelling past him into the carriage - and alight on a ghost. The ghost is old, with crooked front teeth, white, curly hair in a monk-like tonsure, and skin as dry and taut as ancient parchment. The only thing is his name is Nick. I should know. I worked for him for years. And he's dead. - And buried.

I sit and watch him. I can't help myself. He/It is immovable. Not a word. Not an eyelid flutter. The only blinking being done is by the overhead carriage light, on for the tunnel. It's turned him an eerie yellow.

I am sure it is him.

And that makes him the second ghost in two days. I knew who the other one was too. He was alive and well when we left the U.K. and he should still be there - certainly not standing at the foot of my bed at twenty past four in the morning.

Maybe I should join Doogie and the bus people.

After two minutes we break out of the tunnel and into bright daylight once more. The ghost is still there, still as unearthly.

Doogie is still there too, champing at the bit, and as soon as the old locomotive grinds to a halt at Top Points, the shout goes up from the guard: "Ten minutes!"

Doogie's off; camera fixed to his eye and moving like he was a Special Forces guy on a raid looking for terrorists through a night sight.

I spend the ten minute engine changing time being bombarded with useless information: the differences and superiority of 1 - 41 gradients over 1 – 40; how the Western District overcame a fall of three inches in a mile; the merits of three feet six inch bogeys. And a whole lot more I would like to share with you, but my brain went numb at the same time as my eyes glazed over.

My yawn is interrupted by the whistle blowing at full tilt. Doogie appears at the top of a mound of coal on the other side of the track. And he's a hundred yards away.

The whistle blows again: Urgently. The locomotive begins to gather itself once more with a series of shakings, puffings and jarrings.

Doogie is trotting, well, moving as fast as his gammy leg would let him. He is grabbed by the collar and hauled aboard by the big bloke in the blue shirt.

Two minutes later: "Fifteen minutes here! Take fifteen!"

Doogie needs no further encouragement. He's off, leaving behind a chorus of "Eeh!" and "He's a card ain't he?" from the old dears.

Fifteen minutes! God! I cannot stand any more talk of steam pressures in pounds per square inch and the swapping of references from mouldy old manuals: "Mmmh! That's got a chamfered whats-it. What you've got is the Mark MV23AZ. Now I've seen the MV22 - a totally different kettle of fish….."

To prevent me going mad, I decide to talk to the ghost. "I'm sorry to disturb you - but do we know each other?"

"I-don't-think-so," he answers in a monotone voice straight out of the Daleks and Doctor Who.

His eyes don't move: Nor his head. Hell! His lips don't even move. But unless ghosts can talk in the light of day, I guess it wasn't Old Nick.

"All a-board!" Our departure is announced in a sing-song voice.

This time Doogie is scurrying along the platform. He runs past our dog-box. Doors are slamming. He's lost. We're moving. He's panicking now – head on a swivel; bewildered.

A big man in a blue shirt pushes him through our door at the very last second - and we are off.

"Sorry about that," he apologizes. "I get a bit lost sometimes."

Just like our day.

Just like my ghosts.

"Tilly! Here Tilly-Tilly-Tilly!"

2.20 a.m. I am wide awake. Yet another truck has crawled up the mountain using all its gears. Not that I mind our motel room, nor the noise for that matter. It is just I can't work out if the back – hip pain is keeping me awake so I can study the traffic flow, or whether it's the other way round.

In a way it is comforting, taking me back to my childhood when I'm snuggled down under a heap of blankets in my room at grandma's house and lie awake watching the headlights of the night traffic playing across the ceiling. I used to wonder at life going on 'out there,' beyond the frosted panes. Were the cars hurrying their occupants to parties? Was it a police car responding to a break-in? Was it a doctor on a mission of mercy? One night it was the Pit Deputy from the local coal mine, coming to tell us that granddad Reg would not be coming home again.

I couldn't wait to get on with my life. Back then: All those years ago.

2.53 a.m. A speeding car squeals its tyres through the road works chicane. At least I'm getting time to reflect on our time in the Blue Mountains: Some stupendous bush walking along Deep Green Govetts Gorge, with its blue-tongued lizards, frilly-necks and stunning views.

No snakes! But I soon learn it is not the bracing air of the mountains which has made them stay at home, but the clamour and clatter of not-so-tiny feet coming from the opposite direction: A veritable bus-load of faces carefully negotiating a rocky decline in deep wilderness country.

"Is there a bus waiting for us up the track?" enquired the leader, a teacher-type in her thirties, with boots and shorts and knapsack.

As we explained that we had been walking for two hours on a track two feet wide and had not seen another soul, she went a bit pale.

"Oh dear! What to do? What to do? I think I've asked my girls to do too much."

Her thirty or so girls did not have a clue where they were or why. All were sixteen-or seventeen-year-olds, and snakes, lizards, birds and panoramic views were as naught compared to their mobile phones, chatter and constant re-adjustment of their plastic flip-flops. Someone ought to tell them about walking in the Australian bush; certainly the necessity of carrying water and mossie killer. They talked incessantly as their leader dithered. They could have been in Big W or Coles' Supermarkets, for all they cared about the Great Outdoors.

We left them in a quandary. At least we knew where we were going - and that made me feel just a little bit guilty.

Three-and-a-half hours later, on the way for a well-deserved tea break, we saw their bus. We give a 'thumbs-up' to the leader and elicited a worried look, a half smile and a feeble wave. I thought maybe she hadn't forgiven us for leaving her on the road to nowhere - then realized she did not have a single kid with her…..

But we had our own problems: a search for coffee in Blackheath…..

I must have dropped off for a while, as the clock now said 4.21 a.m. The lorry convoy is never ending.

Tea ended up being taken in a converted cinema, built about 1920. Most of the premises were now given over to old books and junk, invariably described as 'antiques.' The little serving counter for refreshments is stuck in a corner fronting the street. It looked meticulously clean and boasted a sparkling new cappuccino machine. In charge was a girl who looked like she should still be in school, but fussing around the place was a middle aged Chinese bloke - a 'New Australian,' as incomers are called in these politically correct times.

"I'm sorry," I said to the guy, as I took my first, longed-for, sip. "This has sugar in."

"No soogar! No soogar!" Belligerent!

I insisted. I had waited five hours for this. "Sorry, but it has. Any non-sugar taker can tell something with sugar in it at fifty paces."

"No soogar!"

"Well, I can't drink it."

"You dink! Is good! You dink! No soogar!"

"Look! If you didn't put sugar in, then the cup mustn't have been washed properly."

"Cup clean! You look! You look at cups!" he said, practically tossing one at me.

"That's not a muguccino. I've tasted cappuccino all over the world - and in Australia….." I added forcefully. "And that's not….."

"Moccachino," he finished the sentence for me. "I thought you said Mocca, not Mugga."

Problem solved, but later, I could not face telling Blackheath's bejewelled and ear-ringed barman that I'd asked for whisky and soda, not whisky and dry ginger.

Guess it must be me.

4.45 a.m. Katoomba is a nice enough little town, trading on the beauty of the Blue Mountains and of the Three Sisters in particular. Like all well publicized natural phenomena [and I put the Three Sisters on a par with Ayres Rock and Niagara Falls], nothing can stop you from being impressed. They somehow manage to soar above the tourist buses and camera-toting, litter-depositing hordes. Yet, it would be nice to see them on your own, or as they were. Dream on!

5.30 a.m. No chance of sleep now. The traffic is at the constant roar level - and although my wife, Patsy, is still asleep, she will want a brew in the next half hour.

But I reckon I can't get up without reliving our adventure at the Botanic Gardens on Mount Tomah.

The car park attendant refused to bend his old back, so, after speaking with a lapel badge 'My name is George,' and being asked to be on the lookout for Tilly, we parked by the Information Centre and café. From the vine-covered terrace we were suitably impressed by the view which stretched for two hundred kilometres before, map in hand, we were off.

At long last our search for a close-up view of the ancient Wollemi Pines was over. Only a few short years ago, a valley unknown to mankind had been found just thirty miles from Sydney. [Think about that for a moment.] And in the valley, the Wollemi Pine - trees which were thought to have disappeared in the Ice Age. And now they are cultivating them here.

Excited, we pass roses and conifers; even tread the Gondwana Forest Trail, dedicated to plants that have evolved in isolation ever since the southern super-continent of Gondwana broke up 120 million years ago.

But no sign of our trees: - And no sign of poor, little lost Tilly, despite calling her name continually.

We end up back where we started - at the car. Ever the opportunists, we have sandwiches before heading off again, map still in hand. "Tilly! Here Tilly-Tilly-Tilly," we sing-song.

We pass splendid rhododendrons in full bloom, push our way through the dense walls of forest, and end up back at the car. No Tilly! No trees!

The map is orientated once more. We see the heathers, the goldfish, even ignore the 'Danger: Road Closed,' signs: But no Tilly and no pines – just the car park and the car waiting patiently: And now, all alone.

This is getting spooky.

The sun starts to dive for the distant horizon. One more go, - but first the loo's and, being sensible, semi-intelligent creatures, we ask for directions at the Information Desk. This time for sure.

The Wild Plant Explorers Walk leads us once more into the ever-darkening Forest Walk, overhung with branches and fronds and animal sounds I did not care to think about. And once more we are back on the car park.

Now exhausted, the Wollemi Pines can wait for another millennium. We head for the exit.

"Did you find your cat, George?" I ask with some concern.

"Cat?" he asks with a growing look of bewilderment. "I haven't got a cat."

"Tilly?"

"Oh! The tiger snakes. I call 'em all Tilly. You've got to be real careful where you tread, especially….."

The foot hits the accelerator.

6.20 a.m: Up and at 'em time. I wonder what today has in store.

As drunk as….:

Nestling at the foot of the Blue Mountains is a tiny winery, and after several days of spring rain the vines were green and ordered and stretched far into the distance.

To sell its wares by the side of the narrow and winding country road, a large corrugated-iron barn had been constructed and filled to the gunwales with wine of every variety: Chardonnay, Cabernet, Shiraz; the lot, and more besides.

Not so impressive was the large cardboard sign pinned to the door, telling us that all the wine was made on the premises by its Italian – Australian patrons. The sign had not deterred the buying public - the place is full of customers heaving the stuff onto trolleys. I reckon this is a good sign and enjoy watching the free-for-all, as they squeeze between the ranks of bottles and cartons and containers. Cars come and go, kicking up dust clouds across the cracked earth car park.

We have found a real beaut-bonza spot here - of that there can be no doubt.

I get stuck into the free samples: A white at two dollars a bottle. It is an undrinkable home brew and I do so wish I hadn't taken such a mouthful. Too many folk to spit it out, so I swallow hard and pull a face as the raw alcohol burns its way toward my nether regions. Shit!

The Chardonnay had to be better.

It wasn't, so I move onto the more expensive, six bucks a bottle, damaged-label reds. Vinegar! I'm just swearing to myself when I realize that the reds were tasting just like the whites. Could that be true? I don't know, as I was blessed with too much common sense to go back and have another go. In fact, I'm stunned. As happy people come and go with armfuls of the grog, I chew a handful of indigestion tablets and mull over some half-remembered news item of long ago about an Italian winegrower who got caught adding anti-freeze to the mix. Or was he Spanish? I could not remember, but couldn't help wondering if the guy had moved out of Europe and started afresh over here.

After a while, the tablets kick in and I come to the conclusion it must be me who is the odd man out. Everyone can't be wrong. So, nothing if persistent, I return to the free samples.

I am the last back to the car and chewing on yet another handful of pills. I drop into the front passenger seat with a, "I don't know what that guy was doing when he lived in Italy, but it certainly wasn't making wine. There must an awful lot of desperate drunks about....." I'm immediately struck by the silence - a somewhat unusual event amongst our happy little band, so I turn to face the rear seats.

I'm not met by people, only by their disembodied hands making rude gestures - the passengers having disappeared behind cases of the stuff, piled to the roof and entwined by nursing, caring arms.

*

And so back to Sydney:

On! On! On forever through wall-to-wall forest: Fifty feet away is virgin country unmolested by man for forty thousand years.

Sydney is calling. It is waiting, as seductive as ever. Through tiny hamlets we rush; sleepy little places where tourist information offices are shut at the weekends and where the little shops, displaying 'Open seven days' signs, are closed tight shut, leaving the geckos to play unhindered in near deserted streets. In fact the only thing moving fast is the poor woman in a coffee shop, who is trying to cope womanfully with a 'mystery tour' bus disgorging passengers in desperate need of tea and 'things.'

Sydney is close now. Signs appear: 'Horse Manure: Dollar a bag:' A sure indication of approaching civilization. All of a sudden the traffic builds, the pace quickens. We see the city from thirty three miles out, proud on the skyline. Sydney, the Excitement City; awaits.

Journey 5
New South Wales

Newcastle and the Central Coast

A Bank Holiday Greeting

In Britain, Bank Holidays are a time to stay at home - for me anyway. I'm at home with a cuppa and derive a malicious pleasure from the T.V. news. Nor am I sitting in a car prone to overheating in a fifty mile traffic jam at Bristol or Birmingham, or any other of a hundred places you can mention on our tiny, crowded island. I am not cursing at road works with their infuriating signs telling me that I can 'Phone-a Cone' [Hotline] if I'm not happy.

And when, or if, you get to your destination, no matter whether it's the seaside or country, tens of thousands of others have beaten you to it.

And I won't mention the weather. Is it a myth that holiday weekends are always cold, wet and very, very long?

And there is always the journey home to look forward to.

Nope! Bank Holiday travel is not for me. Mind you, this is Maundy Thursday and what are we doing? You guessed - Driving on the busiest section of road on the continent and the most dangerous in New South Wales: Freeway 1.

We call in at the National Parks of Ku-ring-gai Chase, to view the Aboriginal carvings in the sandstone rock, and then later at Brisbane Waters for the views. It was around here in 1791 that the Governor of the fledgling colony came into contact with a tribe of Aborigines who lived by the Hawkesbury River. They greeted the Governor and his party of soldiers with "Ga-diay." * To the locals 'Ga-diay' meant penis and, after a lot of pointing and pulling, one of the soldiers was ordered to drop his pants and stand to attention. Perhaps the officer said "Be an Angel James, would you......?"

I have always assumed that 'G'day,' the usual greeting Australian men give one another, was a bastardization of the pleasantry, "Have a good day." So it's a bit of a worry when you realise that for all these years we have been greeted, "Penis. Nice morning." To which I have been replying, "Penis. Nice one isn't it."

But this Easter journey has to be worth all the travel, for our family have populated the mid New South Wales coast since the 1830s, those early settlers having been joined by successive generations of emigrants escaping from the horse and cart jams of a cold and bleak northern England.

The journey here to Blacksmiths, just south of Belmont near Newcastle, was expected to take us about four hours. The traffic moved and every road work disappeared astern in a twinkling. The journey is completed - in four hours.

Our motel is only half full, and that night the television relays pictures from "Our eye in the sky." The traffic is moving and there are "No worries" anywhere.

* The Fatal Shore by Robert Hughes quoting Sydney Cove 1789 - 1790 by John Cobley.

The Brothers

Today has been a good day, thanks to a seventy-seven year old lady. She met us on the veranda of her old, timber-clad house - which lies a couple of hundred yards from the beautiful beach at Blacksmiths - with a huge smile, a hug and a kiss.

That was extra special because we had never met. I don't suppose there is any reason why we should have. A grandmother's, brother's daughter who emigrated to Australia in 1923 is not high on the Christmas card list. She should have been though.

Over a pot of tea, and out of the reach of an angry-at-the-world King Charles spaniel, she revealed a little more of our Thompson family heritage.

"The three brothers came out here in 1922 - Ramsey, Bill and Ned. I had my third birthday on the boat. We went to Kurri-Kurri for the men to work in the pits there."

"They were coal miners back in Northumberland too weren't they?" I interrupted.

"Yes. But there was no work back then. No work meant no money to feed us kids. No rent money, so no house. And, of course, T.B. was rife."

"So that's why they all came away?"

"Yes.s.s....." She drew the word out. A momentary indecision and then: "They wouldn't have come but for the War. They were disgusted by it first and foremost, the way our lads were just used. Then they were disgusted by the treatment the survivors received at the hands of their own Government..... They insisted on reparations by the Germans who had nothing to give us except coal. So they took it and put our men out of work. And after all the promises that were made.....Did you know that all three brothers sat around the front room fire one night and burnt all their medals?"

"No, I didn't. However, I know the Great War affected a lot of men in different ways."

She continued as if she hadn't heard me. "They were finished with England - for good! They never talked about it you know. Never spoke of England again. It was gone, an inconsequential little island off the shores of an irrelevant Europe. It was gone and that was that."

I put in my tuppence worth. "My granddad wouldn't talk about the War. He'd talk under wet cement, but not about that. Back then, when I was sixteen, I thought he was very strange for refusing to tell me about it."

"No. He wasn't strange. I don't think anyone who wasn't there could understand. Another relative of mine:" a little laugh; "Of ours - sorry. When he got out here just after it ended, he wouldn't hurt anything, not even a fly. I well remember his only fruit tree being eaten to bits by caterpillars. He finds one that's fallen to the ground, so what's he do? Only picks it up and puts it back on a leaf." She paused. "We used to get a lot of tree snakes in the coal wagons. He used to take them back up the bush in a coal sack and let them go."

"It must have been a hard life for you at first," I said: "Nothing like your home now with all its mod-cons and the beach nearby."

"Tar paper walls for the house and a tree bark roof. It could get pretty hot too - but no matter how tough it was, not one of them ever talked of going back. This was it - get on with it. We had one thing here you see above all else. Hope! Hope for a better future for the children."

Tears filled her eyes as tiredness came upon her. She rubbed her right arm, disfigured by a stroke many years previously, but wasn't about to bring our chat to an end. She battled on. "But they weren't the first, you know."

"No?"

"No. That honour belonged to a convict called Samuel Asher. He was given 14 years at Nottingham Assizes for stealing clothes, but he died early out here. 1837, I think. Fell off the back of a cart and broke his back. Still, one of his descendants became Mayor of Newcastle. They married into our family of Scott's: Douglas Scott, Master shipwright, but when his wife died he went back to Scotland."

Her voice was faltering by now, the throat drying up. There were still the remnants of tears in the corners of her eyes, threatening to come again.

Despite her protestations, it was time to go.

Food for Free

"The flies will have gone by Christmas," said Bill, as we both swiped at the persistent attackers. Missed again! "They arrive with the mutton birds," continued the ex-navy man hardened by years of sun, whisky, and keeping his mouth shut in the presence of the perfidious insects which seemed intent on checking out my dentist's handiwork.

"What's mutton birds got to do with these **** flies," I asked pleasantly, as I back-handed a big 'un. Missed! "**** it!"

"Get yourself down the beach and have a look."

Good advice. The beach at Blacksmiths is not one to be passed by and it's not hard to get to from the rello's house: fifty yards over the gentle dunes.

The beach was as lovely as ever - long and golden; rocky headlands, crashing surf and a tidemark of shells. A kid's dream and I am in my element - which says something about me, I guess.

But then we begin to have to pick our way around the painful, blue jellies, aptly named stingoes, which have arrived at the water's edge, courtesy of a week of north-westerly winds - remnants of a storm a long way up north. I curse my lack of forethought. If I had remembered to carry a can of Coca Cola [or vinegar - less palatable but equally effective], then I'd be armed with the perfect sting remedy. And of course if you don't pour it over the affected part, you can always drink it.

Then the flies arrived! They buzz angrily around legs, arms, head, mouth, - anywhere and everywhere.

Australia: The Enigma: Beautiful and tainted.

The reason for the flies was immediately obvious - mutton birds: Dozens within a few strides: Dead mutton birds. If what we could see here at our feet was repeated along the nine miles of this one beach, then there must have been many thousands of these unfortunates who had become exhausted by their migration and had not quite made it to their breeding holes on the headlands of Phillip Island and King Island to the south, and, wait for it - Mutton Bird Island further north.

We have good reason to be thankful to these creatures, as their opportune arrival had once saved the early colonists, including the two James's, from starving to death. The breeding colonies inhabit burrows beneath grassy promontories, making them easy to catch. Guess what they taste like? God's manna: Aussie style.

The tide was coming in with more dead; more breeding places for the flies. And it's still six weeks to Christmas.

The Great Escape

The wind had changed direction and for some unfathomable reason most of the mutton bird corpses, and consequently the flies, have disappeared. Unfortunately, they have been replaced by even more stingoes and an array of porcupine fish.

Why?

Harry wasn't really interested. A character who had that certain something which makes you want to smile before he even opens his mouth. Perhaps it was his spiky hair, protruding ears, a missing front tooth, or his booming laugh. He boomed often.

"Don't know, mate," he said. "It's the sapphires I'm interested in see."

"So you sold your house to go sapphire hunting.....in that," I ask incredulously?

"For ten years mate: That's the plan. Guess the missus will be a bit pissed when I tell her, eh?"

Harry and Corrie had indeed sold all for a second-hand camper van and a dream - not that

Corrie was aware of the whole of the master plan yet. The dream was not of striking it rich [gold prospecting and opal fossicking were also on the agenda], but of seeing Australia.

"Didn't you once tell me you don't have a sense of direction?" I asked, as we continued to do a bit of beachcombing. I stop and examine a shell: Common. I throw it down and we move on.

"Too right, mate. I went picking Christmas bells once. It's illegal now: Was then, come to think of it. There I was fifty yards away from the forestry tower cutting like hell. When I looked up I couldn't remember where I'd left the missus and kid: Took me two and a half hours to find her." He boomed; slapping his thigh and seagulls rose in protest. "Silly cow! She should've been whistlin' or summ-it." He paused for a quick breath. "Even got lost on a garage forecourt once....." [Author's Note: Don't ask!]

"Put ya' tongue in a bloody sling, Harry," drawled a long-suffering Corrie.

But Harry was irrepressible. "Did I tell you about the time I was down in Melbourne?" He didn't wait for a reply. "My trouble is I want to know how everything works. Well, the car is in bits and I have to phone the garage. Don't know where nothin' goes, see. This bloke works like a demon: Bits goin' everywhere. 'What's the hurry, mate,' I asks? 'Grand Final,' [Aussie Rules] he says. 'Need to find a telly p.d.q.,' he says. 'Bloody aerial ping-pong,' says I. Holy Snappin' duckshit! Down went the starter motor. Bits all over bloody Victoria and he's off: Bloody Mexicans!" *

Another pause for a well-earned breath:

"Put a bloody sock in it Harry," drawls Corrie, but I take my chance.

"Harry. How do you hope to navigate around Australia without a sense of direction? You've got no four wheel drive on that old vehicle you've just bought and with no roads to speak of, you might just need that. And to top it all you're no mechanic. Aren't you being a bit optimistic?"

"No worries mate. Avoid the Wet and in ten years' driving I've got to get somewhere, sometime."

I wasn't so sure.

*Mexicans is a derogatory term for Victorians. They come from south of the Border. [Down Mexico way.....]

Lake Macquarie

We had not intended to stay by the lake all day, but then the place exerted its magic over us once more and we stuck.

We are on the north shore of Lake Macquarie. The lake is dark blue and surrounded on three sides by a crescent of distant, tree-covered mountains. On the remaining side, a spit of land separates our tranquillity from the ocean's roar. There lies the little township of Belmont - insanely happy with its place in the sun and its role as the supplier of necessities to the fortunate few who call this place home.

Happy! - So it should be. The world's biggest ocean on one side, and Australia's largest saltwater lake, four times the size of Sydney Harbour and stretching as far as the eye can see, on the other. The waters of the lake are untroubled by the slightest of breezes and appear forever frozen in time. It forms a canvas on which ever changing-patterns are created by yacht sails and idle boats, and the reflections of passing clouds.

The kids are happy, up to their knees in warm water. Their squeals of delight only heighten the illusion of perfection.

Mid afternoon: The heat is near unbearable. The very air lies heavy upon you. Only the children keep going, stopping only for repeated applications of sunscreen. The clouds begin to pile: White cotton-wool clouds: One upon another. They build inexorably, and darken: Atomic cloud-like, streaky black at ground zero, heralding rain. Lightning: Savage fingers burst - but silently, out over the lake.

We sit enthralled, as the children flee indoors and the yachts to harbour. The lake, as if in protest, whips up waves out of nothing, causing the moored boats to bob and swing wildly.

Still we sit. The storm approaches, not head on as expected, but suddenly and violently swinging in an arc from the sea.

It hits us. Thunder: Lightning. And it's gone. No rain.

The sun makes a final appearance as it disappears beyond the far mountains. It turns the dark water blood red and the sky every colour on God's pallet.

Braveheart at the Moonee.

I guess Bill Symington must have stood just here nearly a century ago, just before he left for the trenches of France with Newcastle's Own Mounted Cavalry: [Later to become part of the 35th Battalion A.I.F.] Had he stood, if not at this very spot - a hugely impressive slab of coal jutting out into the white-capped blue of the ocean, near the coal ship loading jetty; he surely would have, at least, said his good-byes to the wonderfully, sandy beach of Catherine Hill Bay.

Back then, in Bill's time, the Moonee Pit dominated the bay, as it had since coal started to be mined there in 1873. On the face of it, nothing much has changed; the infrastructure of the mine still dominates the sweeping ocean views, - only now, the number-crunchers in Sydney, or somewhere, have rung the death knell for the mine. There is still plenty of coal beneath the headland and the sea, only it's now uneconomic; there is so much coal coming out of the mechanized, open-cut mines of the Upper Hunter, why bother?

The evidence of the wealth of resources beneath the Hunter Valley of New South Wales can be seen at Stockton Bight, the largest coal-loading dock in the world. It lies about an hour's drive north of Moonee - a place where one-hundred-thousand ton ships from Japan and Korea lie in rows, loading coal from the endlessly-fed conveyor belts and then, within hours, head out to sea again. Moonee never stood a chance. They were still using pit ponies here in the 1970s.

Bill Symington was a miner. He had to be, of course, if he lived on this remote bay at the beginning of the 20th century. He gave his address as 'Care-of the Post Office, Catherine Hill Bay.' The township had boasted its own post office since 1874, but we can't find it today. It's frustrating, as it was the only clue we had into the Symington family.

Frustrating, yet wholly understandable, as the old wooden cottages, once the homes of the miners, are being snapped up as second homes by wealthy Sydneysiders. The weather-beaten, peeling facades and tin roofs of yesteryear are fast disappearing under a deluge of plastic weatherboards and designer gardens.

Bill never returned from the Great War, so his direct line descendants were never in a position to benefit from this, or any other future property boom. They have had to work to create their own wealth, and that leads me to cousin, Doug.

He began his entrepreneurial career at this very pit. With a friend, he acquired an old lorry, which they ran between them for twenty four hours a day, taking coal from the pit head to the local power station. The dollars flowed, but they had no intention of parting with any of the hard-earned cash on lorry maintenance. Anything the vehicle required, they did themselves - like making their own re-tread tyres. That necessity led to the formation of a re-tread tyre company, from there to property development and the sort of lifestyle people envy. Only they don't see the very long, very hard hours, underpinning it all.

I walk on, passing tranquil rock pools and the fascinating industrial relics of yesteryear. Chain hawsers the thickness of my body, girders, rusting pieces of metal which must have had a purpose long ago, all lie each and every way amongst the rocks and the coal, all awaiting a slow death at the hands of each and every tide.

For some, Catherine Hill Bay may represent the opportunity to make a killing in the property market; to others, the challenge is to ensure the uniqueness of the place is not destroyed in the new century. Film buffs will remember the place as the location for Summer City, in which Mel Gibson made his film debut in 1976.

To me, this place means much, much more.

On the trail of teeth:

We are sitting under a large umbrella in the middle of an Italian-style piazza in the new heart of Newcastle on the central coast of New South Wales. We are outside a coffee shop, and I'm busily expressing my views about how the city was changing for the better as it left its industrial heritage behind, when Mark turned up.

Mark is a twenty-six year old Australian, had heard our accents, and so pulled up a chair to introduce himself. He was the cappuccino maker of this establishment and, despite the masses of people milling about in the broiling street, the shade under his brollies was not tempting them to stay for a while. I guess the Novocastrians haven't traded in their steel works, coal mines and dockyard heritage in favour of middle-class Yuppyness - not just yet anyway.

Mark had lived and worked in England for three years - well, Highgate, an area of London - and missed his life there dearly. He longed to return to Britain, even though, to him, London was Britain.

"Shark's teeth?" he mused over the question of where to get some dentures of a protected species for non eco-aware grandchildren. "Belmont, I guess. I know a bloke there who is a shark fisherman: A world champ in fact. Maybe, he'd be able to help."

It should have been us giving him the card, but no, we were the recipients.

'An act of kindness can change a whole life...
A whole lot of them can change the world.'

Thirty minutes later we were back to where we had started: Belmont, one of our very favourite haunts, and the place where a Great White had recently been persuaded to part with various parts of the undigested corpse of a Wollongong fisherman. Perhaps the world champ had copped him......? Perhaps - but it's a no-go on the teeth.

Instead, I wander back into the chemist's shop on the main street - the Pacific Highway, to be exact. Nothing unusual in that, except that it's the third time today I've been in there. On each of the previous occasions I was informed that my film, left for developing, was not ready [despite assurances], and "Come back after....."

It was now the third time 'after.....'

The shop girl was still there and still evidently angry at the world. She would have been about sixteen years old..... Do you remember Doctor Hook singing his hit song, "She was only sixteen, you know what I mean....," all those years ago? I don't think that this sullen lass was what the song writer had in mind: sweetness and light, with overtones of sexual innuendo, she was not.

The queue to pay was a long one, but she studiously managed to ignore it for a full five minutes, flicking at the shelves here and there with a feather duster. Her older companion worked steadily through the queue, until she got to the woman in front of me, who was carrying forty-two bucks' worth of fifty-cent cosmetics in her arms. She also wanted to talk about the local pre-schoolers learning to speak Japanese.

"Name!" An authoritative demand: not a question.

I look round. It had to be me being spoken to - there was no-one else left.

"Name!" Same confrontational tone from the sixteen year old, who was now facing me across the counter. Not exactly hands-on-hips sort of stuff, but you get the drift. This gal had teeth.

"Patterson," I reply pleasantly, giving her my best de-frosting smile.

No luck. She glared at me as she tore the yellow photo-lab tag out of my fingers. Then, after two minutes of rustling under the counter: "Not here!"

"Oh dear," I say. "What time will....?"

"Try later!"

"Could I have my receipt back please?"

Without a word, she thrust it in my direction. With a deftness which surprised even me, I reclaimed my ticket, leaving in its stead Mark's card, reverse side up:

> 'You've been given this card
> recognizing that you are a Good Samaritan.
> Have a nice day.'

I don't think she read it. By the time I reached the heat of the street, I could hear her shrill voice, "Name?"

Home Thoughts:

Travelling four hours north of Sydney, the coastline of central New South Wales has become a very desirable area in which to live. Sun and sand and palm trees and surf and a comfortable living, are proving an irresistible lure to Sydneysiders who have had enough of the rat race; or to 'Pitt Street Farmers' – people with loads of dosh seeking tax relief opportunities.

Whatever, whoever; the result is that house prices are being pushed out of the reach of ordinary folk. We meet three of them on our daily walk to the breakwater; today fascinated by the sight of twenty-three bulk tankers, waiting off the beach to be loaded with Hunter Valley coal.

First of all there is Neville, an elderly man we first came across in 1982. He lives by the beach in an old fibro-cement sheet, single-storey home. Neville has changed; not surprisingly the years are catching up with him - so much so that his legs won't carry him the fifty yards to his beloved beach on the other side of the low dunes.

His home has worn a little better - except for the hole in the living room ceiling which he had made so he could fix a leaking roof from the inside: And the cost for his little palace these days? Half a million dollars! But, as he says, "The old place will see me out," and after a teary pause adds, "Where would I go?"

The owner of the eight year old Alsatian had only been living in the area for three months. He had been lucky enough, or had the foresight, to buy a beach house here years ago, only it had taken him a bit of time to realize he could sell the "pretty ordinary house" in Sydney and move to the coast permanently, with money in the bank.

He made the move, falling on his feet with a job working a crane on one of the new development sites. And there are plenty of those about.

Here's the rub. He is a second generation Aussie, his parents having arrived from Malta after the Second World War. Their seven kids and twenty-seven grandchildren are all Australian through and through, yet the parents still harbour this romantic notion of returning to Malta so they can "Die at home."

They can't of course. Cash and family militate against them. What's the old saying? – The kids can leave you, but you can never leave the kids. Something we can identify with.

We found two nice ladies mooching about an empty property near the surf club: a mother and daughter. The daughter was in her late twenties, and stated quite matter-of-factly that she would never be able to buy a home of her own unless she won the Lotto. Sound familiar?

Her mum needed to live by the sea to help her lung disease and so had sold her home 'Up country' amongst the asthma inducing cotton crops. It fetched a good price - for that area - but she couldn't buy garage space for the money here on the coast.

So they are looking to rent. Jointly they might be able to finance a deal, but their mood is subdued. Even if they could find a place, they might have to forgo things - like food, in order to pay for the property.

All we can do is wish them well, and reflect that the position regarding property is frighteningly similar to that in Britain.

Today I have once more been confronted with the realities of life wherever you happen to be. I guess I'll have to thank my lucky stars and learn to be content with my lot.

Now! Where're the Lotto numbers?

Ethel, Janet and the beautiful Redhead:

The beautiful Redhead had been on our list of places to visit for some time - certainly since we ran into Ethel and her sister, Mary, both of whom run the local wool shop.

As the odd ball remnants bin: 'Sale! Fabulous reductions' - was picked over, I could not help but ask Ethel what the scrawl across the back of the envelope she was holding referred to. I had decided in favour of a knitting pattern, as opposed to a work of modern art; but no!

"It's some plans a local real estate developer wants me to look at. I've four and a half acres overlooking the ocean at Belmont North, but I don't know......"

I did a quick calculation. Quarter-acre blocks of land go for about a half a million bucks..... "Why don't you sell and enjoy the good life. You can't take it with you," I said, putting in my two bucks worth with a little laugh.

She put the map down and rubbed her arthritic fingers, the joints swollen by eighty-five years of knitting, and the cold spell that has just hit central New South Wales.

"I don't know really," she replied seriously. "Our old mum was left to bring us up after dad was killed in the Great War. She made ends meet by knitting and dress making; real hand-to-mouth stuff. I don't want to be broke when I get old."

By now, my wife Patsy and sister Mary were getting stuck into the bowels of the old shop. Something to do with: 'special four-ply suitable for a new baby.' Very rare and well hidden down the back apparently. I managed to overhear "Special customers," but as the whole place smelled of old – and damp wool – I was beginning to think the old girls were having us over.

As the two wool gatherers poked and prodded away in dim recesses, Ethel deflected my suspicious nature by starting to tell me of her life; a life of family; the ageing wool shop in a run down building by the ocean; and now, most interestingly of all, of fishing. Did I know crabs float on the surface of the water at night and can be picked out by using a spot lamp - just like the television crocodile hunters do?

No, I didn't.

Did I know the ocean shelf comes in really close to Redhead Beach, allowing some of the best, but most dangerous, fishing around? "Especially near the sewage outlet, dear."

No, I didn't.

Patsy returns, clutching an armful of wool and patterns.

"Do you know I could have got this lot for a quarter of the price at Big W," she whispers, as we take our leave. "But I couldn't let the poor old dears down."

I didn't know we could get that particular wool in Big W - but there again, the ageing millionaires-in-waiting probably needed the money more than we poor pensioners did.

But at least they had put us on the trail of Redhead.

Next day; Redhead: - So named because the headland which towers above the northern end of the beach has a sandstone layer to it.

It is a beautiful place, even though the storm clouds are piling up and the bulk-coal, super-freighters are queuing up just out to sea. I count twenty-seven waiting for their turn at the loading docks.

Last evening we had visited the pleasant little Hunter Valley coal town of Kurri Kurri for a spot of Scottish Country Dancing. Despite the advancing age of the club members, none could remember my great uncles, the three Thompson coal mining brothers, who had arrived here from Northumberland eight decades ago.

The underground pits they had worked have long since closed, replaced by the vast, open-cast mining of the Upper Hunter - the product ending up in the ships now waiting off Redhead, Blacksmiths and elsewhere.

Did I know that Japan was storing Australian coal in the sea just off their coast, asked Mildred?

No, I didn't.

Did I know they were taking delivery of as much coal as they could get to ensure supplies in the future, questioned Agnes?

No, I didn't.

"Oh yes!" added Rachel. "They'll sell it back to us one day. You mark my words."

"Let's dance," interrupted a bewildered looking Janet. Her bright red hair came out of a bottle in an effort to role back the years, but her legs didn't look any too good, covered as they were in elastic bandages with swollen feet and ankles sticking out at the bottom. "I'll be resting for long enough all too soon..... Did I tell you I'm going to be buried in Maitland Cemetery?"

No, she hadn't. But it was certainly a conversation stopper.

A True Australian Christmas

Several days ago a tropical storm, or some such thing, was lashing the north coast of Australia. Poor old Darwin copping it again - but it is far enough away to be of no concern to us here at Blacksmiths Beach.

Christmas is being planned. A barbee; a swim; beach cricket.....

How foolish! The storm left the Timor Sea, did a left into the Indian Ocean, hooked another left into Western Australia and now, four days and three thousand plus miles later, what's left of it is HERE!

And there is plenty of it left. There is something deeply despondent in seeing huge palm trees bending almost double under the lash of the wind. And rain! Good grief! It knows how to rain in this land of sunshine and desert and drought.

Cancel the swim, the cricket, the barbee. Cancel any thoughts of attending church on this most special of days - none of the rello's know where there is one! Cancel any dreams you have been harbouring of a real, true-blue Aussie Christmas.

Instead, look on the bright side.

It is warm.

And?

The flies have gone.

And?

'Pressies.'

And?

Champagne at ten in the morning!

Charades degenerate steadily, miraculously keeping pace with the rise in alcohol consumption.

It finishes with an uproarious demonstration of Roget's Thesaurus which would not have been out of place at an orgy in ancient Rome.

A great day in great company: A truly splendid meal - marred only by.....no..... Not the weather, nor the booze, nor the disgusting rogering-Roget, but by the Legacy Christmas pud,* which arrived in all its glory, ablaze in brandy, and stayed.... and stayed.....and stayed all night.

* The puddings are sold each year to raise funds for war widows.

The Surfers Jamboree

In my family's dim and distant past there lies a Viking who went by the unprepossessing name of 'The Black Son of a Noisy Thief.' * He arrived on Yorkshire soil near Scarborough - back God knows when - after having rowed across the North Sea in an open boat. Presumably he still had enough energy to go a-pillaging.

Vikings! You immediately think of a Kirk Douglas look-a-like. Someone six-and–a-half feet tall, muscular, and with a beard which makes you think he'd eaten a grizzly bear for lunch. Undoubtedly he is wielding an axe as big as himself.

Is this the description of our bloke? Perhaps not! I cannot help thinking that he might have been quite happy at home with mum and was shanghai'd to make the tea on the way over. Perhaps he was a little fella', the runt of the litter, four feet tall and two stone soaking wet through. You know - the wimp who hangs onto the rudder of a racing eight propelled by testosterone. No raping and pillaging for him; he is happier left in camp doing the washing-up, waiting his chance to filch what he can from his mates' suitcases whilst they are out chasing the locals.

I can't help but think this is the more likely scenario, as I look down at my pale chest, now to be found immediately above my hips. We are at the Surf Carnival on Blacksmith's Beach - some big championship or other. I spend most of the day wincing, as hundreds of swimmers churn through the shoals of stinging jellyfish; hundreds of athletes sprint across the soft sand; hundreds of surf skiers go way, way out to say hello to the basking sharks; and dozens of surf rescue outboards race about like noisy, demented chooks, plucking exhausted victims out of the unforgiving rips. They are the undoubted descendants of Olaf the Bloodthirsty, Sven the Slaughterer and Harald Wal Eye.**

Such close proximity to the bronzed gods, the prima donnas of Australian sport, heightens my awareness of the genetic deficiencies passed on to me by my little black thief. If I worked on it, I could look like these guys....Well, I could get a tan! As for the rest of it, who wants to be a giant with broad shoulders, tight bum; muscular arms and leave an eight foot stride pattern in the sand, as they do a gentle jog along the water's edge just to warm up?

One thing our noisy runt would have had in common with these guys would be the unsavoury habit of exposing their naked buttocks to the sea air. We are told it is to enable the modern day athlete to stick better to the boats' seats as they rise and crash through the waves. Now that is something that the Viking rowers surely must have done. The desire to stick in that boat would have been overwhelming; nobody wants a swim in an icy North Sea. A naked, frozen and wet bum would be a small price to pay.

A common denominator at last: A shared heritage between today's heroes and yours truly. This is something tangible on which I can base my challenge to become a perfect physical specimen. Unfortunately, I don't think the wife will let me expose myself - certainly not to the world; and certainly not until I finish the washing up.

*Dawson: Someone with black colouring, raucous voice and thieving nature. Like a jackdaw.

** Wal Eye: One Eye.

Wind and Wheaty Things

Day two of the Surfees' Blow-out on Blacksmiths Beach and we're looking forward to second helpings of testosterone and steroids.

And it's day one of the new me. I am walking around the house with no shirt on and a pair of skimpy shorts so I can stick to things better. Breakfast from now on is going to consist of the 'Power Generator. A secret formula;' - wheaty things shaped into something like cricket bats with holes in them. The packet carries on: 'You're striving for real performance. This cereal equals energy to push yourself to the limit and the power to do it again and again.'

Wonderful stuff! It won't be long now. By the time the third bowl disappears, I am pushed to the limit; in fact my stomach is responding manfully to the maker's call for 'Commitment that equals success.' Only later do the home truths become evident. Hidden away at the bottom of the box, in very small print, do the gullible learn; 'It's up to you to get up in the morning and train and develop a killer attitude.'

Undeterred, hyper with sugar-induced energy, we set off along the beach toward the bright flags and the distorted voices of a distant tannoy. Only this time we walk into the teeth of a full-blown southerly gale. Walk close to the water on the hard sand and the massive waves, raised by the wind-shift during the night, crash about you. Choose the dry, safer route and the deep sand pulls at your ankles whilst the loose grains blast and sting the skin. Worse! It sticks like glue to the sun block and smears the specs.

We arrive, energy expired, but in time for the surf boat final. No engines of course - just five men and a heavy boat versus the crashing sea - and each other. I'm pleased when the no-hopers' win. Why? Anyone rowing a boat called Aunty Jack deserves some luck. And Aunty Jack has all the luck going as it catches a huge breaker; is literally picked up and hurled ashore, to beat the favourites by a snip.

The favourites are not amused. In fact they are well and truly brassed off. Recriminations and autopsies go on for half an hour. Net result – they are still second. Their super-duper, aerodynamically, wind-tunnel-tested, manicured craft may need a new million dollar sponsor next year. Life's tough for those striving for real performance. Did they read the bit about developing a killer instinct? I wonder...Perhaps I can become the team's highly paid consultant...No luck! Have you any idea what a dag is? I have just been called one and it's not in any dictionary I have.

I know they were upset, so never worry. I have the knowledge now; I have a secret energy source, skimpy jockey shorts, and I'm developing a new physical training technique suitable for anyone's backyard. Take a Hill's Hoist - sort of a four armed, rotary clothes line; fill it with washing on a wickedly windy day, like today; and proceed to chase it round and round, trying to retrieve a pair of your daks.*

Oh! What was it that guy called me up the beach?

*Daks: Ladies unmentionables.

No end in sight

It has been a frustrating day, it really has. It started off well, heavy cloud cover lifting long enough for some sunrise shots from the beach. But since then it has been down-hill all the way.

Cocky's owner was hiding in the shrubbery and jumped out as we approached. He was lonely and wanted a chat, but uncharitably it was his white cockatoo, caged for the last forty-two years outside his front door, that we wanted to see. We would have loved to have been able to talk to him again, to re-introduce ourselves after an absence of three years. We would have loved to have watched his one-legged dance, hear about his wish for a rabbit friend and for him to tell the dog to go for a whizz in the backyard, but we are too polite to ignore the old chap.

We escape, pleading an urgent appointment, and return to the beach. A venomous sea snake has been left high and dry by the tide. I'd love a picture, but the young surf boarder is kicking sand in its face. This is annoying it somewhat and it would probably kill him, given half a chance. Anyway, I don't want sand in the camera lens, so off we go again.

We head off down into the small coastal township of Swansea. It can hardly be anything else except idyllic, standing as it does beside the estuary leading from Pacific Ocean to Lake Macquarie. We need the library; some necessary research on a First Fleet ancestor of ours. It's closed.

Ten bucks on the Lotto instead. Not a sniff.

Ten bucks buys us another box of mangoes - an inexpensive way to feed my obsession. Then the fruiterer tells me mangoes are fattening.

Back home; it's lunch and a think about today's story: The hunting issue - and a clever comparison between the fate of English foxes and the Aussie kangaroo. Did you know that about a million 'roo are killed every year in eastern Australia alone? I really tried to write that story, but couldn't.

So that is abandoned in favour of another beach walk. The snake has gone - probably chasing that kid. The sun is shining on Nine Mile Beach – well, on the far end of it. Above us it's black cloud, the lack of sunlight turning the ocean to a murky, North Sea grey. But at least it's not raining.

Pleasant walk behind us, we return home. Clean the barbecue up for the steak, snags and kebabs. The heavens open! But it doesn't matter - we have the technology and the intelligence to overcome this. We cook in the garage.

Frustration! I have spent an hour now on "me Pat Malone," trying to find an ending to this sad tale...and guess what!

Erik the Startled

It is quite strange really. Yesterday, all the fishermen were up at that end of Blacksmiths Beach and now they are down this end. Can it be that these particular hunter-gatherers are imbued with the Aussie spirit of 'Give 'em a fair go,' and so are looking for dinner from a different shoal? You know, share the misery about a bit. I'll never know unless I ask - and one chap looks as though he wants a chat.

"G'day, mate," says I. "Caught anything yet?"

"Not yet. - Just got here, mate."

And that was that - we idled a very pleasant hour away, ankle deep in warm water. And I was certainly right - he did want to talk. So I took the opportunity to try and learn something about fishing off the beach, a pastime I would certainly take up if I could find a teacher who moves around as much as we do. But I did learn something: like trying to get your line into a 'sweep'. This is the name for the wicked drag off a sloping beach which will pull even a strong swimmer out to sea in the blink of an eye. However, this dangerous real estate is just where the fishermen want to be - slap-bang in the middle of the detritus on which the fish feed.

My new companion is gnarled by the sun and advancing years, yet his bronzed torso shows a dedication to his sport. No! it's more than that: Dedication to his way of life is better. He is protected from the sun only by a woman's dirty, wide-brimmed hat, once pink and now tied beneath his chin with string - and a pair of faded, nondescript shorts. He dresses the same, whether he fishes the beaches here on the central coast of New South Wales or in Northern Queensland, where he over-winters.

His grandfather was Norwegian and my friend is proud to bear his name - Erik Olaffson. Seemingly the original Erik left his four-masted schooner and a life on the ocean waves for a life at Foster, now a nice coastal town hereabouts. Back in the 1880s, however, it was no more than a mosquito-ridden swamp. Why abandon ship there? We don't know. As a family historian I find that infuriating.

By now you will be convinced Erik can talk the hind leg off a cuddy.

Did you know that you are not in much danger from saltwater crocodiles when you go beach fishing in Northern Queensland? Erik swears it's true. They prefer to stick around the mouths of the river estuaries: "It's the brown snakes that'll get ya! See, they warm up on the sand between the rocks." And Erik should know; he stood on one just the other week. "Boy, did I jump!"

Boy, can he chat!

Did you know it is no good going barramundi fishing outside 'the Wet?'

Now my wife, Patsy, is a patient soul - a likeable gal who is quick to help and slow to anger - but it has to be said she has a limited interest in the nuances of fishing techniques - a subject now warming Erik's cockles.

Did you know that you can't use pipe worms as bait unless you dig them off the same beach as the one you are fishing on?

Patsy listens with half an ear as she paddles about up to her ankles in the delightful, lapping waters of this remarkably benign ocean. All day the waves have not risen above six inches in height, as they caress the land's fringe. She half turns, politely feigning an interest in the various worms being offered for inspection. As she does, a rogue wave, a four foot high monster, rises up behind her. I try to speak, to warn her, to protect the gentle mother of my children, but the words catch in my throat. My 'Oops!' arrives just as the dumper smashes down. She's wet - up to the oxters. Now that would have been O.K. if she was wearing her swimsuit - but no, she just happens to be ready to go off shopping, clean blouse, clean shorts, clean knicks and all.

I can tell you now that she wasn't happy. Erik could have told you she wasn't happy. The seagulls rising noisily from the beach can tell she's not happy. Whether it's at my wife running through them on the way to the dunes and home, or whether it's at her screaming "I hate the firking sea," we will never know.

A Night out with the Girls:

"Not sure about the trainers, but the rest of you will do."

I looked in the mirror and hardly recognized myself. Borrowed shirt, borrowed trousers, borrowed jumper. Not quite my style, but I'd been appraised and given the stamp of approval by the rello's.

No doubt about it – I would get into the Sixteen Footers Yacht Club for dinner that night. Standards must be maintained or you don't get through the door.

Fair enough!

I could hardly get through the door anyway. The bouncer was huge - probably in the six-foot-six, twenty-stone range. He was young, shaven headed and as immovable as Baldy's Nob.

I edge past him with a timid "Excuse me," to enter the pall of cigarette smoke and the all-round stereo sound of clattering and tinkling poker machines. I make for the bar before taking in a deep breath. The two feet of lino-covered space around the serving area was designated a 'Smoke Free Zone to Protect the Health of the Staff.' Yeah, right! Some hope in that.

I looked about me, already congratulating myself on wearing someone else's clothes, as they get to wash them, and discover the bouncer is there. It's uncanny. Only his eyes move - back and forth, this way and that, alert for any sign of trouble. He fixes me with an icy stare. It could be that my trainers have offended him; or maybe it's the midi of V.B. beer that has singled me out as a wimp deserving of attention. Or it could be the ill-fitting mishmatch of clothing.

I follow our group heading for the restaurant, only to emerge two hours later, and five hundred bucks lighter, still savouring the glorious food taken in sumptuous surroundings overlooking the winking anchorage lights of the yachts bobbing at their moorings across a darkened Lake Macquarie.

The pokies are now in full swing, the bars more crowded and nosier, the atmosphere crackling with suspense, as the National rugby team strut their stuff across massive TV screens.

The big doorman is easy to spot. He stands immobile amongst it all, letting the noise and action break about him.

A young man falls backwards off his bar stool. The bouncer's eyes flicker, then the prostrate drunk is ignored.

Instead, I get this sinking feeling that he is looking at me.

Two women begin to scream incoherently when the Aussies kick the ball across the screen and a chase ensures. Beer spills.

Ignored!

A gang of five youngsters stagger across in front of the chase. They are obviously under age, and walk as if they are on the deck of a sixteen footer during a stiff gale. Roars of anger directed at them are met with various gestures not designed to create harmony and love.

Two small, inoffensive looking bouncers, hardly older than their charges, escort them from the room to jeers and cheers, whilst the Big Man moves not one jot.

A cheer from the direction of the rattling pokies: Three women and an elderly man are jumping and punching the air with joy.

Now the giant moves. He waddles five paces toward them before grinding to an ungainly halt. Watching! Waiting!

Of course it just has to be my wife and the rello's celebrating winning back three bucks from the club. I just hope they don't win any more.

At last, twelve lungs full of other people's smoke, two wallets empty and six stomachs the size of water melons, we head for home. Man Mountain is there again, blocking the main door just as he had when we arrived.

Our eyes meet, but the prospective staring match is interrupted by the arrival of a taxi. Our hopes rise; our departure is imminent. Then a one-legged prostitute alights.

We know her - well, let me put it another way, we know of her. She works the highway near home and tonight she's worse for wear; smudged make-up, hair in need of a comb and, as she barges past the Big Fella', she pulls her knickers back into place.

Not a word from her. Not a word of farewell to us, as we emerge into the chill, night wind and wave away the taxi. There were no others in sight, but none of us fancied the recently vacated back seat.

The wind was a cold one, blowing in off the lake. We huddle together, hoping..... It is a far cry from the soft, warm rain, fruit bats and a zillion happy frogs of a few nights ago.....

I push such fanciful thoughts far behind, snuggle further into the borrowed down-filled anorak, and take a furtive glance over my shoulder, back into the warmth of the club.

My reward: a thin-lipped smile which breaks into a long, chin-wobbling, silent, belly laugh.

No Name but Burgess.

Just outside the booming twin resort towns of Forster and Tuncurry, which face each other across the estuary leading to Wallis Lake, is the quiet Burgess Beach.

The beach is used in the main by local people, and for the training of up and coming Iron-Man athletes, but we visit because of the name: Burgess. It just jumped up off the map at us. Burgess! One of our main Australian family names - and I am determined to find a connection to our mob.

We ask everyone we meet: "Why Burgess?" No one knew. The best answer: "I guess it's something to do with a bloke called Burgess."

I needed to write that down straight away.

The beach is so far removed from the holiday beaches that before the township expanded, it would have been classed as 'remote.' Burgess! – Remote!

Wouldn't it be something if the swagman, Richard Burgess, who left Queensland for good in 1898 never to return, had come here to set up camp by the beautiful beach that now bears his name?

Not that Dicky's story is a particularly meritorious one. On Boxing Day, 1898, a Michael Murphy, his wife Nora, aged 27, and her sister, Ellen McNeil, aged 18, all set off in a sulky to drive home. They were never seen alive again. The police from Brisbane duly arrived, but found no clues as to what had happened. But they did come across a swagman, Richard Burgess. He was arrested on that good old-fashioned policing principle of 'You'll do,' but eventually they had to let him go for lack of any evidence at all. Dicky took off, never to be heard of again. I wonder..... [Well, it's better than musing over the Forster to Tuncurry Bridge which was once the longest, pre-stressed concrete bridge in all of Australia. Still might be, for all I know, or care. Isn't it funny how much useless information you accumulate as you get older….?]

I was still wondering, tantalizing myself with the criminal possibilities, when later we met Jimmy. Jimmy was a young bloke, carrying a surfboard down toward a near-deserted beach just south of Burgess's Fantasy. His black wet-suit showed off his developing beer gut very nicely.

"No! This beach has no name at all," he says, in response to my query. "We just love it because it catches good surf most of the year."

I was really pleased with our new friend, and we carried on talking about this and that as we hurried along toward the waiting surf. I usually end up talking to old folk who can't get away, but despite the age difference, twenty something or other year old Jimmy was happy to chat - especially when I demonstrated my talent for trivia by mentioning that surfing was introduced into Australia by a young Melanesian gardener who rejoiced in the name of Tommy Tanna. That was in the 1890s - about the same time as Tricky Dicky Burgess did a runner from Queensland.

"Burgess?" He mused over that one for a while: "Nope! Know nothing about Burgess Beach I'm afraid. Can't have any surf on it though or I'd have been there. I do know a little about this place though….." and continued after a little encouragement on my part [necessary, as his attention was wandering as he prepared himself for the water, making himself comfortable in the wet-suit, his eyes searching for the best surf]. "There used to be the ruins of a farm up that end of the beach," he said, nodding toward the south as he hopped on one leg. "But they knocked it down when the area became the Booli Booli National Park. Don't know the name of the property though."

With that our paths parted. The lure of the surf was too strong, so off he went, running, surfboard under his arm.

Then my wife was calling. A large pod of dolphins was frolicking just offshore. Then we, too, were running. A run of Olympian proportions toward the distant car. Burgess doing his runner; Jimmy's dash to the sea; both as naught compared to our departure. The swarm of bees, or wasps, made more fearful by the fact we could hear them, close, very close, but could not see them, ensured our Herculean efforts continued the whole distance of that long, sandy track to safety.

The Entrance

The violent thunderstorms of last night are gone, leaving a cloudless sky. Time to explore a little more, and we are baby sitting - if two girls, seven and six, going on seventeen, qualify as 'babies.' Young lady sitting would be better.

In any event, two of the grandchildren are out from England and mum and dad have flown back to Sydney for the day. Now I thought I knew this area quite well, and that I knew the girls even better. I was in for a surprise on both counts.

What better way to entertain the kids than a day at the beach: Easy to kill ten hours surfing and sand castling and sea shelling.

Beach after beach came and went. They had one thing in common - notices which read 'Beach Closed.' I didn't understand. My wife didn't understand..... And the kids didn't want to understand by the time we disembarked at The Entrance.

Now each small and beautiful beach all along this coastline seems to have spawned a small township and The Entrance is one such place. Each is attractive in its own way, but very much minor variations on a sea, sun and sand theme. You know: pelican feeding at 11 a.m. here; estuaries teeming with fish there; a vegetarian-feminist, decaffeinated coffee house run by lesbians, who make a great cuppa and offer free cake, somewhere else.

So here we are at The Entrance, a place which can boast, according to my wife, the best ladies' toilets around. The notice in the gents - "Don't wash your fish in the hand basins" - seemingly says a lot about men from the feminine perspective.

I hate crowds. Anybody will tell you that. And today the town is full to overflowing. Cars queue; people drift in huge tidal waves every which way. Two rock bands engage in a noisy quarrel across the small park, presumably for our pleasure.

They were awful. The place was awful. But! But I knew of a little beach.....and there is no-one on it. Excitement peaks in this veritable eye of the holiday storm. We decide which rock to sit on, spread towels, place bags, position surfboards and apply sunscreen. I could wet myself with the joy of it all.

One foot in the lovely warm water and OUT! I now understand. My wife understands. The children do not. Blue jellyfish: - The stingoes. Innumerable: Not a few - not even a few thousand. Brought in by last night's storm, the poisonous, hospitalising horrors have invaded and occupied the whole central coast of New South Wales.

We cheer the kids with chips and tomato sauce. They play in a multicoloured paddling pool with other kids - hundreds of other kids - with hundreds of their minders looking on.

I'm depressed. The noise goes on and on. The people swarm. The kids move to climbing frames and bouncing chairs. At last! Time to go!

"Thank you, Nanna. Thank you, Granddad. That was great."

I now understand that I understand nothing.

P.S.   We had a barbecue later. Much better: - Even if Jessica ate all my steak.

Powering through the sands of time:

Now my cousin Sandra is a power-walker. That means she's younger, slimmer and prettier than me, and with her quick stride easily leaves me struggling in her wake.

It's 5 a.m. Sunrise photos from the distant breakwater beckon. Trouble is, the breakwater is at the other end of the beach, the sun is already colouring the sky with every hue imaginable and I feel like I'm walking in sticky porridge as the wet sand sucks testily at my aching legs. The calf muscles can't take much more - action must be taken. Obligingly Sandra steams on ahead. Obviously I needed to take a photo of her footprints in the sand. She returns.

On again: I stop to photograph the sunlight twinkling on the crests of the waves. Many waves came ...and went. Well, you can't hurry a craftsman at his work. The muscles begin to relax, the heart eases down to a terrifying pounding clatter.

On again...I admit defeat. "I'll just sit here and wait for you. You make the breakwater."

"Sure?"

"Sure! I'll be fine."

Sandra powers away.

It is beautiful here. Golden sand, that special warmth which comes with the dawn in the tropics, blue enticing water...God is in His heaven and all is well with the world. - Except that Sandra is nearly at the huge boulders protecting the entrance to the tidal lake with its yachting clubs, marinas and the like.

Huge boulders: When I was a kid we used to go to the seaside on the coast of Northumberland: Mile upon mile of golden sand, deserted even in summer with a silence all of its own. Instead of boulders, concrete bunkers, tank traps and machine gun pill-boxes left over from the once real threat of a Nazi invasion. Now the only protection they offered was to us less-than-hardy souls, hiding from the biting wind continually sweeping in from the Arctic across a very cold and very dark sea. I suppose we must have enjoyed our summer breaks from the concrete alleys of dirty old Newcastle, but all I can remember now was the coldness of the water which even at the height of summer could stop your heart at thirty paces. That - and the peculiar smell emanating from certain spots near the caravan sites spotted about the dunes: Sort of seaweed and sewage. And sand covered sandwiches. It was just impossible to take a mouthful of cheese and pickle without the sand which was driven at you by the whipping wind. The one year my Grandma afforded a canvas windbreak and huddled in behind it, spreading out her feast on a square of red gingham, four delinquent footballers ran passed celebrating life. Sandy sarnies yet again.....

Look out! Here comes Sandra, legs pumping, arms a'swinging. Oh well! I can't remember the beach of my youth playing havoc with my legs, but the present one is infinitely preferable to the past.

We scoot along now. Time is of the essence. Cousin has to go to work...I have to... well, do all sorts of things - make a cup of tea, return to bed...

Journey 6
New South Wales

The Northern Tablelands

Booral

Booral is a little off our direct route to the Northern Tablelands but is typical 'Up - Country,' repeated a thousand times throughout the State. Single-storey houses, self made of weatherboard or handmade bricks and tin, perch on island clearings hacked out of the bush. No mains water here. Every drop of rain is collected in huge storage tanks, or you don't shower, make tea or flush the toilet. It is a different life-style, where travelling distances [say from Birmingham to Oxford], for a meal or a night class, is not even worthy of consideration.

We pass over Cameron's Creek, turn off at the Pioneer Cemetery and visit some great people - our people - for a magnificent lunch. There may be three generations of Australian-born rello's waiting for us, all of us sharing a common gene pool, - although you wouldn't know it, for 'the country' breeds a different type of Aussie from the city folk. Here self confidence and self reliance ooze over the lunch table. They give me the impression that they can deal with the constant risk of bush fire and drought without even giving a thought to the other irrelevances of life - such as poisonous snakes, spiders, stinging bull ants by the front door, and thorny bindy grass in the feet of the unwary.

Community here has real meaning. It has not been bastardized by politicians. The concept of Australian 'mateship', born in adversity, is alive and well. Two of our hosts are volunteer bush fire fighters - splendid examples of how people out here must pull together - for their lives, homes and livelihoods literally depend upon it.

Being here, being a part of it even for a short while, makes you appreciate people and what is around you more. Soccer with the kids, while by the fence kangaroos graze, becoming motionless except for a twitching ear when shouts of joy ring out; beautiful tropical fruit, and a plethora of cakes and goodies, are conjured out of thin air; shrieking parrots; noisy, invisible insects; all welcome friends who have just dropped in from a million miles away.

I hope you haven't had enough of the family history stories, but imagine our delight in finding out that the great, great, great grandfather of our hosts was THE Cameron over whose creek we had earlier driven. He was sixty [he lied and said he was forty-five] when he came to Australia from Scotland with his second wife, who was thirty years his junior. He also brought with him eight of his children from his first marriage. By the time he made his way into the Pioneer Cemetery at the age of eighty-nine, he left 106 Cameron's behind him in this area.

A photograph is produced of a gnarled, white-haired, old man. The face is diamond hard, the epitome of strength and resolve.

The story goes that recently some aged relative wanted another picture of him altered by a professional photographer.

"Can you lighten the face and remove his hat?"

"Yes Madam," came the reply. "We can do that with our digital thingy-me-bob. We can touch in his hair. Now! What side was his parting on?"

"Oh! - I don't know. But you'll see that when you take his hat off."

Tears of laughter, followed too closely by tears of parting.

'Aunty' Jean's Chocolate Caramel Slices:

Combine one and a half cups of self raising flour, 3 teaspoons of cocoa, a third of a cup of castor sugar, a third of a cup of coconut and 185 grams of melted butter in a bowl and mix well.
Grease a shallow pan, about 25cm by 30cm and press the combined ingredients, [above] over the base. Bake it in a moderate oven for 20 minutes and then allow too cool for five minutes before adding the following topping:
Topping:
Combine one cup of castor sugar, 125 grams of butter, 2 tablespoons of golden syrup, a third of a cup of liquid glucose,* [*This is a must,] one third of a cup of water, 400 gram can of condensed milk.
Stir the topping ingredients over a low heat without boiling until the sugar is dissolved. Increase the heat and boil for 10 minutes or until it becomes caramel in colour. You must stir continually for those ten minutes.
Spread over the tray and allow too cool.
Top with 300 grams of melted dark chocolate and sprinkle some walnuts over it.
Refrigerate until it's set and cut into squares.
Unmissable!

The Hunter Valley

I have had plenty of time to think. Well, you know my view on little 'planes and Cousin Doug is busy ferrying my lot up into the Hunter Valley in a particularly small, one engined job. But what a way to arrive for those on a first visit to one of the finest wine regions in the world!

Me? Another tea under a plaque reading "To commemorate the first recorded snow fall on this mountain, July 18th 1965," then I'll drive up. They came from miles around that day - to see snow on this hill of butterflies. But today, it's just the butterflies, Anzac Biccy's and me

*

I'm still thinking. This time sitting quietly by a tiny watercourse through a vineyard and surrounded by the bush. I am waiting for another azure kingfisher to put in an appearance.

I did drive up and passed a sign for Kurri Kurri. Kurri Kurri! - The centre of the early search for coal in the Hunter, where our Thompson brothers began their new life in the early 1920s. Other signposts hereabouts, pointing to other pit villages, are reminiscent of their Northumbrian roots - Morpeth; Pelaw.

I went 'in-bye,' once. Once was enough. I have never been so terrified before or since. Utter blackness: Squirming about in water and filth, with a creaking roof eighteen inches above your panicking head: And the noise. The mechanical cutter at the face screamed like a banshee in agony. If there is a hell, it will be like that.

And now I can add three great uncles to the twelve of the fourteen grandfathers and great [etc] grandfather's who went down, shift after shift, in order for their families to survive. Heroes I'd call them.

I continue. Up through the fertile, rolling hills to Maitland, where our Mary Birkby married in 1854. Her husband was Joe Canon, a pot boy from London who got seven years for pinching a handkerchief. Mary is buried here.

Singleton comes next. Distant, extended family members grazed livestock somewhere around here in 1832 - but that would be a nightmare to sort out in the record offices, so we hurriedly pass on to Muswellbrook.

It was in the mid to late nineteenth century when a Richard Birkby became a policeman here in

Muswellbrook, before being posted in succession to the neighbouring towns of Scone, Murrurundi and the tiny Wallabadah. The whole area is incredibly beautiful and Scone has become one of the richest rural areas in Australia. Immaculate horse stud farms abound..... It must cost a fortune just to paint the white picket fences.

Murrurundi and Wallabadah are inextricably linked to our Birkby's. Richard was descended from Thomas Birkby, a Yorkshireman who had been a gardener on a large estate before emigrating with his wife and two kids aboard the ship, David Scott, in 1834. Thirteen years later he was the Chief Constable of Murrurundi - which must have had a population of, oh! - at least a hundred folk and half a million sheep. Both father and son were policing the area together when, in April 1860, Richard married the under-age daughter of yet another copper called Farrell. How many peelers do you need for an area like this for goodness sake?

A hundred and twenty years later I was having to police a busy town of 70,000 souls with only one more bloke than that. Mind you, I did not have to get on a horse and disappear on patrols for days on end chasing armed bush rangers. My reality was a 'panda' car and home in time for tea, with only the odd mad axeman to contend with.

The kingfisher hurtles past, and the past threatens to disappear just as quickly. Then, a bunch of huge, yellow butterflies come out to play in the dappled shade. The warm, sweet smelling air, the relaxing trickle of the stream and the utter tranquillity allows for contemplation.

My life is in harmony with the present: Jet travel, pensions, career, diet, choice, freedom. You name it. I am a child of my time and I wouldn't change it. Yet my life is so out of touch, so alien to the reality faced by my ancestors, whether out here or back in Britain, it just doesn't seem right somehow.

Tamworth

For one week each January, Tamworth becomes the country music capital of Australia: Nashville, New South Wales style.

For fifty-two weeks a year, Tamworth is the administrative centre of Northern New South Wales, drawing people to it for jobs in the bureaucratic jungles.

For fifty-two weeks a year, Tamworth IS the centre of the world for its fifty thousand inhabitants. It has everything they need: shops, schools, cafes, swimming pools, even a wildlife park, riverside walks and tourist drives. It has everything because it needs to have. An island of civilization set adrift in an inhospitable, vast hinterland.

It may have everything - and yet there is something missing. It took me years to understand what. It is that its people lack somewhere to go. Tamworth IS the eye of the needle, the bright star in an infinite galaxy. People are pulled in to it as surely as a dying star is absorbed by a Black Hole.

Quite simply, there is nowhere else.

But here we are, and with ten days left until Christmas I can find absolutely no sign of the festive spirit. I try to explain its absence by my own tiredness brought about by our journeys.....but that's not it. Maybe it is because we are visitors living a new experience. Christmas is certainly different here. No dark and cold nights; and unlike Britain, where the shelves will be laid bare by panic buying, there is no hard sell here - no buy-buy-buy consumer culture. In fact the shops consider they are staying open late on the Saturday before Christmas by not closing their doors until 4 p.m. But I don't think that is the reason for my lack of joyful expectancy either.

It could be that Santa does not travel well. He is still walking the streets of down town, or sits in snowy grottos wearing the traditional boots and fur-lined clothing. He "Ho-ho-ho's" along to the strains of a herniated rendition of 'In the deep mid winter' - a long way from Carols by Candlelight in an ancient Cotswolds' church. Yet it is infinitely better than a modern Aussie Christmas 'Carol,'

which goes something like:
> "Here comes Santa in his big black boots,
> All done up in the back of a Yute."

We look on in our shorts, stinking of sun cream and munching a fistful of paw-paw. It's just not Christmas for us, so I decide not to apply for a job that is on offer in the department store: 'Wanted - Grotto Assistant to help Santa Claus.' We decide promotion prospects are a bit limited and instead make a wish by throwing good money into the grotty well. I wish.....I wish.....I wish that sweaty Santa over there sprinkles us with some of that artificial, magical snow that the kids are all covered in.

Well, it might work.

The Tots of Tamworth

Kids! I love 'em. Christmas, and Tamworth town is heaving. The main street is decked with bunting. Hot, excited children, and even hotter parents, await the event of the season. Thirty-five degrees, but their ordeal is about to end as the Grand Parade approaches, Scottish Pipe Band to the fore: Stirling marching music, swirling kilts.

Then Santa: He is waving and happy and fat and red. His sweating face matches the colour of his robes. But all the careful, behind-the-scenes planning and the work of months vanishes with......his horse! Surely this must be the most broken down nag in all of Australia. It is so old it can't raise its whiskered head. The kids don't notice. They cheer and cheer. The rest of us smile whilst Santa glares and the horse plods.

Shopping and Santa satisfied, it's time for a swim. Fifty littlees train under critical gazes. Seven training sessions a week, fifty-two weeks a year should you want it: More Olympic records await. A country town - with two Olympic-sized pools and full-time trainers! Eat your heart out Britain.

A tiny tot dives in and swims his first ever length. The last fifteen yards are hard to watch. Shouts of "Grab the rope!" are ignored as Maddison plods on as slowly as the horse earlier. "Grab the rope!" shouts the coach. But the bobbing head continues, occasionally breaking the surface and sucking air - hard.

He makes it. Maddison's mum is pleased. The coaches are pleased.....We are pleased. This kid's got it - the killer instinct. Perhaps I should introduce him to those cricket bat things.

Time's up. Out! Next lot - in! Move on! More to do!

The basketball courts reverberate with the noise of hundreds in competition. Enthusiasm knows no bounds. All display a will to win, even when 40 points to 12 down. Some have their shirt numbers cut into their hair. All work hard for each other until they have no more to give.

Baggy-eyed exhaustion - and that's just me. I'm shattered just watching this hectic round of normal life 'up country.'

Good night Big Dog.*

Good night Thomas**

* Big Dog is a man-sized puppet whose appearance on the telly at about 7.30pm used to herald kid's bedtime.
** Thomas, our godson, wants a mention.

Techno-man

I could not help but smile last night when the printer bit of a friend's computer went berserk, spewing out page after page of unsolicited material across the floor. The computer will resume normal service when I leave here the day after tomorrow. How do I know? Well - experience.

Technology and I just don't mix, and I define technology as anything invented by man for the use of man.

After fifty [very odd] years, my tool box consists of a small hacksaw - unused since I permanently scarred the forefinger of my left hand; a hammer - unused since I left an impressive, if unforgiven, line of bent nails in the wall of the front room on which photograph frames refuse to hang; and a pair of secateurs, which regularly draw blood. My wife, wherever she goes, now carries our two screwdrivers with her. She keeps them deep in her handbag, "Just in case." I guess she means just in case I get my hands on them.

In fact my battle with technology can get rather alarming at times. For instance, one night when the grandkids were staying over, my wife woke up in a panic. She dreamt of being caught up in a fire with two of the girls - so I was despatched to see if everything was all right. I checked the house over and after five minutes returned to the bedroom. As I passed under the fire alarm, the damn thing went off. So I reckon: [a] the wife has some genes of one of her ancestors floating around in her - someone called Lucky Hog, a Scottish witch; and [b] I am a bit of a Jonah who gives off electrical impulses to balls things up nicely.

So, I sit in this lovely sitting room, looking at the brooding mountains and smiling at our friend's attempt to gather up the uninvited paper mountain from the polished hardwood floor. Having said that I am a Jonah, I was prevailed upon to enter the twenty-first century recently - to abandon the tired sit-up-and-beg typewriter with its oceans of correction fluid. How else could I compete in the cut-throat world of publishing? How could I live without an 'Intel. Celebrity 200J with monitor and scanner bundle?' - Especially when it has a 56k v.90 full duplex whatsit and a 3x pci 3xi SA slot. [Or should that be clot?]

So this new thing sits there frowning, with functions unknown to me. F's this and that and an 'alt ctrl,' which the handbook helpfully explains: "These keys have varying functions on their own or when used with other keys."

God help us! All I want to do is write something. First thought! Let's go to Australia and do some more research. I can write in a book and use a pen. My wife decides it is cheaper for me to study the dreaded handbook. Who designs these things - with chapter headings like: 'Pccillin Scan,' 'Defragment Hard Drive', and 'ESD Precautions.' I close the book when it gets personal: 'Removing a Dimm.' Research is sounding better.

So here we are, twelve thousand or so miles from the dimm removing machine. I can afford to smile. The fax, or whatever it is, is still spilling its entrails and the telephone help-line is needed urgently. Instead of a helpful human who can recognise a Dimm: "You have six choices. How to join: Accounts: Information on other products: Blah-Blah. Technical Advice:" We decide between us to go for the technical guy.

"You have six choices. Blah-blah: Blah-de-blah...or number six. - Ring back at 8 a.m.'

I, too, have a choice. Godson number one takes charge of the computer and summons up a herd of reindeer - who proceed to fart out a chorus of 'We wish you a merry Christmas.' It ends with Rudolph doing something you do not want to know about, but somehow it seems a fitting conclusion to this particular ode.

Slasher

'Slasher Ahead,' said the first road sign of the day as we travel the short distance from Tamworth to the neighbouring town of Armidale.

But who, or what, is Slasher? What is he or she doing up ahead? Slasher! Perhaps he is the ageing leader of a Glaswegian razor gang - transported for his crimes no doubt. Perhaps he is the Zorro of Australia.

It is the type of country where your imagination can run wild. Now that we have breached the Great Dividing Range, we are 'Up Country' and into 'The Dry.' Everyone says the drought is bad everywhere. Rain is urgently needed - but everything is green. And it's raining. Maybe everywhere is somewhere else?

We reach a small, rural town: Population one hundred, according to the sign outside the store. Could Slasher be found here? It looks promising. There is a tired horse, saddle intact, at the hitching rail outside the pub. An old pub, if the layers of peeling paint are anything to go by. Trouble is, the horse is standing in the back of a Ute, legs tethered; head drooping; tail still - despite the hovering fly cloud: A picture of abject horsy misery.

The eye is drawn into the darkness of the bar by the sound of clinking glasses and mumbled conversation. It is the only sign of life in town. We enter through a swing door. The ceiling fan is as listless as the horse - a perfect statement about the alcoholic ambience of the place. All conversation stops as we enter and heads turn in our direction. My wife shuffles nervously – there is no sign of women in the bar. And it's quite obvious that any cleaning which does get done; is done by a man.

Meals? The barman examines something out of his ear. Reluctantly: "Maybe later." No community centre this. No bingo or tea: - Just beer and conversation for the hot and tired workmen.

No obvious Slasher. We didn't dare ask.

We move on, hungry. The only sign of 'the dry' is that the cattle are grazing 'The Long Paddock' - that's the road verges, where they wander deafly from one side of the highway to the other in search of something greener or more tasty. Cattle dogs lie disinterestedly behind the herd, ensuring that they only move one way - at the oncoming traffic. There is not a drover in sight. No prizes for guessing where he was.

We pass a wet Thunderbolt's grave: Then a stormy Thunderbolt's hideout amongst huge boulders miles from anywhere - but conveniently positioned right next to the highway's edge. We know our Slasher is not the same guy as Thunderbolt, for he was an infamous bush ranger, the Ned Kelly of the New England Plateau. If he had been alive today, then for sure no one would have been stupid enough to put graffiti all over his cave.

Two days ago, the news had reported that the Wizard of New Zealand had visited Tamworth. He had worn a stupid hat, a stupider grin, bashed cymbals, shook a rattle, and called upon whatever spirits were around to end the drought: All this whilst he did a Red Indian war dance. The newscaster called him a "Whacko," and I suppose the modern-day Merlin must have taken exception to this - or the fact the local Cattlemen's Association refused to pay him for his unsolicited efforts on their behalf.

Now it is raining cats and dogs, so I guess they must be feeling guilty for not greasing the Whacko's palms.

So we arrive in a rain lashed Armidale. Thunderboltless, Whacko-less and still very Slasherless.

Button Bashing

Armidale, a small, once prosperous university town, lies on the Northern Tablelands and is an excellent base for exploring the numerous National Parks hereabouts. It is Boxing Day, the big day for the opening of the January Sales everywhere. Everywhere except here, that is. We walk the town's single mall and not a shop, not a coffee bar, is open. Even the pubs are boarded up.

Worse still, there is not a soul about. A veritable ghost town, if it were not for the lonely, middle-aged lady reading aloud from her Bible. Her audience is an empty and silent street; her voice, caught by the gentle breeze, wafts and echoes around the empty shop doorways. We plonk on a nearby bench, unwittingly destroying her own particular reality. Well, we are immersed in our own thoughts. My wife is undoubtedly cursing the absence of anywhere open so she can save some money [this time it is rather nice wine glasses], whilst I am secretly pleased that nothing else is coming my way to pack into the two, overburdened travel bags.

The god-lady falls quiet, gives us a less than godly thought, and begins again. We leave around Mark's Gospel, Chapter 9 - but where to? We have already tried the town's arboretum, a less than inspiring place where the highlight is the sign which reads: "To see waterfall, press button and wait five minutes." We did - couldn't resist it. A trickle through the green algae became a deluge, the muddy, litter-choked puddle that passes for a lake, churns wildly for a few moments...and then it stops. Press again for a repeat performance: Hardly Disney. But to say something positive about Armidale's answer to Kew Gardens would be that it is better than the park in the neighbouring town of Tamworth - with whom there is something of a rivalry. The only thing memorable about Tamworth's park is that it is, well.....unmemorable.

We decided to walk back to the 'digs,' our family's little cottage next to the army depot of the 12/16th Hunter Valley Lancers. It was during this part of our route march that we met John, an old chap with gammy legs who was propping up his gate post watching the world go by. He would have rather been watching the cricket match being televised from Melbourne, but rain has washed play out - naturally.

Anyway, John is a nice guy who had served in New Guinea with the 1st Field Regiment of Australian Engineers during the Second World War - a fact about which he is justifiably proud. Warfare in the razor-backed, five thousand feet high mountains, which were cloaked in heavy mist and almost impenetrable rainforest, would have been bad enough. Add in a savage and determined enemy who could be invisible just four yards away from you, then one ought to recognise how hard things were for ordinary people like John.

Anyway, John enlivened our walk with his stories and humility, and eventually directed us to the Oxley Rivers National Park, about twelve kilometres out of town. And we were pleased he did. The distance was probably measured in country miles and no mention was made of the unsealed roads covered in various breeds of cattle, including bulls, which did not move for us; horses which did, skittish, scattering every which way, including straight at the windscreen; and kangaroos, which couldn't move 'cos they were squashed flat.

But the prize at the end was worth double the effort. We could have spent the day staring in amazement at the timeless, impregnable mountains, the two thousand foot vertical drops, and played forever with the fat lizards amongst the huge boulders of a placid river. The wildlife was incredible. I particularly liked the gentle butterflies, choosing to ignore the spiders' webs across the narrow paths, and the enormous number of fat skinks which sunned themselves on the warm rocks. And what eats skinks? Snakes! That's what! And that alarming fact kept going around my brain like a mouse on a plastic treadmill.

Of course we never saw anything nasty - just the single spider on my shirt. It died a sudden, violent and unnatural death just before I did. I was troubled by the thought of the spider, even by the invisible, lurking things. I was troubled by the little handrails and narrow, crumbling paths beside sheer drops. I was more troubled by the fact that I was no John and never could be. He and his mates' endured malnutrition, disease, exhaustion, fear - all in conditions far worse than these. And he did not have a car waiting somewhere back there, to scoot him home in time for another enormous dinner.

Despite the recent yule-tide rain, the park's masterpiece, the huge, majestic Wollomombi waterfall, which normally drops a river out of the clouds into an unexplored valley far below - a valley where dinosaurs could still be walking about - today only produces a mere dirty trickle over algae-covered boulders.

I looked everywhere but, regardless of my recently-acquired jungle craft, I could not find the button marked "press and wait five minutes....." Now if John were here...

Danny's Dinner Dissertations

The spider was a big 'un – grey, with long front legs, and about the size of the palm of your hand. It was busily running about the rafters of the garden pagoda, a rickety structure affording some protection from the elements to the charcoal barbecue. I was told to sit down; it was a friendly character named 'Danny Long Legs' and without him dinner outdoors would be impossible.

"What if he wasn't about then?" I asked. "How come we don't get dinner?" I was convinced it was a wind up.

The reply was unsettling. "Then the red backs get ya.' He eats them 'afore they get to us."

Thus reassured that I am safe from one of Australia's nastiest species of spider, I return the twenty yards to my recently vacated seat and, by implication, to my recently abandoned, 'tee' bone steak.

The rest of the evening was taken up with grog, grub and plenty of chatter, most of which revolved around the 'What-If' syndrome: That and one eye on Danny. With the other eye looking for my food, the fellow guests must have thought I had some sort of a peculiar affliction. However, the evening gave me the idea for this chapter - and before embarking on it, I should say I have been a bit selective about the material appearing here from last night's offerings. I have left out people such as politicians or other notables about whom whole encyclopaedias have been written. Instead, ordinary people who are part and parcel of Australian folklore.

What if....:

What if Robert Patterson had not completed the overhead telegraph from Port Augusta to Darwin in 1872? 1,973 miles across a perilous expanse of territory; – which until only ten years earlier was deemed "uncrossable." All had gone pretty well to start with, but when the 'Wet' came, things started to fall apart. Aborigines constantly attacked the expedition, killing one man at Attack Creek. [Don't you just love the names?] Then there were the sandflies, mosquitoes, floods, malaria and starvation. These inconveniences did not stop the men, only slowed them down a bit. What did stop the work dead in its tracks was the first recorded strike in the Northern Territory. On 7th March, 1871, the blokes had been without "tea, sugar, soap, salt, 'baccy and grog with nothin' to fill our guts 'cept weevily flour," for some time. The boss stupidly said that those items weren't necessary - and the strike was on. Patterson not only took it upon himself to get some proper food and rations for the men, but when the northern and southern lines met, he found that the wire was two feet short. Undeterred, he grabbed both pieces of wire to try and squeeze out the last few inches...and electrocuted himself. [On this evidence alone, I claim Robert Patterson as a relative.]

What if Celeste Mogador had not come to Victoria in 1854? Well, for sure, her French Consul General husband, Lionel Comte de Chambillan, would never have been remembered in the history books. He did nothing special - but Celeste was a different kettle of fish. At fifteen she was a vagrant; in a brothel at sixteen; and at seventeen, an erotic dancer in a couple of notorious shows in Paris. She had also been her husband's mistress for years and only married him shortly before sailing to Australia. She had written a book about her colourful past, so everything was out in the public domain. She was only in Australia for a couple of years before having to leave for France to sort out her husband's debts. However, she'd fallen in love with Australia and its people, and wrote many novels about "that harsh land." With the cash she made, she ensured medical care for the orphans and soldiers of the Franco - Russian war.

What if Lucky Jim Johnson had died with everyone else aboard the 'Dunbar' - a ship which sank whilst trying to enter Sydney Heads in rough seas and gale force winds at 11.30 p.m. on 20th August, 1857? Lucky Jim was on deck when the ship foundered, claiming the lives of 121 people. He clung to a narrow ledge on the vertical cliff face for thirty-six hours before being rescued. He got a job as a keeper in the lighthouse at Newcastle on the central coast of New South Wales, and was working away when the S.S.Cawarra sank there on Oyster Bank on the 12th July, 1866. Only one person out of 59 survived - Fred Hedges - the man who saved Lucky Jim nine years earlier. Only a coincidence? - Or something in the stars?

What if.....A young stockman was minding his own business one day when a wagon floated past, caught up in flood water. Three people were on the wagon and in obvious danger, so the young stockman, John Conway Brookes, effected a daring rescue. One of the rescued just happened to be the man who had been handed the task of completing the overland mail link between Melbourne and Sydney. No easy task was this, as the Aboriginal Woradgery Tribe killed any white they could find in an area which extended from just forty miles outside Melbourne for 160 miles toward Sydney. Brookes took the job as the mailman and set off on his first journey on 1st January, 1838, with two long-barrelled pistols in his belt, damper bread in his saddle bags and fifteen pounds of mail. He covered the 160 miles in six days - and continued to do so uneventfully. However, he did have a store of stories, like when his horse got stuck in river mud. He managed to get ashore without the animal, without the mail, and without his clothes. He then had to run for his life, as a pack of fifty hungry dogs descended upon him. He was still up a tree, surrounded, and planning to stay right there, when a settler appeared with a shotgun. Instead of shooting at the dogs, the man threatened Brookes, who hurriedly explained that he was the postie. The settler replied, "Don't think much to your uniform: Any letters?"

I hope you are not getting bored, but these little ditties are true - and anyway I'm enjoying them...

What if little Clara Wilson had not needed to pee in the early hours of the morning of 8th April, 1865? What if Black Dan Morgan, a bushranger of fearsome repute and not noted for his compassion, had said, "No! Do it here?" But he didn't - and so ended a notorious career. Between 1862 and 1865 he had murdered and robbed his way through southern New South Wales and Victoria, initially with his partner, German Bill, who ended up dead in a shoot-out with the cops. Anyway, Black Dan had held up the homestead where little Clara was a servant. He kept everyone prisoner overnight, making the family sing and dance for him. Presumably he spent so much time there he let his guard drop, let Clara go and gave her the chance to earn the £1000 reward, placed on his head for the murder of Police Sergeant McGinnety near Wagga Wagga. Black Dan was shot to death by police as he walked out of the family home he'd invaded. What if Clara had got to keep the reward? What a difference it would have made to her life. Alas, none of the folk at the barbee knew the answer - we just hope she got the cash... - but don't you just doubt that!

What if an Aborigine by the name of Dooley, who was fossicking about in the Kimberleys, had not met up by chance with a guy called Don McLeod? Dooley was angry at the treatment of Aboriginal stockmen who worked for little or no pay, sometimes only receiving their food and drink. But he didn't know what to do about it. McLeod did, and spent weeks instructing his new mate on how to organize a strike. This was 1946 - the year when six hundred native stockmen went on strike for thirty bob a week. They won - and how Dooley managed to coordinate matters in an area the size of Ireland, without the use of telephones, etc., is still a source of wonderment.

What if the seamen aboard the pearling vessel, 'Crest of the Wave,' had thought their captain, a man called Porter, had gone mad and refused to obey his order to cut down the ship's mast? I reckon we would all have thought he was nuts, as that day in early March, 1899 was a beautiful day, and the crew, like the thousand other men of the pearling fleet, were relaxing in Bathurst Bay after a week of fending off sharks and heavy work aboard ship. I would like a beer and a chat, put my feet up and have a snooze in the sun. Instead, "Chop the mast down!" The men didn't know that a hundred miles off Cooktown two cyclones, Mahina and Nachon, were meeting up. Captain Porter didn't know either; there was no communication with the outside world, but he must have had a sixth sense, probably stimulated by the silent lightning of the previous two nights: So the mast came down, the anchor went out and everything battened down. His actions meant that his was the only ship in Bathurst Bay to survive when huge waves arrived unexpectedly and crashed over the ships for nearly eight hours. Without her mast, the 'Crest of the Wave' continually righted herself and eventually lodged up on a coral ledge. Three hundred and seven died that night - a night which boasted some incredible survival stories. For instance, two women swam all night with their children clinging to their hair. The kids died from exposure - cyclones are not noted for happy endings.

[Pearling fleets were also destroyed in 1908, 1910, 1929 and 1935.]

What if Henry James O'Farrell had shot to death the Prince of Wales in Sydney on 12th March, 1868, instead of just wounding him? The first shot struck Queen Victoria's lad, the second missed. The immediate reaction at the scene was: "What will his mother say?" Perhaps if O'Farrell's aim had been better, she may have pinched a line off one of her rello's, who reputedly said with his dying breath "Bugger Bognor." She could have said "Bugger Bendigo-Baby", or something like that - and Australia could have been a republic long ago!

What if...What if Santa didn't come at Christmas? The world of Australia's railway children was an austere one, lived in isolated places, often under canvas and always in a harsh landscape. Ron Ryan was a railway worker and one of Santa's little helpers. Each year he dished out pressies to the kids from the back of a train. Now he was supposed to give the presents to the children of railway workers only, and each year he annoyed the hierarchy by stating Santa did not know the difference, handing out gifts to every child who answered the train's whistle. In 117 degrees, dressed in his red outfit, Ron was met at the tiny settlement of Nunjikompita in Western Australia by seventeen dogs and thirty-one kids. He only had twenty-three parcels designated for that stop, so he gave out the parcels for the next stop as well. Of course the next stop came and he was short of gifts, so the children were treated to the sight of Santa Claus racing from the train to the local shop to buy whatever he could. When the train stopped at Karkoo, the whole school turned out and sang carols to him. Ron was so moved, he gave the kids the rest of the day off. The teachers were annoyed, being too slow to catch the children as they disappeared quicker than rats up a drainpipe. 11 p.m. 25th December. The train is late, very late, when it arrives at Thevenard. Santa Ron is surprised to find the children still waiting at the station. "How long have you been waiting," asks a concerned Ron?

"Twelve months Santa," came the reply.

What if Santa hadn't arrived.....

The stories go on; the Aussie revellers prove more resilient than yours truly. They did not seem to care that Danny Long Legs has turned in for the night, leaving the field clear for the little redbacks to have a feed. And so to bed - the plight of those railway children - still waiting at eleven o' clock on a Christmas night pulling at the heart strings.

Once upon an Aussie Christmas

For those of you who have been paying attention, you will know already that we have spent more than one Christmas in Australia.

By now we reckon that the advertising men promoting Oz throughout the world as THE tourist destination are earning their corn. Who cannot identify the Sydney Harbour Bridge or a gleaming Opera House fronting a brilliant blue sea? And the sun is always shining.

Yet the images of barbecues, beaches and burning bodies are nothing like the reality of Aussie Christmases despite the relatives saying "You should have been here last year." However, we do read the newspapers, and watch the telly like everyone else; and last year six people died in the southerly gales which devastated the Sydney to Hobart yacht race. To us Christmas means cold rain and no sun - and I am not talking about Britain. We head to Australia to escape all that, sold on the idea of the sea and sand and the sun of advertisers' dreams. And I'm sure it's just that. Dreams! One of our Christmases consisted of the remnants of a cyclone which proceeded to bend palm trees double and dump enormous quantities of rain on top of us: Cold rain, of course.

Despite the occasional inclement weather, if I lived here permanently, then I would have to live on the coast, if for no other reason than access to the wonderful array of cheap seafood. It appears I am not the only one engaged in this fetish. During the last two days before Christmas, the fish market in Sydney has sold ninety thousand kilos of prawns - huge, delicious pink things. Mouth watering ecstasy...! Of course we are in Armidale, on the high plateau of Northern New South Wales. It's a long way from the coast and the smoked trout looks more than a bit iffy. Ah well!

A family Christmas in Armidale is accompanied by "Well above average rainfall and near record low temperatures." When you know the record stands at 12.3 degrees, you will realise it's * cold for high 'summer' - all courtesy of a low pressure area about fifteen hundred miles away. Being forever optimistic we have been stupid enough [again] to bring only shorts and tee shirts. For some reason we keep living in hopes that one day we will see an average temperature - anywhere around that elusive 27 degrees would do.

In the meantime, I need someone to blame for these goose-bumps and lack of a lovely warm sweater, cords and a wax jacket. Americans! I could blame them for changing the world's weather patterns because of their prolific use of oil. Perhaps that is too generalized. I know! Weathermen! They're a good target nowadays - ever since Michael Fish of the B.B.C. reassured Britain that there was no hurricane coming; the Dutch meteorologists had got it wrong. A couple of hours later a bit of a breeze flattened southern England.

Great! Weathermen will do very nicely. You will be pleased to know the same high standards of weather prediction have been reached in Australia. It's true that they are real good turns when it comes to them filling a five minute spot on the telly. Plenty of banter and they leave you laughing. But it's not so long ago that one of them looked at his computers, instruments and seaweed and decided to take a break for a smoke. Fag finished, he returned some twenty minutes later to find that a storm had sneaked up on him and caused two and a half billion dollars worth of damage to parts of Sydney: Twisters, hailstones the size of footballs, the lot - and no warnings 'cos he took a 'smoko'. He is probably checking weather balloons on Norfolk Island or some such isolated place that used to be the preserve of the difficult, recalcitrant or hopeless during the days of transportation.

The outlook for the next week is 20 degrees and showers. The good news is that the weather pattern for the Northern Tablelands will change next Thursday. The bad news is that by then we will have left Armidale far behind.

Mount Kaputar National Park near Narrabri

And so we are off again, out toward the interior this time, where some pretty hostile places are waiting for us. On our way we visit the small town of Bundarra, which sits on the river of the same name. It lies at the foot of the Nandewar Mountain Range, our next destination. It is a place to which those Blessed Birkby's somehow found their way in 1848, before moving to the more accessible town of Inverell.

However, we have no intention of fossicking for precious stones. Our destination awaits - Mount Kaputar National Park. Of course it's on the other side of the mountains, a long way from anywhere - and those roads.....!

The first thing to strike a note with me was the solitary headstones. They stand in pools of shade cast by solitary trees, and mark the passing of the pioneer generations. They are the people who worked and toiled to make a success of their lives and of this place. Now long gone, they have been buried on their land beneath the towering, extinct volcano of Kaputar by their people. Here they remain, on ground sacred only to them and theirs. No doubt they would rest even more easily if they could witness their legacy - a wealth earned from the vast cotton fields, fields planted by them on the ground they cleared. An achievement beyond comprehension, had they stayed in a subjugated Britain.

The dirt road deteriorates steadily as we climb and climb, until most of the four thousand and odd feet of Mount Kaputar, beckons at the near-side tyres. Sweating profusely, we arrive. Once again I have to admit that the sweat is fear induced. I began praying that it didn't rain until we got down again - or suicide was on the agenda.

But once there, the log cabins welcome you with all the comforts of home. Heart rate subsiding and vision clearing, I begin to realise just how beautiful and special this ancient place is. The bush walking is marvellous - good tracks which lead to exciting rock ladders that herald stunning views.

Fabulous sunsets over yet another million trees: I'm getting blasé about the tree millions on this desert continent. Smoky barbecues by the cabin retreat, whilst industrious cockroaches, vigorous mossies and yob kangaroos all threaten to invade 'our space.' Such human arrogance!

Ah! - To be at one with nature - and where better to commune with it than from inside that instantly recognizable building. That one! Over there! The interior is the same throughout the western world. It is only when you peer through the wooden circle that you gasp and hold the child tight. It must be thirty feet deep. And is that something slithering about down there? If the child falls through that vital hole, there is no way back. Mossies rise in anticipation of a meal.

Welcome to the Long Drop.

Welcome to the Bush Toilet.

Lightning Ridge

"Don't go to Pilliga."

We didn't. Well, who would want to go to a place the name of which in Aborigine means 'Swamp Oaks.' Every time we saw an occasional termite-ridden sign for the mysterious Pilliga, we turned away from it.

My brother was being 'helpful.' He was worried by our first trip inland on unmade dirt roads. He was worried! He wasn't here, and we didn't know where 'here' was anymore. I do not know where we went wrong, but it became obvious we were lost. How? Well, the skeletons were a sure give away. More than you could poke a stick at. Kangaroos, wallabies and lumps of noxious things we couldn't recognise. The road was loose, rutted sand, the sun fierce and the heat intolerable. Our single, half-empty bottle of tonic water was looking pathetically inadequate. The petrol tank was becoming worryingly low and we were still nowhere. Some bushmen! Ill prepared and starting to panic.

Another great hole in the track sent our little car off through the scrubby desert once more. This time we managed to scatter a lethargic emu family.

Having already flattened two brown snakes which refused to budge, and nearly being flattened ourselves by an immense road train, we ended up in a quarry. At least it was a sign of mankind; we were no longer alone on the planet.

I ease my wet and sticky shirt out of the hot car and into the blast furnace of the 'out there.' The man was sitting atop the biggest tyres I have ever seen, and as I approached I just hoped he was more tolerant than that road train driver. Had he really not seen our frightened little Nissan blocking the track? Sorry! - His track.

"Back up the trail three k's mate and turn left at the fence line. Twenty k's and you'll hit the tarmac."

The fence line was laughable: A few stumps here and there which the white ants had not quite finished off yet. They marked nothing in a lonely desert. Yet they were there, and we were never more thankful for good directions.

We were lucky, and that is all there is to it. People frequently die out here for failing to look after themselves, and so some well meaning tips:
1. Driving in Australia is different; any similarity with Britain disappears with driving on the left. You must prepare for any journey outside urban areas and off the highway. For instance, in some remote areas the roads simply disappear, especially in 'The Wet.'
2. Do not drive in the country at night unless you have to. Kangaroos make for the short grass of the verges and make an incredible mess of both vehicles and their occupants.
3. If your vehicle breaks down, STAY with it. It gives you shade and it's easier to be seen.
4. Ensure someone knows where you are going, the route and relevant timings.
5. Take enough fuel and water with you. The water requirement is a minimum of four litres per person per day. [Not half a bottle of tonic.]
6. Should you run over a snake, check your rear view mirror to ensure it comes out from beneath the car. They have a habit of giving non-vigilant drivers something of a shock when they open the bonnet later.
And oh!
7. Road trains take no prisoners. Get out of their way.

Huntin' the Opal

I will have abiding memories of Lightning Ridge. We are standing in a moonscape in forty degree temperatures and it is ten in the morning. There is not a bit of shade on this patch of opal rich dirt. No shade anywhere come to think of it. Countless hummocks, the spoil of human moles, stretch out as far as the eye can see; abandoned pieces of machinery rust quietly: Uniquely photogenic.

It was here, waiting for Jenny, that I met my first bounty hunters - two of them, looking totally normal. Not huge men, not violent and not a gun in sight. Maybe I watch too much telly. They had been working Lightning Ridge, the nearest thing to a Wild West town I've come across. Success meant a murderer was now in the local caboose awaiting transport to Sydney. My question about police inactivity met with shrugs and nothing else.

It is estimated that only a quarter of the actual population here is on the electoral role, pay taxes etc. One can only surmise why. Not so long ago bodies were dropped down abandoned mine shafts, dynamite down working ones. Thankfully those days are over. - More or less.

Jenny arrived, delayed by a messy baby. She matched the land - large, sunburnt and tough as nails. All her desires in life revolved around two things: her family, and the black opal for which the Ridge is famous. She answered all our questions with a smile, as we descended shafts and clambered from one vaulted cavern to another.

"It's only three hours to the doctors 'n shops. It doesn't bother us, we don't go much."

"No. Opal doesn't bring bad luck. The only bad luck involved is not finding 'em."

"Yes, there's money here. Put it like this. A schoolgirl started collecting so we could have a swimming pool. Kid raised half a million bucks inside a week."

Stunned silence:

"Does that answer your questions?"

"Err, yes. Thank you."

Impertinence dealt with, we feel privileged to have been allowed an insight into the hardships of, and the beauty claimed from, this unbelievable place.

Willies and Wallabies

The natural springs just outside Lightning Ridge are hot and sulphurous and after twenty minutes they make you feel as though you could run a mile: Remarkable, when I blanch at the thought of running for a bus.

There is something faintly Alice in Wonderland-ish about the experience though - sitting up to the neck in hot water, wide-brimmed hat perched above a red, red face, and being watched quizzically by wallabies coming out of the bush as if to witness some secret rite.

Somehow, the Aboriginal Dreamtime tale, centred on Lightning Ridge, does not seem all that far fetched. Not sitting here in such a bizarre setting. According to the legend, the Supreme Spirit had two wives: Mother Nature and Teacher. Off the two girls went for a swim, probably in these very springs, as we have seen no other water. Unbeknown to them, the bad guy in all this, Guria the crocodile, was following on behind and when he got the chance, swallowed them whole. The Supreme Spirit, called Bhiame, found his wives' willies. [No, come on! It's a belt made from hair.] Anyway, these two willies had been abandoned by the springs and he guessed what had happened. So he tracked the crocodile down and speared him. As the croc died he thrashed about for a while and as he did so, rain began to fall. A rainbow sprang up and got trapped between his scales, and as the crocodile's skeleton turned into Lightning Ridge, the rainbow turned into opal. Bhiame cut the croc open and his wives got out - no doubt p.d.q. and very thankful.

I just love happy endings, and to ensure our expedition was going to end the same way, we leave for civilization the long way around. The all Tarmacadam, boring, safe way, with one eye staring at the infinite line of thirty feet tall water-depth markers that edge the highway, and the other on the gathering clouds.

Carrot Cake Conundrum

We arrive back in the oasis of Tamworth and drink in civilization. We let it overwhelm us and are so thankful Tamworth exists.

The second pot of Earl Grey arrives. I must resist a second helping of that carrot cake. The world passes the coffee shop by, and the fatigue and stress of the last few days start to drop away. Eventually we face up to the need to talk, to get it out of our system and rationalise our experiences on what T.S. Elliot aptly described as "Rock, no water and the sandy road."

We are here, trying to follow in the footsteps of some of our ancestors: Ancestors who lived in places like we have come across heading inland a-ways. And now we know that they must have been very special people indeed, to endure the 'out there.' And of course there was a whole lot more of it back then.

Even today, I don't know if I could cope with that blistering wind, the all pervading dust, the endless miles, with nothing to break the horizon except maybe the occasional creaking of a rusting wind pump or a stark grain silo; and the loneliness. I know in my heart I would be hopeless - worse than useless in such a seemingly hostile and totally alien land.

Worse is to come. Realisation dawns that I will never be able to make any real connection with our forebears; never be able to share a common experience......none of us can. We are all products of our own time and place. If I'd been born on the dust plains or salt flats, perhaps I would have stood a chance - but surely not now.

And it does not just apply to us W.A.S.P.'ish townies. For instance, this land once held over six hundred Aboriginal tribes. I don't know how many there are now - in the wake of disease and extermination which followed the path of European settlement - but for forty thousand years those tribes didn't just cope out there; they were at one with their environment in all its passions.

We have just been witness to boarded up shop frontages, the world weary pubs, the weathered, peeling houses, the sullen eyes that follow your passing with a cold hostility. It is as if you are somehow personally responsible for the plight of those folk left out in that dust bowl.

Perhaps they are right. Outsiders like us pass through those forlorn outposts in a cloud of dust thrown up by our vehicle's wheels - outposts forsaken by all but the most exact of cartographers. We contribute nothing. We are of no consequence.

Today, some of the inheritors of frontier land - whether of the original Aboriginal people or of the early colonists, are unable to cope in a changed and ever changing world. Somehow they have become interminably lost. That does not mean we don't wish the best for all those who are trapped in, and share in, that common vale of tears. We can only hope that they face the future together, because there is no other way out there in the tullies, where the rainbows fall to earth as stone, not gems.

Strangely, that idea cheers me up no end. It's not so fanciful - nor merely academic philosophizing..... After all, didn't the First Fleeters arrive in Sydney Harbour when the great boondocks started at the quayside? Together they made a whole, wonderful nation.

The footsteps of our forebears might be fading, being slowly extinguished, but it is not by the sand, or the dust, nor the hardships of the 'out there.' The footsteps will eventually disappear, done to death by the carrot cake and tea of the ice cream parlours.

Having said that, you must try this one! Another favourite:

Carrot Cake: [The Easy way.]

You will need a food processor. In it, mix together two eggs, half a teaspoon of bicarbonate of soda, half a teaspoon of ground cinnamon and two roughly chopped medium carrots. Keep going until the carrots are finely chopped up.
Add in 185 grams of melted butter and a good three quarters of a cup of brown sugar.
Process it some more until it's all combined.
Now stir in one cup of wholemeal self raising flour and one cup of sultanas.
Grease a loaf pan, about 14 cm by 21 cm which has had its sides and base lined with grease proof paper. Put plenty of grease around.
Now pour the mixture into the pan and bake in a moderate oven for about 50 minutes. Leave it to stand for a further five minutes before turning it out and allowing too cool.
Feel free to butter ice it if you want.

Journey 7
Northern New South Wales

To Coffs Harbour

Poor woman: Panic encapsulated. One train a week to Broken Hill via Sydney and a train, now deceased; blocks the single line south. Her connecting train is now a bus, which is nowhere to be seen, and our train is thirty minutes late. We are going north - hopefully. Then, with a whispering sigh, the North Coast Express is here. Excitement rises within me, uninvited. The reflective windows, impervious to our stares, hold out the fulfilment of promises of thirty degree temperatures in the Banana Republic of Coffs Harbour.

We leave Broad Meadow Railway Station near good ol' Newcastle with an unrivalled smoothness. Accumulated rusting junk and miles of grain silos fall behind, to the accompaniment of an Italian lady from Sorrento called Mary O'Toole. True, I swear! She dictates recipe after recipe to an imprisoned Australian lady who steadfastly refuses to record them.

"You sure you don't want to write this one down? I've a pen and paper if you need them."

An Aboriginal man, obviously disinterested in one thousand and one things to do with pasta, snores in the next seat: Soporific Mary at work.

For hour after hour we pass through trees. Literally a billion have been planted and the Government has pledged to double that number. We pass a tiny hamlet in the forest. It's so small we can't see any houses - but there is a soccer field. It supports a roofed stand large enough to accommodate all of fifty people and is surrounded on three sides by a massive graveyard. Talk about desperate for support!

The tannoy over-rides Mary and the snores. "We regret to announce that we are proceeding slower than normal. There is a problem with the engine."

With that we judder to a halt amongst clouds of acrid, blue smoke. The trees momentarily disappear.

"I hope this won't inconvenience our customers," continued the guard, unperturbed.

Horror stories about train journeys reverberate around our carriage.

"Not again!" someone says. A simple but disconcerting statement when you think about it, and especially so when you are in the middle of nowhere. All of a sudden the trees seem to be closing in on us.

"I knew this woman once. She gave birth on this train. The conductor was a bit miffed. He told her she shouldn't have got on the train in her condition. 'But I wasn't in this condition when I got on,' she replied."

The oldies are still the best.

The car attendant walks by collecting rubbish in a large black plastic bag. I remember my brother telling me that once the rubbish was collected, it was thrown out of the back of the train before it arrived in the next station. I didn't believe him, but developed a crick in my neck by journey's end.

Within minutes we are on our way again and the stories subside. Either the driver is a mechanical Einstein or he'd left he handbrake on. Mary just continued - on and on. The snoring continued - on and on.

There was a subtle change around Mount George. The first sign of the drought which has plagued this part of Australia for four years appears in an instant. Poor looking cattle gravitate to pools of shade. The mountains are sunburnt; the fire-blackened trees droop. Water sprays the wood yards continuously to prevent fire. It looks hot beyond our air-conditioned haven.

We pass a small, pink church with its own barbecue area, as if standing as a symbol of hope to a community under siege. Indeed, it did give a miracle, for within seconds of Mary disembarking we were passing water-filled rivers and creeks as we returned to the coastal plain. Even the sight of water exacts its price. A cow has fallen to its death down the steep river bank and lies bloated only feet from the water it craved. Houses are now on stilts for fear of floods. There is luxuriant foliage, fat cattle, tidal creeks and palm trees.

Rubbish intact, we arrive.

From Taylor's Creek to Tourists

Coffs Harbour is a misnomer. The man who founded the place was called Korff and his shelter from a storm is over a mile out of town.

To be perfectly honest, we have been a bit disappointed in the borough on this visit. But why: The weather is great and the town full of good shops. Great beaches abound, sparkling like their names: Emerald, Sapphire. And there is plenty to do for families and people of all ages. Disappointed? Not in the people. They are still typically Australian: friendly and generous. "Borrow my flask." "Borrow the car." ".....the bed" Borrow more or less anything except the wife.

What then?

It was 1982 when we first visited Coffs, the new home in the sun for a new generation of immigrants out from Britain. Looking for gold – yes: But no longer in the creeks and river beds. Now gold is to be found in the professions - and dentistry is no exception. But back then the whole area had an intangible sparkle; an appealing rawness still laid its hand over Coffs Harbour's aspiration to become 'The Holiday Coast.'

Now, its charming naivety has succumbed to the power of money and 'progress.' Gone are the zoo keepers in flip-flops who kick vicious wombats into their allotted places, with a smile to the paying public. Gone from the museum is anything politically incorrect. No sign any longer of the early twentieth [yes - twentieth!] century licence authorizing the bearer to shoot kangaroos, wallabies, rabbits, emu, etc., etc., and Aborigines.

Now money talks - mainly in yen. Holiday villages have spawned along the incredible coastline. More are planned. Dual carriageways speed the impatient traffic between more and more shopping malls, with a hundred and one ways to spend your tourist dollar. A university has been born. The latest jet aircraft connect with Sydney and Brisbane, and there are plans afoot to go 'international.' The quaint attractions, like a visit to a working banana plantation, are now more professional and have lost something in the transition.

The resident population has burgeoned to over fifty thousand in the last two decades and is likely to continue to explode during the next two - a new, assured gold rush for the waiting professionals.

It took thirty-six years for the first thousand tourists to visit the area, i.e. between 1884 and 1920. Now it wouldn't surprise me if it were a thousand a day - out of season.

The history of Coffs Harbour has been one of exploitation and change. The timber industry fell. No big hardwoods left. The dairy industry failed - soil exhaustion caused by over grazing. The port was eventually laid to rest for commercial traffic in 1975. It lasted longer than the gold. It petered out after four tons were removed from Eleven Tree Creek - and at Taylor's Creek in 1899, the gold was so thick you could just pick it up off the ground.

In its rush to find something else - tourism - Coffs is running the risk of exhausting its resources yet again. This time it is water. Because of the insatiable appetite of the ever-expanding housing- and tourist-related developments, consumption is quite simply out-stripping availability.

As we arrive, there is fourteen weeks supply of water left in the dam. No rain is in prospect and the tourist season hasn't even started yet.

Sawtell

I could see by the light in her eyes and the way she moved that she was aroused.

I wasn't. I stood there, outwardly as solid as a rock, as dependable as ever; inwardly I was in turmoil. In fact, the panic was near overwhelming. This cannot be true. I've made a mistake - and a big one this time.

"I can live here. It's beautiful."

"Don't unpack dear," I said.

Unhearing, my wife continued. "It's gorgeous. It's clean. And look, honey eaters."

I looked all right - not at the courtyard garden, lovely and private, with the sound of the sea the only accompaniment to the array of tropical birds paying us a visit - but at the accommodation brochure: "Very nice, Patsy. Just leave everything alone!"

I was talking to the wall. My wife muttered something intimate to the inside of a cupboard as a myriad of freckled blue butterflies did a fly-past.

"Out! Now! This can't be the right place. Let's sort it out with the agent.....Please."

But I need not have worried. It was the right place. More importantly, it was the right price. Large, airy rooms: kitchen, dining room, lounge, laundry, shower, double bedroom, garden; all inclusive of electric, water, garbage collection etc. And it's cheaper than home.

"O.K. love: You can live here."

Sawtell; our base for a wee while: As late as the 1940s it was no more than coastal scrub out of which a dairy farm had been cut. The site of the farm had rested solely on the fact that there was a freshwater creek running from the distant hills out to the ocean. Now the small town has every amenity, but is more than happy to remain in the shadow of Coffs Harbour, a couple of miles or so to the north.

Sawtell; the place doesn't bother with tourist information offices; does not promote itself. It seems to be quite happy to remain one of Australia's best kept secrets, languishing as it does in its sub-tropical, never-too-hot; never-too-cold climate. I'm not arguing; content to enjoy the fabulous beach in peace..... Cheaply!

Save Water - Drink Beer!

Last night's electric storm was out over the ocean. No rain fell on the land. This morning, the press is full of the ongoing drought, spurred no doubt by the disappointment of rain being so close yet so far.

The Coastline Review has the best quotes. "On current weather forecasts there is no worthwhile rain expected until at least autumn." [And autumn is six months away!] "Things are crook!"

It has to be said that we have seen very little of the drought along the coast. Our paper 'boy' is all of seventy, with a history of heart attacks. He now delivers by throwing the papers from his passing Datsun onto green, manicured lawns surrounded by green trees.

But we are assured this is not the case elsewhere. A farmer in his early sixties, disfigured by skin cancer, is trying to stay out of the sun on his seaside holiday: Just one more living statistic which makes Australia the world's leader in this particularly vile disease. We meet at the Bottle Shop, under a sign doing its bit for the environment: 'Save water - Drink Beer!'

With a tear in his eye he tells me, "Had to slaughter half me cattle. Just not enough water or feed for the poor buggers."

I remember the good intentions spread across acres of newsprint. "No time for complacency." "Politicians act! Hose-pipe ban comes into force today." [Yes folks! Four years after the drought began - a hose-pipe ban. This may seem a little unbelievable to the long-suffering British public, who face water shortages after two weeks of sunshine.]

I am foolish enough to mention this outcry to my new friend. Now, I don't know about you, but I am always fearful when apoplexy is about. The farmer seems to have it.

He blows. "* * * * hose-pipe ban: It's the * * * * Pollies." [It would appear politicians have the effect of inducing words with a lot of 'ing' endings.] "They talk tough and do nothin'. This country depends on farmers and what do they do?"

I try to look knowledgeable, but does apoplexy involve a swelling, red face and blue neck veins which stand out half an inch? I still haven't answered his question but there is no need to worry. He's going full bore.

"They spend nothing on what matters and * * * * millions on * * * * art festivals in * * * * Melbourne."

As we part, united in anti-pollyism, the storm clouds gather again. Maybe the drought will be broken, if only for a while, leading to the countryside becoming awash with a surfeit unwanted 'ings'.

PS: It didn't rain.

The Bush Fire

It was the first really hot day for the North Coast, the stiff westerlies bringing with them the desert temperatures. By midday even the birds had fallen silent, leaving the rasping wind unchallenged.

Rugby and cricket vied for attention on the telly: Just a normal Sunday.

4 p.m. "Someone's got a garden fire," stated my wife, matter-of-factly.

"Shouldn't have," I replied. "There's a total fire ban." Yet I can smell it too.

I was not the only one. A flock of black, yellow-tailed cockatoos, twenty or more, screeched overhead. They headed south, away from their home on the wooded headland.

"Bush fire?" I had wondered aloud, but surely not. Such disasters are confined to television screens, aren't they?

We walk to the beach, where not one, but two, and then unbelievingly a third - fires announcing themselves with billowing black, white and grey smoke. The acrid smell of burning was everywhere. Hot ash was blown into our eyes before it died in the sea. Sirens wail and then wail again.....and again. It looks close to the houses backing onto the reserve - and guess where we live.

We return and immediately are caught up in frantic activity, played out against a constant background of sirens: Fire engines and police everywhere. The fire has a good hold. It's a hundred yards away: Plenty of noise and smoke from the invisible monster. No sign of flames yet but you know it is there. Oh yes; it's there; and this fear grabs you in the pit of your stomach.

Hose-pipes are played on the houses and nearby trees. Garden sprinklers are working the roof tops. Guttering is blocked with newspaper and then filled with water again and again. Sparks fizzle and die on the roofs - on our roof. Fear now grabs at your throat as your stomach turns again.

The roar gets ever louder.

Twilight: Hungry flames are now very much visible. Licking: Devouring. The fire fighters and home owners aren't winning.

Fifty yards: Dear God!

"Wait till it hits the tree tops - then watch it go," says a neighbour, senses dimmed by drink. "Then it's fireball time," he adds.

It's not something I want to hear, nor see. But my wishes do not enter into it. Thirty yards away a tree explodes in flame. The laconic fireman next to me remarks, "This is getting a bit exciting." I smile nervously and work the water. Don't think - just work the water.

Then the fireman is no longer the laid back guy. "Evacuate: Now!"

In thirty seconds we pack. Passports; photo's, clean undies and OUT: Funny - practically everyone in the street saves the photo's and undies. What would a psychologist make of that?

Relegated to the role of bystander, a series of images takes over as if I were watching a movie, projected, as in the olden days, with a flickering lamp. A line of fire fighters kneel at the edge of the bush, inactive hoses in hand, waiting for the moment experience will dictate to strike back. Outwardly they are calm and disciplined as a seventy foot wall of flame advances toward them. Now, in total blackness, men are on roofs, inadequate hose-pipes still in hand, silhouetted against the towering flames.

Incredibly, cars still pass along the road through clouds of sparks hot enough to blister their paintwork.

Walls of fire now on two sides: It's hard to breathe; impossible to leave.

Images: A man searches for a tame bandicoot: He thrashes about hopelessly in the undergrowth. A woman sits and cries. Firemen are running - back-burning, literally fighting fire with fire. An ancient Digger displays the Tobruk spirit. "I ain't goin'." He's carried out of his home, still in his armchair, fingers dug deep in the material.

Just as remarkable is my wife. Patsy is more than a bit fearful of dogs and now she holds and comforts a stranger's collie - and the dog lets her! Now that is weird.

8.15 p.m. We witness a minor miracle. The wind, fickle all day, now blows even stronger, but from a true westerly direction. In response, the flames veer away - less than ten yards from people's homes and dreams - and charge down to the sea- to oblivion.

10 p.m. Sirens blowing, and the brigades, most of them volunteers, leave us to the embers of our own particular brush with hell.

I could not bring myself to take photo's of the potential disaster facing ordinary folk - people we had come to know as neighbours and friends. However, I am sure, without evidence, that our ain' folk back in our benign land far away, will never believe the savagery, horror and extraordinary power of a bush fire.

*

An uneasy night: Watchful, yet grateful to have a bed. The bush is still red, the air heavy with smoke.

Morning breaks. In the grey half light I fall over the still packed passports, undies and photo's: You know - just in case. Tables and floors have deposits of grey ash. Smoke gently rises from the hillside. The burnt trees, one only feet away, bear silent testimony to just how lucky we had been.

I use the word 'we' advisedly, having exchanged a little of ourselves with these remarkable folk. Once again, I realize just what a tenuous hold humanity has over this enigmatic continent.

Still the sirens wail, this time courtesy of the morning news. There have been bush fires from Sydney to Cairns. We don't rate a mention.

*

The wind has died and, with it, the apocalyptic sound of alarm bells. The bag is unpacked at last. Smoke-stained windows are cleaned, yards swept. The polish is out and the wallabies have abandoned the naked beach from whence they had watched their homes burn. A large blue-tongued lizard heads home across the now quiet and empty street. The cockatoos are already back.

It seems they don't mind their nuts being roasted!

Marco the Polo

5 a.m. I am already late. The sun is a couple of minutes ahead of me as I reach the beach. It is truly beautiful - a sight being shared by a few walkers and joggers.

It was then I stumbled into Marc and his teenage daughter, who had just completed a three- mile run along the sand, and were busy doing press-ups and sit-ups and other energetic things down amongst my ankles. As I was seriously embedded in the camera lens at the time, we all decided it was nobody's fault.

Apologies over, Marc and I got talking - to the evident discomfort of the young lassie. Adolescence, sweat and strangers don't mix.

Yet for me, the fortuitous meeting was a memorable one and for all the right reasons. Marc is a new Australian and epitomizes what this country stands for now, and has stood for in the past. Released from gaol in a communist Poland after serving a sentence for pro-Solidarity activities in the Gdansk shipyards, Marc left his home and Europe behind forever. Within ten years he had learned to speak English like the Aussie he has become; has a successful business associated with the burgeoning tourist trade; got himself several Aussie kids and a home with a swimming pool...... and dawns such as these.

He also has a pride in his new country which is nothing short of inspirational - much like our own migrant families.

I find it hard to tear myself away, but we all have more running to do. They have three miles of sand to cover before breakfast and work or school, and I need to find a spot to zoom in on that pod of four dolphins who have just decided to cruise the shore.

Grafton

The road to and from Grafton, following the coast is called the South Pacific Highway: Route 1 - the equivalent to Britain's M1.

For thirty-five miles we have travelled through forest decimated by last Sunday's fires. Smoke rises from both sides of the road, so thick in places that it blots out the sun. An occasional flame bursts from the ash carpet - a sight to re-kindle strange feelings in the lower body.

A forlorn signpost - a charred survivor - shows the way to Minnie Waters, seventeen miles down a minor road. Minnie Waters, cut off by the fires, where homes were lost and several badly injured fire fighters had to be air lifted to hospital.

The signpost brings it home to you, and my feelings of relief at being spared from our own brush with nature's venom now make me feel very guilty indeed.

The scale of devastation is enormous. No wonder we didn't rate a mention on the news channels.

*

We had company at lunch and didn't mind a bit. The elderly farmer and his equally wrinkled wife were a fountain of information and stories: sixty years of fighting the land before retiring to Coffs Harbour and civilization.

"The Big 'Un," he nodded at the still, brown water behind me.

And the Clarence River is a big 'un. Discovered by Richard Craig, an escapee from the brutalities of convict life, it destroyed him. There he was, full of relief at getting away, full of hope for the future. He would find a boat or walk to China – only to find the width and might of the Clarence an unassailable barrier. He gave himself up.

"I've seen it miles wide."

"Eighteen times dear," said the long suffering wife. She'd heard all this before - probably more than once. "And the rest of the time, shared baths, careful with this and that, carrying the washing-up water out to the veggies."

I got the distinct impression she was pleased to be living in the city now, with all the mod-con's; - like water that comes out of taps. There is no way the Water Board is going to get this lady to save water by drinking beer.

The old man didn't hear her. "When it's like that, the force of the fresh water pushes the salt right back to the sea."

"How come Grafton ended up being built here....? Thirty miles inland," I asked.

"Trees: Red cedars. Gone now, of course," he replied.

Yet Grafton has not just exploited. It gave something back. As long ago as 1873 the city fathers' had gone green. There are now six thousand trees in the three hundred streets of this beautifully-preserved town. It must be like living in an arboretum: Trees with wonderful names like London plane, Illawarra flame, Biblical fig, ombu and many more.

But none can compare with the jacaranda. From between two to three weeks each November its mauve - hyacinth blue flowers fill the air with a sweet, sickly scent and carpet the pavements with spent petals. When you drive down the city avenues, it is as if you are driving through a blue haze. Wonderful: Intoxicating.

"Your boys didn't want to keep farming then?" I have this annoying habit of allowing my mouth to operate without first engaging the brain.

"No!" It was the old lady, her voice strident: Adamant. "It's too hard a life for anyone." The tone softened. "I don't blame them."

In my usual way I had blundered into something best left alone.

"No," the old farmer said slowly. "It was hard: Very hard at times, like now. No rain means no grass; but I keep on coming back."

By the Clarence, picnicking under the shade of the jacaranda, I could understand why.

To worry, - or not to worry

There is something about an outstretched towel and carefully placed shoes lying on a deserted beach. You see them and you become a mental wreck. Your eyes display a will of their own as they frantically search the ocean, then the beach, then the ocean. You start to pray you will see a head bobbing in the water - then you realize that you don't want to see anything in the water at all. In particular, you don't want to see someone lying on their back with an arm raised: the code for HELP!

I am not a strong swimmer. Even the granddaughters out-swim me. What could I do? Go and get them?

Still no one on the beach - and it's three miles long. Still no one in the water - and it stretches to Hawaii.

Has the rip got him?

Do I report the towel and shoes?

Please let me see someone, or no one.

Nothing to do but walk on!

Hours later the towel and shoes have gone home: Another mystery on a perfect day in paradise.

Some tips from a booklet entitled: 'How to survive the summer.'

The usual things: never swim alone; avoid the rips.
But how about this one: "If the shark alarm sounds, do leave the water."
As if they need to worry.....

Rain at last

Australia! Land of Sunshine! And what have we got? Rain! Four days of it.

News flash! Bush fires are now out. There is enough water in the reservoir for another sixteen weeks. The locals are happy. Australia is happy. Even the weatherman on the telly is happy - even though he didn't see it coming. Everyone is happy - except me. Selfishly, I like sun.

Rain: The grass has greened overnight. Even the charcoal bush is sprouting.

Rain: It's hard to sleep. Water now fills an old wallow outside our window, and the frogs and toads, buried alive in mud and unnoticed for years, now fill the night with their songs of freedom and love.

Rain: Lashings of it. We meet an old chap on the beach: Shorts and a brolly - the Australian answer to humidity. He's lonely. We're wet, but what the hell. We stand talking, ignoring the deluge, and the sweat trickle down our backs.

Rain: It does not deter the surfboarders. Young and still bronzed, they hurry past to the warm water of the South Pacific, with no time for anything except a 'G'day.'

Rain: No worries.

Dreamin'

What do Sawtell in New South Wales, and Aberystwyth in the Wales of the United Kingdom, have in common?

On the face of it - not a thing!

Sawtell: Sunny, twenty-six degrees, the sea like a warm bath and today, the near-deserted beach has captivated a child. He was all of two years old, and with a spade in one hand, and a small pail in the other, he imitated "Dadda."

Sun-tanned, slim 'dadda,' was dressed only in skimpy bathers and his ego. He is the sort of bloke that you just hate. Even in his near-naked state he was as flash as a rat with a gold tooth. Anyway, he held his spade tight in both hands, and with his bucket strategically placed, he dug furiously here and there as he tried to unearth [or should that be unsand?] worms to use as bait in a later fishing expedition. He tells us, pleasantly, that "They're biting," but as you know by now, not being a fisherman I thought he was talking about the mosquitoes.

Anyway, dadda went this way whilst the kid chucked sand that way - all over their kindly old dog. The dog shakes itself noisily. Father turns around to see nothing but harmony. He continues to dig - child covers dog again, and then helps out by whacking the long-suffering canine over the head with his little shovel. The dog shakes itself and lets out a little wheeze. It is either too old or too comatose to bother.

Dad looks around, to view nothing but harmony.

Child smothers a passer-by, who is not too pleased to have his sun screen plastered. Dad digs on oblivious.

A nice little cameo - which brought back memories from years gone by and from a world away.

Aberystwyth: July. Cold, windy and wet: It is impossible to get onto the beach without frostbite or exposure setting in. The miserable holiday break is enlivened for eternity by a dear friend and his less-than-dear dog.

Take our friend, who, totally lost in his own world, is attached to his docile, old Labrador by a long, leather, umbilical cord. Together they wander the rain swept streets, mirror images in remoteness. We tag along behind as they indulge in frequent doggy stops, where the dog does the usual things that dogs do, usually involving bodily functions and the smelling thereof. The day saunters away.

Imagine a bus stop. A queue of the wet and weary: Pale faces protrude from cagoules and plastic rainwear. A more complete picture of misery I cannot easily imagine. The dog stops again. The owner stops, still staring vacantly into the future whilst idly picking his nose.

Now, Labradors are big dogs - and when they decide to cock their legs in earnest, they can pee buckets. And this one did.

Heads turn aghast. A dumb struck silence hits the queue as the lady's shopping bag, brimming with bread and milk and stuff, fills to overflowing. The unbelieving silence continues as the dog finishes off, smiles [I swear it] and then leads off its unmindful owner into my reminiscences.

When things go wrong

What a day! Hardly one to remember for the right reasons, yet on reflection it wasn't all bad. Reflection, aided by the consumption of a bottle of chardonnay - a most necessary palliative, to help in the relaxing process, after yet another round of bureaucratic blunders which have caused the stress levels to rise.

Cock-ups! Yes! But hardly in the same league as those perpetrated by a Mr Warburton back in 1873, who between April and December, had travelled across the country from South Australia to Western Australia. He was the first white man to do the journey, but was so bad an organiser and leader that his 'team' had to strap him to his horse and travel like blazes by night to avoid the certain death he had in store for them.

No. Not that bad. But answer me this. Why is it that people seem to be unable to complete the simplest task required of them? Is it just since the advent of computers that we, as a species, have become brain dead? Or is it the much heralded decline in educational standards, so that now 'A-B-C's and '1-2-3's have become academic Everest's?

I know this will strike a chord with every reader, for who hasn't stood at a supermarket checkout and waited, and waited, and waited for the operator to prod the machine into subtracting one dollar fifty cents from two dollars?

But I'm babbling. A page gone already - so I had better get on with it. So what happened today?

First, the credit card had a melt down. I will say it was not my wife's fault. It had nothing to do with her punching wrong button after wrong button at the hole-in-the-wall banking machine - all in front of an ever-lengthening queue. She suits a red face which turns scarlet when the machine asks her "Do you need more time?" "Press yes or no:" No, that was nothing to do with it.

But that was the overture. The main event consisted of an illiterate who had rented out accommodation on which we had paid a deposit month's ago. To rub salt into the wound, he now wanted to double the previously agreed rental. I cannot stand people not doing what they are paid to do, and this guy has got me drinking beer instead of afternoon tea. A first!

A swim: A meal: A bit of shopping: The renewal of old friendships - but all overshadowed today by idiots, computers and/or both.

Three beers and several wines later I begin to wonder. In truth, in an alcoholic haze, I begin to question my initial arithmetic. Perhaps it was me misreading the invoices: It could have been an eight, not a three: Perhaps I'm the modern-day equivalent of Warburton the Wally.

Fruity Footy

At last it's here: the sporting event of the decade, if not in the whole history of Coffs Harbour - if you can believe the hype that has been going on for weeks.

A record crowd of eleven thousand, eight hundred and seventy-nine fans - plus my wife Patsy - eagerly pack the International Stadium for a double header. Not some obscure Aussie game, but two games of Rugby League back-to-back. It's enough to make grown men swoon and Patsy yawn. Some of the best rugby league teams in the world are on show. The Brisbane Bronco's take on the Dragons from Wollongong way - and the Newcastle Knights are pitched against the big time boys from Sydney.

Thirty seconds into the first game and Patsy realises, "It's just like rugby in England."

"Yes love."

"But I don't like rugby in England."

"Ah!"

At this point I must admit to a little obtuseness to get my wife to come to the games. Somehow she thought she was going to see an Aussie Rules match. After all, she had enjoyed a red wine called 'Aussie Rules' and in her alcoholic debility had said, "Why not?"

"Come on Ref! Get a grip!"

"Look at those kids making a slide on the mud. I'd kill our John if he came in covered like that."

"Oooh! The winger's dropped it. What a ....." I was enjoying myself immensely.

"He's plastered."

I tear myself away: "Who? Not the winger surely?"

"Him! That's seventeen cans of beer he's had already."

"Don't point," I urge. He was bigger than me. "Brilliant. Did you see that, love? Incredible skill:"

The cheers rise to the twelfth try of the night.

"Oooh look! Fruit bats: They're after the insects in the floodlights," said my wife, still pointing.

"By the heck he's a hard man. Did you see him? Four blokes he took out."

"The grog shop is being stocked up again. That's the third time..... And that drunk's back."

"Don't point. Look at that number five run, Patsy..... Patsy! Where are you going?"

"It's trying to rain."

"It won't be much. Come on you Knights."

"If it's not going to be much why are people wrapping themselves in tarpaulins? And look at that drunk. He can't get his poncho on." She started laughing uncontrollably.

"Oooh! What a tackle. Did you....."

"Can we go home?"

"But....."

One cold stare was sufficient. It contained enough ice to send the fruit bats into hibernation. But this is a man's game and I know how to deal with the situation.

"Yes love," I replied manfully. "Only stop pointing at....."

Animule Tales

"Where have you two been?"

"To see some animules," answered Emily, six years old with lively, flashing, dark eyes and close-cropped brown hair.

"And what sort of animals have you seen?" I prompted.

Jessica, a year older than her sister, twisted her long fair locks around her index finger. "Dolphins," she said shyly.

"Yes, dolphins," added Emily not to be outdone.

"Were the dolphins nice?" their Nanna asked.

"There wuz three of 'em."

"Were Emily," corrected Grandma.

"Were what?"

"Were three."

"Yes, three."

"And we touched them," interrupted Jessica, no doubt trying to restore some semblance of sanity.

"And stroked them:" Emily again.

Then Jesse: "And fed them."

I was getting a bit dizzy, even before Nanna asked, "What else did you see?"

Then the words came like a torrent, tumbling over themselves in excitement.

"A seal called Nicky."

"You know he kissed all the girls."

"He smelled of fish."

"We stroked the fairy penguins."

"And fed them."

"And a walla.....I can't remember," said Emily, looking chastened by her failure.

I do my David Attenborough impersonation: "Wallabies."

"Yes! That's it!" Her Celtic gloom disappeared immediately.

"We stroked them as well."

"And pelicans."

"I liked the dolphins best. Bucky....."

"Zippy....."

"And Calamity," stated Jessica with some finality. "We didn't want to leave them, did we Em?"

"No," agreed Emily, with a pensive frown that quickly changed to a cheeky grin. "But we fed a shark!"

"Two!"

"You fed sharks?" I was aghast: "How?"

"Oh, you just hold the fish like this....." Both kids extended their right arms and pinched first finger to thumb.

"Oh!" I didn't want to know. Change of subject. "What else was there?"

"Mmmh," mused Jessica, forefinger pressed to her lips: a study in concentration. "Kangaroos:"

"We played with 'em," said Emily.

"Them Emily! Did you remember what granddad said about the 'roo's?"

"Yes, Nanna.....Only approach a 'roo from the side: - Never in stand in front, or behind."

"Well done!" I said. I'm not a fan of kangaroo. Not quite true - dead ones are O.K., especially smoked and done up in a plum sauce. But live ones can be nasty beasts, disembowelling the unsuspecting with an uppercut kick. Just in passing, and totally irrelevant, male kanga's frequently chase and attack female joggers: Something to do with the monthly cycle.

"What about koala's? Did you cuddle one?"

Two crestfallen, watery-eyed girls: In unison, "No Nanna."

Jessica takes over. "The man said they get stress, so we can't touch them any more."

I think the world has gone mad. In fact, now I am sure of it. I defy anyone to think of a less stressed animule than the dopey koala. It sleeps twenty hours a day, drugged up to the eyeballs on eucalyptus leaves - the hippy of the animal kingdom.

I shake my head in disbelief. Feed a shark - yes. Play with unpredictable kangaroo - by all means. Get kissed by a sea lion with large teeth - that's a good laugh. Zoos put platypus on display, caring less that the 'exhibit' will die within weeks. Who cares? Pop in another one - they pull the crowds.

BUT DON'T CUDDLE A KOALA!

The kids see my dismay. "It's alright, granddad. They've all been rescued."

"Rescued from where my loves?"

"Silly granddad! From the wild of course!"

Think about it!

The Yarn

We have been around Australia enough to know something about 'the yarn.' Australians tell a good story about everything and anything, from historic pub fights to ordeals in the Outback. Some are perfectly true; others embellished 'a bit.' Who's to know?

The rain, well cloudburst, showed no sign of running out of cloud. We flee to the clubhouse. 'Greens Closed' signs unnecessarily sprout and blossom in our wake. As gutters fill and the road pools, we drip, and sip shandy in the company of other refugees. The weather is a great ice breaker and before long I'm tempted to recount a yarn.

"On a day like this I can believe the story that one bloke had to sit up a tree for two weeks with water swirling around his feet. For food he lived on green snakes that floated past. Wrung their necks and ate 'em raw."

Freda, a happy widow, ["He left me very nicely thank you"], and Eric, a balding fugitive from stress inspired by technology and a former wife, proved far better storytellers.

"That's not unusual," said Freda taking up the challenge. "I used to live at Narrabri....."

"Been there," I encouraged.

"Well, you'll know then that it's on a plain: Flat as a pancake with mountains all around. It had been raining like this for days."

[On our visit, Narrabri was one of the driest places we had ever seen - narrowly pipped for the honour by the Sahara Desert.]

"Well, two in the morning it was, and we were woken by someone banging on the door. It was a policeman. "Water's comin'! Get out now!" he shouted, and was off. No chance of using the car 'cos a wall of water was coming from everywhere, draining off the mountain ranges and filling the plain like a sump. It was frightening, I can tell you. You want to run but can't and just have to watch it come. Only one thing for it. We grabbed bedding, some bread and cans of baked beans and stuff like that. And water. We spent three freezing nights and three burning days under a blanket on the unfinished roof of the new two-storey school: Holes in the roof everywhere. No fun with three kids let me tell you."

Not to be outdone, Eric joined in. "You've been to Lightning Ridge haven't you?"

"Yes," my wife and I replied in unison. Nervous sweat sprang immediately onto my forehead and my twitch twitched.

"Remember those flood level marker poles stretching for miles and miles along the only road?"

"How can we ever forget; it gives you the jitters. One eye on the road and one on the sky, just in case it looks like rain."

"Well, I never did get to the Ridge," Eric continued. "I started, but the rain came. Just as heavy as this it was. The water must have been fifteen feet deep. When I couldn't get no further I stopped and made the mistake of getting out of the car. Mossies! Big as blow flies covered me from head-to-toe in seconds. An old bushman told me once that there was only two ways to deal with them. Let them drink their fill - or cover yourself with mud. Neither seemed a good idea, but I reckon I was a pint of blood short by the time I jumped back in the car. I ain't been back since."

I looked at the torrent outside, sighed deeply and thankfully sank my schooner.

"Another beer anyone?"

Life's hell!

The Storm

The good news is that a couple of nights ago the sunset was memorable. The sky was Lucifer red, with sinister fingers of long, black cloud glowering over a black and sullen sea. The swell moved listlessly, as though the entire ocean was comprised of a thick oil slick. The whole scene was eerie. In fact, looking back now I think a better adjective would be malevolent. It was as if some hellish creature was stirring itself, before easing out of the ocean depths to reek vengeance on the unsuspecting.

However, at that time I saw no harbinger of evil, and apart from a silent curse at not having my camera with me, I did not give a second thought to the signs revealing themselves. Maybe I should have - although actually I could not have done anything to alter the course of events.

The bad news is that what we had witnessed was the approach of a low pressure system heading slowly down the coast from the tropics. A tropical cyclone, force three, was coming our way. When you consider that a force four destroyed the city of Darwin on Christmas Day back in 1974, you should understand why our bums are starting to twitch. A cyclone this far south is unusual but not unknown.

I remember someone telling me that the last time that this had happened it had taken a train, three-and-a-half days to reach Brisbane - a mere six hours north. Tourists on a day's four-wheel drive adventure had been cut off by raging rivers and fallen trees, their planes leaving without them.

This time; seven inches of rain: Not too bad - but in the first hour! And hailstones! Not the golf ball-sized ones we were warned about - but hail, nonetheless. And it is as hot as Hades. Unbelievable! Our other experiences of bad weather and bent palm trees are as of nothing compared to this. One person has already died in the floods. Brisbane is cut off from the south. The Pacific Highway, the main arterial north - south route, is closed all over the place because of landslides, lying water and collapsed bridges. Schools close early. Our harbour is closed as twenty foot high waves break across its entrance. The coastguard issue a warning: "Anyone stupid enough to go out there, are on their own: We aren't coming to get you."

Strangely, the winds accompanying Cyclone Violet are not frightening. Sure, there is a good blow on, with trees down, banana plantations flattened and cars turned over; but they are not the gut wrenching, howling, fearful winds of our imagination.

So we brave the elements, as the rain eases to a respectable one inch per hour. We can take it. We have walked the Northumbrian coast in January - and anyway, we want to look at the sea. At first I don't recognize it as our ocean, a place to walk, to hold hands whilst you dawdle along, or a place to splash in the shallows. To a round-the-world yachtsman I suppose it would not amount to much, but to me it is mountainous and hateful, and has the unrelenting noise of an express train setting records.

Needless to say, what is left of the beach is washed clean of people and deserted, except for the seabirds. They stand forlorn, backs into the gale, and don't even bother to move as we walk through them in a bemused search for the missing sand dunes. Millions of tons of sand, several feet in depth, have just gone.

Even the Aussies, who for so long have prayed for rain and welcomed every passing shower as their saviour, have had enough.

Lost in Wild Cattle Creek

"I must be as thick as a plank." I cursed myself, my fellow lost souls and Australia for the hundredth time that day - under my breath, of course. To curse out loud would brand me as a "whingeing Pom," but uncharitable, unspoken thoughts are non-punishable. So I suffer in silence.

In fact, the day had started well enough: A pleasant walk in good company in the forests of Wild Cattle Creek, following a trail of red ribbons through never ending eucalyptus. Why? To find Arthur McQuilty's tree, of course - a monster somehow missed by the marauding loggers of yesteryear.

I thought the red ribbon trail a charming gesture to eco-tourism. Not that any tourist would find Wild Cattle Creek, let alone this particular tree. We are here, courtesy of friends and members of one of the many local walking clubs.

Anyway, we found Arthur's tree. And a very fine specimen it is, too. We joined in a peculiar Australian custom by holding hands around its base. It took nine of us with outstretched arms to encircle the giant, soft-barked tallowwood. Even with the observance of this rite completed, no one seemed to know why Arthur, a bullock driver and axeman, should have a tree named after him. Of such, yarns are born.

So far it has been as easy as a Sunday afternoon's walk in the Cotswolds and happily off we go down the Bopan Road to a hidden waterfall. Now, don't let the word 'road' fool you. 'Road' seems to be defined as anything from a Sydney freeway to, as in this case, a dried up and collapsed riverbed on which no tree is growing - for the moment.

But our goal is Battery Falls. Set in the middle of a sub-tropical rainforest, on the Little Nymboida River, they are well worth seeing: Australia at its very best. The falls also provide the highlight of the day - a surprised five foot long goanna. Just too please us, it promptly fled up onto the lower branches of a tree, from where it nonchalantly observed the excited crowd far below.

At this point the day started to go downhill fast - just like the ample rump of the rock-climbing lady. Unfortunately, I was next in line to make the ascent and, purely in self defence I placed my hand on her toppling backside. I may as well have put a twig across the path of a tidal wave. Down! All I got was what felt like a dislocated wrist and moments later a dirty look from the imitation, upturned turtle.

Taking my chance, I shinned up the rock face without trouble, until a very nice lady with a walking stick took fright at being followed by a Pommey Bum-Toucher and let fly with a whippy branch. Smack! Right between the eyes! I wanted to cry. Instead I swore - quietly - just as I lost my footing, parted company with the rock and tumbled back to make two fat bums at the bottom of the little cliff. Worse! I had let go of the expensive sunscreen, which slowly toppled with a final plop into the green, slimy stink hole. Hand in water, with a silent prayer of thanks that all I got for my courage was a single leech. Remove it and swear.

After all this, I would not have been surprised to learn that the Battery Falls had got their name from assault and battery. But no! Instead it was derived from the rock-crushing equipment used by the gold miners of a hundred and some years ago. I am pretty convinced no one has been anywhere near this place since. Certainly none of our group has, as we are soon LOST.

More goanna's and small brown snakes disappear grudgingly from our path as we crash through the virgin bush. I wonder if I'm the only one who has the equation - small, baby brown snakes equal large mummy brown snake - going around inside his head. The snakes disappear under fallen, charred trees - trees which happen to bar our way. Question: Over or around? As the detour could be several hundred yards - uphill - we all become champion hurdlers. Leeches, and barbed 'wait-a-while' thorn bushes, add to our woes. All I need is the ferocious stinging tree to really make my day. Their venom has horrific effects on the skin and respiratory tract. "I must be as thick as a plank!"

Pleasingly, I'm not the only one having doubts, as evidenced by one of the Australian ladies who, for no apparent reason, comes out with: "I've got to go to Harvey Norman's this afternoon." I feel like telling her that there is no chance of getting to his furniture store when, in answer to her prayers, we stumble across the old forest track we had left nearly two hours before. It had to be the right track – there is only one - and there we are, fifty yards from the cars and nowhere near where we thought we were going. But who cares! The relief is wonderful.

Relief - and a lesson learned. It is strange how vulnerability creeps up on you. It is easy to remove yourself further and further from any sign of civilization, and by doing so you unwittingly accept more and more responsibility for your own safety and actions in a totally alien environment. More frightening still is the fact that you don't even know it's happening until it is too late.

Deep in the forest, and now under the spell of the wondrous calling of the bell birds, we mentally and physically fortify ourselves over a relaxed, if late, lunch. The hardships of this land disappear as quickly as the chicken drumsticks.

The day finishes at an abandoned saw mill by a creek in Timmsvale - a surreal experience, where machinery made in Birmingham and Wolverhampton, twelve thousand miles away, rusts in perfect silence. There is a monument to T.B. Timms nearby, which celebrates, "This pioneer's frugal and simple life:" A monument to ordinary people who cut a life out for themselves in the wilderness, even if it is a wilderness of indescribable beauty.

They deserve such memorials.

Dorrigo

Gob-smacked!

Every time I pass through Dorrigo it happens. I need to explain, and yet how can I, when I don't understand it myself. I find words so difficult at times.

The township sits atop the Great Dividing Range, and the best said about the only road to it from the coast, clinging perilously as it does for its very existence to the mountain side, is that it has very nice views - if you dare look. Waterfalls cascade across your path before disappearing into the dense jungle on the other side of the road. These rivulets continuously feed the beautiful and serene Bellingen River, several thousand feet below, where the delightful and historic village of that name nestles at the foot of the mountains, giving no inkling at all of the tortuous journey ahead.

How on earth anyone got a road up here in the first place is a miracle, yet it's a great pity those early settlers never came back to finish it. But if you want to go inland - to experience the joys of giant boulders and waterfalls and swamps in the National Parks at the Guy Fawkes River or at the Cathedral Rock - then up you have to go.

And Dorrigo awaits. It is centred on a crossroads where the imposing edifice of the pub takes pride of place - or would have done, were it not for the War Memorial slap bang in the middle of the road junction.

This country has many testaments of remembrance. Some are the national treasures at Canberra and Melbourne; others are to be found in every tiny hamlet throughout this vast land. Remembrance of the war dead is part of their living heritage - a people proud of their past, their courage and their achievements. Of course, an argument could be made that it is exactly the same in Britain, and I am not arguing against that fact. But what is staggering is that here we are two-and-a-half thousand feet up a mountain, overlooking tropical forest which falls away to the very shores of the South Pacific. Up here life is a struggle - even now. How hard it was a century ago is unimaginable to me. From here, Europe is as alien as the dark side of the moon and just about as relevant. Yet from Dorrigo, and a thousand places like it, men left everything - families, land, homes, - for European wars which had nothing to do with their reality.

Now, some are names in marble, yet they still have an effect on the Australian psyche, even today: And on me. I have a mixture of feelings. I feel humble and grateful; and in me there is stirred an affinity to this place which passes all understanding.

The current crop of politicians are talking and acting as though the only relationship that matters is the 'special' one with Asia. Sorry fella's! You might like it to be, but we are bound together by much more than cash flows and balance sheets.

Forever Lost

As you know, two of our grandchildren are out from England on holiday. So far they have been 'misplaced' in Taronga Park Zoo, overlooking Sydney Harbour, and at a rather pleasant vineyard in the Hunter valley.

In fact I understand the eldest, Jessica, is getting a complex about it all. "You know granddad, sometimes I think mummy and daddy want to lose me."

Today we are all doing the Wonga Walk in a World Heritage-listed rainforest near Dorrigo. It is set high on the Great Dividing Range, with wispy clouds caught amongst the tallest trees, and is home to about a hundred and twenty bird species. The bell birds are in raptures, and the waterfalls fill the valleys with the noise of rushing water and rainbows: A truly beautiful, enchanting, magical place.

A half-shout and I turn in time to see seven year old Jessica clinging by her fingertips to the crumbling edge of our path. She was slipping in slow motion down a near vertical, fifty-foot drop. Oblivion awaited: Mum races to the outstretched hand and hauls the whimpering young 'un back in.

Well done, mum! The myth about trying to lose the kids has been well and truly put to rest.

Not only that, but I remember having to do the same for Jessica's mum a quarter of a century ago. Mind you, that was in Roundhay Park in Leeds, where the only thing to fear was a few scratches from the thorns of the waiting rose bushes.

Different in the rainforest: Survive the fall and start to worry about the creepies: snakes, spiders, giant ants, hairy caterpillars and, possibly worst of all, the endemic stinging trees.

Not that we have seen any wildlife. Having pointed out the stinging trees to the youngsters as something to be avoided at all costs, the morning was constantly punctuated by shouts of, "There's one! There's one!"

"I saw it first."

"No you didn't."

"Yes I did!"

"There's another one."

They enjoyed the 'rude' story about how early explorers used any large leaf as toilet paper. They used the leaves of the stinging tree only once.

Noise equals no wildlife, but I didn't care. At least the kids could identify the tree which has been known to kill, or more commonly cause great pain for up to six months. They were safe - then Jess fell over the precipice.

Safe! How stupid of me. I have often mentioned the Australian, 'devil-may-care' attitude. I admire it for the most part, but it can be taken too far. Maybe it's my Englishness showing through, or my paternal instincts, but dangerous paths, and poisonous trees growing over them, do seem to be a little extravagant when you are encouraging families to go walk-about in a rainforest.

Back home, safe and sound, to find a baby goanna, just four foot long, mooching around by the back door.

Trial Bay, near Macksville

Trial Bay was named after the brig called Trial, which was shipwrecked here in 1817 after being stolen by convicts.

And what a place to be washed ashore! This is yet another piece of heaven on earth. Not a cloud in the sky and the water as warm as a hot bath, as it gently laps the sandy bay.

Out on the bluest, clearest water, several hundred small sailing boats paint an ever changing picture with their multi-coloured canvas. A living Ken Done masterpiece blessed by God Himself: A joyful, fantastic place which brings a tear to the eye.

I turn and face the headland. The walls of the convict prison stand tall and strong, even after all this time. The building is bleak and chills the mood immediately, but its evil pull is all-powerful. You cannot resist entering. The cells and cages still smell - of damp, of fear, of bodily functions. The flogging posts scream, but silently now.

Up on the sunny ramparts we walk in the footsteps of the exiled guards, and all the while I am beset by emotion and questions. Did our James Moresby have to endure such cages, such punishments - if not here, then in similar penitentiaries? Would our Jimmy Angell feel at home walking such walls as these? Or would he be appalled by the cruelty of a system he was helping to perpetuate. Was that why he deserted?

I look down from the stone parapet at the ghastly horrors at my feet; then turn to gaze out over unsurpassed beauty.

Australia: Once again at its enigmatic best.

Chasing Shadows

There are two photographs I have wanted to take in Australia.

The first is for sentimental reasons. We married in 1966, with five quid in the building society - all that stood between us and the poor house. So skint were we that we used to have to hide from the milkman when he embarked on his weekly cash-collecting fetish.

I was on the night shift. Now the life of a uniform beat constable back then was not made of the stuff which fills our television screens today. There was nothing romantic about working from ten at night until six the following morning - time spent shaking hands with shop door handles. Those were long, dark, cold, wet and windy, frequently lonely, Yorkshire nights.

I used to interrupt my patrolling for as long as I dared without incurring the wrath of my cunning and ferocious sergeant. The unscheduled stop was always to peer into the cheapo, arty-farty shop. The reason: a framed picture of the sea. I could stare indefinitely at those serried rows of huge breakers rushing the beach. Every blue imaginable, tipped with the expectant white froth of a wave ready to explode.

On that miserable, litter-strewn street with only rats and cats for company, the vision freed my spirit, gave me my dreams.

The picture cost four pounds, nineteen shillings and eleven pence old money. We bought it. The poor milko had to wait.

We bought it - the picture and the dream. It graced our home for years - hard years in many ways - but it never failed to give us joy. Eventually it faded and took its leave.

Now, thirty odd years later, I record wave after wave with my pocket instamatic, seeking to reproduce our perfect picture - or perhaps our youthful dreams. One day I'll get it right and the result will grace the walls of our old age.

Photo number two fires my creativity - what little of it I have. This one thought dominates every beach walk.

Lend me your imagination for a minute. Picture a deserted beach, nothing to impinge upon its perfection: yellow sand, an ocean without ripples, all stretching away to infinity. Between the bright yellow and the sea is a strip of dark, wet sand left by the retreating tide. It mirrors the sky. Add a flight of gulls skimming low, creating patches of quick moving, dappled shade across nature's tapestry. I want a picture of that! It shouldn't be hard - should it?

I've failed. Failure! For eighteen months! There have always been birds. They fly too high, or, camera shy, they veer away. They sneak up from behind - and depart before I get to think about camera settings. They have even refused to fly as I approach, madly flapping my arms and shouting. They look over their shoulders and waddle away, with disdain showing in every feather.

I have had kids, other people's dogs and even my long suffering wife, chase hordes of them - only for them to rise into the air and leave - but always waving two fingers at the camera.

The good news is that today was the perfect picture - what I've longed for, planned for, craved. Simply mind boggling as seabirds came from miles around to engage a shoal of fish in mortal combat. The shadows, the beach, the sun, all conspired to make for perfection.

The bad news is that I was in the surf and twenty yards from the camera. Ever tried to run in four feet of water?

Lusty Love

The bus stop is a good place to meet people. The naturally friendly folk want to talk during the usual Dee-Dee inspired wait.

Today has been no different, except that we are now convinced that the British Navy must be responsible for half of the emigration to Australia. We have just met the fourth bloke who came out here courtesy of the British taxpayer, saw, and said, "You've got to be joking. I'm stopping right here."

The Irish ex-Royal Navy man still spoke with the broad, singing Gaelic lilt after forty years of life down under. "Met my first wife on the Thursday and we married the next Tuesday. Eighteen-and-a-half years, good years, we had before she passed on to bigger and better things."

The American - Australian blonde, sitting to my right and therefore two seats away from Patrick, leaned forward. "I'm divorced."

Patrick continued, oblivious to the heaving cleavage. I wasn't oblivious to the naked breasts dangling in my lap - nor to the wife's hackles rising. I'd better look out. Better – I had better look anywhere except down.

Paddy: "My second wife is a good 'un to. We were married three days after we met and that was twenty years since."

The blonde sank back, taking her invitation and her breasts with her.

I was relieved, especially as the hackles by my side subsided.

"We separate once a year," he continued. "She goes off to her kids in Melbourne for a break and I just go off wherever Clancy's fancy takes me."

Revitalized by this availability the blonde sat forward again, her boobs even more dangerous. I was safe though - it wasn't me she was homing in on.

"I lived in the U.K. for fifteen years," she said. "I love it."

"I'll bet you do," murmured my wife uncharitably.

"Love to travel," she continued, pretending she hadn't heard. "I can't stand this heat. Ugh!"

Her hand wafted across her face. Patrick adopted an even more hang-dog look. "I can't afford to travel now. The Government took everything: My youth, my money. Everything except my accent and they ain't gettin' that."

Offer not so much rebuffed, more unnoticed, Miss America 1939 gave up and sank back in her seat, no doubt silently pleading for the bus to come and remove her from her failure.

In passing

Eighty-one days have passed since we stopped our wanderings around Australia. Eighty-one days without research, without worrying about our family's fading footsteps. For eighty-one days we have lived as Australians do, and for most of that time the days have been full of kaleidoscopic colour and tranquil, hallucinogenic shade.

The sea is always with us beyond the dunes: Ceaseless: Restless. Its voice carries to us on the summer breezes. The water will be incredible - as ever. You don't have to be on that crescent of sand to see it, to know its truth. A mosaic of deep indigo blue, giving way by degrees to turquoise and aqua where sandbars and hidden rock intrude on the vast blueness. And everywhere, the effervescent white tops of the rolling Pacific breakers.

The sky goes on forever. Blue. But for a pencil line of indigo, it would be impossible to see where it falls into the sea: Blue on blue. The clouds are high and wispy, at times cotton puff-ball white.

Sometimes, late in the afternoon, a storm builds over the mountains of the Great Dividing Range. The cloud balloons and darkens until it boils over the mountain tops and careers like an avalanche down onto the coastal plain, racing wildly to extinction in the all-consuming ocean.

Sitting here on a shaded veranda surrounded by the eucalyptus and banksia, parrots and lizards, it is easy for those who don't know to say, "Bor-ing." But boredom can have a special flavour all of its own. For the traveller, life is what you make it, wherever you are. Be alive. See what is about you and be content with it. Enjoy.

We have encountered nothing but friendship here. The Greek philosophers knew friendship as a special kind of love, philos. We feel blessed, as our lives have been allowed to touch the lives of others a world away. And yet we find similar desires, the same concerns and hopes and fears.

No, we cannot complain about our days here.

The nights we share with each other. A bottle of chardonnay or shiraz; occasionally a beer: A meal. All to the backdrop of deepening pools of light, which act as an oasis to a myriad of the living unknown. A frog and cricket symphony rises with the darkness. The night has a character of its own. I do not fear it, but my trouble is that I think too much. Sugar gliders and possum feeding on the tin roof become, during the drowsy, half-sleep periods, monsters devouring the ceiling tiles. Insects, hitting the fly screens with the force of charging second row forwards, force themselves into my dreams - funnily enough, dreams which have been transported from home, a world away. An animal or bird shrieks in fear and I become restless, longing for the dawn.

We phone home. The conversations are as clear as crystal. It is as though we are speaking face-to-face. No static. No twelve thousand miles. No satellites spinning in outer space. It is wonderful to be close to those you love the most, however briefly. Yet, the very contact you desire has the perverse effect of heightening your awareness to the fact that you are now on the periphery of their life. You are still wanted, but no longer needed. Fellow travellers beware.

The anxiety soon falls away, like a shawl from your shoulders, tranquillized by the ocean and sky and sun.

The mournful call of a distant train reaches the veranda and reminds us that our time here is at an end. I do not want to leave. And yet I do. Confused? So am I.

On the morrow we resume the mantle of research. We will be seen once again as holiday makers, or worse, tourists: Tomorrow we will begin our journey again - a journey which will lead us eventually to our other life in another place.

Southward Bound

The railway station at Sawtell must be one of the smallest ever built anywhere. The single platform is so small that the train has to continually nudge along so as to let people off and on. "Passengers in cars A, B and C please make their way to the rear of car B or the front of car C. Passengers in D, E, F and G make their way to crackle, crackle of car crackle or the front of car crackle." Was it D, E or B he said? For those who manage to disembark, no taxi awaits, no phone to get one, no staff to point, no toilet, no barriers, no tickets, no town centre, no nothing.

We find we aren't the only ones hailing the train and so heave a sigh of relief. Putting one's arm out to stop an express train on a deserted single track had not filled me with confidence. We need not have worried. Twenty arms waved. The driver waved back: And stopped.

Off south then: No, the compass has not gone awry. We forsake the heat of the Holiday Coast of New South Wales to backtrack. We need some time in the south of the state, and despite the critical remarks of the elderly about the need for conscription, the student travellers unknowingly entertained us throughout the journey.

They were obviously suffering the after effects of an end-of-term shindy, for almost at once bleary eyes closed and they were gone.

The resplendent conductor, polished brass buttons and all, was not impressed. He was not a party animal and took a malicious glee in waking each youngster in turn for a glimpse of the all-important ticket.

The rest must have done them good, for once they were awake their stomachs were on overtime. Each consumed croissants, crisps, biscuits and scones - with cream and jam, of course. All were devoured with frightening rapidity.

"They must have bellies like boilers," remarked my wife, as the famous Aussie meat pies arrived.

The knife covered in jam and cream spread the tomato sauce over the steaming pastry tops, before being used to stir the coffee: Three sugars.

By the time lunch arrived I felt as though I had put on three pounds in weight just by watching them. One orders lasagne. The others drool, straining their necks over seat backs to see that which is denied unto them. One grabs the lid of the micro-waved meal and licks it clean. Three others try to sub money from the contented lasagne eater. No good. To be fair, he had already coughed up loans to the tune of five dollars. The three disappear, only to return within five minutes with one coffee and one sandwich to share between them.

They have another five hours to go before we approach Sydney and they have no money left. Their long-suffering parents had better put a lock on the fridge.

*

It has to be said that it is not one of the great train journeys of the world; the journey down the central coast of New South Wales, that is. During the four-and-a- half hours from Newcastle to Wollongong a slow transition takes place, from areas of great beauty, to places where luxurious homes are embraced by coastline, lake shore, forest and rivers. It seems as though such places have no right to be replaced by a sullied suburbia. Then the coast once more: repeat the pattern, apparently ad infinitum.

And if I get bored, I like to people-watch. I make no bones about that - but I do get uncomfortable when it's me on the receiving end. A woman, you know - one of those nearly seventy year olds but will do anything to be fifty types - is sitting about two rows in front of us and continually turns and stares in my direction. From the way she is looking down her nose, she desperately wants Australian trains to adopt Britain's class segregation. She is definitely a first class kind of person - well, obviously rich; nobody wears shoes like that unless they have more money than sense: Sort of 'gold lame', with three-inch heels. The three ugly sisters would die for a pair of them. She doesn't compromise either: If she wants to wear a dark blue dress with matching, lined jacket, straight out of the pages of some fashion magazine, then the weather had better fall into line. It hasn't; it is hovering around the twenty-eight degree mark, but she shows no sign of discomfort; sweat is left to us lesser mortals. Anyway, she can't sweat; it would spoil her meticulous make-up - even though it has been applied with a trowel. Her hair looks a rat-tailed mess, but I bet it cost a bomb.

She looks again. Perhaps she doesn't like us eating cheese butties and drinking tea out of a flask at ten in the morning. We are obviously lowering the tone - but she is not to know that we were on the beach at five. This is our lunch time. It makes no difference. She tuts; turns to her husband and gives him grief. He looks over, his eyes appealing, like a real old Labrador about to visit the vet for the last time.

Her dangling, gold earrings jangle as she turns toward a new quarry. Four Yah-hoo's have arrived in the carriage. They look like death warmed up, probably been partying all night, but are still in good spirits, laughing and joking and mimicking the broad Scottish accent of the train driver each time he announces an approaching station.

More tut-tuts. More hubby haranguing. She sees nothing right with the young; I see nothing wrong with their generation - except I'm not one of them.

She cuts another look across at us. Could it be my wife's red and white legs, victims of hastily applied sun cream?

The insistent beep-beep-beep of a mobile 'phone saves us from further scrutiny: A business man tells the world where he hid his filing cabinet keys before he returns to the clack-clack-clack of his laptop computer. The beeping and clacking continue unabated for nearly four hours - even the unamused tutterer is worn down - eventually.

And so it continued. A sneaky look at us - could it be the matching white, lawn bowling hats? Her evident displeasure with life surfaced again and again. She did not like the Vietnamese woman who told everyone within earshot that she didn't like the Chinese and would rather live in Vietnam than in Australia. She did not like a pretty young thing [sex unknown], who paraded the length of the train showing off his or her body piercings. The double assegai in the belly-button was particularly nice. That got an extra tut - as did the hippy with no shoes, the unshaven, fat and fifty something alcoholic, and the loud New Zealander with a line in dirty jokes.

It was a long journey for Madam Tut; definitely longer for old Labrador-eyes who looked like he needed help. His face was by now as red as an Illawarra flame tree, whether from embarrassment, temper or blood pressure, I couldn't tell.

It was our turn again - and this time I got it. Odd socks! That's right! I was wearing odd socks. Now this might not matter much in England, where I have unwittingly been known to participate in this eccentric practice; long trousers cover silly mistakes....But in shorts!

There is nothing I can do about it but recall a story from my police days, involving an odd Detective Superintendent who had been sent at short notice to take charge of a large police station - a uniformed post. Now he had been in plain clothes for something like thirty years, and no longer had one piece of uniform which did not look like it came from the Boer War. It didn't fit anyway. His twenty-six inch waist, suitable for a young man joining from war-time submarines, had given way to the C.I.D. belly - a boozy fifty-six inches.

Jack couldn't see a problem; he had no intention of wearing uniform anyway. Then Remembrance Day came around and he had to attend the town's cenotaph with other civic dignitaries. A flustered search began: A borrowed shirt here; trousers there, and, from a cobwebby cupboard, a jacket complete with medals. So there he was, all done up like a turkey cock, except for his shoes: Brown, not regulation black. Not a pair could be found. "It'll be right," says Jack to himself. "Nobody'll notice a little thing like that. Nobody'll know I'm not in uniform. Nobody'll know the shoes must be black."

He put his doubts behind him and paraded down the street. A man approached - an old veteran, wearing the fabled red beret, "You're a brave man," he says. "Let me shake your hand." Jack is red-faced. He'd been discovered. He should have known better than to wear brown shoes. Still, nothing he can do about it now, so he spends a couple of uncomfortable hours worrying about his appearance.

"I'd like to shake the hand of a brave man," says an eight-foot tall Guardsman, as he slaps to attention in front of Jack and flings up a salute. The local press photographer sees a potential photo and snaps away.

Jack is upset, his hackles rising: If the Chief Constable sees that picture.....He's ready to fight his corner. "How do you mean?" he retorts to the bemused soldier.

"A Military Cross is one thing," comes the reply. "But an M.C. with Bar is something else. You're a brave man." He salutes and marches off.

"Er! Thank you," replies Jack to the retreating back and curses his borrowed jacket.

I return to the present. The four Yah-hoo's have fallen silent. Reason: a woman has entered the carriage; a startling woman, in fact. Black, wide-brimmed hat plonked on top of long, black matted hair; a man's see-through, black string vest; black shorts. If that is not enough to startle, add several tattoos. She cradles a rather scruffy baby in her arms, who turned from whingeing to yelling in pretty short order. The four Larakins acknowledge they are in the presence of greatness; respect must be shown to the dirty Madonna and Child, and so their silence continues.

The woman sits. The baby is obviously hungry and so a grimy breast is popped out for all to see. The child refuses to suckle the scrawny thing, despite repeated attempts by a perplexed mother. Eventually she holds the baby at arms length, looks directly into its eyes and says, in a Glaswegian accent which would have been more at home on a Saturday night in Sauchiehall Street, "Do ye want this or no? If no, ah'll gi' it that man ower there."

Old Tut-Tut's mouth falls open, eyes widening with incredulity, as her husband leans over and whispers in her ear, "Don't - say - another - bloody - word."

Journey 8
Southern New South Wales

Wollongong area and the coast

Pampered Pedigrees

Take twelve friends. Add five kids. Sprinkle liberally with alcohol and what do you have? Pandemonium: Hilarious pandemonium.

Once more we visit home-town Wollongong for another round of steaks n' snag's. Beneath a darkening sky we talk and laugh as only old friends can, yet wary of the careering, ankle-high Evil-Knevils'.

Stories come and go. Tales of yesteryear tantalize me - I'm always a sucker for a good yarn.

Transported from the south of England for poaching the fish of the rich and famous, a relative of one of our gathering had ended up working the land of someone else, rich if not famous, in the Hunter Valley. A herd of pedigree cattle is ordered to be sent from the old country, but the ship is wrecked off the coast and everything believed lost.

However, several months later, word came through to the property in the Hunter that these easily identifiable white cattle were roaming the bush south of Adelaide. Obviously they had swum ashore. So the storyteller's granddad and another bloke are sent by ship from Sydney to Adelaide, and from there went off and rounded up these poor, bemused, no longer pampered, pedigrees.

It took months.

Returning to Adelaide, they were in for a shock. The unloading procedures at the port consisted of throwing any animals into the sea for them to swim for it. Loading was a bigger problem: there was none. So off the intrepid stockmen go and surely this is a testimony to their loyalty and character which England did not need; they drove the herd back home - nearly two thousand miles!

"Stop it! Now!" One of the mums at screaming pitch.

No worries. It has nothing to do with me - just two three year olds getting into it with fists and head locks and toy swords.

"You'll both get one in the mouth."

That sound, logical reasoning worked well with the littlees, who commenced drag racing with their sisters' prams: Now sisterly tears.

"Don't know how they did it," rejoined the storyteller's mother-in-law. "I've been up that way on holiday and if two of you walk out of the cabin together, before the second one is through the door, number one is covered head-to-toe in mosquitoes. I couldn't cope!"

Maybe not, but I am sure the storyteller could. Born in the bush in the mid 1940s, his family had known hardship. Living in tents by a railway line, the family forever moving for work, they lived wherever and however, they could: Whitewashed newspaper for walls; braving snakes and floods. Yes! I'm sure the storyteller, like his granddad, could cope manfully.

Unfortunately, I couldn't. The mossies of the interior have sent their cousins to feed off my legs - and I'm wearing jeans - so I'm off indoors.

A Family Favourite for when you need a change from Steak n' Snags:
Butterflied Leg of Lamb: Serves 6.
Get the butcher to bone a leg of lamb for you. [To butterfly, means to cut the flesh diagonally every inch or so for about two-thirds of the way through the joint: The butcher will do it in seconds.]
Marinate the meat with the following:
One-third of a cup of Olive Oil, half a cup of lemon juice, 2 tablespoons of red wine vinegar, 2 cloves of crushed garlic, 2 tablespoons of fresh parsley, one teaspoon of oregano.
Put the marinade in the diagonal cuts as far as possible and then wrap the whole thing in tin foil.
Cook it on the barbee for about an hour or until ready.

From Lucker Street to Wongawilli

"Have yer seen the paper?" said Tom, as I walked in. His tall, rangy figure sprawled across the poolside chair - and despite his eighty-odd years, he was still in disgustingly good health, with a handshake fit to break fingers.

My eyes couldn't focus on the waving newsprint until he rejected it in favour of his twentieth 'nice cuppa tea' of the day. It was 11 a.m. Even then, I didn't know which piece he was referring to. It was a big news day and plenty of bold headlines vied for space: 'Croc attack! - Man loses arm!'; 'Child rushed to hospital' [spider attack]; 'New Jello found!' [New species of blue jellyfish:] - 'So vicious it must be on steroids', says victim'; 'Pathetic Poms!' [Here the Australian Government are being urged to deport the English geriatric cricket team, or charge them under the Trade Protection Act].

I decide to ignore the latest in cricketing disasters and instead start talking to Tom about his life.

"How on earth did you manage seventy five years ago, Tom? Mother Nature still seems to have the upper hand even today."

"It was hard, especially on the women folk," he mused.

"But there you were in Wongawilli, newly arrived from Lucker Street on cold, wet and dirty old Tyneside. No crocs there to have your arm away....."

"Nowt 'cept the pit: Plenty of accidents down there. When the men went off to work at four in the mornin' you never knew whether they'd come home again."

"But that was a fact of life; our people were born to it. But you, your family - to be dropped at Wongawilli, like spacemen into the Australian bush: Sun, spiders and all. How did you cope?"

"Well you had to. And you learned fast. It doesn't take you long to find out you'd better look under the chook first before putting your hand in for the eggs. Could be a snake in there first having his breakfast see? Brown, black or king - it doesn't matter. You look, boy!"

"And the family lived by the pit and the coke ovens," I stated. "There's a place called Bedlam in the Ironbridge Gorge where the Industrial Revolution started. It's rural Shropshire now, all peace and quiet, but the old coke ovens are still there, cut into the rock faces giving a hint of what it must have been like."

"Aye well! You really can't imagine what it was like out here. Coke ovens and a hundred degrees in the shade don't mix well. The Aborigines must have known what was coming to this place when they named it Wollongong. Know what it means?"

I shake my head.

" 'See! The monster comes!' - I don't suppose they were far wrong."

'26th November, 1834. The Government Gazette;
Town of Wollongong: Notice is hereby given that a site has now been fixed for the town.....'

It is incredible to think that, only six years earlier only thirteen white people had been there at all, living on Charles Throsby Smith's farm around the harbour. He had wanted to call it Bustle Town, which gives the reader an indication of the activity and pace of change, as coal, steel and industry boomed and then boomed some more.

A monster unleashed, given free reign. Displacement and disease reduced the local Aboriginal population from "about three thousand," in 1820 to thirty-three by 1899. Some monster!

I stop day dreaming. "Did you have all your own animals, Tom?"

"An old horse to get to town on and a cow: The cow was so full of ticks we used to get 'em in the milk. 'Spit 'em out,' said mother. 'They'll not hurt yer!' "

"Did you have your own house?"

"Aye - after we built it. Started off in a humpy - that's a one room wooden shack with a chimney. The cooking and living was done in that one room. We slept in the barn: Seven of us, bedroom furniture up one end and hay on the other. Used to lay in bed and watch the rats run the rafters. No toilet. Dig a hole and bury it: Didn't even get sewers around here until 1975."

"1975?" I ask incredulously.

"Yep! Built all these estates without sewers: The Dunny Can Man came once a week and carted it off: Unless they were on strike - which they were - often. Can't say I blamed them mind. When that happened it was back to burying it in your garden. He used to go to the pub for lunch and nobody batted an eyelid. He did stink rotten!"

[Let us try and put this in perspective. Can you imagine the suburbs of a major city only an hour by train from London - say Oxford - the housing estates of which had no sewers - in 1975?]

"It can't have been all hard slog and doom and gloom, Tom."

"No. We were better off here than in Lucker Street after the First War. Dad, as you know, was born in Scotland, like your grandmother, and the family moved to Tyneside – for work I guess. Whether that's what made him into an adventurer, I don't know, but he'd worked his passage to Australia, South Africa and America before the war. He joined up but was gassed and ended up back in Newcastle, where we went hungry. And, of course, there was the T.B. Everyone was frightened of that. I lost a sister to it. There was so much disillusion then. Even I remember it: But not here. We never went hungry and never heard of T.B. Do you know I'd never seen sausage strings hung up in the butcher's until I came here? I remember saying to mother, "What's them Ma? Coo's tits?"

And we laughed the day away, in the sun, by the pool. Lucker Street was a long way away and we were thankful for it.

That Photo!

I'm quite excited. On the beach at Shell Harbour today, flight after flight of sea birds [I dunno' what sort] skimmed the shimmering sand, their fleeting black shadow mesmerizing and imprinting the scene forever upon the eye of the beholder. Black shadows over a sea of every shade of blue imaginable; black shadows on brilliant yellows fringed with effervescent white. I have waited for this day for a long, long time. My photo is here - and today I'm going to get it. I blast off reel after reel of film, giggling like an excited schoolgirl.

Mind you, I had to work at it. For some reason, each clutch of birds veered away from the camera time after time. Tantalisingly close to perfection, but not quite right.

And I had to pay for it to. My wife and her cousin chatted and chatted, ignoring my pleasure, oblivious to the frustrations. On and on they walked, never pausing, leaving me trailing in their wake. Mind you, the gulls were flying into the wind, forcing me to walk backwards along their flight path. They were fascinating, so absorbing, I hardly noticed the waves reach my shorts, then the shirt. Shame about the hat, but never mind, I'll keep it on 'til it dries to the shape of my head.

Still I retreat. The girls had long gone around the tussocky, windswept headland when I fell backwards into a **** great hole - a trench so deep that a Sapper of the Great War would have been proud to put his name to it. Fortunately, it was half filled with brackish saltwater, so that my fall was broken rather than my neck. As I stuck my head over the parapet, my head was nearly shot off by a salvo of cormorants firing along the beach and only about two feet off the ground.

After so many years, the perfect picture: They could not see me in the hole; why had I not thought of this before. I snap away as happy as Larry - wet, but happy.

Too soon the birds have gone and so I start the long trek back. Around the headland, over burning rock, stabbing shale, ankle twisting pebbles, stinging bindy grass, rock pools with things in: it was horrible. It hurt, but it was all going to be worth it. I hobble to the car where the girls chat away. They decide to ignore my blood trail and I'm forced to prise my beach shoes out of my wife's hand - the ones she kindly held for a moment whilst I took a couple of photo's, an hour ago.

I just hope...

PS: It's three weeks later and the photographs have been developed. And the result.....Need you ask?

The Monk Market

The Buddhist Temple, with its ochre pagoda and the red tiles of its curved roofs, has become something of an attraction to people arriving from Sydney by road. Set on a hill overlooking Wollongong and near the ocean, it is totally out of place in a modernized western culture.

I like it for one reason.....I know to leave the freeway and turn right for the family home.

In Asia, temples blend into the landscape. They are an ancient and integral part of the fabric of that society. The monks have renounced all worldly possessions in an effort to become part of the all encompassing 'I.' In return they receive blessings of food from their grateful and understanding fellow citizens.

Not here. The lone monk, shaven headed, sandaled feet and flowing saffron robe, should be an ethereal figure – timeless: A teacher and a guide.

Not here. The sight of an Australian monk conjures up different images. I become transfixed by his hurrying gait and heavy load of shopping. Milk [skimmed of course,] tea bags and loads of cans, which I desperately try to catch sight of. Wouldn't it be good if it was beer - or a bottle of Coke? Anyway, it is all in the less than environmentally friendly, supermarket plastic bags.

So, unable or unwilling to rise above the worldly, we engage with others in a shopping frenzy: Kids' clothes at a dollar, being sorted through with as much finesse as a Great White fancying a surfboarder. Cries are heard above the melee. "At this price, if it doesn't fit I'll give it you:" Our daughter in Heaven.

Now there's a chip off the old block.

The Bush fire, the snake and a couple of sharks:

It has not been a good day for the local Water Board. And the company's top guys are worried.

It is 33 degrees [again] - somewhat unusual for late winter hereabouts - and jumpers have been discarded in favour of reddening flesh. The scorching sun is also enticing the unwary onto the golden beaches - and beyond into the bright blue, but still cold, sea. To the casual observer, everything looks real good.

In fact, from where I am sitting, I can see two surfers frolicking in the heavy swell, the breakers being piled up by a strong offshore wind so that they froth and crash about the rocky shoreline. And then there is the fisherman. He's on the low, basalt rock prominence, where the ocean crashes and breaks before boiling and rushing forward toward him. It kisses his feet, tugs at the ankles and swirls around his knees before receding, only to come again. Now I reckon he should worry, because those very rocks, situated beneath the smoke stacks and plumes of the huge steelworks, seem to have become a Mecca for the local Great White shark population. They cruise about here, close to the shore, and wait. Sooner or later there will be a chance..... maybe a nibble of a surfer's leg...... or worse.

A couple of months ago, a fisherman - a bloke from the steelworks - stopped on his way home from the early shift for an hour's fishing. Instead of catching his tea, stocking his freezer, a freak wave took him off that very same, dark, volcanic shelf and into the ocean – and into the path of a Great White. Weeks later, the shark was caught off the Central Coast of New South Wales, around Belmont. In its stomach was one limb and a head, [undoubtedly wearing a look of surprise]. Ah well!

But back to the Water Board and today's story.

Now imagine this: The winter has been a dry, mild one: Very little rain. That means the bush is tinder dry and the 'Big Fish' in the Water Board is worried. We all know that, as he's on telly every night telling us so, and urging people to stop watering their gardens. Sixty percent of all domestic water goes on keeping the grass green, and he is running out - of water, that is. So, "Please stop it!"

His pleas last night immediately followed the Government-sponsored advert by the Rural Fire Service telling people to rake their yards clear of the highly inflammable, dead eucalyptus leaves, and too keep their grass well watered to prevent fire.

To add to the Water Board's woes, today is 33 degrees and sunny – again. And their problems are about to get a whole lot worse before the executive's T.V. performance tonight.

One of his maintenance crews is out and about, 'doing' in one of the Sydney suburbs that has plenty of fine, new homes cut out of the bush: A paradise on earth - until the men of the Water Board show up. On goes the crew's camping gas stove. On goes the kettle for a welcome brew. But then someone needs a hand in the gulley nearby. There's a snake, a red belly, in the inspection hatch, and the bloke's not doing too well at encouraging it to leave.

Within seconds of being left alone, the flame under the kettle is hit by a freak gust of wind. Momentarily the flame moves a few inches to the side, where dead eucalyptus leaves wait. They explode, and within seconds fire engines from miles around are hurtling to the scene, to deal with the huge, raging bush fire.

The maintenance crew, [and the snake] get out alive, but eleven houses are burnt out. T. V. cameras appear in the faces of people who have just lost everything to the vagaries of nature - or think they have.

Now, I do not know if the unfortunate eleven families were phlegmatic enough to remember the fisherman and his fate, but they are wise and angry enough to immediately enlist the help of the T.V. crews to put pressure on the Water Board boss.

And the publicity worked. The T.V. reporter needed a comment to complete a rounded piece, and so runs the 'Big Cheese' to earth. He's at lunch in a fashionable restaurant and not drinking water. [Presumably to conserve it]. Live on telly, he is informed of the local disaster. He asks questions: "Where?" "Is that in my area?" – Then follows up by asking what a maintenance crew was before clarifying a few minor details, like: "Is it my fault?" After a long explanation, he apologizes, promises to pay compensation and asks if he can finish his lunch now.

I would love to know what he was eating. Wouldn't it be great if he was having flake, [shark] and chips; it would sort of round the whole story off. But knowing the celebrity status of that particular restaurant, somehow I doubt it.

Time for Old Time

The storm was directly overhead now. Mid afternoon and it's as black as night. The electric light flickers wildly as the hail, as big as bullets, hammers down. It is fair to say that it is not an afternoon for the beach.

'Police open fire. Man flees!'

The headline, resurrected from 1963 by the storm and the boredom it brought with it, grabbed the attention. It had to, really, as there seemed to be a dearth of police stories in the old newspapers. In this case, a man had stolen a car and was cornered in a dead-end street. He decided to run off. Wrong move. Shooting him was possibly a little O.T.T. by the cops. Been watching too much telly, I suppose.

The storm showed no signs of wanting to leave us, so, with a couple of hours to kill, I thought I'd have a look at the newspapers around two significant dates on my journey through life. December, 1963 - the date I joined the police back in England; and April, 1982: when we first journeyed as a family to Australia.

1963! Was it so long ago? The Beatles: Britain involved with Rhodesia; Australia with Vietnam. Patsy and Ian fall in love. In one way it seems a lifetime ago; in others only yesterday.

I hit lucky. A couple more paragraphs buried deep on the inside pages. In Melbourne, police broke a man's arm in a fight. Fair enough - it could have been accidental, and he probably deserved it! But the second snippet is enough to make anyone wince. A twenty-stone cop ruptured a bloke's kidney when he 'accidentally' fell on the prisoner in his cell. I suppose it was an accident as the policeman was too drunk to stand up.

Now, I am not pretending the police in England were angels back then: we weren't. We were as rough and ready as the next gang on the block - and proud of it. The difference between us and the 'baddies' was that we had an encyclopaedia full of believable excuses and reasons as to why.....

I well remember my old sergeant, nicknamed Rip, taking me - the rooky who was hardly old enough to shave - for a walk on the main street of a rough Yorkshire mill town: - My first Saturday night of pubs kicking out and drunks' lashing out. I think the walk was so that he could have a second look at me after the acute embarrassment of our first meeting earlier in the week. [Well, my acute embarrassment, not his.]

"Good morning young man. I'm Sergeant Keating."

"Good morning. I'm Sergeant Patterson."

And me one day out of training school: I wished the floor would swallow me.

Anyway, this Saturday night a drunk comes up to us and starts practising Kung Fu moves in slow motion. He pretends to kick at the sergeant's kneecap - and stops, two inches away.

The sergeant smiles: "Go away, son."

This idiot, not knowing his 'victim' had been the British Army Boxing Champion, punches at Rip's face, the heel of his hand coming to rest two inches from the officer's chin.

Rip's fist didn't stop. In one continuous motion the elbow followed the fist through. Two hits with one shot. It's always a delight to watch a professional at work.

The yobbo collapsed into the waiting gutter. Walking away as if nothing had happened, I knew then that if repercussions arose, the excuse would be found on page 1 of the manual entitled: 'How to keep of the shit.' The drunk had simply fallen over and broken his nose on the kerb.

No. We were no better than anyone else: Probably, worse. However, I do remember that the police in the U.K. were under scrutiny from an enquiring press and a complaints system was up and running.

Flicking through the newspapers - as people, now aware of the hailstones, rush about trying to cover their vehicles with blankets to stop dents in the bodywork - I come to 1982. New South Wales was talking about a Complaints Tribunal and press reporting was confined to facts: A novel approach to journalism. No critical leaders. No investigative reporting. No causes to be fought for.

Don't run away with the idea that this is a piece of academic research. Far from it: Purely personal observations as the lightning flares, the blankets blow off car roofs and people run this way and that. Still I'm in here.....

While I'm at it, in the sixties there is plenty of world news reported alongside local issues in the Australian press. Things like mossies from the Hexham Swamp stopping work on a building site; and sharks closing Bondi Beach.

The storm heads for the ocean. The hail turns to torrential rain as I read on.

The Aussies seem to have become more insular in the intervening nineteen years. Sure, we are told of Reagan and Brezhnev playing a game of nuclear poker, but more space is given to rain being needed and Sydney Harbour Bridge's 50th anniversary.

1982: Complaints and Discipline had become my speciality. The growth areas in the British Police Service - investigations into everything from drinking on duty, to the grudges of convicted child murderers being turned into 'causes', by a press now fine-tuned to individual rights.

Between the establishment and the watchdog press, the mentality of the British police had been forever altered. The ingrained sub-culture which led to the situation of endemic corruption was confined to history. Thank goodness! Thank goodness we said goodbye to an ethos which gave rise to statements like: "Lend 'is a fag 'til the shops' shut." And it wasn't a joke!

1982: New South Wales. They are still talking about setting up a tribunal to look into police corruption. Ah well! I suppose you cannot hurry these things.

The storm is gone, leaving in its wake wet yards, full swimming pools and the silent, eerie flashes of lightning which continue to paint the sky: Beautiful now, no longer a threat.

I might get to see the rugby on telly after all.

The Reivers are alive and well

"Excuse me, Madam," said the smartly dressed young man, who looked like he should be in school. "Would you mind accompanying me back into the store? You have goods in your bag that haven't been paid for."

Well, the lady did huff and puff a bit, denying any such thing, "How could you...," "How dare you...," etc. All hoy-tee-toyt.

Her protestations seemed convincing. She was, after all, well dressed in a charcoal grey business suit - looked like a well-to-do solicitor, or something like that - and I should know, having a quarter of a century of police experience behind me. Yes, a mistake had obviously been made by this youth, who was not even shaving yet. The old guy sitting next to me, on the shopping mall's benches for forgotten husbands, nodded in agreement. As he did so, a half-an-inch of fag ash fell off the end of the broken cigarette which was hanging limply from the corner of his drooling mouth. "Bloody kids," he murmured. There could be no doubt - this nice lady was a victim of mistaken identity.

At that point, just as I was exchanging a thumbs-up sign and a knowing wink with one of Australia's finest, the pimply young accuser smiled sweetly and pointed to the tail fin of a toy aeroplane sticking out of an unfortunate tear in the woman's plastic supermarket bag. The world's favourite airline, no less!

Her fate was sealed when a smartly dressed, middle aged guy, who had been standing invisibly some fifteen feet away, took off, running for the side exit. He was promptly pursued by a security guard, who was just arriving to add some authority to the proceedings. Now the Invisible Man may have gotten away, but he was none too bright; he couldn't work out how to open the emergency door - kept pulling at it for some reason. But I couldn't watch for too long, as our elegant and eloquent barrister lass uttered an oath which started with, "Oh for" and finished with "sake." In between went some words I reckon you wouldn't hear in a convent. She was led away, cursing like a paratrooper yomping through an Iraqi desert with a full pack, leaving in her wake old iron-lung shrugging his shoulders, and my thoughts flying back over thirty years....

Back to my fledgling police career, my training entrusted to an old chap, florid of face, fat of belly and long of service. There was I, back in the dirty old mill town of the West Riding, a place famous for nowt except for being mentioned in the Domesday Book. God, it was a depressing hole, where the senses were assailed twenty four hours a day by the sweet-sour smell of the mills – and, of course, the noise of the looms. An industrial pimple in that green and pleasant land, where gypsies roamed at will with their horses and carts, 'tatting' for scrap metal.

This one rainy, grey day, two-and-a-half thousand quid's worth of copper went walk-about from a builder's yard. The suspect: anyone with a pie-bald horse and a low sprung cart. The good news was that we found all three moving slowly along the canal towpath. The two-legged offender was a swarthy chap with an earring, who vehemently denied any knowledge of the heinous felony and was equally insistent his name was "Spider Royan, Sur." I'll never forget the address he gave: '123, Blackman Lane, Leeds.' Even my dormant suspicions began to light up. My experienced colleague knew just what to do. No! He didn't throw him in the canal, as was an accepted police technique of the time. [We had to stop when two suspects drowned. True!] No, instead, nose twitching, up onto the back of the cart he went, and burrowed his way into the piles of innocuous and legal scrap which covered the stolen copper. As his ample rump disappeared beneath an old gas cooker; "Here lad!" Mr Royan spoke. "Had onto that." The reins were pushed into my hand. "I'm just gannin' for a piss."

And he did just that. He pissed off - never to be seen again. My punishment: "Sort the 'orse, lad." Ever after, the seized property cupboard had this strange smell that neither disinfectant nor time could remove.

Obviously this high standard of on-the-job training stood me in good stead. Move the clock forward five years or so and by now I am the fat-bellied tutor. Tonight a rock and roll band with a reputation for being somewhat naughty, is playing in the Town Hall. The rockin' starts and so do we eager beavers. A search of the band's dressing room is an obvious necessity; the public must be shielded from long haired wantonness. A search warrant? - Don't be silly, this was the 1960s and legal niceties weren't in vogue - at least with the police. A solid brown substance, all neatly packaged, openly [and therefore legally] presented itself for inspection. Actually it was taped inside a guitar which was found on top of a wardrobe behind some other stuff - but who was to know.

"And what's this?" was the question on everyone's lips. Now this was a heart-felt, non-rhetorical question, as law enforcement was in total ignorance of the developing drug scene. To us in Yorkshire, drugs were aspirin and booze. Illegal substances were found in London, not here.

"So what's this, pal?"

The great unwashed, in torn jeans, black leather jacket and baseball cap with the logo, 'Road Manager,' replied, "Vegetarian sugar, man."

"Oh! O.K. then:" We were disappointed, yes.... But whereas vegetarianism may be a strange practice, it wasn't illegal as far as we knew. So we shrugged our shoulders, returned the sugar for their tea and headed for the door.

It was years later before I realised I had handed back a half a kilo of Moroccan Black – enough cannabis resin to put an illegal smile on the face of the whole town.

The Australian shoplifting duo? No idea what happened to them, but I can give a word of advice to the Invisible Man – the accomplice; good advice that was given to me whilst once holding an 'orse:

"Don't walk through life pulling doors marked push."

Procuring Peaches

Just after the Second World War, the Australian Government adopted the policy of 'Populate or Perish.' They did not have this in mind: The fore-finger of the right hand thrust out at our little car as we toddled along a little road in the middle of nowhere. It belonged to a twenty-something year old woman whose face looked, well, shall we say, lived in. Her skin was pock marked, the eyes black with mascara and sleeplessness.

It was eight in the morning and we didn't stop. We were on our way for peaches: ten bucks for twenty-two pounds at a little place atop the Illawarra Escarpment. Until a week ago we may have thought the lass was going peach-picking too; may even have offered a lift up the dirt road with the two thousand foot drops and hair raising bends. But any such charitable thoughts had disappeared with another pointed, imploring finger on the main road into Newcastle about a week ago.

"That girl shouldn't be doing that," says I.

"She could come to harm," added my wife. "It's not safe to hitch-hike these days. Let's give her a lift. Anything could happen to her."

Uncle Bill cast a shadow over our concern. "There's only one thing likely to happen to her - and it's going to cost a lorry driver about ten bucks."

My wife is bemused. Several seconds elapse. "Oh! Oh dear!"

I'm even slower on the uptake. "Oh! Ugh!"

Oh indeed. How things have changed. Seventy years ago the good city councillors of Illawarra were discussing public decency and decorum in public places. Men and women must swim separately. The 'goings-on' between the sexes under the spreading branches of the five hundred year old fig tree on Mathew Ryan's farm were exposed by the investigative journalists of the time. A photograph was taken - proof positive of unspoken things. How dare a man embrace a woman whilst both are fully clothed and wearing hats?

We travel on in our little car up the little peach road - a little road that's getting littler by the way. Tree ferns begin to encroach; kangaroos hop wildly away....Any moment now we will see something horrible scurry out of the bush.

Just then an appendage appears. It is attached to a nice young man who was doing something behind a Blackboy fern. He sticks it in our direction. Ugh! He's no peach picker! But is he interested in my wife - or me? I know I'm not an attractive sight at eight in the morning, but I'm equally sure I don't look like a trucky. Not many of them wear bowling hats tied beneath the chin!

How things change. A generation before the shock-horror of a cuddle under a tree, twelve Wollongong women were cocking-a-snook at the Establishment, forcing out society's parameters. The Wollongong Twelve were not suffragettes; these ladies were the fore-runners of surfism. Down they went to the beach, right to the water's edge; where, in fashionable hats, long dresses with full, puffed sleeves and carrying handbags, they dared to expose their naked ankles to the ocean and the world.

My wife has finger-pointed in her past. She may colour in embarrassment all she likes, but it is better out than in, as my Aunty Edna used to say. I saw her myself - pointing out of the window of an R.S.L. Club a few weeks back. True, she was only pointing at the fairy penguins on the harbour's breakwater, but the three or four rough looking seamen seemed to be forming a queue for some reason......

But that's another story....Now, where are those peaches.

Symptomless Shoppers

"Have you written a story about yesterday love," asked my wife innocently.

She knew I hadn't. I find a day's shopping in mall after mind-numbingly-similar mall less than inspiring. I guess that's the difference between most men and most women.

For men, the novelty of shopping for cheap mangoes instead of our boring old bananas; Super Wheaties instead of anything Kellogs, soon wears off. And it is worse for the guys who live here permanently - they don't even have the novelty factor.

Then there are the dress shops. How many outfits does one person need?

Ideally I'd like a change of swimmers, perhaps underpants, and that's about it. But that's a forlorn hope as the unseasonal weather closes in. Grey sky and drizzle out there, so I guess I am better off in this air-conditioned shopper's paradise, looking for more... - stuff.

Life on the mall is enlivened by a brief encounter with a refugee from the troubles in Belfast, back in the 1970s. Now fifty-something, she has lost none of her lilting accent, as she tells us that the problem with Belfast is, "It's full of Catholics and Protestants and no Christians." Here-here!

But hold on...the gloom lifts. We've left the shopping to others, released into the...wait for it... sun. The sun is out; the rain has gone and, despite the humidity, we are heading for the beach. My life is on the up.

We walk the beach, paddling in warm water whilst I ponder one of the mysteries of the universe. We have just passed a sign outside the open-air swimming baths, the pool itself being continually washed by the Pacific rollers breaking over it. The sign gives the usual warnings, you know: no running, diving, etc; no drunks - that sort of stuff. And then the imponderable: 'No one admitted with an offensive complaint.'

Ebola! I suppose that's one: Foot and mouth? How about festering pustules? Or anyone shouting: "I want to make an offensive complaint against all politicians."

Trouble is; I have a limited imagination. Can you help me out here?

Happy Days?

There were three generations of us sitting chewing the cud over a breakfast of fresh mangoes, pineapple and paw-paw.

The conversation centred round the local news headlines of the previous evening. 'Disgraceful',' etc. shouted the press. Seemingly, a 'bus load of teenagers had trashed some cars as they celebrated the end of the school term.

The younger generation shrugged their shoulders. "It's not right, but what do you do?" "It's a sign of the times..." "Things can only get worse...." "We're not all like that."

The middle generation: "It wouldn't have happened in my day. We'd have thrown toilet rolls around - perhaps a bucket of water over an unfortunate or unpopular fellow pupil. And we'd have cleaned it up....." "No! Things were better then."

The older generation are perhaps a little more knowing. I contribute: "We had a teacher once called Mister Naughton, a maths master with a malignant nature and a huge leather strap. As an incentive to get your times table right he used to smack this thing down onto your desk. Horrific! I still get cold sweats."

My wife joins in. "And don't forget Mrs. Askew, the nearest thing to a witch I've come across. Thirty-two kids in her class and if she asked a question thirty-two hands went up. Not that anyone knew the answer - but you only had a one in thirty-two chance of being picked to answer it. No hand meant that for certain you'd be explaining your ignorance at the chalkboard before a much-relieved audience."

But we should not forget the science master called Eliot: For some reason he 'lost it' when Andy Anderson set fire to the curtains of his laboratory. As the building burned to the ground, Eliot forsook evacuation, 'phoning the fire brigade, or pressing the alarm button, in favour of knocking seven bells out of the miscreant with a big leather, studded thing. The cops came and took the whimpering teacher away. He got six months, whilst Andy became sort of a cult figure. Eliot's successor ever only pointed at the Bunsen burners, saying: "If you were allowed to use them, then….." [So and so] "would happen."

Happy days! The teachers were ogres and the kids frightened to death, channelled into an acceptance of their lot in the world. Is that better than a bit of yahooism?

I don't know...you choose.

The Garbage Guy:

I like eccentrics - especially genuine, made-in-Australia ones. They attract me, just as their revered or feared or persecuted forebears have attracted generations of others throughout history. And this one, approaching along the pavement above the beach outside the St George – Illawarra Steelers Rugby League ground, must soon be elevated to the status of god-like.

He is careering along on an old bike with wicker basket out in front and dating from when bread and meat and the like were delivered to your front door by boys from the local Co-op shop. The pedal cycle is also towing a home-made box with huge, protruding, ill-matched wheels. The box itself is quite large - coffee table size - and I suppose it must have once been painted blue, or red, or tan, at one or another stage in its life. The paint is now peeled and dry - just like the skin of the rider.

He is old. His shorts display bandy legs and white knees. On his head is a leather Second World War aircrew cap, the sides of which dangle and flap in the wind stream like basset hound ears. He is even wearing Biggles-type goggles. And he's flying!

I spread my arms and dance about the roadway in front of him. The bell tinkles and tinkles some more. I decide on discretion and step to one side. He passes by without breaking the rhythm of his pumping, rickets-affected legs, yet he smiles and shouts something which is lost in the wind behind him, and the rattle of the old iron and metal pieces which fill the box to overflowing.

An hour later the apparition appears again, only this time from the opposite direction. Like a fighter plane pilot he attacks out of the sun. Instead of machine guns, there is the incessant tinkle of the bell.

Once more I bar his path. He is too much of a character not to have a yarn with. Only this time I enlist the help of my wife and companions: four idiots, dancing about to try and deter the fly-past.

This time he stops. He's not angry, but smiling happily at the world and has time to spare. It's only after he squeaks to a halt that I realize he is not wearing goggles, but pebble glass specs: Magoo, not Biggles.

It is his daily run - collecting rubbish from around about where he lives, taking it along the coastal path passed the pioneer graves, where he doffs his hat, and passed the luxurious bars and outdoor cappuccino tables of the rich, where he doesn't.

As we chat, I have time to examine his contraption further. The lights are torches fitted inside cardboard toilet paper tubes, and pieces of string and wire seem to hold most everything in place. He didn't say where he had dropped the garbage, but on the return journey its place in the not-so-clean box trailer had been taken by milk, bread and biscuits.

He leaves with a hearty "Hi-ho Silver!" happy as Larry and leaving the world a better place in his wake.

Gabby Two Dogs: Coniston Beach.

The European settlement of Wollongong dates from 1815, although it did not become a township until 1834. The centre of the community has always been the harbour of Belmore Basin, where, even today, the fishing fleet is blessed by the church before the season begins in earnest.

Immediately above the harbour is Flagstaff Hill, formerly known as Stockade Point - so named as that is where the convict-labourers were locked up for the night. There is now no trace of the stockade; or for that matter, of the old harbour master's house which was built on the same site. And that's a shame, for a distant relative, Sadie Thompson, used to live in it.

No matter! The building was knocked down to make way for a war memorial dedicated to those who died in the Vietnam War. And here is one of life's little ironies: one of the inscribed names is that of Tom Phillips, whose family had married into that of our Thompson's – the vintage who'd arrived in New South Wales in 1923. I will concede that Thompson is a common enough surname, but I like these little quirks of fate. They give life a kind of continuity and a glow of belonging.

From Flagstaff, the massive steelworks at Port Kembla are easy to spot; impossible to miss really, as the chimneys and stacks bellow forth huge clouds of grey and black smoke, with occasional blasts of flame which sear the clear blue sky.

The steelworks has provided employment for generations of our folk and deserves a closer look - only this time I let it put its best foot forward by approaching along Coniston Beach.

And that is where I met Gabby Two Dogs, happily playing in the surf with his Jack Russell terriers. The sun was warm, the water beautiful; a day to be enjoyed. Somehow the massive, grotesque works, alive with flame and muted industrial noise, just seemed a natural part of it all.

Gabby was in his early thirties, had thick, black curly hair, and features that spoke of an Aboriginal heritage within - even though it was well diluted by generations of Irish and Scottish genes. He knew our family; had played soccer and rugby against them in his younger days, and worked alongside them in the coke ovens and marshalling yards. He didn't have any hobbies. He no longer played sport; too old and carrying too many injuries. He didn't fish off the beach, didn't drink, and had no time for the talented sportsmen in any field who didn't have the tenacity to succeed when they had been blessed with talent.

His passion was now confined to his terriers and what pleased them. And what pleased them was the surf.

We parted, he ankle deep in the warm water, following in the wake of his dogs and inevitably heading in the direction of the giant works. I remained, waiting for another quelching of the coke which would produce towering plumes once more and make for a great photograph.

I was sorry to see him go; I could have got to like him quite easily. And I suppose that's the point. There is continuity here: of people, of place, of belonging.

If only you look for it.

Surprise at Bass Point.

The first surprise was just how special the marine and headland reserve of Bass Point near Shellharbour is.

Hard on its heels came number two surprise - a real eye-opener: the park ranger. He was young and broad shouldered, tall and built like an athlete. Dressed as he was in a light khaki uniform of short-sleeved shirt and knee-length shorts which showed his suntan off to perfection, he managed to turn the ladies' heads.

Despite hating him immediately, I admit he looked the consummate professional and did seem to know an awful lot about the place. Unfortunately for us, he was softly spoken and no match for the intermittent screeching and rumbling of the chainsaw wielded by his mate, who was tidying up the straggling tea trees which overhung the path to Red Sand Bay. Softly spoken maybe, but his laugh was infectious as he answered our innocent query as to where the red sand was. After all, the bay was rock and pebbles: Black rock and black pebbles.

"It's there alright. You'd be surprised," and went on to explain, "It's the banks at the back of the beach that are red - but they're covered in bush, so you wouldn't know." He added a warning after a moment's hesitation. "But don't go poking about in there. You'd be surprised at what's lurking on the reserve."

We had to take his word for it; no sign of the seventeen thousand year old Aboriginal habitations on the headland and no wildlife at all, save for a couple of bright, red-tailed finches.

In fact, I had just convinced myself that the natural inhabitants of the park [except the deaf finches] all knew how to hide from the chainsaw gangs and gawping visitors, when I met the feisty crab. This guy was no bigger than a thumb nail, yet it leapt at the intruder's boot, clawed at the inquisitive digit poking it and angrily spat sand in my direction: A crab with attitude. I just love an Aussie battler - especially the tiny spiders and caterpillars and snakes - and now crabs that will do you in, given half a chance.

Spirits boosted by the encounter, we take a short and easy walk across the finger of land to Bush Ranger Bay. And here there is yet another surprise. The bones of a shipwreck poked up through the sand between the jagged rocks - a terrible reminder of what happened here, despite sixty years of ceaseless battering by an invincible ocean.

The bits and pieces of unrecognizable wreckage are all that remain of the ship, 'Cities Service Boston,' a nine thousand ton American forces tanker, which was deliberately run aground at full speed when it began to founder in raging seas in the dawn light of 16th May, 1943. Luckily for the crew, the Australian Army had thirty men of its Sixth Machine Gun Battalion in the area, and it was they who set to, with nothing more than raw courage, ropes and whatever they had to hand, to get the sixty-two man crew off. But not without incident. Ten men were swept into the sea, four, all Australians, never to be seen again.

All the American crew survived, some of whom later returned from homes in California to dedicate a memorial and remember the men who had given them back their lives.

Bass Point did not look particularly dangerous, at least not today, although the rocks jut out like fingers into the vast and deep blue ocean. The ranger popped up again and, after standing silently in the background for a while so as not to spoil our moment's reflection, eventually spoke. "This is just one of the hundred and fifty or so vessels which have come to grief in the area."

I know the headland reserve is small in area, but uncharitably I was becoming suspicious of his motives for wanting to ripple his muscles and flex his chain saw in front of our girls, resplendent in the day's short-shorts. He might just have wanted company - visitors are rare - but it was time to put him to the test. I removed my jacket and challenged him there and then.

"Tom Thumb!" I cried.

He looked blank.

"Tom Thumb!" I repeated the name of the eight-foot-long boat belonging to the explorers, George Bass and Mathew Flinders, and crewed by their helper, William Martin.

Still blank, so I tried an easier one. "Was this the point they rounded in Tom Thumb in 1798 before capsizing and being swept ashore at Towradgi?"

No reply, so I went in for the kill. "You must remember the story of how one of them, Flinders – he trimmed the beards of the Aborigines who'd met them on the beach, so as to distract them whilst the other two blokes dried the guns and powder. You know, just in case."

He didn't know, mumbled something about not being old enough to remember and went back to hauling branches.

My companions looked sideways at me. "Isn't that Tom Thumb Lagoon?" A finger pointed across the bay in the direction of the distant steelworks.

"Oh really! That's a surprise."

The Aftermath

When I saw the sign, 'Last pub for a hundred yards,' I knew we would be in for a good day.

I wasn't wrong.

We dodged the attentions of the huge mosquitoes which had made Crooked River outside of Gerroa home; delighted in the Shoalhaven Estuary, where hundreds of black swans were over-wintering; and adored the brilliant reds of the Illawarra flame trees, which were everywhere announcing the imminent arrival of spring.

We returned, safe and well, from a remote forest track where the bodies of three murder victims had been deposited over the last several years [no sign of an arrest], and negotiated the remnants of a recent humdinger of a storm. Everywhere the skeletons of shallow-rooted trees were being subjected to the attentions of chainsaws and tractors. Even the corrugated-iron roof of a house, rolled up by some invisible hand into the shape of an opened lid of a tin of sardines, was being battered back into place by many a willing hand wielding ropes and hammers: Lots of hammers.

And our journey had certainly been worth it. The Seven Mile Beach at Geringong, protected by the stunning promontory of Black Heads, is silent in the cold aftermath of the departed storm front. Even so, it is hard to imagine the scene from seventy years ago, when the beach saw its largest ever invasion of people.

Why? To see VA-USU parked on a tarpaulin and being prepared for an international flight to New Zealand. The plane was the 'Southern Cross,' piloted by Air Commodore Charles Kingsford-Smith, who, with two crew members, faced a journey of twenty-two hours sitting atop 412 gallons of petrol and 30 gallons of oil.

The crowd watched the fuelling on the afternoon of Tuesday, 10th January, 1933, and although it wasn't reported how many were still there when the intrepid airmen took off from the beach at three the next morning, I suspect there were more than there are today. Present company excepted, not one person is braving the cold sand and blustery showers. Even the welcome sunshine, peeking through fast-moving clouds, is weak and hasn't encouraged anyone out of the cafes and bars, unless it's to run the hundred yards to the next.

Still, seven beautiful miles all to ourselves is something to be thankful for.

Red Santa's in the Sunset

Christmas is coming and the silly season is here. We are in an R.S.L.* club in the pleasant little coastal town of Huskisson on Jervis Bay, a day of warm seas and the whitest sandy beaches in Australia behind us.

We were welcomed into the club by the largest striped marlin in the world - dead, stuffed and mounted of course; all eighteen feet and eight hundred and sixty-eight pounds of it. It hangs forlornly in a passageway, denied even a view of its former home, the majestic bay which is six times larger than Sydney Harbour.

We have the best of both worlds here. We have the view from the panoramic windows of the club's restaurant; and we are just about as stuffed as our friend, having just seen off the best sea perch available anywhere. We are content to sit and watch the dying day. The harbour lights begin to twinkle in the gathering dusk, the boats bob gently at their moorings and all is well. Except one thing is puzzling me: an irritant niggling at my mind when I should be at total peace.....

Why have a couple of dozen young people with a couple of dozen eski's** full of booze let the large whale and dolphin cruise ship leave the jetty without them? The answer becomes obvious five minutes later. Santa Claus, in full festive regalia, arrives at the quay. No reindeer - this is coastal Australia. No! This one arrives in a rubber dinghy complete with outboard motor. He fills the boat to capacity, adds some more, and then more again. Everyone is standing - they have to, as there's no room to sit. With a hearty cheer and a wave of beer bottles, they're off. The rubberized craft head-butts its way out of the protected little harbour and into the rolling waves. The revellers must be having second thoughts about their version of a cheapo bay cruise by now. They hang onto one another as the boat rises and falls, slips and slides across the rollers, spray everywhere. They've gone pretty silent, more scared than silly now.

Santa heads out to sea. They pass a sandy spit of land - an excellent spot for a private barbee party. They pass a lonely, rocky outcrop surrounded by sea and lashed by spray - hardly a nice party spot, but certainly something to boast about later when sober. But no, they just keep on going, out into the darkening, empty bay, toward the home of striped marlin and a silly Santy who must have rocks in his head.

*R.S.L: Returned Servicemen's League clubs. In New South Wales they are an excellent place to eat cheaply, the food being subsidised by the gaming machines.
** Eski: A cool box.

Jervis Bay

As I put pen to paper, I have no idea how to deal with the plethora of images that Jervis Bay throws at you at every turn.

Just this morning we've seen wild kangaroo, white sandy beaches, incredible rock formations, botanic gardens, lakes and lagoons, and hand-fed parrots whose colouring would have stunned a rainbow. We've fed on paw-paw, pineapple and the local speciality: sweet cherries the size of ping-pong balls. We've marvelled at the soaring sea eagles and been astonished by the yellow-headed boobies skimming the ocean with wings touching the wave tops.

And then, of course, there was the Warrawong Ladies Bowling Club outing. They boarded the dolphin cruise at Huskisson Jetty without a care in the world, if the noisy laughter and chatter was anything to go by.

"If any of our passengers can spot a dolphin before we do," said the captain, "Then you're on for a free trip." That was enough for cousin Noel to do his titanic Kate Winslow impression, standing high on the sharp end of the boat. And, of course, he won the freebee. I'll swear his ancestors were either native hunters or soothsayers.

Anyway, the dolphins were smashing. They did their dolphin things, like eating cuttlefish - and were quite happy to show their babies off like all proud parents do.

However, the rotund ladies of Warrawong were not impressed. They never moved from the food nor the booze, content to laugh and talk and ignore the waiting world outside the warm cabin.

The dolphin experience was good; not great, just good. We've done enough wildlife chasing to know animals of any description don't line up for a photograph like the one in the booking office for the cruise: six dolphins surfing through a breaking wave. It just doesn't happen - well, not to this photographer, who has been known to get bored after a two minute wait.

No! The whole experience of Jervis Bay was incredibly good. However, things can be very different in this spectacular place, memories triggered by the remnants of a shipwreck, the hulk rusting quietly away amongst the rocks and just out of the reach of today's inoffensive surf.

My cousin Doug used to race ocean-going yachts. He nearly lost his life just there, in this tranquil bay near that wreck. A storm like he'd never seen before had sprung up from nowhere, causing him to seek the protection afforded by Jervis Bay. He just had time to furl the sails and switch off the electrical supply when bolts of lightning began striking the water within feet of him. He still remembers the water boiling, the stink of sulphur and the helplessness he felt as he lay curled on the deck, the yacht drifting toward the waiting rocks.

Luck was with him that day - as it was with cousin Noel, whose fishing trip nearly ended in disaster on the other side of the bay near the Naval College. He could see the shore clearly, the white sand beckoning, and yet had to run for his life when the innocuous waves all at once became very large and threatening - large enough to broach his dinghy, which suddenly had become very small indeed.

Jervis Bay: wonderful yet terrible. The cliffs guarding the entrance have claimed the lives of nineteen fishermen - perhaps revenge extracted by the gods for the indiscriminate taking of the dangerous, eighteen foot long, grey nurse sharks who seem to favour Doug's Bay.* Their numbers are now down to three hundred; the belated attempt at conservation may be too late to save them hereabouts.

Australia at its best: So much beauty, yet there is always that underlying, darker side. And it is this unseen danger which heightens the sublime, an intrinsic, God-like duality which makes Australia what it is.

Not that philosophy ever entered the minds of the Warrawong ladies. They saw nothing, had a great time and, whereas they walked onto the boat, the crew just about managed to pour them off.

*Shark Bay:

Lake Conjola

I will have abiding memories of Lake Conjola. Tranquil: Blue. Set as it is amongst a eucalyptus forest, it also backs onto miles of sand which fringe the ceaseless ocean.

However, it wasn't really the setting, the perfect unity of it all which fired my imagination. No, that was left to my wife's delight as the hordes of multi-coloured parrots covered her and our veranda, demanding a breakfast of sunflower seeds and bacon fat.

And then the boundless pleasure at our two British granddaughters, who live miles from a cold sea and who have taken to 'boogie-boarding' as if born to it. Mind you, their parents are doing a pretty fair imitation of a couple of surfees too.

Friends: Kids. Barbee's: And a lifetime of sausage and steak. Memory Days! – Get as many as you can. This fragile life of ours is not a trial run!

*

Of course, I could do the nightmare version: of hand-sized spiders; mosquitoes that need an aircraft carrier to land on; kids with nappies full and overflowing; a sleepless night in 'motel style' accommodation; and our granddaughter, Emily, blowing snotty strings down her nose after being dumped on her head by a malicious wavelet.

But I won't.

The Whales of Eden

The klaxon blared and people began to flee the Whaling Museum, situated in the pleasant little coastal town of Eden.

"Fire?" I half shouted the question at anybody prepared to listen as we joined the runners. "Fire?" Looks which say, "Idiot!"

No. It's whales in the bay. Car doors slam, the car park empties and tyres scream in protest at the unexpected rush on this hot, sleepy day. No need for directions as dozens of locals have joined the exodus. Not even I can lose this stream of vehicles.

We arrive on a headland just outside the town. We're impressed. Binoculars, tripods, telescopes, gigantic zoom lenses appear in a trice. We are in the presence of professionals, or well-prepared scouts and guides, who generously allow us a good view through their equipment.

Anticipation and excitement at fever pitch.

"There they are!"

'There she blows' may have been more appropriate in this old whaling town, still visited by God's great sea creatures between May and November each year.

"There're two..... No three! No four of them."

One wag at the back mutters that the whales hereabouts always have this habit of breeding quick.

Humpbacks? Rights? No one knows for sure, but then no one really cares that much. Seeing the whale, or whales, is all that matters.

"I once saw eleven right whales without a telescope. Really close they were."

The forefathers of the speaker had helped decimate the whale population and by doing so consigned the fantastic blue whale to extinction. I wondered if she knew how the Right Whale got its name. Not from Mister Right, but because that particular species was the right one to kill. It was slow to dive and floated when it died: an easy target.

The whalers of this particular town on Twofold Bay allegedly had help in their hunt for the 'right' whales. The story goes that killer whales used to round up any of the other species and drive them into the bay for the human hunters to dispatch. In exchange they were given the four ton whale tongue and lips, a delicacy to be enjoyed by the killer shepherds at their leisure.

Now whaling is unacceptable within Australian waters - and rightly so: [Forgive the pun.] The pulling power, the majesty of these magnificent beasts is such that a living can now be made out of keeping them alive. Tourist hordes will pay big bucks to be allowed the privilege of just being near these denizens of the deep.

Long may it remain so!

Budderoo National Park

Up through the rolling Jamberoo Valley, the award-winning Minnamurra sub-tropical rainforest awaits. A gentle walk, a gentle rise and before you know it we are into the tree canopy. Giant Moreton Bay figs, thousands of ferns of all kinds, crystal clear streams, darting fish, and then an eel slithers around a submerged boulder, giving ample evidence for the Aborigines' naming this place: 'Minnamurra - plenty of fish.'

Until now the walk has been easy: A mirage, my friends. The track to the falls becomes vertical - and then steeper still. Olympian mountain goats train here. It takes a never-ending, lung-bursting feat of endurance in the rising heat and humidity to reach our goal - a wooden bench. As the pain subsides, between the gasps, we can see the falls are truly magnificent. They add life to a tranquil fairy glade at the foot of the Illawarra Escarpment. Yet on other days, after extended rainy periods, the atmosphere of this special place would be distinctly different - threatening in its intensity, as evidenced by the huge boulders and galleon-sized tree trunks discarded this way and that.

Heart rates normal, and memories captured by Japanese technology, we retreat on leaden legs for a gourmet lunch - tea and Aussie meat pies smothered in tomato sauce.

Journey 9
Southern Highlands of New South Wales and the Australian Capital Territory

Molly Lolly and Polly Lolly

Bundanoon is to be found in the Southern Highlands of New South Wales and is the very epitome of Scottish settlements in this part of the world. Every autumn, Highland Games are held - and even though it is only early summer, the skirl of bagpipes heralds our entry into the main street. The shops are full of tartans, clan histories, shortbread, tea shops and pictures of snowy glens, where proud stags stand on rocky outcrops proclaiming their kingdom. The Australian summer has even turned Scottish for us - it's wet, windy and cold enough to don a cardy - made in the Shetland Isles, of course.

But it is not Scotland - not with place names like Yellow Rock Creek, where families from outlying homesteads meet on a Sunday morning to pray in one of the three adjacent churches by the rickety road bridge. Catholic, Presbyterian and Anglican ministers all competing for the sparse business of gathering souls. On a rough headcount I would say the R.C.'s are winning hands-down.

In such a rural area, where a high percentage of the far-flung residents are apparently regular church goers, it appears incongruous to have an establishment in their midst called the Bang Bang Motel. I can't help but be reminded of a small township in Pennsylvania, a centre for the strictly religious community of the Amish people, whose fore-fathers decided to call the place 'Intercourse.'

Ah well! There's no accounting for taste. Taste! It's hardly an inspired link, but it is through an extended tasting of cheese, various cakes [orange, poppy seed and lemon]; liquorice, and twenty-four different types of ice cream at the cleverly named, 'Old Cheese Factory,' that we got to meet up with Molly Lolly and Polly Lolly.

You think I'm joking don't you? It's quite true, though. Both were in their mid - late fifties, dumpy, happy types and wearing, wait for it - dolly hats. You know, those frilly, lacy things, happier on the heads of 1880s serving wenches.

Molly was the talker, twenty to the dozen, and was quite happy with the division of labour. She talked. Polly worked. Molly still travels a lot, any and everywhere in Australia, and loves it as much as I do. Whether it's whale sharks out west, or saltwater crocodiles on the Daintree, she doesn't care. Polly is equally adamant. She has never left the Southern Highlands and will never do so. Polly works at home and here, in this grand old cheese making factory. Molly goes off and leaves her to it. It seems to work for them.

It's hard to say goodbye, but we have bought most of the shop's stock whilst we've been picking at the merchandise and chatting - and we've still got the Fitzroy Falls to visit.

The water plunges something like nine hundred feet over red and grey rocks eroded into fantastic shapes by the never ending force of the water. The views are spectacular, reaching out from the vantage points to places worryingly called 'Wilderness this' and 'something or other Wilderness.' At least we're led to believe that is what's out there, over the precipice - if we could see further than five yards through the low, drizzly cloud.

Well! What do you expect in Scotland?

Question time at Canberra

Now two hundred kilometres south west of Sydney, we pass through Goulburn, a pleasant and thriving little city and the location of the headquarters of the New South Wales Police. I don't know if it is significant - that transient Thomas Birkby of ours - the one who became a copper - was a gardener here in 1835. He may well have imbibed at the Riverside Coaching Inn before it was classed as 'historic.'

1835. Law and order was only ten years old outside Sydney's boundaries. As settlement extended into the more remote parts of the colony, mounted police were used to combat the problems with bushrangers, escaped convicts and hostile Aborigines. Their tasks included the patrolling of the three main roads to Sydney, including the one through Goulburn.

We push on to our goal, Canberra, set within two hundred square miles of the Australian Capital Territory. The site was chosen in 1908, but with typical bureaucratic urgency it took until 1927 to get the politicians to move here from the delights of Melbourne. Mind you, only politicians and bureaucrats could establish Parliament at a place called 'Tits' in Aborigine.

The city was designed by an American who had never seen the place. He was given a clean sheet of paper and started to draw, undoubtedly taking his ideas of grandeur from Washington D.C. He replaced sheep runs with a collection of fine buildings and vistas, waterspouts and lakes - but somehow failed to make the place come together. It has no soul, no character.

Yet Canberra is a must for everyone, if only for one reason - the National War Memorial. It is without doubt one of those great experiences. As you walk the portalled Great Courtyard, the enormity of the cost of war assails you from every side. The name of every fallen man-at-arms since the 1860s is inscribed around the stone walls. Men dead at Gallipoli, where the ANZAC legend was born - one of ours, Bell. They stand side by side with those who did not return from Europe, the sands of North Africa or the jungles of Vietnam: More of ours; too many: Patterson, Phillips, Drewe, Symington, another Bell. This is a mighty people in arms.

Names! The list appears to be endless. Serried rows of names, some highlighted by the sun's rays, as if man and nature were conspiring to nurture the lost spirit; others in shade wait their turn for illumination, to be singled out in remembrance. The place touches the most hardened, cynical of hearts with its peace and sadness.

Humbling.....

You look down from the shrine on Mount Ainslie with a million silent questions at your back. You look down the mile of ANZAC Parade and you see Capital Hill and Parliament House in the distance; the decisions of politicians and the subsequent results superbly connected.

A nice touch that - and one which I am sure would find favour with those remembered here.

Coughs, colds, sore holes and pimples on the nose:

I know people, as individuals, are different the world over and that you can't generalize. [Can you feel a 'but' coming on?] But you have to speak as you find and, without exception, my experience of Australian country-folk is that they are an open and friendly bunch who make time to welcome strangers.

By way of example, let me introduce you to Ella-Mae, a village shopkeeper somewhere in the Snowy Mountains. We had left the main highway because of the 'Cafe' and 'Shop' sign tacked loosely onto one of the dead blue gums which was being used as a telegraph pole, and headed off down the gravel track.

We stopped by a delivery truck parked out in front of the wooden store, and for a while paused to take in the silence, broken only by bird song and croaking frogs. The caged cockatoo refused to talk, despite the best intentions of a couple of Poms.

"He's called Henry," said the delivery man, kicking open the metal, fly-screen door with a crash. "He might not be able to fly, but the bastard sure can bite."

With that he started unloading his cargo. Beer: Pallets of the stuff filled the three tonner.

"Is that all for the shop?" I asked incredulously.

"Sure is! The boys get a might thirsty after work."

"Need a hand?"

"Nah, Mate. You'll have the Unions down here on a demarcation dispute," he laughed.

I pushed the door to the store open and entered the darkness beyond, to be met by the sound of a television and laughter coming from off to my right. I peered round the boxes marked 'water pumps' and 'machine parts,' to be greeted by my first sight of Ella-Mae.

She was sitting in the centre of the store by a table [the cafe?], watching an old movie whilst munching on a sandwich between peels of laughter. "Oh no!" she'd say, then more hefty laughs.

She sees us and waves. "Have you seen this movie?" she asks, beckoning us over. It was 'The Party' with Peter Sellars. "It does make me laugh."

We joined her in time for 'Oh Goodness Gracious Me.' I didn't mind a bit. I am not an old movie buff, but it gave me time to study her unobtrusively. Early 60's, grey hair that probably hadn't seen a comb that morning, and a face which held plenty of laughter lines. That made up for a lot and I knew instinctively she would be easy to like.

A customer came in down the far end.

"Hi Helen."

"Hi Ella-Mae."

"That stuff you wanted just came in. It's by the register. Help yourself."

"Okay. Thank you......By the way, old Mr. Tate is 90 on Sunday and is having trouble with an ulcer on his leg: Any ideas?"

"I'll have to have a think about that one. Catch you later."

"Bye."

"Bye...... Now then, what can I get you folks," she asked, turning her attention to her visitors.

I thought I'd try it on: "Two large cappuccinos, a pot of decaf. English tea and a chilled pineapple juice please."

"No worries. Have a seat here and I'll get it now."

She left, leaving us with her open handbag. A simple act of trust and much appreciated.

Surprisingly, the coffee was very passable, although I could have done without the hair hidden in the froth. I had passed the time waiting for the order looking about the place. Well, I'd been sitting for five hours. The place had everything: paperback cowboy books with titles like 'Gutless' and 'Fearless in Dodge'; bug sprays and agricultural poisons next to the nappies and ointments; tinned peas and water pistols. Any spare inch of wall space was covered by photographs of the customers: men shearing, men drinking, men on the backs of pick-up trucks, women with kids.

"Well, you certainly seem to have everything," I said. "But where do the customers come from? I haven't seen a house in a fair while."

"Oh, they're about. Hills are full of 'em."

"Could I have one of those expectorant cough medicines there, please?"

"What's wrong with you?"

I could have started with an itchy scalp and worked down through the body to a sore right ankle, but whilst I was working out what to concentrate on, she must have thought I was being shy and so prodded, "What's up? Al kicked in?"

"Al," I asked, looking around in growing confusion.

"Alz-heimer," she helped. "Come on! I was a nurse until I took this place on thirteen years ago. What's up?"

"Sore, constricted chest. Picked some bug or other up on the plane I expect."

"You know why I'm called Ella-Mae?"

"No-ooo," I answered suspiciously.

"Because Ella may, or may not, sell it ya. You don't want to be spending twenty bucks on what those pharmaceutical blokes produce. Here! Use this stuff," she said, as she thrust a brown bottle into my hand. "We used to give it to the old blokes in the home when they couldn't get their breath. There, try it! Tastes like shit, but real medicines are supposed to."

With that recommendation I had to part with my three dollars to purchase 'Doc. David's Galenicals Ammonia Mixture: 'Good for coughs, colds, sore holes and pimples on the nose.'

"So, Ella-Mae, can you recommend something to open the bowels?"

"Just drink plenty of that stuff. It'll get you one way or the other."

The Sub-Nivean Explorer.

Threadbo, high in the Snowy Mountains, set below the towering bulk of Mount Kosciuszko, the highest mountain in Australia, is a thriving ski town. The one thing you notice as you sip your over-priced cappuccino in one of the open, sunny squares, browse the expensive boutiques or queue for the ski lifts, is that the people hereabouts are predominately young - just like the town itself.

Threadbo only came into existence after the construction of the Snowy River Hydro Electric Power Scheme, which began back in 1949 - an event which drew people from all over the world to work here. The northern Europeans saw the potential of the alpine slopes immediately and, now, new chalets cling to the sides of the mountain, car parks fill and people shop, despite the hidden costs and hidden dangers.

Hidden dangers - such as the land slides which claimed several lives in the village back in the 1990s. But hidden dangers would have been the bed-fellows of Paul Strzelecki, born near Poznan in his native Poland, and who, between 1839 and 1843, explored vast areas of New South Wales discovering Australia's highest mountain, [which he named Kosciuszko in honour of the Polish patriot, Tadeusz Kosciuszko,] along the way.

As Paul went about his business of discovery, he found the odd fortune of gold, silver and coal here and there, and in his spare time became a recognized 'ologist:' Geologist, zoologist, meteorologist and mineralogist, that is.

And today, there are plenty of folk following in his well-beaten tracks. For one, we're tracking up Mount Kosciuszko in the snow. It was a choice between walking above the snow line and with it the chance of some great photo's, or taking the lower level walk to the evocatively named Dead Horse Gap - so known because once upon a time, a mob of wild brumbies perished there in the deep winter snows.

I was intent on becoming an 'ologist' too. Not many birds about this high up, so strike ornithologist; but I know the native cockroach; the one with the reddish colouring, is being counted by some university types, and the bug is bound to be hanging about beneath the snow somewhere. By the noise coming from the innumerable bogs and tussock mounds, flattened and discoloured by the melting snow, there must be thousands of them winding up for the breeding season.

Plenty to discover then. I know; I've read the Kosciuszko Today newspaper and I'm sure the current crop of 'ologists' will be glad of any help yours truly is willing to give. I've been watching them. They are knee deep in snow, busily hauling plastic tubes and other modern gadgets about the place. If this hadn't made Strzelecki stop and scratch his head, then maybe the explanation would. Instead of telling me they are counting bugs and stuff: no! They are - wait for it; 'monitoring the sub-nivean space to check on the dusky antechinus.'

It took a lot of time to get this explanation to you. That space they are talking about is to be found between the snow and the actual ground, purportedly inhabited by a host of creatures. I've still no idea what a dusky what's-it is, but its mates include the brown rat, the broad-toothed rat and a host of skink-type slithery things.

Other experts are trapping feral cats, who are eating the rats - and also poisoning the foxes, who are eating the cats who eat the rats who pee in the snow and poison really nice people - like the sister of a close relative, who drank the sweet water from the fast flowing streams above the snow line, fell ill and remained sick for months. First contribution to the ecology debate: don't drink diluted rat pee. But a question immediately raises itself in my brain: 'Did Polish Paul have to bring bottled water up here with him too? If not, why not? And did he get sick?'

My thoughts were interrupted by the sight of a red and shiny bug, which was presenting itself for inspection on a moss covered rock, around which icy cold water flowed.

We had reached 6,500 feet, and at this altitude the gap between the melting, slushy snow cover and the ground, or rushing water beneath, was variable. Still, the bug looked to be stranded on that rock and should be an easy target for the requisite photo, for identification to be made later.

I move with precision; a little lower. Lower. The lens zooms and whines. The camera is moved a little this way, a little that..... The 'solid' ground under my left foot proves a trap for the unwary. Weakened by the sun, eroded from beneath by the rushing water, the ground suddenly becomes a bog. I sink six inches; then more. I panic; I topple; I lose balance - and disappear into the sub-nivea.

My second, and final, contribution to the ecological debate surrounding Mount Kosciuszko: "The sub-nivea region is wet and smelly. It is best left to its own devices."

The men of Alice Chalmers:

Sawpit Creek could be a million miles away from the walk up Mount Kosciuszko. But it's not; it is just a couple of thousand feet lower and tucked away in a cleft of rock so that it is always sheltered, even when there are one hundred mile an hour winds whipping the snow into a frenzy on the mountain peaks.

Its location has meant it has always been sought out. First by the Aboriginal people, the Monaro's, who lived in the majestic ash and eucalyptus forest which covered the valley floor; then by white settlers, who used the sheltered location to set up a sawpit. A sawpit should not be mistaken for a saw mill. To create a sawpit, the settlers dug a hole, dropped a huge tree across it and then two men, one working from above, one from below, would push and pull on a double-bladed saw until the tree had been turned into planks. No machinery, at least at the start. Hard men! [Just pause for a moment and think what it was like for the poor bloke working from down in the pit.]

We chose Sawpit Creek - or rather we stumbled across Sawpit Creek, after dropping down the mountain from Perisher, an aptly named and purpose built ski resort, because of our companion's search for his roots.

His father had been one of these outback hard men long before getting a job in the late 1940s on the Snowy River Project - a visionary construction of a series of ten major dams, 120 miles of inter-connecting tunnels and a host of minor dams. For sure he had worked on one of those smaller dams, or pondages, at the nearby Island Bend Camp.

The work gangs would move to their designated area in the utter wilderness, where no man had put a foot since the beginning of time, by using the simple expedient of taking a compass bearing and then driving in their huge, American-made, Alice-Chalmers TD24, bulldozers. They simply smashed their way in, moving everything in their path.

Once in, the men lived under canvas, whilst other equipment arrived for use in the construction of roads and tracks. It was hard and dangerous work, but not without humour. The cook at Island Bend Camp was expected to vary and supplement the men's diet with whatever he could take from the bush. One day, he'd managed to catch a waterhen, which he duly plucked, gutted and threw into a pan of boiling water. To weigh it down in the pan, he'd put a stone in its belly. He boiled it and, feeling quite pleased with himself, served it to the men that night. Unfortunately, waterhen doesn't cook; it remains the texture of rubber, no matter what you do with it. It is said the men preferred to chew on the stone.

Shortly afterwards, one of the workmen was called to see the supervisor and was challenged: "I want to know who called the cook a bastard." The workman replied: "And I want to know who called that bastard a cook."

Humour aside, it was hard and dangerous work. Many men died as their vehicles plunged over precipices in the dark; others died the most horrible of deaths when they were caught in the concrete pours and were left entombed in the dam walls; many more perished when the 'dozers simply rolled over.

The bulldozers rolling over must have been commonplace, when you see the steepness of the gorges and mountain sides. In fact, so steep was it, that two 'dozers had to work in conjunction. As one went down the perpendicular slope, pushing back everything to virgin rock, the other acted as a counterweight and went up. That sounds good in theory, but I certainly wouldn't like to abseil strapped to a huge bulldozer.

And as we walk, picking our way along an overgrown track in an attempt to follow the course of the fast, snow-melt, river, I keep looking at the house-sized boulders towering above us. The enormity of what these men achieved here suddenly comes home. The whole area is covered with these huge devil's marbles, once ejected by an exploding volcano way back in the mists of time. It is beyond imagination how the plant equipment managed to move them.

Our walk is good, the woods full of flowering tea tree bushes and other plants I can't identify; full of parrots and red breasted warblers; and memories of those hard men who lived and died in this wilderness.

The Gold Diggers' Ball

Early Sunday morning, and there is hardly a sign of life along the modern main street and shopping area of the high tableland township of Adaminaby. A dog is taking itself for a walk, and a fat man waddles from the newsagent's shop clutching an armful of newspapers, no doubt contemplating a day of inactivity. And that's it!

Adaminaby's predecessor, an old nineteenth century country town, now lies at the bottom of one of the Snowy's major reservoirs; but I would lay good money on the fact that those old stomping grounds of our one-time timber hands and farm labourers didn't have a thirty foot high, plastic trout dominating the main road into their town.

In the twenty first century, Adaminaby is touting for the tourist dollar, but trout fishing isn't my thing - I suppose a hang-up from my youth, when I could see no point in sitting by the side of a foul canal in foul weather. However, book shops are a different matter and a particularly decrepit one caught my eye. More precisely, the reproduction of a nineteenth century 'flyer', stuck across the glazed front door, drew me in. It was advertising the coming of 'The Australian Masonic Waltz.' Apparently this was an annual event and much looked forward to.

The pictorial scene displayed on the old advertisement fascinated me. Imagine a grand ballroom, with impressive Doric columns bedecked in flags and bunting; and above the dance floor a tier of private boxes from which the well-to-do peer down on the energetic dance scene below: Men in black ties and winged collars; women looking like something out of 'Gone with the Wind.' At the bottom of the flyer, the legend reads 'Melbourne, 1867.'

The shop is locked, but still the scene holds me.

It is said that Captain Cook introduced dance into Australia by making his sailors keep fit through the dancing of jigs and hornpipes. That may be so - I don't know enough about Aboriginal history to dispute the assertion - but I do know that dance is as much a part of the human condition as.....breathing. In fact, dancing in Britain is supposed to have started as part of an act of worship, where people moved around a sacred tree, touching it to ward off evil: [hence: 'touch wood']. I presume the Aboriginal people did something similar?

But the nineteenth century gold diggers had no such philosophical interest in the roots of dance. They just wanted to enjoy themselves - and why not? To our gold diggers of Victoria, the Bulford's and Reedhead's, we can now add our Burgesses from around here - and we can be sure they used to look forward to the Annual Gold Diggers' Ball. But mainly their dances were make-shift affairs, dancing taking place between the rows of tents, or, if they were on a property, behind the shearing sheds.

A lack of women saw bearded men pairing off for fast polkas or for a Highland Schottische, all to music issuing forth from a band which usually consisted of four men playing the swanee whistle, a leather squeeze box, a violin, and a set of drums made out of kangaroo skins stretched over a wooden frame.

And the dancing would go on all night, right through until dawn, when the people would walk, or ride, up to thirty miles back to their homes - to begin the work of a new day.

A Real Mongrel of a Place:

We passed through a real mongrel of a place: Kiandra. Sitting high in the Snowy's, it doubles up as part of a snowfield [the Selwyn] and a goldfield. Unfortunately, the two don't go hand in hand, snow melt defeating any attempt at sinking meaningful, productive shafts - at least with the technology available to the first miners back in the mid-nineteenth century.

But apart from invisible gold, and the memories of a family member who tried his hand at mining out here on this desolate moorland, the area holds no attraction for me. This probably has a lot to do with the fact that the cloud is so low I feel like I can touch it - and it is issuing marble-sized hailstones, along with the torrential rain and jagged lightning bolts.

I cannot imagine the determination of those first people up here; or the grim necessity of a life which drove men to try and seek a living in this God-forsaken place. It is truly awful.

Then, seventy-seven kilometres from Tumut Town, we drop down from the high country and into the six hundred feet deep valley of the Yarrangobilly River. Here we find ourselves in a different, certainly gentler, world. We weren't drawn here by the cave system, with its spiders and insects which are to be found nowhere else in the world. Nor was it the parrots and cockatoos that claimed our attention, even though their antics did raise our spirits - after Kiandra. Neither was it the vast tracts of native bushes flowering red, white, yellow and purple, filling the valley with a near-overpowering scent: nor the exquisite river itself, with its rapids and falls, and thermal pool with its hot water, bubbling up from far below.

No! For us it was the pobble-bonks who stole the show.

From fifty yards away, the erratic, non-harmonious clatter of a thousand pobble-bonks meant that the large, green males of the banjo frog fraternity were breeding fast. Initially, the commotion made me stop in mid stride, as your mind tries to cope with something new and strange. Could it be the river making that noise? You know - the fast moving water bashing tin cans over the rocks. But no! As you get ever closer, concentrating hard, an individual call, 'pobble' - 'bonk,' emits from the ooze alongside the river bank. That one call sets off a cacophony of similar calls from every other male frog ready to fight to protect his space; after all, you never know when a female may happen along.

The frogs like the 27 degrees of the thermal pool and are prepared to share their sperm, eggs, tadpoles and green slime with the hardy human interlopers who feel the necessity to swim amongst it all. It might be 27 degrees in there, but the changing-rooms are fifty freezing yards away - probably so placed by the sense of humour of the prisoner chain gang who constructed the infrastructure hereabouts in the 1960s.

We press on, leaving the caves to the more adventurous, and head for the small township of Tumut. We find the six and a half thousand population enjoying a Sunday lunchtime session in the town's seven pubs. [Well, the men that is. The ladies are noticeable by their absence.]

We park in the street outside the Royal, next to a Ute displaying a 'Honk if you Bonk' sticker. Despite the growing reticence of my wife and her cousin, Maggie, in the face of so much blatant machismo, we head for the hotel. Had we not been driven by hunger, there is no way the girls would have entered the noisy bar.

A deep breath and we're in. It's packed. The local angling club is getting stuck into steak and snag sandwiches and middies of ale. The noise dies immediately, just as it had done when we got too close to the pobble-bonk colony. The silence reigns for a long second, then stretches interminably into two, as the two females, who'd had the temerity to enter the male bastion, are scrutinized. The noise switches back on, as the barmaid explains that there's no food to be had. Hard to believe, as the meat juices are now running down the jowls of the locals.

It was just about certain that we were on Guinness and crisps for Sunday lunch, when Joe Doyle's lad intervened. He was small and wiry, dark haired and sunburned and with a ciggy in one hand and a beer in the other, he looked a contented man, perched as he was on the edge of the high bar stool.

I never did get to know his Christian name, "Everyone just knows me as Joe Doyle's lad," he responded to my question. I would also have liked to give you a more lucid account of our conversation, but unfortunately I understood only one word in every ten he spoke. I don't know if it was the local dialect of pobble-bonk he was speaking, or whether the combination of sun and beer was making him punchy, but he sure was hard work to listen to.

For the sake of decency, the swear words have been omitted too, which means that one word in every fifty is hereby recorded.

"Have you lived in the town long?" I asked.
"Dead now."
"Longtime! Here! You!" I emphasize what I'm saying with a pointing finger.
"Enough......Years."
"Did you work on the construction of the dams around here?"
"Bad.....Goodfella's.....Bad.....Yes."
"Was there any other work hereabouts after the dams were finished?"
"Factory.....Bra's and Steppin's"
"And you worked there making these corsets and stuff?"
"Nah! Timber.....Sawmill."

Then, gold dust: Our companion was getting attuned to the accent of his youth and it transpired that in earlier days, Joe Doyle's lad had known and worked with our mate's father.

"......Your mother, Mavis......Worked here behind bar."

In the wake of the breakthrough, others join in and the conversation rapidly assumes the proportions of a reunion for a wayward son. Even we nonentities are being treated like minor celebrities. Steak sandwiches appear: even the girls happily munch away, their thoughts of dirty blokes in a dirty bar being put on hold by the generosity being displayed - and the arrival of more booze from a distant admirer.

But time was pressing, and when the barmaid offered me a taste of the local speciality - deep fried Dog's Bollocks [true I swear it], it was definitely time to find the door through the crowd of well-wishers.

As the shadows lengthened, we headed for Gundagai, and home, singing chorus after chorus of that well known chart topper, 'On the Road to Gundagai':

> 'There's a track winding back
> to an old fashioned shack
> along the road to Gund-a-gai.
> Where the Blue Gums are growing,
> the Murrumbidgee's flowin'
> beneath the South-ern Sky.
> Where my Mummy and Daddy are waiting for me,
> and the friends of my childhood
> once more I will see.
> Ne-ver more will I roam
> ' cos I'm heading back to home
> Along the road to Gund-a-gai.'

Ah! The old tunes are the best, as me mother used to say.

The Gundagai Guys

Now Gundagai is not very famous. It lies on the Hume Highway, between Yass and the evocatively named Wagga Wagga. However, it does have 'that' irreverent song named after it from years ago which is now a firm family favourite.

Its recorded history begins with the first settlers fanning out from the coast in an ever increasing search for land. They ended up by the Murrumbidgee River - a beautiful spot, with land ripe for the plough. They built their houses and made a start at a new life. Then the floods came - the worst ever - and their houses were on the flood plain. Now don't run away with the idea that they were being stupid, because, believe me, when the rains come in Australia, they come. Ordinary, benign rivers can flood tens of miles wide.

But they stuck it out and now the area supports farms and vineyards, and the fishing is legendary. It is the place to go to hook the whoppers.

"Do they bite well here then?" I ask the barman over a midi.

"Bite well!" he says, helping himself to another beer. "Listen! I've seen the time when you had to hide behind a tree to bait yer hook."

I didn't believe him - and anyway, the fish are perfectly safe with me.

But why are we here? Well, the War Memorial at Canberra was the initial attraction as it holds the names of many of our people – including two brothers, James Joseph Thomas Bell and his brother, Louis Augustus, both of whom came from Gundagai. Both had perished in the First World War; [obviously:] - J.J. at Gallipoli and Lew in Belgium. Both descended from James Angell, one time marine, failed agriculturalist, prison guard, deserter and rake.

We aren't learning much; their footprints are too faint, and our journeys around the rolling countryside are more of a pilgrimage. Yet we feel it's something right for us to do.

And whilst we're this far, it's only another eighty miles, following the course of the Tumut River to Tumbarumba, where the Burgess clan - more men of the Angells - used to go bare-knuckle boxing around the local pubs and fairs. It is strange how the life of families here reflect the experiences of those they left back in Britain. Back there, we, too, have a history of bare-knuckle boxing - but in pit yards and back street pubs, where the rounds only ended when someone was knocked to the floor, and the combatants continued with broken limbs and horrendous injuries.

Just looked at the map! Much swearing and many expletives: " * * * * it!" We're only two hundred and fifty kilometres from Ned Kelly's High Noon at Glenrowan in Victoria. Haven't we been there?

Must back-track: - And quick.

*

The early explorers and settlers made damper bread as a mainstay with their meal. Try it now as something different with your barbecue, but make it the same day.

Damper:
Put 3 cups of self raising flour in a bowl and rub in 90 grams [3 oz] of butter until it is like fine breadcrumbs. Use your fingers.
Make a well in the centre and add three-quarters of a cup of milk and about one-quarter of a cup of water.
Mix it with a knife using a cutting motion until the dough is sticky.
Turn it out onto a lightly floured surface.
Knead lightly and shape it into about a 6 inch round before placing it on a greased oven tray.
Make two x half inch cuts in the round so that wedges will be marked out.
Brush the top with milk and if you want, sprinkle some cheese on top.
Cook in a hot oven for 10 minutes and then reduce the heat to moderate and cook for a further 15 minutes.
Something different: - A shared experience with the past - and very eatable.

The Great Australian Shoe Mystery:

Shoes! Dozens of them: All shapes and sizes, odd ones and in pairs; all dangling on a wire stock fence in the middle of nowhere. No town. No village. Not even any sign of human habitation - except for the fence.

The spectacle stopped us in our tracks, but not for long, because the bush walk had proved longer than we thought - the consequences being that we were drenched with sweat. My underpants were sticking to me most uncomfortably and, once stopped, we became the target for the blow-flies: big, buzzing things that sought out your nostrils, eardrums and mouth.

We walk on, but I can't stop thinking. I have never seen anything like this before. I've heard of 19th century gypsies hanging up chicken bones in their homes to ward off evil spirits; and certainly, in the 17th century, people in Britain buried the shoes of infants under the floor, usually near the hearth, for similar purposes.

But surely, those explanations don't work out here, not in the bush. So - why?

Could it be that, over the years, tourists have been murdered hereabouts and their boots hung up as trophies? You know - something like the notches on a gunslinger's pistol. But no, I don't think so. Murder is as old as time itself - the Bible shows us that - and Australia is not immune. There have been the occasional reported cases of a murdered tourist here and there, but mostly it is home grown crime.

For instance, just yesterday, the newspapers reported that a woman had murdered her husband, jointed him like a side of pork, boiled him up with a load of veggies, and served him to the kids. From her prison cell she is reported as saying: "I've never been happier."

Not only that, but in all our time in Australia we have never been frightened..... Sorry! I tell a lie. We've been scared stupid by snakes, spiders, cockroaches, ants, sharks, crocodiles, kangaroos, floods, heat, fires, storms and outback 'roads' - but once, only once, have we felt ourselves in a difficult situation with our fellow man. So, I suggest we discount dozens of murdered tourists as a source of the fence mystery.

Perhaps the shoes are the worldly remains of swagmen - you know - the Australian equivalent of a gypsy. Maybe they've passed through here and camped without a licence - and suffered the ultimate consequence.

But no, that won't work either. The Aussie home-grown vagrant types are more laughable than frightening. An example from the other day: We were walking along a main street, discussing with friends just how much wine we needed to take to a lunch-time party, when this dog suddenly started barking right behind me. Startled, I jumped a foot in the air and swung round to face the four-legged foe. Only it wasn't a dog, but a middle-aged man, with short stubbly beard, and hair that hadn't seen a comb since his mother died. Through tobacco-stained teeth, he half-shouted, half-laughed: "Don't get drunk! Don't get drunk!" before skipping his way across the road between fast moving cars.

Now, in America, vagrants seem to have developed aggressive begging into an art form. Try walking past the guy in Santa Monica who waves a 'Jesus is Love' sign in your face without dropping something in his cup. You'll see what I mean. But, no! The helping of Australian vagrant types to pass into the hereafter is not plausible. Now, had it been America......

That means I'm out of ideas. Perhaps you could come up with a couple of your own before proceeding. I'll wait for you.....

[1]

[2]

Hard, isn't it? However, in your absence I reckon I've got it: Just now, my wife and her cousin, Maggie have subjected me to another rendering of: "There's a track leading back, to an old fashioned shack, on the road to....." That gave me this idea: the best yet. You see, there's this deranged Pom who thinks he's an Australian. He goes off, wandering all over the continent, and every time he comes across someone singing "On the road to Gundagai," he does for them and hangs their boots up for all to see – all done in an attempt to exorcise that damn tune from his mind.....

No? Well, I give up. You figure it out.

Journey 10
Queensland

Brisbane and area

Down and out Downtown

We didn't sleep too well. Whether it's too much travel, too much excitement for us oldies, or just the first night in a strange bed, I don't know. Take your pick.

However, we saw the dawn break over one of Brisbane's 109 parks. This one is directly outside our plush hotel window on Whickham Terrace, just down the road from the Convict Treadmill. The park is lush and verdant and full of massive old fig trees. As the city clocks chime, almost in unison, from the century-old towers of the 'English' churches which abound hereabouts, the city yawns itself awake.

And as the sun came up, bright and beautiful again - Brisbane has about 300 days of sunshine a year - so the men came. One by one they arrived at the park entrance, inexorably increasing along with the distant rumble of invisible traffic.

We thought they might have been waiting to be collected for work. Could we be witnessing the black economy in action? You know, 'the draw the dole and work for cash' lot. But they can't be. Mostly they are too old.

Could they be members of a club? Jogging, walking perhaps? Health freaks who start the day with activity rather than with oceans of caffeine? But no: they are too well dressed. However, the shorts and business shirts did give the appearance of a uniform of some type.

We had just given up the guessing game when the soup kitchen arrived. I was aghast. I was in the throes of finishing my four-star luxury cup of tea in order to go across and have a chat, maybe even partake in their walk through the park.

I was even more aghast with the 'full-English-breakfasters' at the other tables. They never noticed. The knives and forks never missed a beat.

Well done, Brisbane. Not only are your streets litter free, your fine buildings free from the madcap antics of the graffiti merchants and your air unpolluted by smog and siren, but you also have the healthiest, cleanest, most orderly and best dressed down-and-outs I have ever seen.

Ossie Rules

We walked on. It was pretty warm and muggy. We were both tired, legs aching and backs hurting - but on we walked. It's a good job Brisbane is small enough to be seen on foot - but in this humidity.....

The aspirin hadn't helped much, but we are a determined pair, if nothing else. No shower. No room service. Not until we find one.

It may be something to do with Queensland's conservative past - but bottle shops [off-licenses] in Brisbane are as rare as hailstones in summer.

Eventually, success! We stumble into one by accident on Edward Street. Two bottles of red, chosen because of the name 'Aussie Rules,' and the hotel's air conditioning is beckoning. But wait! Edward Street! Wasn't that where General MacArthur once had his headquarters? It was, you know. And there's MacArthur's Chambers, the old nerve centre for the planning of the war in the Pacific.

Brilliant! I am really pleased as it gives me a chance to retell a little story about a bloke called Ossie Bates. Seemingly Ossie was a soldier in the Second World War. He was on leave in Brisbane, his home town, and had his mate with him. Both were in uniform, slouched hats n' all, and were stood outside this very building when MacArthur himself emerged, followed by his hangers-on. As the senior N.C.O. present, Ossie threw up a salute, which the General acknowledged with a touch of his cap and a "Good morning, Aussie." Ossie's mate gasped. He'd been shown all over town, met all Ossie's family and friends, but this took the biscuit.

"Blimey Oz." he says. "You knows every bugger!"

Thought of the Day

Sitting here in the shade of the biggest umbrella I have ever seen, and looking down from the headland at the sluggish expanse of the Brisbane River, I find it hard to comprehend that it was only two weeks ago that this area was under two feet of hailstones.

I know it's true, as I saw it on telly before we got here: pictures of people in flip-flops pushing cars out of 'snow' drifts.

Yet today we have none of that. Warm breezes enfold us, as we picnic at the world-famous Lone Pine Koala Sanctuary, about twelve miles up river from the city. The kids are inside, stressing the inmates to death, leaving us time to reflect on......on..... - The weatherman.

There is a great bloke on breakfast television. Today he was broadcasting from down the Murray River and the commentary went something like this:
Weatherman: "I've caught you a couple of whoppas, Sharon."

Now Sharon is in the studio, make-up immaculate, hair done, fingernails that have never seen a sink full of dirty dishes.
Sharon: "Oh! What are they? Show them to us."
Weatherman: "It's a European carp." He holds up a still twitching fish. "Just caught it!"
Sharon: "It's a nice looking fish."
Weatherman: "Yeh! Well it's not. It's a feral fish: A real mongrel this one. Only one thing for it....:" [Whereupon he takes a hammer and proceeds to bludgeon the creature to death in full view of millions.]
Sharon: "Don't! Don't!" she shouts, through the strangulated sound of her being sick.
Weatherman: "No! It's got to have it." Bang! Bang-bang! "Gotcha!"

Can you imagine the outcry in a super-sensitive Europe, where even fish have rights now - that is, if you can find a fish amongst the irradiated, polluted cesspits we have which pass for water.

In Queensland, conservation does not come naturally. For many years the ultra right-wing government up here was a joke to the rest of the country and nothing, but nothing, got in the way of 'progress.' Up here, people are encouraged to swerve their vehicles across the roads to squash the cane toads, and so the road sign for the koala sanctuary, emblazoned with the legend "Conserve Nature: Pickle a Possum," has a certain ring of truth to it.

Nearly time for the boat back to beautiful Brisbane - but before we board the river cruiser, a quick thought for the day. Brisbane came into existence purely as a prison colony and purely by chance. The colony was supposed to be at Redcliffe, about thirty-five kilometres away to the north east of the city, but the local tribesmen took the hump and chased the interlopers back to a more defensible position by the river.

There the newcomers settled and prospered, exploited and exterminated - just like the imported feral fish and feral toads.

Tangalooma Island

There is an anchor on Tangalooma from a ship wrecked here in 1862. Always on the lookout for a link, however tenuous, the migrant ship was called the 'Everton,' out of Liverpool. Here's the connection. I had a great uncle who played for Everton in 1892.

However, there is a closer hook-up. Remember the wild dolphins at Bunbury? Two days of no-show. Well, here we are again, sitting on yet another beach with yet another crowd of dolphin well-wishers.

"There's only been three nights in the last five years that they've not come in to see us," said the lady researcher-into-what-dolphins-do. [How do people get jobs like this? I want one!]

Nothing doing!

Long silence: We stare at the empty sea.

"There's a wobigong shark - just a metre off the beach. Can you see it?"

Interesting black shadow departs - but it's not what we've come for.

"I'm sorry if you've got yourselves a dinner reservation. They aren't usually so late."

Still nothing!

People, stomachs rumbling, start to head for the grub.

I sense an embryonic panic beginning within the researcher-cum-announcer. Can she prevent a stampede to the local watering hole? Nervousness hits her throat and her voice raises a couple of octaves.

"Perhaps if we all concentrate very hard we'll reach them by telepathy."

It's starting to feel like Bunbury all over again - only this time the expert is clutching at straws. Telepathy indeed!

But we're desperate. For five minutes there is total silence. Then little Emily, with a wisdom far beyond her years, says "My brain's ran out."

I know the feeling well.

Then! A single dorsal fin!

It's working? We all start doing matching mantras:

"Ommm.....Come-dolphins-come.....Ommm....."

And they did. Six, all told.

We're in the ocean, smelly fish in hand, like rats up a shutter. [Not quite, but you get the idea.]

I will forever remember the eyes; intelligent, full of life-force and so very, very different from the emptiness of those killers, the shark and the crocodile.

Being up so close to those graceful, gentle mammals has been a true privilege.

*

What can I say? The word 'incredible' springs to mind on this ordered, paradise island. But that word, 'incredible', is yet another that is being worked to death. Remarkable....., exquisite....., magnificent - it is all of those, and much more besides. Perhaps 'awesome' comes closest.

I suppose I should tell you about the fish feeding. Last night, dolphins: today, fish: An awe-inspiring array of sizes and colours, tearing food out of your gloved hand. The fish range up to the dreaded size sixteen - but no need to worry, it only has a size eight mouth. I feel as though I've fed every animal and bird species in Australia in one way or another - but the fish take one's breath away.

To snorkel around the eleven sunken ships at the northern end of the arc of sand was another privilege. There was no natural reef here, so create one and let nature do the rest. Protected from the rolling Pacific breakers by the bulk of the island, it has been like swimming in the heated indoor pools back home - only here, the water is not full of chlorine, but reef fish. They are incredible in colour, number and diversity. How confusing it must be for them to witness the bungling attempts of would-be mer-people, Charlie-Chaplining forwards in flippers, and then choking constantly when foolishly breathing through the nose instead of the mouth. They must be confused, as why else would they crowd around the stranger instead of fleeing? Then one nibbled my ear and I knew then that they hoped I was lunch.

The snorkelling expedition had not been spoiled by the rainstorm which hit. That too, was stunning both in ferocity and beauty, the deepening blue sea and the vibrant island colours being devoured by blackness. Yet the sun, before being overcome, blazed defiantly one last time, imprinting vivid images upon your very soul.

The rain didn't stop. This land of sunshine is awash: Cloudburst after cloudburst arrives at ten minute intervals. We do the only sensible thing - we take off our clothes. Sorry to disappoint - it's for an afternoon of water sports. Ever tried to get back onto an upturned inflatable banana in the middle of a heaving ocean?

Weak in the arm, and even weaker in the head, we must have given the impression that we were having fun, as the queue for the fruit ride just grew and grew.

Later, dry and warm, no-one expressed any surprise, concern or even anguish at the revelation that Moreton Bay is renowned for the size of its Great White sharks. They come to eat the poisonous swarms of stingrays - and it's stingray season.

Now that is incredible!

Rain-rain; go-away.....

We visit the island's sandy desert interior: a wet and soggy sandy desert.

Rain drips from awnings, from forlorn barbecues. But it cannot detract from the beauty that is Tangalooma.

And here it is again: Enigmatic Australia: Outward perfection with an unseen edge to it all. You look at nature's wonders and marvel, overcome by them. Yet they cloak the sinister, the dark side. No mention is made here of the island's Aboriginal past which spanned millennia. No mention of why they should suddenly abandon their homes in the face of growing European interests.

There is, however, a bleak and constant reminder of darker days: the remains of the fleshing deck, dedicated to profit from the slaughter of whales, stands in the midst of the resort. Derelict it may be, but its presence casts a worthy shadow over our pampered existence. Maudlin', perhaps.....

I blame the rain.

*

The sun is setting over the bay at the entrance to the Brisbane River and the tropical paradise of Tangalooma falls quickly astern. Shadows lengthen rapidly across our wake; last photographs are taken, cameras raised in some kind of farewell salute.

The large sand island stretches to about two hundred square kilometres and is swathed in banksia and eucalypts, thanks to thousands of years of nature at work. But somehow it's the fringe of palms which seems to stand out in the evening light. Not the lush forest nor the bleached white beaches, but the green fronds against a green hillside. Most strange!

The Ngugi tribe had once lived here, in a time before the first convicts arrived in the bay. The locals were described as: "the happiest, healthiest and most self-sufficient race on the face of the earth."

After our visit to a true paradise, I can see why.

Chicken Man:

Just to the north of Brisbane lives 'chicken man'. He's well over seventy, grey haired and grey bearded and complains that "My legs have gone."

It doesn't stop him being up before six each morning, to do battle with a huge Moreton Bay fig at the bottom of his garden. The branches are as thick as a man's body, but he's decided to reduce it to a pile of twigs. This morning he's thirty feet above the ground, sawing like crazy before his wife wakes up. [She wants to keep the tree.]

My guess is that the tree is still winning, but it is early days.

However, it's his chickens that bring purpose to his life.

I reckon it must be his deafness that allows him to ignore the local council - 'No more than six chooks,' they've told him.

"I've got seven," he admits, smiling conspiratorially like a naughty seven year old.

His eyes light up when he talks about the hens. They are pets, although he appreciates the occasional egg they still produce: Remarkable, when you learn that the youngest hen is pushing eight years old.

One has to be hand fed. "It's got a crook leg," he explains. "And the others pick on it."

"That one over there - she likes porridge, so I make her a bowl each morning."

"That one there knocks on the door every morning asking to be fed; and that one there," his index finger is working overtime, "that's the one I found the baby budgie under......"

Lucky the budgerigar now takes pride of place in the porch, kitchen, lounge, - wherever he happens to be.

The trouble is that 'chicken man' is becoming forgetful. The chickens can undo the lock on their coop, the budgie the door on its cage. The top mysteriously comes off the chicken food barrel kept just outside the back door and the mice are welcome to help themselves.

"Shouldn't you......" I ask? The furry critters are running along the skirting boards and shinning up the metal sides of the container without effort.

"Oh! They're fine. Lovely little things aren't they?"

Perhaps! Cute is in the eye of the beholder. But the fly screen door is always open and I'm now an expert on Aussie wildlife: I've watched all the shows on the telly - especially the ones on crocs, sharks, and snakes. We are safe from the first two, but isn't it a fact that mice eat chicken food - and wherever mice are, snakes turn up for a free feed too?

I shut the screen door yet again and go check the kitchen floor - you know, just in case. And today I'm in luck. It's only a giant cockroach.

A Night to Remember

Tonight the gods have conspired to fill us with a sense of wonder and awe. It is warm and sultry and we've got a glass of champagne in our hands – Australian, of course, and it's very, very good.

We are on the top of Mount Coot'tha, or Honey Hill, the tallest of Brisbane's eleven, and witnessing something special. The city is spread out below us, sparkling in the blackness as though all of King Solomon's jewels had been emptied out and scattered at our feet. The buildings and the seven bridges over the inky black, majestic river stand proud, be-decked and be-jewelled by lights of every conceivable colour. Ruby, emerald, citrine, diamond white - they are all there.

Brisbane is my kind of city. It is clean, unpolluted, with a nice mix of old churches, monuments, parks, stone civic buildings, as well as incorporating a touch of the glass and concrete towers of a downtown anywhere. But here it works. The city is enough in itself. Especially here: Especially now.

But beyond the fleshpots, out toward the invisible coast, a silent lightning storm takes the breath away. It is as if God is showing His majesty, saying, "Anything man can do....." And He is right. His apocalyptic backdrop to the city is truly awesome, enhancing the spectacular beyond belief.

And that's not all. Look up! The countless stars of the southern skies are at their timeless best, their eternity; their truth, crisscrossed by belfries of flying fox chasing a night full of insects: Mere extras in a heavenly extravaganza.

If I hadn't believed in God before tonight, I would now.

The Basilesk of Brisbane

What would our John Moresby, Royal Navy, make of this city and coastline now? As captain of H.M.S. Basilesk, he was up and down this coast like a rash back in the 1870s and must have come to know the insecure, infant colony quite well.

I wonder if he is up there now, although somewhat higher than Mount Coot'tha, peering down on Brisbane's lights, and feeling the atmosphere of a people who in safety and security enjoy the night's revelries in the restaurants and lantern markets along the banks of the great Brisbane River, or who take in the fantastic views from the cliffs on Kangaroo Point or Wilson's Outlook. It's a shame there's not a 'Johnny's Knob' or a 'Moresby's Knoll' to remember him by.

But if the city would perplex him now, how much more so the barren coast of his day: A place where the Aborigines tended to dispatch the unwary: where mosquitoes, sand flies and swamps, and the diseases they spawned, made it imperative for the Navy to keep out of harm's way by remaining out on the ocean - unless you ran out of fresh water or the ship needed to be beached for repairs.

Now the unsavoury reaches, south of Brisbane, have been transformed into forty-two kilometres of hotels, houses, marinas, theme parks and shopping malls, where the spending of money by the three million visitors each year has been elevated to an art form. And all the while the golden beaches and warm sea pull at you, whilst the rainforest of the hinterland beckons. These places are no longer to be avoided, but enjoyed.

No matter how splendid an adventurer John was, he would find it difficult to cope now. But of course he doesn't have to - he can leave us to enjoy his legacy in the here and now.

Bribie Island:

We had spent the morning on Bribie Island, with a remarkable woman who had been confined to a wheelchair since a car accident many, many years before. On top of that disaster, her husband had left soon after, in the company of a bar maid, so it fell to her to raise their three children, all under ten, alone. And she had coped admirably, not only maintaining her independence, but becoming a very accomplished artist to boot.

I didn't know the lady [yet another distant relative of Hogg descent] well enough to pass comment, and it would be wrong to do so. All I can say is that she appears to us outsiders to be a coper with life - someone with enough about her to teach herself art to a high standard, keep an immaculate house and produce well-balanced grown-ups.

The how's and whys of someone else's life are not my business, but I can't help compare her tenacity to that of Ron, whom we met later on the island's Woorim Surf Beach.

The meeting was accidental. Patsy trod on his toes, trying to evade the in-rushing king tide, which had already stolen several billion tons of sand from the beach and reduced the shoreline to a mere six-foot strip, backed by high, near- perpendicular dunes. So there was not much room to manoeuvre. However, it made for a certain coziness for those of us trying to squeeze the last few minutes out of the dying day.

We apologized to Ron's toes and the sprightly seventy-eight year old accepted it with relish. He needed someone to talk to. Since his wife of fifty-two years had died recently, he had bought a Volkswagen Campervan and taken off on a never-ending, lonely journey around Australia. As the coastal highway stretches as far as from London to Hawaii, it takes a bit of time - but his home was - had been - Bribie Island, so he touches base occasionally.

However, he remains tied to the beach, here as elsewhere. The sea and shore, their incessant movement and sound, seem to exert some sort of spell over him. Whatever it is, they certainly have him in their grip, as evidenced by his deep, all-over, tan.

In fact, you would never guess he was a Brit., born after the First World War in Wolverhampton in the industrial West Midlands. He had emigrated to Australia after serving for years in the Shropshire Light Infantry.

Perhaps this is why we immediately hit it off. Until comparatively recently, the Light Infantry depot had been in the county town of Shrewsbury - our adopted home for many years.

Ron seems to cope with his loss - of wife, of home, of regiment, of everything he held dear - by talking of the past and was soon telling us of his wife's family, timber-getters in the 1920s, somewhere in the interior of Queensland, inland from Nambour. The valleys were full of trees back then: ironbarks, grey gums, blue gums, tallow wood.

The broadaxe men, working in pairs, sweated the trees into railway sleepers and bridge girders for use throughout the state. They would set up camp near a stand of trees and within distance of drinkable water. The camp itself consisted of a ten foot by twelve foot calico tent, set under a large flysheet which acted as a cover for a tucker table and cooking galley. This double-sheeted tent could withstand weeks of rain - provided the inner layer didn't touch the outer.

Living was primitive. Water was collected in old kerosene tins which, of course, tainted everything. The bread, flour, tea and sugar were kept in a tucker box to stop the goannas, dingoes and crows from helping themselves. The meat, bacon and cheese were suspended from the ridgepole in a meat safe [a box with mesh sides, so the wind could blow through it,] to keep it away from ants. The cooking fat, butter and cheese would turn to liquid when the weather became hot, the meat remaining fresh for only a couple of days. Consequently, corned beef was favoured, pickled in brine and covered in coarse salt. It was slowly cooked in an old kerosene tin over an open fire and when it started to go off, the men flooded it with black Worcestershire sauce to make it edible.

Ron would have talked forever, but the tide had reduced the foreshore to almost nothing and all this talk of food was making me hungry.

We parted. I watched him across the car park, his van now standing alone as people departed for their homes. As he slid open the side door to his vehicle to begin yet another lonesome night, I could swear he had tears in his eyes.

It's Murder in Redcliffe.

To the best of my knowledge and belief there are no members of the Ningi Ningi Aborigines left at Redcliffe, the small, historic township situated a little to the north of Brisbane and where the first whites had landed in Queensland.

The original inhabitants of the area were an unfriendly bunch, seeing off those first European settlers who had been deposited there by the brig, Amity, in 1824. Admittedly, there weren't many intrepid settlers - just 29 convicts, 21 officers and men of the 40th Regiment of Foot, together with 19 of their wives and children. Soon they were heading for a more defensible position - present day Brisbane - put to flight by the Ningi Ningi warriors, dysentery, scurvy and all the rest.

I suppose we shouldn't be surprised by the British failure at Redcliffe. One of the first constructions they built was the flogging post - no sign of the working together in the face of adversity which would have been an essential to any success.

In fact, the army officers commanded only 16 men-at-arms, or 'rankers.' With such a small number it proved impossible to clear their settlement perimeter, let alone maintain and defend it.

These military matters were in my mind only because earlier in the day I had spent time with Pete, a sixty-five year old ex-S.A.S. man and Australian hero of the Vietnam War.

He was short, clean shaven, his frame still muscular and his handshake firm - despite, in his time, having suffered several gunshot wounds, been riven by various tropical diseases, and, more recently, two strokes.

In Vietnam, he had been the best mate of a recently deceased Hogg relative - hence the visit. He was more than happy to devour his wife's scones and talk of old times. But no secrets divulged. Drat! He's not a kiss-and-tell type and will take what he knows to the grave, thank you very much.

He did have certain, unequivocal views on the performance of the U.S. forces in South East Asia - like their inability to secure their defensive perimeters and a whole lot more.

Like at Redcliffe. I turn my back on the Pioneers' Memorial in the park by the ocean in order to watch one of the whale watching cruises disembark. Hundreds flood down the jetty to join the thousands thronging the choked esplanade. The car park slots are full; the Greek tavernas, Italian restaurants and German bratwurst sausage vans are all doing great business.

Thinking is difficult, what with the sound of oompa-music and the nerve-jangling warbling of an 1890s hurdy-gurdy competing to overwhelm my senses. But I can't help but raise a cynical smile at the thought of the Aboriginal warriors sitting around a fire on the beach saying: "Well, that's got rid of them for good."

The noise and crowds become too much; I dive for cover by the seashore, where the murder of hundreds of beached stinging blue jellyfish is taking place. Genocide carried out by young children wielding pointed wooden sticks. They stab; then pile the bodies high before running for more: Ghoulish, maybe - but infinitely preferable to the candyfloss atmosphere all about me.

It's no good. With no respite possible from the insane clamour, like many before me, I must flee.

You are my Sunshine.

Set inland, Nambour can hardly be said to be on the Sunshine Coast, although it does boast that it's only a fifteen-to thirty-minute drive to all the delights and sights on offer there. In the blink of an eye you can be amongst the crowds and the malls, the touristy things and the new housing developments of the Beautiful People at play.

But the town of Nambour has none of that; the Beautiful People are but a lost race out here in the hinterland. They would have no interest in the belching smoke that emits from the sugar refinery in the centre of town; no interest: nay! - be appalled at this 'Man's town' of tattoos, beer and stained singlets.

Nambour is without doubt a rough-and-ready place, disinterested in the superficiality of the Sunshine Coast and ready to face anything the world throws at it.

And we like it; like the rawness and are enamoured with Ed. In a plush hotel, in a city centre somewhere, he would be a uniformed and polite concierge. Here, in his obligatory vest, stained with sweat and strained to the limit by his rolls of fat, he is a propper-up-of-a-newspaper-by-the-cash-register in a run-down motel. His enormity should be of concern both to him and his chair, swamped as it is by wobbling buttocks.

In the working town of Nambour visitors are few, so there is no need to update or modernize.

"We leave that to them lot down the coast," he explains disparagingly, his finger stuck in his mouth trying to dislodge a grape skin from between his back teeth. "There's no need for us to do much here. No competition to speak of, see. There's a room above the pub - but it's a bit rough."

So we accept his invitation to stay the night, content to put up with the influx of the harmless Christmas beetles in our bedding, whose urine stains won't wash out, and accept the damp patches on the ceilings and walls.

"You need to git out of this here town," Ed says with a feigned American drawl: [He's a country and western fanatic, you understand:] "Nothin' much doin' unless yer fancy a lock-in at the pub up town."

He gives us a withering look when we reject the offer of an all-night booze-up and instead mention a Scottish country dance. We obviously deserve closer inspection now. He studies us, to make sure we weren't taking the Mick, then, satisfied that we weren't, flattens a fearsome rhinoceros beetle with the heel of his hand. "Try the Maroochy River, down Mooloolaba way," he advises.

That sounds suspiciously like a line from a song, but I say nothing, opting to explore the town. There followed thirty confusing minutes. The centre of town held a railway line along and across at least three of the main thoroughfares, down which loaded sugar cane trains hurtled. They were unrestricted by traffic lights and were in a hurry, stopping for nothing.

As were the men of the town: They propelled their battered Ute's, reinforced with 'roo bars, at speed along the main street. They drive as if they have somewhere to go, oblivious of careering trains and wandering pedestrians.

Thirty minutes was enough. We take Ed's advice and try Maroochydore.

Now, I don't wish to be unkind, but the tiny, river-mouth township situated in the centre of the Sunshine Coast offered nothing to us. It is but one more example of the affliction that has hit coastal Australia, seemingly from Cairns to Melbourne: unfettered development - an unstoppable drive to build one mind-numbingly, boring shopping mall after another, one housing estate, one apartment block after another. Then there are the roads, choked with traffic. Worst of all: the inevitable caravan and camping parks, blighting once beautiful and near inaccessible places.

To add insult to injury, these monuments to modern man have been awarded exotically sounding names by the owners in an effort to aid sales. Words like, 'Pacific,' 'Blue,' 'Waters,' 'Pelican,' 'Beach,' 'Palms,' 'Tropical,' 'Hideaway,' are used interchangeably.

Okay! So ninety percent of Australia's population lives within reach of the sea - and that fact has to be lived with. Add in the vast amounts of cash collected from superannuation schemes that have to be found a home [excuse the pun] - and there is no better investment than property - so it's no wonder so much land is becoming urbanized. It is just that I can't help but feel that, in the process, Australia is losing something of itself.

I reckon that's why we liked Nambour. It harks back to how Australia was: raw; exciting; different.

I am not the first to recognize the dangers involved in the urbanization of Australia. Many years ago, someone called George Johnson warned, ".....It is as if we are unaware of the peculiar beauty of our environment."

I think he was right. His 'gypsy's warning' echoed in my brain, as we experience a crowded riverside walk, accompanied by the sights and muted sounds of the incessant traffic of the Sunshine Coast.

With a stress headache threatening, we retreat to the delights of a Nambour lock-in - complete with urinating beetles and sweaty vests.

So refreshing!

Obi-Obi to Kin-Kin

The interior of Queensland, once away from the hullabaloo of the coast, is apparently unaffected by time.

Pobble-bonk frogs call from their hide-outs by the Mapleton Falls, where the crystal waters disappear over the edge of the plateau into the Obi-Obi Valley far below.

Poisonous black snakes, dangling at head height from trees overhanging the only path, add excitement to the bush walking, and goannas strut the tracks as though they own the rainforest of the Kondalilla National Park and falls: Which, of course, they do.

The people are different up here on the Tablelands - a far cry from the hedonistic lowlanders. More relaxed, with more time for......well, just about everything.

I think it is incumbent on me to try and learn something of the prevailing attitudes of the locals - not something I can do justice to in the time allowed to us by the ever present need to make miles. So, over coffee, I turn to the local newspaper, the Hinterland Voice, which is leading with the Kin-Kin Carnival. Surely there can't be anything more parochial?

Amongst its adverts for local eating places, general stores, bric-a-brac stalls and all the rest, I find an article and a series of letters as to what health care means out here to those who choose to turn their back on conventional dictates. All of a sudden you realize there is no escape from 21st century issues.

A local woman is expecting triplets. [I suppose that's a cause for celebration, although we found having to cope with one at a time hard enough.] Anyway, none of the local GPs will take her on - in fact they are not accepting any more pregnant mums at all. It is much too dangerous to the doctors' pockets if anything goes wrong during the birthing process.

The triplet mum finds an obstetrician in Brisbane - provided she pays a one thousand dollar, non-returnable, insurance premium.

This scandal has provoked a comment or two on the lack of government funding for the interior:

"Wherever you find a trough, you'll find pigs."

"Bureaucracy has finally caught up with the piggery technique - a free trough for those with snouts long enough to get into it."

"They" [the Government] "say the results" [of their policy] "are getting through on the ground. I say bureaucrats and porkers are getting obese and the public are cottoning on."

From the obsession with pig references, I suspect the same hand behind the letters. Either that, or there are a lot of swineherds in these here mountains.

In any event, it's nice to see the seemingly parochial Hinterland Voice is speaking with so much universal appeal.

Bald Rock

Now Queensland is bigger than Britain, France, Spain, Portugal and Italy all put together and there is no way we are going to be able to visit more than a fraction of it. But we've got to start somewhere, so we head up the Brisbane Valley, following in the footsteps of the settlers who left the security of the fledgling city behind them for the rich, black soil of the Darling Downs.

The town of Warwick dates from 1848 and lies in the Cunningham Gap beneath the Great Dividing Range. It became home to some of those blessed Birkby's - prolific breeders in both numbers and locations throughout Australia and who, with their gardening roots in the heavy soils of a wet Yorkshire estate belonging to Lord and Lady What's-it, must have been delighted by the conditions here - and on their own land.

There are none of our breed left hereabouts, but it is still a handy spot for us as we make our way to see two natural features lying a little way to the south: Bald Rock and Boonoo Boonoo.

*

We emerged from our enforced walk through dark, dense forest and stopped. We had no option. The rock was there, close enough to touch, towering above us before losing itself in a blue, blue sky. Bald Rock: Well named. Blinking furiously against the sun's sudden attack, we looked again at the world's biggest granite monolith, standing naked and unashamed against the world. It was immense and exuded a magic. It put its arms around you, drew you in; demanded your attentions, tempted. And yet, until just now, its hugeness had remained completely hidden. We had known it was there; the Prospectors' map said so. But we had seen neither hide nor hair of the mountain throughout our journey along unmade tracks infested with kangaroo and frilly-necked lizards.

Until now, that is. We hesitated. It invited with a siren silence. We lingered. It seduced and called us to the rock.

Still we lingered. It would be a fair old climb. What's further up? How would we cope with the exertion in the heat? How would we get back down? Shut up, fool! We've come a long way for this, so get on with it. Doubts cast aside we succumb to the alluring face of the virgin.

It took some time. Fifty feet up and stop. We share our pain with the non-panting lizards. Whereas our lungs are fit to burst, they are having to lift their feet high and in a regular order to prevent them being burnt. Our heartbeat rate returns to something like 120 a minute; time for another fifty feet. Stop and watch the dancing lizards. Is this a good idea?

The top! Incredible! Awesome! I've run out of adjectives again, but it was a good idea to come after all. Good! No, it's better than good. Huge, perfectly round boulders sit like giant marbles on the back of the hand of a colossus. We sit and look out, like sailors from a crow's nest, onto a never-ending sea of green. As far as the eye can see, there is nothing but the tops of trees: Million upon million. This is my desert continent and I love it.

Sandwiches on top of the world: Elated, we float back to the civilization of small town Tenterfield.

*

Still high on the adrenaline rush of success, we brave another exciting drive further into the wilderness - until we have to abandon the car. We take to a walking track, half hidden by the encroaching bush, unheeding and uncaring. We are on an all time high - invincible after Bald Rock. Just the sort of attitude you don't need to take with you on a bush walk.

We reach Boonoo Boonoo and the falls are exquisite. However, two questions rise within me and start to eat away at the old grey matter. First! In the Aboriginal language, Boonoo Boonoo means 'poor game.' Which Boonoo means poor and which means game? To us 'outsiders,' I guess it will remain a mystery. Secondly: "Where the firk are we?"

Bob's Place

Millmerran is in totally the opposite direction to Bald Rock. It had to be of course, as one of the chief characteristics of our family would be best described as ornery or cantankerous. They certainly don't make it easy.

But we find Millmerran, recorded as the home town to the MacClean and Birkby families, who ran sheep on a property an awful lot smaller in size than Belgium.* But the small town is still a long way from their old place down on the Condamine River.

The river itself is interesting, in that it is one of those predestined to self destruct in the interior. It rises in the mountains of the Great Dividing Range, but instead of taking the short, easy route to the sea, it heads inland, where the unrelenting sun goes to work draining away its life force. Now the river dies in a dam before the desert plains are reached, but it dies nonetheless.

The family and the river would no doubt have got along famously, sharing the same characteristics as they do.

*The largest sheep property in Australia is about the size of Belgium.

*

Bob's place was a near dust bowl, despite some recent rain and the presence of the river. The sun was relentless, the heat enough to stun the senses. Taking in oxygen was like doing deep breathing exercises inside a bread oven, but we had been invited to visit a property and it would have been churlish to refuse. Because of the bad state of the wool market, exacerbated by a long drought, Bob was having to think 'tourism' to try and get some cash flow going, so as to keep the bank off his back. It was proving to be an eye-opener for all involved.

We followed him to the silent shearing sheds. These are simple structures - four walls and a roof - but not only are they central to the farm's existence, they are also central to Australian legend, mateship in adversity, and the country's economic foundation.

The whole building shook with the violent kick he gave the corrugated iron door. The sound reverberated across the vastness; white and pink gulahs took fright and rose squawking into the stillness. I raised my eyebrows. He read the question. "Snakes," he said: "Gives 'em a chance to go."

Bob, big in every way, wasn't overly communicative. Too many problems out here, I guess. I don't think he really wants his farm invaded, and certainly he had a lot to learn about his fledgling flight into the tourist market.

"What was wrong with the sheep back down the track?" I asked.

"Birthbed's come out."

It certainly hadn't looked too good, the animal lying on its side, bloated and fly blown.

"I'll shoot it later."

I thought uncharitable thoughts and held my peace. Another guess – he had no intention of wasting a bullet on it, as they cost money. Having said that, it is fairly obvious to anyone that it's a hard life out here - and I have no right to make judgements on what I don't understand: But tourism?

Change of subject called for. "Not much livestock, Bob."

"No. The breeding stock has gone south. No feed here for them. If I hadn't sent 'em I reckon I'd have lost the lot. As it is....." He shrugged his shoulders disconsolately.

"How do you feel....?" Inane query: Why do I do it? I hate those reporters who always seem to ask that dopey question. I try to repair the damage. ".....About the place being so deserted, I mean."

He was generous - obviously a quick learner.

"Relief, really: I know I'm not in charge, but at least they are getting plenty to eat."

"Must have cost a bomb to transport them out of here: - what with the drovers to pay and all."

"Mmmh!" Thoughtfully he stroked his bristled chin: Still no smile. "But we can walk 'em back."

Business man to the last.

What Guzzunder

Aunty Dot has spent sixty or more of her ninety-something years in Australia. It was one of her proudest boasts that, in all that time, she had only ever seen one snake. That was before her family bought a property 'up-country' - meaning it was way out in the bush. The place was equipped with all mod cons - like an outside dunny: a sentry box-sized bush toilet made of galvanized iron. Unfortunately, brown snakes, king snakes, tiger snakes [those are the ones that chase after you] and practically every other nasty [i.e. deadly] reptile and spider called the place home long before our mob did.

Night-time trips to the loo become the stuff of nightmares for aunty. Tired out by not sleeping too well, a nap in the afternoon sun was called for. As she dozed the afternoon away, a tiger snake snuggled into the pool of shade created by the sagging, canvas bottom of her deck-chair.

I don't know if the family ever dared to tell her.

Not quite as bad, is the tale about an outback expedition my baby brother took in his hardier days. Camping out, under the Southern Cross, somewhere in the 'Red Centre,' he used the old Sundowners' trick of hollowing out a piece of ground to allow your shoulder to fit into, and then wrapping yourself into a groundsheet. Seemingly this is a comfortable way to sleep. [Myself, I prefer.....]

Unfortunately, during the far reaches of the night he twisted and turned and couldn't get comfy. There was always something sticking into him: A long, uncomfortable night, the grey dawn a welcome release. A cup of steaming coffee in hand, my bulky [but lovely with it,] sibling turns a deathly shade of white, but he needn't have. The large black snake, which had fancied the centrally-heated hole fit for a shoulder, had been squashed to death.

These little tales remind me of a yarn about a couple of mates out camping in the bush.

One of these guys - a real big fella' who had never had a day's illness in his life - wakes up one night, moaning and groaning with terrible pains in his lower back and legs. He can hardly move for the pain.

His mate, we'll call him Old Bobby, wakes up but doesn't know what to do except sit beside him and feed him cigarettes. He sits and sits - for hours he sits. Moans and groans, sporadic anguished cries and plenty of smokes.

Dawn is about to break when Old Bobby, despite the deep mournful 'Ohhh's' from his mate, starts to drop off to sleep. He wakes with a start as his ciggy rolls under his mate's bunk.

Now the bunks consist of Hessian sacks stretched over two poles and with the weight of the occupant, sag perilously close to the floor.

Bobby, on hands and knees under the bed, comes face to face with a bad-tempered, sleepless porcupine. Each movement from above, another quill penetrated the sacking in retaliation.

"Right, I'm off then," says Old Bob, getting to his feet.

Please! "Don't leave me. Ohhh! Don't leave me like this out here. Ohhh!"

"For Gawd's sake! Get out of yer bunk and get unda-it. You'll soon be better."

The ill man made a remarkable recovery - matched only by his remarkable language, which had as many points as the porcupine.

Australia!

And talking about snakes and other creepies.....

Queenslanders are supposed to be the most Australian of Australians. The manly frontier spirit lingers on, and for a generation the state kept on electing a peanut farmer who was dead set against conservation, permissiveness and human rights. He was authoritarian, barred demonstrations, had protected buildings demolished and had a finger in many a corrupt pie. In fact Gough Whitlam once described him as "The dumbest premier of them all."

This was my brush with Aussie politics:

For the sake of argument, and to prevent me being sued, we'll call him by his nickname of Kipper - a name earned by him being spineless, two faced and smelling badly. He was sitting behind his uncluttered desk and must have had a good lunch. His tie was slightly askew, he managed to stifle a belch and his shirt tail peaked out from below the folds of fat. He stood to greet me and I took the limp handshake. His breath was alcohol laden and he had nothing to do - except me, that is.

The whole episode reminded me of a promotion interview I'd once had. In a drunken slur, the chairman had called me a cross between Geoffrey Boycott and he of the 'V' sign, Harvey Smith: Both good Yorkshire lads. Thinking it was a compliment, I was quite surprised when I didn't get the job.

Like twenty or so years ago, I was annoyed with myself. I didn't leave; I actually felt flattered - this time for being asked to meet this particular parliamentary spokesman, who was ostensibly seeking information about the British policing system.

I should have known better. We should all know better. I've met a few royals and a few politicians in my time and have only found two that I have instantly warmed to. One was later branded a racist [wrongly]; the other, a 'wet.' I don't know which is worse - but both meant a political death.

Kipper was no different to others on the greasy pole. Give him his due, he could talk for an hour and say nowt. The reason for my visit became evident fairly early - to provide free accommodation to him on his forthcoming, all expenses paid, trip to the U.K. No chance! But I smile, the politicians smile, and don't say yes and don't say no.

I leave, cursing the loss of an afternoon and wondering about the necessity of politicians worldwide.

The Science of Politics

State Election Day provides me with the perfect excuse to give the light of day to some clangers I've gathered over the years and which, I suspect, the politician authors would like to forget. [They are all true.]

Foreign Policy:
When referring to the Khamer Rouge guerrillas who were threatening to behead the first Australian they could capture, in 'retaliation' for the Australian Government's support to the Cambodian Government, it was said: "My advice is to keep your head down."
The Dole:
"They [spongers] ought to get their heads down, their arses up and earn it."
The Breathalyser:
"I don't agree with lowering the blood alcohol limit," said the politician.
"Why?" asked the reporter.
"I can drink a bottle and a half of red wine, and I'm still O.K. to drive."
Road Deaths:
Whilst denying the interviewer's assertion that there was a direct correlation between the high number of road deaths and the lack of any speed limit whatsoever: "The problem is not the speed limit. The problem is that we've got more Aborigines than anyone else."
Crime:
"If the system stuffs up, the system pays up. That's democracy."
This was said in relation to an Aboriginal man being released from prison after serving seven years for a murder he did not commit. Sceptical after years of British cases hitting the headlines? Not this time. The bloke was in gaol when the murder was committed, so it was a pity no one bothered to check the custody records sooner.

The argument against Abortion:
   "The girl's more scared of the calf than she is of the bull. That's the way it ought to remain."
Your guess is as good as mine:
   "As Aunty Beryl said, 'It's the bit on the end that counts.' "
Politics:
1. "Australian people are bloody minded sheep."
2. "Democracy is the art of running the circus from inside the monkeys' cage."
Re-Election:
1. "I don't care what I have to do to get re-elected."
2. "Vote for me. I'll keep the bastards honest."
3. "I feel we did take some risks in the election by leaving the results to the electors."
4. On finding that the City of Geelong in Victoria had been won by the opposition:
   "Geelong has copulated."
A comment on a parliamentary statement:
   "This is the greatest heap of bullshit since Marx first enunciated his Mein Kampf."
I know you'll want to know who won the election today. – Well, the government did: - It always does.

Brisbane

We head out of Brisbane for the day: North to Burpengary. Sounds like it should be a movie title.

The train is modernish and electric. One of the utterly boring, international metal tubes we all know so well - but this one is well used, clean and very cheap. It hurtles like a thing possessed for the few seconds between interminable stations.

Brisbane as a city reputedly covers one of the largest areas in the world, and I for one begin to believe the statistics: For nearly an hour we stop-start our way through a tangle of suburbs with nary a park or river to lift the spirits. Plenty of boarded-up factories and fields full of rusting cars. Miraculously, between the heaps of rusted metal, a lone sheep or cow grazes unconcernedly. I suppose it makes a change from the vicious guard dogs of British scrap metal merchants. And everywhere a monotonous trail of mindless graffiti defaces inner city and outer suburb alike.

Yet surely every city in the world exposes its nether regions to the train traveller. Just out of sight can be the wonders of the world, - but train users are given a great big moonee.

So it proves. Burpengary is a pleasant place with pleasant houses set in pleasant gardens. The relatives are nervous. The best china is out and they've probably heard I can wreck furniture at twenty paces given half a chance and a couple of wines.

We stick to tea and the time just flies.

Journey 11
Central Queensland

Gladstone

'A city with a difference,' as the guide books would have us believe.

In fact, what they are disguising is that the city is a working class, industrial town with major works and refineries dealing with alumina, oil shale, petroleum, coal and much more besides. And they all use the deep, natural harbour to export their wealth, the tankers rubbing shoulders on the sparkling water with racing yachts and vessels ferrying passengers to and from the Great Barrier Reef.

The place may be industrial in parts, but is none the worse for it: Beaches, tidal rivers, muddy inlets, a wild hinterland; the reef, all within touching distance. It's a good place to be.

The City Council also keeps the place clean - always a recommendation in itself - and its residents remain friendly in the face of the cash-heavy hordes of visitors, who merely use their town as a convenience to get to and from the reef. Yes, it's a good place.

To get there, we drove seven hours south from the National Park at Cape Hillsborough, on a road which soon turned away from the coast; and the busy sugar cane fields with their smoking refineries, until we ran for mile after mile through open eucalypt woodland and grass: cattle country.

The traffic is very light, the road long and uninteresting. The crosses at the roadside, dedicated to the memory of accident victims, grew apace: Boredom Kills!

Oncoming traffic, in the main, consists of army vehicles, which are full of personnel and their equipment: bulldozers, explosives, ambulances, tanks, bridges, all of it heading north - to Townsville, and the one supposed threat to Australian sovereignty - their near neighbour, Indonesia.

The troops are American Marines, but the sights and sounds of so much military muscle provoke the mind into action, establishing connections where perhaps none exist.

We have not long left Townsville, the home of our cousin [a retired Australian soldier], and instead of concentrating on the road, I recall our shared conversations over a beer or two.

Connection one was Ned Kelly, Australia's most famous bush ranger and folk hero. Our Wollongong family have a claim to him: one of their Devlin's acted as blacksmith to the gang. Now, our Townsville mob, who are from a completely different family line, tell us of their Harris kin. They actually rode with Ned before he became such a notorious villain, dropping out of the limelight when his misdemeanours began to mark him out as a serious target for the cops.

The Harris clan moved out of Victoria and made their home in the desolate Pilliga Scrub in the west of New South Wales. And that's the second coincidence. Patsy and I got totally lost in that semi-arid desert on the way to Lightning Ridge. Getting lost in a trackless wilderness wasn't much fun - indeed we reckon we were lucky to survive; but here it is the cause of so much disbelief that the cousin is on the phone in a flash, calling the rello's in Pilliga, to pass on the information about "These useless Pommy Bastards," that were having a beer with him.

Fortunately, we've travelled sufficiently throughout Australia to know that such a description is an endearment: [Usually.] However, 'useless' is a different matter, but something about which I could hardly argue - especially when you know the Harris story.

They were a rum lot. Twenty-five children, twenty-three of whom survived to adulthood and, from the age of nine, made their living by splitting railway sleepers. The lucky ones went off in boxing booths which toured Australia once upon a time.

Four unmarried brothers lived and worked together in the Scrub and were a little too fond of a tipple and a fight. After a night at the pub, all four would fight each other to a standstill for the right to drive home. Once in their yard, they would fight again to see who went into the house first, and then fight again if anyone showed any inclination to go to bed instead of staying up for a nightcap - or two.

True spirit; and a toughness they took into the Australian forces. During the Second World War several brothers joined the 9th Australian Division and saw action at Tobruk before being sent to New Guinea. None of them suffered any injury. However - another brother who was under age - decided to run away and join up too. He couldn't join the 9th with his siblings because they would 'dob him in.' So he was with the 22nd Brigade when Singapore fell. He celebrated his fifteenth birthday in the infamous Changi Prison.

Another tank transporter rumbles past showing more urgency on its journey than we have so far. The foot hits the accelerator, and with it the past lives and times are put behind us: At least for a while.

And along came Joan.

Gecko Valley Vineyard lies at the end of a dirt road and atop a small eucalyptus-covered hill just outside the city of Gladstone.

We were too early for coffee, but along came the owner, Tony, happy enough to pass the time in an amicable fashion. He busily pruned the vines as he spoke. With a full six acres of shiraz and chardonnay to do on his own, there was no time to stop.

So we walk the rows with him, keeping pace with the clicking of shears. He tells us that he still works full-time at one of the local aluminium producing companies and that his way of keeping fit is by rising at five each morning to spend two or three hours at the vineyard.

After work - repeat!

He certainly has plenty of commitment, not only to the present mind-numbing work, but to his small hillside property, which extends to something like a hundred hectares.

And Tony has plans. Eventually he'll extend the rows of vines to cover twenty four acres of Mount Biondello's gentle slopes. As it has taken him eleven years of trial and error to produce a half decent portfolio of wines on the present six acres, I point out that he will be pushing ninety by the time he achieves his dream.

A shrug of the shoulders: "No matter, mate. It's a lifetime's work - and the next generation is coming along nicely."

He was working quickly and, although self taught, gives the impression of being a confident professional. He could not care less that we were leaving his wife further and further behind. Clip. Clip. Snip! Move on.

We hadn't met his wife yet - he'd only shouted to her to get the coffee on. And therein lay a dilemma. Learn more about the grape buds and the trapping of feral cats, or enjoy a leisurely sit in the shade?

Suitably refreshed, it's time for a look at the other side of Mount Biondello. Over there lies the eighty three hectare site given over to the city's Tondoon Botanical Gardens - Tony's recommendation, and they were indeed impressive, with an array of lakes, streams and fern-filled gullies, alive with red and blue dragonflies, butterflies and the calls of unseen birds.

A true Garden of Eden, a place of rest and.....

"Spider!" I shout a panicky warning to my wife, who hadn't noticed the hand-sized beast dangling two feet above her right ear.

"Snake!" she shouts her warning simultaneously.

There followed one nerve-wracking moment, neither of us knowing which direction to flee in. Instead, we freeze.

The spider didn't move a single, bristle-covered leg, content to sit and look malevolently at us.

The snake did move: Slowly: Out into a patch of full sun and away from the shady, fern-covered base of a tree. It was barely a yard away before I saw it. It was truly beautiful though, showing off its yellow belly and black back decorated with blue crystalline markings. It sensed our presence, its tongue working overtime. It raised itself in defence to an impressive three feet high and blew its head out like an Indian cobra.

We were transfixed: One eye on the snake; one on the spider - which was now twitching as if ready to do something. Decision time: To move or not to move? If we moved, could we do it quickly enough to prevent being bitten by one or the other? Or both!

I felt as if we'd been turned to stone forever, before Angela came along. Angela was one of the park's ecosystem guides and had her tuition group in tow.

"It's harmless!" she stated, as if this was an everyday occurrence. Whether it was for her group's benefit, or ours, I wasn't sure: "Just a common tree snake!"

Her dismissive tone made our exciting predicament, our adrenalin rush, kind-of disappointing. And the spider?

"Oh! That little thing! You ought-a see the mother. Come along children." She beckoned to an assortment of five to eight year olds to follow on.

And we did, too - follow on - at the back - sheepish and hoping she wouldn't notice.

"Did I ever tell you about the time I frightened a taipan to death?" She half shouted the information over her shoulder as she walked. "Now that IS a deadly snake, and all I did was scream. It keeled over right there and then in front of me."

Marvellous! And all this time, here am I thinking snakes were deaf.

But the day has been a delight. As evening draws in, we sit in an urban garden surrounded by butcher birds, kookaburras, parrots and a whole lot more. We sip wine; the barbecue smoke tantalizes the senses as we await the arrival of our host's niece, all the way from England: Her first visit.

And along came Joan. Joan Brown. She may have been twenty pounds heavier, but there was no mistaking her. It was THE Joan Brown, the one who had been our classmate, forty years ago, in a dire Newcastle upon Tyne schoolroom, and whom we'd not seen since the date of our release into the big world.

The untamed Lion:

Volcanic Mount Larcom - 'The Lion Mountain,' or 'The Sleeping Giant,' depending on whom you talk to - rises some two thousand feet above sea level to the north and west of Gladstone.

It is a bush walk not for the faint of heart - five hours through eucalyptus forest and razor grass - and, in places, both hands are needed when the paths suddenly become climbs.

It should also be said up front that we never had any intention to try for the summit – more, a gentle plod was on the cards, to see what we could see and get a feel for the place.

And first impressions are favourable. The total silence of the forested mountain slopes, broken only by the calls of kookaburras, is totally enchanting. But reality soon breaks in. There is not a breath of wind to ease the blistering heat, and the trees offer only an illusory shade, as the path perversely winds far enough away from them to keep you in the full sun.

Yet the bush is at its best. We're encouraged on by the sight of a six-foot long, deadly brown snake which slithers across our path. The walk had hardly begun and already nature is producing its best for us.

We sweat.

Kookaburras laugh.

We pant, ever upwards, stopping frequently to sip water.

In places, the path becomes just one giant ants' nest. It needs to be big, for the inhabitants are large - and evidently hungry. We watch, fascinated, as a couple of hundred tear at the remains of an unrecognizable carcass: Perhaps a skink – but impossible to tell.

Meat-eating ants! It's getting better and better. So we press on. Our water consumption increases as the foothills wind and rise. Our shirts, once wet with sweat, are drying on us. The heat is horrendous; it has to be experienced to be believed.

A tawny frog mouth breaks cover. This beautiful – ugly, silent bird swoops low and lands in the tall grass. It is hunting for food, which in the main consists of frogs and snakes. Only there is no water here - so make your own choice as to what's on the menu.

This is marvellous stuff: undisturbed wilderness. No one appears to have been up this track for ages.

We tolerate the sunburn. There is no option - we're already creamed up to the eyeballs in 30+, tropical strength, nothing-can-touch-you stuff, but we're being burned through our shirts.

Time to turn back?

Not at all!

A short distance more and the bush is in flower - vivid yellow flowers we don't recognize, set against fire-blackened trunks: Incredibly beautiful - and somewhat hazardous to photograph.

We press on, ignoring the fact that the trail seems to have lost its way [or we have], as the markers on the tree trunks thoughtfully provided by the parks and wildlife people have gone walkabout. Any hesitation on our part disappears as a frill-necked lizard runs along the path in its endearing, leg-lifting, isn't-this-ground-scorching-hot, fashion.

Then came the grass: sharp, razor-tipped spears which overhung the track. We force our way through, urged on by the blizzard of grass hoppers we'd disturbed. But even they aren't enough. Common sense prevails.

A decision has been forced upon us. We need to retreat. Not because our bare legs are scratched and sore thanks to the razor grass: nor because of other inconsequentials like sunburn or fast emptying water bottles. No! Fear was the deciding factor: A fear of the unknown. The grass is now too thick and too tall, reducing the line of our path to mere guesswork. Visibility is measured in feet and inches and anything could be 'Out there!' - or - 'Just here!' Anything!

Imagination is a fearful thing at times - and in Australia, imagination and reality merge far too often, conspiring to put the unwary into perilous predicaments.

So we stop, content to let Lion Mountain remain untamed and unsullied this day. We drain our water bottles, take in the silence for one last, lingering moment and scurry away toward safety.

And oh! How the kookaburras laughed.

There's no place like home

"You must go to Tannum Sands," said the rello's unanimously.

"You must go to Tannum Sands," said the Canadian bartender at the bottle shop: "Better than all the rest."

So we travelled the twenty kilometres south, looking forward to seeing the "perfect place for a swim in water that's twenty one degrees all year round."

Everyone was being helpful, yet for some reason no one mentioned the vast, brooding aluminium smelter which dominated the approaches to the resort - nor the beach notice board: 'Beware: Stingers and Saltwater Crocs!"

Still, we venture onto the narrow beach choked with seaweed. People are carefree; happy antics in the brownish water, cheering and laughing as the treacherous rip hurtles along the edge of the beach and snatches at their ankles.

This can't be right! Can it?

We head for the Information Centre, which proudly displays a sign on the glass door 'Open seven days.'

"Can you sign my book?" asks the elderly lady, adjusting her specs. She seems relieved to have an entry on a blank page. "Now!" she asks, once our duty is done. "What can I do for you?"

.....

"Mmmh! Something to kill a couple of hours or so, you say...." She mulled over the answer for quite a while - something I found a little disconcerting. "Well, you must see our Millennium Esplanade. It cost three million dollars and not a penny on the rates. We've got a great council."

'That's a first,' I think to myself: 'Someone who approves of a local council.' I hold my peace, not wanting to disturb the helpful old dear now she's in full swing.

"You can take some fish and chips and eat them down there."

By now alarm bells were definitely ringing about the way in which the day was heading, but we smile thankfully, get directions and off we go.

Three million bucks has created a monument to crass bad taste. The esplanade runs along the narrow foreshore behind the actual beach and gives no views of the ocean. There is nothing to stimulate the senses except empty barbecue areas, car parks and the awful smell of ordure coming from the public toilet block which sits in the full glare of a sweltering tropical sun.

We walk a-ways, scratching our heads as to what people do for amusement hereabouts. No cafes. No bowling greens. No pubs. No businesses. No life. We can't even find the chippy. Maybe the locals just battle the crocs and stingers and rips, and then retire to a life of hired videos behind closed doors.

Then, there is life. We spot a couple of ageing ladies sitting under a fig tree. Our spirits soar. In desperation I ask, "Is there anywhere we can get a nice cappuccino?"

"Oh!" That stumped them. They looked from one to the other. "I suppose you could try the fish and chip shop," said one.

"Yes!" added her companion. "They'll fix you up with something."

Try as we might, the chip shop evades our best efforts.

We return to Gladstone, to our shady back garden with its laughing kookaburras and sweet talking butcher birds, rejoicing in our deliverance from the day over a bottle of wine.

Cop Kenny

As cities go, you would be hard pushed to find anything quite as charming and serene as the old Queensland city of Maryborough. It has fine old buildings, the pubs and bottle shops are closed by ten at night, the evening streets quiet and near deserted.

And maybe that's the real reason for Kenny Burnett, [same surname as the surveyor who explored this area back in 1842] to want to move back 'Up Country:' To Longreach, to be precise - seventeen hours' hard driving into a setting sun. A journey he does often, to take part in fishing matches.

"I belong to that country," Kenny says philosophically, speaking of that vast pastoral area of the Outback. And who could argue with him, when he looks the part of an ageing pioneer: old and sweated bush hat atop a straggle of over-long, brown hair tinged with more than a little white. It was hard to guess at his age, what with his features being disguised by a full, dark beard, again flecked with age, his skin tightly puckered and creased around his kind and gentle eyes.

He spoke as he worked, chipping tiles from the bathroom wall of a holiday unit under refurbishment. I had plenty of time to study the gnarled hands of a lifetime's hard work.

"It was a mistake moving down here," he confided. "Okay! So I got a property at the right price, but I need to go home."

I thought Kenny was a very lucky man - to know what he wanted out of life.

Once upon a time, one of his many jobs had been that of a policeman out west, before his itinerant lifestyle had brought him to the coast of Queensland. With a shared past, we swapped cop stories.

"I remember one family all right," he began, a smile breaking out to display less than perfect pearly whites. "I used to lock at least one of them up for fighting every Saturday night."

"Yeah!" I agreed. "I reckon every town everywhere has at least one mob like that."

"One night," he continued, "I was taking this Jimmy character to jail when I got called to another job. So I drop him in town and tell him to put himself in the cells – and he did."

"The old days, eh!" I added. "My first arrest was three blokes fighting outside a pub. I take hold of two of them..... I was never much good at maths, but even I worked out that left one drunk free as a bird. So I just told him to follow us to the nick. And he did. Couldn't get away with it now, could we?"

"Too right. But I reckon I can beat that," Kenny came back with another tale. "This family I was telling you about: Jimmy, Harry and a few more. It got so regular to lock 'em up, that we got a routine going. Good Catholic lads they were and wouldn't miss church on a Sunday. So if I'd put them in the cells Saturday night, I'd leave the door unlocked so they could go to early Mass. They'd be back in their cells by the time I came on duty to bail 'em out."

But times change: Even Maryborough is slowly changing, and not particularly for the better. Its position as the 'Gateway for Frazer Island', whale watching, and a whole lot more activities for the tourist, is forcing change upon it. As with most places, chasing the tourist dollar is becoming all important, and like the rest of the Eastern coast of Australia, the old city is caught up in the throes of one almighty property boom.

Good news for Kenny. Becoming dollar rich is his way back to the bush - his way to return home - and 'good on 'im.'

However, for me, something of the essence of Australia is being lost and, like old-time policing, once it's gone, you're not going to get it back.

To Rockhampton

I promise not to mention the string and paper kite that passes for an aeroplane here in central Queensland.

Instead, I concentrate hard on some funnies at the Brisbane hotel before we flew out. Things like when little Emily, who, when she didn't like a fly landing on her spoon, flicked her wrist. The fly went all right - but so did all the Rice Crispies and milk. And such a nicely dressed crowd in the restaurant too.

Keep thinking! Ignore the smoke coming into the cabin through the overhead luggage compartments. Why is everyone else ignoring it? Think!

Or granddaughter, Jessica: "Can I get some fruit salad, mummy?"

"Of course you can love. Help yourself."

Five unsupervised minutes later: "Mum? Why is there lettuce stuck to my strawberries?"

"Because you've taken the decorations off the chef's meat display.....Why is the meat all in a heap dear?"

The smoke is only the air conditioning. Good! Think!

The kids are just like their mother. She's on the phone at the hotel reception desk talking to someone at the City Cinema - start times for Star Wars and such like. Then directions.....
"Just a moment, madam," says the voice at the other end.
She holds.....
Somewhat disconcerted by a tap on the shoulder, she turns to find the concierge handing her a newspaper advert about Luke Skywalker's mob.
"I think this is what you need, madam."
"That's very helpful of you. Many thanks, but I'm actually talking to the cinema now."
"Actually madam, it's me you've been talking to for the last ten minutes."
A chip off the old block: And if you have any doubts about the genes chasing about in our female generations.....

'Nanna' enters the sophisticated, tenth floor cocktail lounge overlooking the city lights. She's not used to walking on such carpets. The three-inch wool pile catches at her heels and she ends up spread-eagled across the blue and gold pattern.
She might have got away with it but, "Look! Nanna's drunk!" cries Jessica with glee.
All heads turn to watch nanna turn a deep red as she splurts out from the hands and knees position she's adopted, "I haven't had a drink yet!"
Nothing to do with Rockhampton - our destination - from where our family have had stories to tell: People like Charlie Hogg, who survived the war against the Japanese before taking a job as a cane cutter. A fatal cancer got him at a young age. Or the Drewes, who lost a son, shot down over the Mediterranean and never seen again. Or the descendants of the Maas family of Amsterdam, leading lights in the Dutch Resistance against the occupying German forces in the 1940s. What stories there are to tell......
Rockhampton! First impressions! Good grief! I know Rocky sees itself as a progressive city - but any town with a railway line running through its centre has to have a question mark over it – until it proves itself to my satisfaction.
The motel room is pretty average. It's not too clean, not too smelly, and not too many 'things' rush about in and out of cupboards before disappearing behind the cracked tiles of the bathroom when you put the light on. But we do object to three in a bed - even if the frilly-lizard was here first.
Have we made a big mistake?

Life in the raw

The Beef Capital of Australia!
Mmmh?
The Sapphire Centre of the World!
Mmmh?
Screech!
"What's the matter now?" I ask myself.
Screech!
"Clutch love," advises my wife kindly. "Use the * clutch! - At least until we're out of sight of their office."
The hire car slips easily into gear - it does with the clutch engaged - and we move off.
The car stalls. That's O.K! Anyone can make a mistake - only it's not advisable half way through an illegal 'U' turn on a busy road.
"For * * * * sake! * * * * it!" Roughly translated as: "I'm terribly sorry: I'll get the hang of this in a minute."

We jerk our way through the day, a day punctuated by cries of "Clutch! Clutch! For * sake, use the clutch!"

In fact the day has been fascinating. Leave the city environs, dare to turn off the main Bruce Highway [contrary to the hire car company's instructions,] and meet Queensland in the raw. No apology. No effort to encourage the timid or deflect the foolhardy.

Meet Queensland in the raw. Pubs are full at nine in the morning. Wooden mail boxes at the side of the road are riddled with bullet holes. Tourist 'attractions' are to be found down dirt tracks carried away by flash floods.

The rivers are muddy and sullen, capable of momentary violence. The sea is in turmoil. It's not blue here, but an unhealthy, yellowish brown. You don't need the signs: *"Beware! Box Jellies. Flood the affected area with vinegar and start mouth to mouth resuscitation,"* - to know that every kind of unmentionable is at home hereabouts.

The remains of extinct volcanoes and lava tubes remind you of an equally raw time somewhat further back in history.

Rockhampton! It's great!

Great Keppel Island

Light, fluffy scones, be-decked with butter, strawberry jam, whipped cream and fresh strawberries: And Earl Grey tea.

Now I know what you're thinking - but I deserve it. I do! It's twenty-eight degrees, we're burned to a cinder, we've been ravished by sand flies, and climbed a blessed mountainside to get here. I deserve it!

And I've walked half the island.....And I'm carrying a bucket of sand around with me, blasted into the sunscreen by a ferocious wind. No! I do deserve it - and that's that.

We have had a good day on Great Keppel. It might not sound like it, but we have. The island lies a mere thirty, storm-tossed minutes from the mainland; but the ferry is big and fast and can take the punishment. So we've had a good day visiting Fisherman's Beach, Monkey Beach and Long Beach - remarkable, deserted places, which give up their secrets only to those willing to leave the shaded, pampered isolation of the decadent, beachside resort.

No sand flies at the resort – but, there again, there are no sandy-coloured goannas blending in with their island habitat. We have skinks too - and butterflies by the bus load. We have discovered Aboriginal shell middens near the oyster beds - a constant source of food for five thousand years, until colonization. We have seen rocks deformed by the power of the wind and the ocean, shaped into weird formations. The whole island is a photographers dream.

Then came the mountainous Monkey Point: I suppose it got its name from the fact that you have to be able to climb like an ape, grasping tree root after slender branch to haul yourself up it. And THAT was the path.

Yes, I deserved my scone and a chance to think things through again.

It was in the June of 1872 when our Captain John Moresby actually came here to this very island and, by so doing, unwittingly sowed the seeds of a future whirlwind for the natives to reap.

John had left the rolling hills and secluded valleys of his native Somerset some thirty years before, forsaking them in favour of a life in the Royal Navy. By 1871 he had risen through the ranks to become the Master of H.M.S. Basilesk, a 1071 ton Paddler with five guns. He had been sent to Australia, "that most interesting station under our flag offering possibilities of exploration and discovery." Obviously the powers-that-be weren't quite as enthusiastic about the Queensland coast, as it was left to him to scrounge a pocket compass with which to do the surveying.

John treats us to a description of our island back then:

"We feast our eyes on the fairy island rising from the still blue water. The white coral beach has little native huts which sit like birds' nests between the trees.

We were half prepared for disappointment and landed fully armed as we knew nothing of the inhabitants' disposition to strangers. Judge then our pleasure on seeing a group of fishers, young men and women, move toward us without fear, shaking our hands in welcome. Their stature is far above the average and are physical perfection with massive shoulders, pale bronze in colour like that of Greek athletes. In every house we entered clean mats were spread for us and we were offered bananas and cocoa - nut milk."

Sounds good for the crew of the Basilesk: This must have been like a dreamtime fantasy for them. Now we, too, share in it.

Saving nickels and dimes

Today, my wife's horoscope read,

*'You will have to re-think
your budget - and don't
expect to be popular when
you start doing the slashing.'*

My promised Akubra, rabbit-skin hat hit the dust first. I didn't mind. As the old adage goes, "You can't have it and spend it."

So we have a pleasant, restful, and very cheap day. Every little counts, so where better than the botanic gardens - they're free.

To be honest, we didn't expect them to amount to very much. I would have thought that this small, rough and ready, would-be, city would have had little time for such extravagances. A little place, where huge, cattle-filled lorries called road trains hurtle by; where locomotives haul half-mile long freight cars through the shopping centre; and pubs, with their accompanying drunks, don't sit well with the vision of majestic ferneries and lakeside, palm-fringed walks.

We were impressed. We like little Rocky more than ever. The place is a real Aussie battler. The City Fathers set aside 96 acres of gardens on the slopes of the Athelstane Mountain Range, only to see them repeatedly devastated by cyclones, floods and droughts. But the gardens grew and, until the next time nature has a tantrum, will continue to be well used and an integral part of the town's life. So much so, that these are the only gardens I know where you can drive into them and park where you want: Very laid back and very user friendly.

Two features raise the gardens above the ordinary. One is the Cenotaph, still wreathed in flowers laid at the last memorial ceremony. I applaud the vision, for about the monument is an avenue of pine trees raised from the seed of the actual and fabled Lone Pine at Gallipoli, where the ANZACs paid a terrible price for their acknowledged heroism.

The second is the Murray Lagoon, a wildlife sanctuary since 1902. The lake is covered in water lilies, red dragon-flies, multi-coloured butterflies and a host of unrecognizable 'things' - some with wings and others without: A wild beauty: Tranquil.

Now, my horoscope today read,

*'You will be dreaming of travelling
to interesting places, but that is
no more than a pipe dream.'*

To be honest, if today we'd travelled further into central Queensland, as planned before the cash crisis, we'd have been the losers.

Fossicking for Thundereggs

Central Queensland would not have been high on my list of places to visit one hundred and twenty million years ago, as the whole area seems to have been born of exploding volcanoes. These upheavals have left us a legacy. We've visited one of them - the natural wonders of shallow seas surrounding holiday islands - and today we've discovered another: Thundereggs!

I would like to be able to tell you what they are. I have had it explained to me - I've even read the literature. Scientifically, it's something to do with gas bubbles in lava flows. But not to worry! I prefer the simpler and more logical explanation: that they were dropped from the sky during rainstorms by the legendary Thunderbirds.

I'm rambling? O.K. - I'll start again.

Mount Hay is a good place to go fossicking. They give you a crash course in what a thunderegg looks like - anything roundish from between the size of a fingernail to the clock-face of Big Ben. And oh! They'll be covered in muck and gunge.

O.K. so far?

Now for the bad news: They could be lying anywhere on a moonscape the size of several footy pitches - or buried in some strange-looking rock formations: Very hard rock formations, which give off contemptuous sparks at the puny strokes of our heavy pick-axes - which strangely got heavier by the millisecond. Add a burning sun, sapping humidity, red ants which bite and mosquitoes with an appetite, and you can see we started to wilt quite early on. If that's not enough, now walk up and down a mountain for an hour or so.

I'm fairly sure, like us, you'll say, "Bugger this for a game of conkers," or, more politely, "I'm not cut out for this!" We all want to ask; "How do people do this for a living?" Yet people do: Gold, sapphires, emeralds, opals. Just last week a bloke made the newspapers by finding the biggest opal rock ever recorded. He'd been looking for years amongst the stuff rejected by previous generations of like-minded, hard men. But he found it. Now he's rich, he will probably buy a site like this and let us 'nuggets' pay to look around for him whilst he sits in the shade and counts his cash.

For years he looked. For us, an hour is more than enough. We had collected a pathetic half-dozen, pea-sized, would-be gems. Well, Patsy had. I'd seen nothing. My bag was empty.

"What's that?" asked Mrs Fossicker, with a half laugh and derisory point of a broken fingernail.

"I don't know," I answered, as I dropped the beat-up, half brick into the bag. "But I'll look a complete prat if I go back with nothin'."

So we lugged our heavy finds and my bleeding knee back up the mountain, for most of our collection to be rejected out-of-hand by old Bert - a seventy year old character who has fossicked here for the last twenty-seven years.

"Could be worth looking at."

My chest swelled with pride. It was my knobby.

For twenty minutes we waited for the cutting to be done. Watching and waiting, and experiencing for that short while the same luscious anticipation of the true prospector.

Our knobby slowly revealed its secrets from prehistory. Seven multi-coloured air bubbles frozen in time miraculously appear.

Exciting - yes! And pretty. But not worth a tinker's cuss.

Who cares! It was a tremendous thrill.

Farewell to Rocky

We didn't go any further inland. I had no intention of ever visiting that dot on the map called Coniston, which lies about one thousand kilometres away in the 'great out-there' - a place where the temperatures can push fifty degrees centigrade. Now it might be a nice place - and there must have been a reason hiding in our Hogg antecedents for someone of that ilk to make the trip. It must have been a compelling reason - a story somewhere? But you go! I'm not! Call me a coward if you like, but it's a bit of caving and then back to the cultured civilization of Brisbane for us.

Coniston! As Henry Lawson would have said, "It's the best country to get out of that I was ever in."

*

"It's very unusual for it to rain like this. May is usually the best time of the year - but we were flooded last week."

The Brisbane taxi driver's words rang in my ears all afternoon. His smarmy smile irritatingly continued to appear in my mind's-eye as I fumed silently. The over-charging git! All those carefully nurtured cents gone in a flash.

My mood was not helped by the rain. Rain! It now lashes against the windows of our City-Link river ferry, nearly blotting out the impressive gold and blue high rises of the cityscape along the river banks.

I look around. The cabin is large and comfortable. Carpets match the aircraft-style seating arrangements. Rows of faces stare - not at me, but at the rain drops racing one another down the Perspex. Not too many sunny smiles today in the 'Sunshine State'.

I hate those tours that tourists never fail to do. You know, the ones where you sit imprisoned on a bus or vessel, and where the tour guide goes on and on.....and on and on.

"Coming up on the right is a house worth a million dollars. On the left....." [is something else invisible, or meaningless, or both.]

We've hit on a way around that. For a few bucks you can travel as much as you like up and down the muddy waters of the Brisbane River. We settle for a comfortable, and dry, couple of hours of do-it-yourself sight-seeing. Then - just as I'm congratulating myself:

"On the right is Kangaroo Point. Do you remember what we did for the first time there, love?"

It was the sixty year old, balding guy in the next seat - the one with the Brewery Tour ticket sticking out of his shirt pocket. I suppose it was the lunch-time beer talking - his wife didn't - talk, that is. I know not whether she remembered Kangaroo Point, as her glazed eyes gave nothing away. In fact, I can't make my mind up whether one of them is made of glass. It is certainly a different colour.

We were treated to the alternative guided tour of Brisbane.

"On the left: Them-there gardens! We've had some good 'un's in there. Remember honey?"

She didn't - remember or talk.

I decided to switch off and do some remembering of my own.

It's only four hours since we left Rocky - and I miss it terribly. To the last, the place tickled my fancy. A deserted airport at checking-in time: A closed departure lounge, complete with apologetic security guard. When the lounge was eventually opened: "Would you like to go in now?" Nothing unusual in politeness, only the guard had to walk around the terminal building to find us.

He found us with the fat cook who was making sarnies, and had been since 7 a.m. He was more than happy to have a chat over a cuppa with the only customers he was likely to see for a while. [There were no planes due for hours after we leave.]

Now, we're back in 'civilization' with 'Captain Beer Belly', when we could be dicing with death.....

"There's Captain Cook Bridge....." he shouted to the whole boat. [My mind frantically raced to discover what they could have done on the bridge].....".We drove over that.....remember,

Honeykins?"

Agh!!! He's-a drivin' me crazy!

Rockhampton: So much more to offer. Sure we were disappointed at the nine foot high waves which stopped any chance of further exploration of the reef: That and the fact that the stinger season has extended itself this year because of a low pressure system hanging about somewhere.

But little Rocky had more to offer: We visited bat-filled caves, from which a twenty foot layer of guano had been removed. Now we have visited caves before: Note: I said, 'visited caves', as opposed to 'went caving.' Worming your way through a claustrophobic sludge of bat corpses and bat shit has the same appeal to me as visiting Kangaroo Point with Mrs 'Beer-Belly'.

So we've visited caves. Some, pretty mega-impressive: Others, so far removed from civilization, pale into insignificance in the face of the journey to and from them: Dirt roads with unfenced, thousand-foot drops - that kind of thing.

We have also been treated numerous times to 'Cave Black.' In total silence all the lights are extinguished. It is so black you literally can't see your hand touching your nose: Always a humbling, somewhat unnerving experience. Whenever it happens, I automatically think of two things. Being buried alive is one. Coming from a family of coal miners, disaster underground was a fact of life. One great grandfather and his son were buried alive with their friends and workmates after a roof fall. As the water rose about them they sang Silent Night as they prepared to meet their Maker. The water level stopped when it reached their necks and thankfully they were rescued later that same day. A shared experience – hardly? They are going to turn on the lights in a minute and we'll walk out to the coffee bar.

Following hard on the heels of my first thought is another: What sort of people were adventurous enough to hold onto a burning besom and slide down into the unknown, disappearing into a black void? Did they emerge covered in guano - but happy? What if the rope broke.....?

I know that the pioneer, a bloke called Olsen, who had found these particular caves in the unexplored territory north of Rockhampton, was astute if nothing else. He kept his mouth shut, marked a tree well away from his discovery and called for the surveyor from Brisbane to grant him his 160 acres around the selected gum. After five years the land was his - it was as easy as that once upon a time – land which included the caves. He opened them to the public and they have made money ever since.

Olsen's Caves are a little different to most we've seen. There's Capelec, for instance - a wild fruit bat who guards the entrance. We were told the reason for his screeching all the time was the fact that he liked human company and craved attention. This seems to me to be a bit of an old wives' tale, as the verbose, bull-like, animal-loving German tourist seemed to screech as loudly as the bat when Capelec bit him.

Once past the upside down, swinging teeth of the sentry, the cave system was interesting enough as caves go. Different certainly - we climbed up into them. These caves were not under the mountain - but inside it. The expected blackout was unexpectedly wonderful. As the lights dimmed and died, we listened in awe to a recording of the Phantom of the Opera: Acoustics unbeatable anywhere. I was pleased they didn't play Silent Night or there would have been a flood of tears.

The music ended - turned off: something we couldn't do with our shipboard guide.

"On the right - just here! We stayed in a hotel. There it is.....That one!....That one there.....Do you remember what we did love?

I wish Capelec were here - or better! I wish I were Capelec.

Journey 12
Northern Queensland

Cairns: Then and now.

It was the early 1980s when we first arrived in the tropical far north. We had just missed a cyclone which had whirled itself into a frenzied death out in the Coral Sea. Talk about lucky - plenty of rain, but not a full-blown, mind-paralysing storm. Everything is wet; wisps of water vapour rose from the ground in the stifling heat to cloak the tree tops in an ethereal miasma. The humidity is enough to leave you limp just a few yards from the airport door.

Everything smells different up here: musty, earthy, exciting. Everything is different. Tropical forests cover the mountains and crowd down to the coast. Tidal mud flats and mangrove swamp grab at the city centre. Not far to the north, the tarmac road just simply peters out. The whole ambience of this 'frontier' city makes the tales of saltwater crocodiles appearing in the town centre, courtesy of the huge drainage gutters, wholly believable.

The airport: It's not so very long ago that jumbo jets were landing their unsuspecting passengers here without the help of radar. I can still visualize Bruce in the control tower fiddling with his binoculars whilst scanning the skies.

"O.K. Jack! I can't see nothin'. Guess you might as well give it a go."

It's that type of raw paradise.

Tips for the Far North:

1. To make the most of your stay you must consider the seasonal and climatic factors: May - October is considered the best time weather-wise, as it is outside the recognised cyclone season. Paradoxically, the deadly box-jellyfish infest the coastal waters at this time. Mind you, so do the sea snakes. Early April is a good compromise, but do seek advice.

2. Treat the far north with a healthy respect. For instance: take notice of the 'No Swimming' signs. There are a number of crocodile attacks each year. Also, the sun will catch you out. It will burn right through wet 'T' shirts, so consider buying the expensive 'Rash' swimwear, especially for the kids.

3. Cairns is an excellent centre for the traveller seeking to explore the Great Barrier Reef and Northern Queensland. The reef trips are not cheap, but a must. However, Green Island, only twenty-seven kilometres from Cairns, is comfortably priced and attracts a lot of tourists. The island should be everyone's idea of paradise - but we found it spoiled by a pointless and distressing commercialism.

No going back for Joey.

Joey used to be a jockey. Now he rides a cab and wishes it were a horse. He yearns for the past, to be back in the saddle on home territory - the grassy tablelands of northern New South Wales. And he wishes for a whole lot more.

You can still tell he used to be a jockey; he is small of stature, but wiry and strong. He's not carrying an inch of fat on him anywhere, but still bemoans his weight gain before remembering the past.

"It was hard back then. Four o'clock starts every morning for us apprentices: Bed by seven every night, with only Sunday afternoons off."

"It certainly sounds hard," I replied with feeling, stealing a look at the taxi's illuminated dash.

It read 04.20.

"It was hard," agreed Joey. "They knocked all the cheek out of you in those apprenticeship years. Five years taught you respect. Not like kids today. It was a lot harder - back then."

While he chatted away about the jockeys he knew, his father [a leading hand in a racing yard,] owners' inspections and all the rest, it occurred to me that he was just getting old.

Trust me! I know these things from first hand. Talk to anyone with their youth fading and you will find it was always harder or better - back then. For me, it was a police career - and I know it was harder. No radios. No cars. No back-up. But say that today to my detective son-in-law and he would scoff. For our son, it was the army that beckoned. He'll tell you that the current crops of recruits are not of the same standard as when he joined. It was harder - back then.

I am sure it's the same for you, for everyone, no matter what path through life we've chosen.

It has taken nearly a quarter of a century, but we're back in Cairns. I recognize the mountains and the mud flats, but little else. Hotels have spawned along the Esplanade in our absence. Shopping malls have sprouted. Traffic roars and the sky is full of holiday jets, which follow each other nose to tail down onto the tarmac of the International Airport. [Now complete with radar, taxi ranks, public telephones and people. A far cry from the way it was.]

From the terrace above our swimming pool, we can see the charter boats out on Trinity Bay heading for the Great Barrier Reef. You just know that their operations are now so professional that there is no way they're going to leave snorkelling tourists behind to drown, as was once the case. No way! Not in this day and age.

Cairns seems to have lost that rawness it once had - that feeling of excitement that rose up inside you because you had arrived somewhere very, very different. That has gone now, replaced by that mind-numbing sameness which means you could be anywhere. For us, Cairns is the worse for it; passed its mantle as a frontier town on the edge of a wilderness over to Darwin or Alice.

Yes! Cairns was much better - back then!

Live for Today:

A walk along the esplanade in the brief tropical dusk between a scorching day and a sky full of stars, was enough to put a doubt in my mind: perhaps you can go back?

We pause on our stroll to watch the sun sink behind the mountains with a final, fiery farewell; those same timeless mountains which grab at the shores of Trinity Bay and which we remember from so long ago. The ocean fades through pink to near black, in an effort to harmonize with the mud flats and mountains. It doesn't succeed, for soon the moon breaks out from behind slow-moving clouds, to bathe the bay in silver.

Captain Cook, who visited Cairns in 1770 and named the bay Trinity Bay, never returned - not as far as I know, anyway. But others did, finding plenty of fresh water and firewood for their ships.

The potential of the Cairns area as a site on which to develop a township was not spotted until 1873. The decision to develop was taken in the face of the popularity of nearby Port Douglas, an established township closer to the goldfields; but Cairns had no intention of being outdone. It prospered and, by 1923, had a population of ten thousand, including our new friend's family.

Rod must have weighed twenty stones, courtesy of beer, bad diet and his job as a driver. He'd had no need to return to his city - he'd simply never left; not once in his forty years. But that hadn't stopped him noticing the changes and beginning his campaign of prophesying looming problems.

It wasn't the growth in tourism that bothered him: Nor the infrastructure to support it. No! Drains! That was the problem exercising his mind. The huge, deep storm drains are gone; the homes of wayward crocodiles now replaced by parking spots and council-owned meters.

"We haven't had any real rain for years," he says. "Just wait 'til we do. Them blokes in City Hall will have some explaining to do."

That may be so, but the same officials have transformed the esplanade from a place inhabited by society's misfits and their mayhem, into a safe haven for evening strollers and joggers. Now there are whispering palm trees; wildlife, and public barbecues which fill the evening air with mouth-watering smells: To this can be added the sounds of happy children enjoying a splash in the idyllic bathing pool.

Yes! It's so much better now.

Gwen, and her husband Billy, would agree. Originally from Glasgow, for twenty-five years they had lived in Western Australia and were holidaying in Cairns for the first time. Somewhat awed by their modern, palatial hotel - the necessary counterpart to the fine, old buildings still to be found in the central business district [the Qantas building, dating from 1923, is but one example of many] - they couldn't get over the beauty of this Northern Queensland city. They'll come back.

Finally, we meet a fellow Geordie. Well, Liz was from Sunderland in County Durham - close enough to be accepted into the Geordie fold when you're so far from home. At 51 years old, she had emigrated to Australia, fetching up in Cairns. Why? Her husband's midlife crisis, that's why! He didn't want to be an engineer for the rest of his days. Instead - sell up in over-priced, insignificant Britain, and start a bed and breakfast business in a tropical paradise. It has taken all of their savings, and then some, to live for today. Now, flat broke, and with Aussie bureaucracy dragging its feet over final approval for their B & B, try telling them that they aren't living life on the edge.

We turn and make our way back toward our hotel. Under the brooding mountains, lights are coming on in the bars and street cafes. Out in the bay, baby mangrove trees are silhouetted against the gleaming ocean - a beautiful, yet real, threat to the imported sandy beach someone thought the tourists would demand.

Pitch dark, except for the moon and the distant strip of lights from the restaurants and bars, people are still walking and jogging the paths in perfect safety. This is a far cry from yesteryears reality – no sane person would be out here after dark. So, on reflection, maybe I'm wrong in my initial assessment of the new, modern Cairns.

Okay! It's not the raw city it once was, but that doesn't make it bad. It's just different: Just moved on.

Port Douglas

Port Douglas lies about seventy kilometres north of Cairns. It has wide streets and old colonial buildings, which make it an interesting spot. From here, all sorts of exploration possibilities open up - from the Outer Reef, to a wonderful, primeval hinterland.

However, our exploring is not to be done by means of a pocket compass; nor is it as dangerous as it was for the crew of H.M.S. Basilesk, who came to these waters only to face death at the hands of a white squall. It happened just off the coast of nearby Cooktown. They survived and put in for repairs.

Cooktown: In 1874 it was a rip-roaring place - a port of thirty thousand people, where race riots between the white and Chinese gold miners took place on a regular basis. Just to add a bit of spice to life, marauding Aborigines killed both. I am reliably informed they preferred killing the Chinese: they tasted better! But we're not supposed to mention such negativities today, in the face of the growing Aboriginal Rights Cause.

Then the gold ran out. It was to this dying gold-rush settlement that our irrepressible Birkby's came, marrying into Irish stock [yet another Ryan family] and taking up the challenge of wild-west style policing. They also tended the local caboose. They would have worn military style uniforms and carried carbines and pistols - and probably have used one or two local Aborigines as trackers.

As the town declined, the family were moved to other parts of the state, tragically losing one of their children to sunstroke at Ingham, a township to be found on the road south of Cairns.

When a cyclone knocked Cooktown flat in 1907, nobody even bothered to report it to the Government. The jungle crept back in - but the town didn't die. There are still hardy souls who call the place home and make it worthwhile to visit the location where Captain Cook was forced to beach his ship, after the unforgiving reef managed to put a hole in the hull.

And it's to the reef we now go - on a boat. Let's hope......

*

We were close enough to see its eyes: deep soulless, black holes. And their owner was still closing in on us. And I knew it had teeth. I had experience. I've been a matter of inches from those razored rows. And hey! I survived! Admittedly it might only have been at the shark tank in Sea World - but this time it's for real. Worryingly, out here there is nowhere to go. I suppose the shark had been attracted by the noise our snorkelling tour was making: A number of us [well me,] were tiring and therefore making sounds like a very large fish in distress.

Suddenly it changed its mind. One look at twenty-four thrashing flippers and flailing arms was enough for him. He must have thought he was under attack by a flight of drunken Kamikaze porpoise or something. Or he wasn't hungry. Either way, with one stroke of his extraordinarily powerful tail, he turned and fled through the coral stacks.

We tried to follow. Can you belief that? I can't now, looking back. But then we were mesmerized by the sight of so much prehistoric grace and power. But it was no contest. He was gone. Someone 'up there' must have been praying hard for me. For one unthinking moment I had tried to be a Jacques Cousteau - and that Noah* wouldn't hurt me. We were living in a dream, surrounded by fish of every conceivably colour, some very small, darting amongst the waving coral; others, very, very large indeed. But the shark had stolen the show.

"Reef shark," said the marine biologist, as our heads bobbed back up into the sun. She got more questions then than at any time during the last hour-and-a-half.

"Are they dangerous?"

"Not usually."

[It's a funny word that, 'usually.' Should I find it reassuring?]

"I didn't know sharks were on the inside of the reef?"

"Yes. The reef has channels through it. We get all types of shark in here. But we keep it quiet."

Some dodo walked into it. "Why?"

"So you'll come on the tours of course," she said, smiling from ear to ear. "I'd be out of a job else."

And what a job! Swimming on the Great Barrier Reef, with or without Jaws Junior, is a remarkable experience. One moment your face is inches away from multi-coloured, living coral swarming with tiny fish, and then, with one feeble breaststroke, you are out over a sixty-foot deep canyon, still able to see the starfish or stingray clearly on the sandy bottom. Words defy the spectacle. It is not possible for such kaleidoscopic beauty to exist. But it does, it does.....

The reef means memory days that will stay with us, sustain us, throughout the rest of our lives.

*Rhyming slang: Noah's Ark – shark.

White Water Rafting:

My wife's veneer of confidence evaporated in a twinkling.

"Just sign the form to say that your death or serious injury is not our fault."

The light-hearted banter by one of the group's leaders, a sun tanned, hippy type, did nothing to hide the stark truth on the brandished forms.

"Sign the forms and you'll know that adrenaline really is brown," he continued, not realising that Patsy was already beginning to know that.

I went to work reassuring my better half, her hands so cold despite the searing heat. Her face was beginning to whiten. It was bad. I work quickly and well, but was undone - this time by the signpost at the point where we were to enter the Barron River with our rubber inflatables.

"Beware! Crocodiles!"

Now it was really bad. I laboured to get the life-jacket over her struggling shoulders. My gibbering wreck, the mother of our children, coped womanfully. That old Northumbrian determination set in: "I-am-not-coming-out-of-THAT-raft!"

Everyone else did at some point. Teenagers swept away at the 'Alarm Clock' - the first rapid of the day and guaranteed to wake you up. Others left unannounced at the 'Waterslide' - a mere ten-foot drop, and as straight down as you can get in a torrent crashing through rocks.

The only injury of the day just happened to be sustained by the instructor with the big mouth, who somehow managed to crush an ankle. It didn't stop him shouting continually, "Steady! Get the line right!" "Bounce!" "Paddle:" "Paddle NOW!" "Stay off the bottom of the raft:" [Submerged rocks under rubber equals broken knees.]

Patsy stayed put through boiling waves and bruising boulders. Good on yer!

Lunch was barbecued something or other in an untouched, primeval, World Heritage rainforest, where we were surrounded by magnificent trees, hurtling water, the crashing sounds of possum above our heads, and the screams of the injured guy as he was unceremoniously hauled up the side of the gorge from our sandbank, presumably to some unseen track.

Then more of the same: Rocks, water, screams - but of delight this time - and the intermittent clutching at hand-thrown safety lines.

End of the day: Feelings of fulfilment, of self worth and of satisfaction at a job well done. - And Patsy? She experienced all of those positive achievements and basked in their glory.....But no! She won't ever do that again.

Cape Tribulation

Sven was our guide and mentor on our journey into the rainforest of Cape Tribulation, some forty kilometres south of Cooktown. In his mid-fifties, he was as weather-beaten and reliable as his old Landrover. When not dealing with paying, gawping passengers on expeditions into the wilderness that is the Daintree, he eked out a living removing crocodiles from the local golf courses. His Swedish, or perhaps Danish, accent grated after a while, and on occasions his sense of humour left something to be desired. For instance, dangling a dead snake over my wife's shoulder as we stood motionless watching intently the movements of a live one, could have had an embarrassing consequence. Talk about jump! But for all that he was good, taking us to places only the very fortunate will ever see.

Stopping to examine a bridge made of uneven wooden planks under serious termite attack, he brought the polite conversation about the weight ratio of the Landrover to the efforts of a billion, busy insects to an abrupt halt with the urgent waving of a hand.

"Listen!" he whispered.

With an effort, our inexperienced ears eventually picked up grunting and squeaking coming from the undergrowth somewhere near the giant strangler fig. The noise grew louder but we could see nothing; the forest canopy shrouded the area in gloom and the aerial roots of the fig made any visibility impossible.

"Back up! Quietly!"

We did. I didn't stop until I was inside the old, battered vehicle with the doors securely shut. Nose pressed against the glass, I ask uncertainly, "Pigs?"

"Feral pigs! Unpredictable and dangerous boo-gars."

I think he was swearing.

"They'll fight a bool," he continued.

"Good hunting though, Sven?"

"Necessary hunting rather than good: Reckon we got about three million rooting around. They do terrible damage: Can't even eat the boody things: Full of wooms."

On again: Thicket gives way to thinnet and we're out onto the beach. Crocodile slither marks make dangerous patterns on the sand. They actually add to the incomparable beauty set before us. A beach of bouncing stones, something to do with reverse magnetism, and one of only two places in the world where they are to be found. Fresh, refreshing coconuts lying on the white sand are broken open to assuage our thirst; a swimming pool secreted in a palm forest; a volcano, long since dead and filled with rainwater, now a home to a lost legion of animals and birds.

And finally: A visit to a crocodile farm - a bit touristy, but nonetheless fascinating. The narrator was in the enclosure, standing three feet from the edge of a murky pool. No sign of any croc and so she talked away to us with all the enthusiasm her five feet two inches could muster. Her subject: 'Scalies' or 'Saltwater Crocodiles', and just how dangerous they were.

"Up here a dog really is a man's best friend. Any dog! I always take mine camping and tie him up so he has the best view of the river - that's between me and the water. If he's a good dog, he'll wake you if there's a croc about. If not, the croc gets him. Crocodiles always eat the first thing to hand. So your pretty average dog saves your bacon and becomes a good dog - posthumously."

As we laughed dutifully, she stamped her foot and in one mercifully quick movement headed backwards toward the fence. Mercifully, because the previously invisible crocodile came out of that muddy pool like an Exocet missile, its jaws snapping at head height where the girl had been a half a second earlier.

A breath-taking display: Not a trick, nor the actions of a trained animal. This was a wild, fifteen feet long monster trying its best to kill: A salutary lesson.

We returned to our creature comforts, still in one piece thanks to our professional guide, yet somewhat shell-shocked by the sights and sounds of Australia in the raw.

Grub for Henry

Just to the north of Ingham, and on the coast road to Cairns, lies the little town of Cardwell - famous for two things. Firstly, it services Hinchinbrook Island, the largest and wildest of Queensland's island chain. It is a magnet for the explorer, with its rainforests and mountains rising to over three thousand feet. Secondly - somewhat less well known is the fact that back in 1872 it woomed - sorry, wormed, its way into our family history.

On 5th February that year, H.M.S. Basilesk was passing with considerable difficulty inside the Great Barrier Reef and heading north. The crew were watching "Great water snakes at play, languid in the heat," when they found a sinking ship with "two or three wild figures wasted to the bone in the stern. There were many dead, dried blood was everywhere and the planks had been marked with axe strokes."

The survivors were taken to Cardwell, where it was learned that the unfortunates were Melanesian Islanders, who had been taken from their homes as slaves. They had managed to throw their captors overboard, only to find they couldn't sail the ship from the western world. They had drifted, and slowly died, for eighteen hundred miles.

Whether they were delighted to arrive at Cardwell we'll never know. The town was surrounded by "Aborigines who were the mortal enemies of white men whom they murdered."

Cardwell: 9th March. Our captain, John Moresby, learned of a disastrous shipwreck on the Bramble Reef, some thirty miles out to sea. Seventy-five young men were missing and so the Basilesk went off to carry out a search and rescue mission. By working out the tides and winds, it was decided to head for Cooper Point, about seventy miles from Cardwell. Here, eight half-naked and near-starved, ulcerated survivors were found. They had been cared for by the local Aboriginal tribe, who had fed them with fruit and crushed ants. They were lucky. Another boatload of their friends had landed on a neighbouring beach - and had been murdered.

Today, hopefully nothing like that fate will be waiting for us at Townsville, Australia's largest tropical city and an important centre for those intent on experiencing the reef. It's a nice town, with parks and cousins and friends.....

*

The mining town of Charters Towers is also easily reached from Townsville. After all; it's only a few hours drive due west toward the interior. Unfortunately, we aren't going to get to see our cousin on this trip. Their river has risen thirty feet overnight, cutting off the town. Guess we'll just have to content ourselves with the ocean once more.

The 'ferry' turned out to be a two-masted yacht which could have done with a coat of paint and some Royal Navy spit and polish. It was quite a bit smaller than the Basilesk, and I know one heck of a lot slower, as Captain Henry had brought his Fijian Islander's happiness to his work. A big man, and recently retired from playing rugby to international standards, he had hands and feet the size of dinner plates. His feet he used to steer the advertised 'Express Service' ferry along at a leisurely pace, whilst his hands lay inactive over a burgeoning belly. His only reaction to the boat being overtaken by a school of flying fish was for the first order of the day to be issued to the only crew member: "Get the guitar out."

His helper, a slight young woman in a shapely halter and shorts, began to pluck at the remaining two strings of the battered instrument. Henry was content. Less charitably, we were happy when the discordant banjulele was discarded in favour of the anchor being thrown overboard. It was an unscheduled stop - but what the hell - we're obviously on the infamous Fiji time.

We had stopped at a tiny coral islet, which poked its head only inches above the water. If the ice-caps do melt because of global warming, this place will surely be the first in the world to go under. Bewilderment gave way to immense pleasure, as we were invited to slip beneath the calm of the ocean and immerse ourselves once more in the coral gardens and precipices that make up the reef.

But this time we were swimming with a purpose - to try and keep pace with Henry, who has been transformed. It's obvious he must have been a dolphin in a previous existence, for he is in his element. His strength is enormous. The reason for our expedition soon became clear, as he pushed and prodded his small trident into rock crevice after inviting hole.

Fourth go and success! A great pool of inky-black goo flooded ominously out of the coral stack and, as it slowly spread, Henry emerged through it with a squirming octopus impaled upon his spear. Even with his teeth clamped over the snorkel's mouthpiece, you could see his smile back in Townsville.

Henry had his tea.

The Housing Crisis

After two days of constant cloudburst, today is HOT. We are breathing water-laden air, living in a sauna and now know what it really means to live in a tropical region. It brings to mind a yarn that I know to be true, and which tends to highlight one or two problems faced by property owners in such a climate.

Once upon a time a man and his wife had a house. It was a particularly fine house, built of wood, and had an authentic, rusty old tin roof. It was perched on top of a hill surrounded by trees and birds and animals. A wide river wound its way around their hill on its way to the nearby ocean.

One day, the man and his wife decided that their house was not fine enough. A veranda would be nice, with a swinging seat so they could sit and watch the sun go down over the river. And a swimming pool to cool off in on those long, hot days.

Off they went to see the bank manager.

"Of course you can borrow the money. Build your dream. Pay us later, sometime, never. Just sign here - and here. I look forward to coming to see our - err, sorry - your, very fine house."

The builder was a very nice man and went to work with a vengeance. Off came the rusty, old roof.

"Oh-oh!"

The snakes in the roof were eating the mice and the frogs. The mice and the frogs were eating anything they could - including the electrical wiring, and the fearsome, white ants, better known as termites were busily eating the house.

The builder cut, and cut some more, trying to find solid wood. Any piece would do, just so long as it would support the veranda. No solid wood in the roof: None on the first floor; none on the ground floor.

The builder was worried. The man and his wife were worried. The pest control man was worried - he shook his head. But the bank manager wasn't worried - he didn't know.

Nothing for it! A bulldozer pushed the nice house down the hill and into the bush for the termites to eat at their leisure. Foundations were dug, concrete poured, snakes removed.

And then the bank manager came, clutching his swimming trunks in one hand. He turned the corner - and turned pale. No swim! No pool! No house!

"No worries," said the builder. "I have the technology. I can rebuild her."

And he did.

Cocky-Doodle-Don't

No account of a tropical paradise could be complete without mentioning the unmentionable. The wildlife is fantastic and ranges from exotic birds to surfing dolphins, to mysterious reptiles. But there is one thing guaranteed to freak-out my Patsy: One unmentionable. Cocky! And I do mean freak. Not a gasp, not an 'ugh!' - But a blood-curdling, fear-for-my-life, scream accompanied by goose bumps the size of peas.

The humble, cocky-cockroach is a survivor. It's no good squashing them - as they die they automatically eject their invisible eggs as a going-away pressy; so houses are sprayed regularly with toxins strong enough to fell an elephant. But, you guessed it - they are still here. Not many, maybe a couple a day: - But the size! They only make 'em in two sizes: - Very big and their parents.

At the appointed scream, I arm myself with a double-barrelled slipper, or broom, depending on the location, when what I really want is a .38 police special.

Now most of the time these wonderful products of nature are found by my wife: Sometimes they hang there and stare at her nakedness from the inside of the shower curtain; at others, they sit on your breakfast bowl, just daring you to shift them. But worst of all is the 3 a.m. loo patrol. As they skitter about beneath Patsy's feet, she screams and I do my bleary-eyed Sir Galahad bit. At that time of night I don't care. I blast the perfidious creatures into a dusty extinction - eggs or not!

This ritual has gone on uninterrupted since our arrival in Australia - until last night. Slap! "Oooh-nooo." Thwack! "Die you little.....!" Slap-slap! Thwack-thwack-thwack! THWACK! "Got yer!"

I raised my head from the pillow to be greeted by a huge smile and even bigger goose bumps than normal.

"I did it love. I got one without waking you."

Two K's to Paluma.

About two kilometres from Paluma you will find Windy Corner. Believe me! - The name has nothing whatsoever to do with meteorology - more the anxious moments when your car rounds yet another hairpin bend, only to hang over the unprotected edge of a three thousand foot drop to the valley floor below.

Paluma likes to call itself a township, even though it only has a population of thirty people. These permanent residents exist in almost total isolation, atop a mountain range which is now designated a 'Wet Tropics World Heritage Area,' just north and west of Townsville.

I say almost total isolation, as the mountainous area, cloaked in mist and clouds, draws people as moths to a flame. And for those brave enough, it is a journey of over twenty kilometres to climb that three thousand foot massif which towers above Big Crystal Creek flood plain, with its eighteen-foot tall water-depth markers lining the only road.

Put that worrying thought behind you - it hasn't rained in ages - and concentrate only on the road. It demands attention, as every twenty yards or so it hairpins out of sight. The 40 k.p.h. speed restrictions are laughable - then the tarmac runs out. Add in precipices, falling boulders and cars on the wrong side of the road..... Not that I'm complaining of cars on the wrong side. I'll be doing the exact same thing on the way down - hugging the mountain and avoiding the crumbling edges - and a very long drop.

When you do arrive, you WILL need the double shot of caffeine awaiting you at the Aussie Smoko Café in the pretty little village.

"You should see it in the Wet," says Steve, the co-owner with his wife, Karen.

He's on leave from his job as a paramedic to an Aboriginal community and, despite his 60th birthday rapidly approaching, is working harder than ever. He still has time to sit – there aren't too many customers today, or any other day for that matter - the place is for sale.

He continues his description of the Wet. "Waterfalls across the road: Everything alive and green."

We both look wistfully at the encroaching forest. Leaves are fluttering down as if it were late fall in New England. Here, even at three thousand feet above sea level, it is warm, the trees drooping in the unrelenting heat of the spring sun.

The listlessness seems to affect the birdlife we are here to see in this ornithological paradise; only a common McLeay's honeyeater deigns to put in an appearance, whilst we devour damper bread smothered in rosella jam: Sort of comfort food.

Not to be outdone by the lack of uncooperative birds, Karen decides to help nature out by playing taped bird song.

Steve raises his voice above the dawn chorus. "Yes, you want to see it rain here. You'll have seen nothing like it. We'll have a storm soon though, I reckon."

We look at the gathering clouds; he with anticipation; me in palpitation.

We had better move on, do what we've come for, and get down the mountain before the flood markers start earning their pay.

We bush walk, surrounded by the calls of invisible bell birds and whip birds. Otherwise, total silence.

"Bugger!"

I spin round to find my wife attached to a giant strangler fig, its tentacles looped around her head. "That's the trouble with wearing hats in the tropical jungles," she said, matter-of-factly. "You can't see the head-high obstructions."

"Look on the bright side," I quip. "At least your hat'll keep the leeches out of your hair."

"Ugggh!"

The walk to Cloudy Creek is a lung-buster, but worth every muscle-searing step. The tranquillity is awesome. Butterflies feed on the large red flowers of the cocky apple, drawn to the flash of colour amongst the invariable green hues which line the creek banks. Only these are no ordinary butterflies. They are as large as a man's hand: Red and black; green and turquoise; orange and white, brimstone yellow and almost every variation in between.

The place is timeless. There aren't enough superlatives to do justice to the place, nor to the feelings it generates within you. You just feel at one with eternity.

And of course, I needn't have worried about the return journey. The rain held off, which meant no walls of water to negotiate. Somehow, I just didn't fancy driving directly beneath the thundering cascades so that the weight of the water hits the roof of the car itself. In this way, the downward pressure of water on vehicle keeps the tyres in contact with the road surface and you don't get swept sideways. The locals know all the tricks. Still…..

As we reach the plain and head for the coast, I steal a look in the rear-view mirror. Thick, grey cloud is beginning to descend across the tops of the ranges, cloaking them with an eerie air of mystery.

Suddenly, Paluma, its forests and creeks, the sounds of its birds and waterfalls, somehow exerts a presence over us, insignificant mortals.

It demands a return….. Only we dare not listen.

Fever pitch at Ross River:

If I said to you, "Where's Ross River?" - You know, the place famous for its biting, disease-ridden mosquitoes - would you have any idea?

I'd have guessed somewhere in the deepest recesses of a swampy Northern Territory, or a baking backwater in the vastness of Western Australia.

Wrong! It's about a hundred yards away; there are holes in the fly-screen mesh at our window and we are having to sleep, covered head to toe in mossy killer and prayer.

Ross River Fever you don't want, because once you've got it, you've got it for a long time. And it's not uncommon.

And the river is just there!

Where?

Townsville! - The reported 'Gateway to the Tropical North of Australia,' and famous for having one of the only two openings out to the ocean through the Great Barrier Reef.

I must say the rello's were very good about it, but it was my fear of the mossies feasting in the twilight that did it. On reflection, I guess they wished they hadn't asked me to move the car. But they felt perfectly safe: I hadn't had a drink, and they were too drunk to notice the fear in my eyes.

Still, I did as I was asked - after a fashion. I found the reverse gear of the hire car all right - but during the time I'd been inside their Queenslander home for introductions over a cuppa, someone had made a raised garden and installed a water meter in the centre of it. I didn't reverse over it hard - just nice and smoothly - although it did get a bit bumpy getting the car back out of the eucalyptus bush and off the subsequent water spout.

No, be fair, they were very good about it, sank a couple more scotches over their new fountain and promptly phoned the Water Board, to blame them for faulty workmanship.

The authorities promptly ignored the problem, quite happy for the street's new water feature to really take shape. [It was looking pretty impressive by the time we left, two days later.]

Townsville is like that: pretty laid back; yet modern in outlook. It is happily bereft of skyscrapers, and is full of restored old buildings and superb, innovative amenities for its citizens. One such, The Strand, running alongside the ocean, boasts walkways and swimming pools and remembrance parks and beaches and art, - and, best of all, is enjoyed everyday by people of all ages.

One cloud on the horizon is Timmy the Train. It whistles kids round and round the mall, but looks an awful lot like Thomas the Tank Engine to me. It's a bit naff, but no matter. Old couples, [devoid of such litigation worries,] barbecue steaks for lunch under giant figs; school kids are bussed in to enjoy the water parks; the brave ignore the signs and vinegar-dipping stations,* to dive about in the stinger-infested ocean.

We meet Max. He refuses to talk to us, as it's the first time in a week that he's been for a walk. He didn't know his owner had been poorly and so is making everyone feel his displeasure. Max, the parakeet, has clipped wings to prevent him enjoying the outdoors permanently - and oh how he enjoys being out, even if it's only for a breath of fresh air taken on the shoulder of his mistress. He might look cute and friendly, but you'll be lucky to get your finger back - on a black-mood day that is.

The temperatures soar and we retreat to Ross River. Our host's garden, which hasn't seen water in years, is now flooded and turning green. Don't you just know it - there's now enough of a pool to encourage gleeful insects to call home and settle down for a breeding session. And it's right outside our window.

I make a decision. Tonight I'll join our hosts in a bout of the 'Green Death.'** If I drink half as much as they do, perhaps it will help me ignore our plight.

*Vinegar, and Coca Cola, are the recognized antidotes to jelly fish stings, and so the beach front has several locations where vinegar [only] is provided with which to douse yourself.
** V.B. beer, so known because of its green label.

Left cold in Cardwell:

1872: Captain John Moresby took the survivors of the brig, 'Maria,' to Cardwell on the coast of Northern Queensland.

Twenty years later, another member of our extended Yorkshire families, one Richard Birkby, arrived there as the local policeman. Richard had married into another of our 'names' - the Ryan's - and in Moresby's time of exploration, the husband and wife team had together, been enforcing law and order in the rip-roaring, gold mining town of Cooktown in the Far North.

Gold had attracted about thirty thousand people to the area, their needs being met by no fewer than 94 hotels on Cooktown's main street: So, plenty of work for Richard and his wife, she being the town's gaoler.

By the 1890s, Cooktown was virtually a ghost town, and as the population waned as quickly as the gold, so did the need for the police. The Birkby's moved south, to Cardwell - and later, a little further south once more, to Ingham.

Our visit to Cardwell, a place of such historic importance to us, proved disappointing. The township today consists of nothing but a straggle of ill-assorted buildings hugging the road from Cairns to Townsville, a beach with, 'Keep off: Crocodiles!' signs and a windswept jetty pointing out toward Hinchinbrook Island.

Now, Hinchbrook has always held a fascination for me. Well, ever since I realized that what you see are merely the pinnacles of now-submerged mountains - three thousand, five hundred feet tall mountains. This submerged range, with its forest-covered peaks, is separated from the mainland by a narrow passageway, about which Captain Cook once remarked: "No one can sail through Hinchinbrook Passage and not believe in God."

The Barrier Reef Aborigines also attach a theological significance to the place: what you see is the lid of a chasm in which the rains and winds are secured. From time to time a malevolent devil lifts that lid, to let a storm or a mist come roaring out. Not that they've been released for some time – it hasn't rained properly here for over two years.

Lid-lifting devils, Captain Cook's awe and today's beautiful blue sky can do nothing to conceal my disappointment. I usually get a feel for a place, an echo of the past: But not here and not today.

Maybe I expect too much, too often.

White Tailed Rats and Cassowary's:

Greg looked like he had been dragged through a hedge backwards. His lifeless brown hair was unkempt and spiky, and the three-day growth of beard did nothing to inspire confidence in the Australian Customs Officer's uniform he was wearing. The uniform had seen better days too - an unbuttoned, stained jacket and no tie revealing a tidemark of dirt around the collar of his open-necked, once white shirt.

In his defence, he would never cut a dashing figure in uniform. His five feet, four inch, rotund frame would always militate against that. And he wasn't expecting company. Tucked away, in what looked like a couple of old freight containers joined together and converted into office space, and situated at the end of the bulk sugar loading dock in Mourilyan Harbour in Northern Queensland, isn't the posting you want as the pinnacle of a career stretching back too many disillusioned years.

"Hello," he said pleasantly, in a surprisingly deep voice, carefully wrapping his half-eaten sandwich in greaseproof paper. "Sorry about the state of the place. You caught me at a bad time."

My eyes ran over the disorganized paper chase covering the double-sized desk which overlooked the wharf's activities.

He hardly paused for breath. "Rats!" He explained. "Overrun with the buggers. Eating everything they are. All the electrical wiring..... Everything! Still, what can I do for you?" he asked, coming toward me with an outstretched hand.

The handshake was as firm and manly as his voice.

So I explained that I was following in the footsteps of a distant relative, Captain John Moresby of H.M.S. Basilisk, and that he'd named this harbour after his Navigating Lieutenant called Mourilyan: Hence our presence, standing in the ramshackle shack on a little pier in the middle of nowhere.

I finished by saying, "I hope my Captain John wasn't responsible for depositing your rats' ancestors."

"Doubt it," he replied. "These buggers aren't your European browns or blacks. These buggers have got white tails. But go on."

He listened with growing interest as I retold the tale of the 19th century shipwreck of the 167 ton brig, 'Maria,' on Bramble Reef, thirty miles off nearby Cardwell.

"Two boatloads of survivors," I continued, "made it ashore south of the Johnstone River, but were separated by an estuary. The ones on the Cardwell side were murdered by the local Aborigines, whereas the ones who landed further north were actually looked after by the natives."

"And how does your Moresby fella' fit in?" he asked, not knowing the story.

"Well, he set out to rescue the survivors and found the eight being cared for by those Aborigines. They were emaciated and ulcerated, but had survived by being fed on ants and fruit."

"And you want to know what beach he rescued them from?" he guessed correctly.

"I was kind-of hoping someone might know."

"I don't think you'll find anyone who'd know....." You could tell he was intrigued; this was something out of the ordinary and he could kill rats any day of the week. "Let's have a look at some maps and see what we can do?"

The large-scale, coastal maps were produced from a map cupboard and he began to pour over them. After a few minutes of silently rubbing the stubble on his chin and doing something with a protractor and compass, he stuck a stubby finger on the map.

"Got to be there, I reckon: Can't think it could be anywhere else, not with the tides and currents."

I peer closely at the map. Etty Bay!

Etty Bay, at the foot of the rainforest-covered Moresby Ranges [must have been his turn to have things named after him that day,] is now part of a wildlife conservation area, but comes complete with caravan park and a typical country shop, which sold absolutely every essential from fish and chips to hair shampoo.

We found no commemoration to the rescue of the survivors from the Maria. Instead, a plaque declaring that during the Second World War, the bay had been used by the U.S. Forces as a place for R. & R. during the Pacific War.

I can just imagine 500 battle-fatigued G.I.s, having faced fanatical Japanese attacks at Guadalcanal or elsewhere, being told they were to have some time off in a tropical paradise. The joy! The elation! Then they're told not to go in the beautiful water, "'Cos if the crocs don't get ya', then the stingers will."

Now it's a wildlife refuge, notably for the endangered cassowary, a six feet, six inch tall black, flightless bird with a bad attitude problem. Advice is given on yet more notices: 'Back up! Place something between you and the attacking bird!'

I wouldn't mind betting that Greg's really pleased that it's just rats attacking his cables. He'd really have something to worry about if the culprits were bigger than him and wanted to fight.

A Happy Ending:

[The Whitsunday Islands:]

It's good to learn something new every day. And today, "Sand flies," Cousin John was saying: "Millions of them around here. They don't bite - just urinate on you. It's the acid in it that burns your skin. In fact, they're one of the main reasons the Queenslander houses are built on stilts. The flies only operate to a height of three feet from the ground you see....."

Cousin John was very informative on a whole range of subjects, but unfortunately his house is a bungalow. And it's a sand fly night on the quiet hillside above Airlie Beach. Warm. No wind.

"Oowoo!" The undulating sound conveyed anguish in any language. "Oowoo!"

It was an inhuman sound, somewhere between a scream and a moan. It was so close, so loud, that Patsy jumped like an Olympian. Two feet up she went - and two to the right. It put her on the bed. Her "Agh!" joined the unremitting Oowoo's.

For a moment, I'm back earlier in the day, back on South Molle, an island resort in the Whitsunday Group of islands. I'm surrounded by obese people devouring chips and burgers, with fat running down their chins; inhuman screaming from their kids, who were doing their 'bombing' best to empty the swimming pool of water. I am surrounded by resort guests wandering vaguely about the place with paper, tour lapel badges: 'Hi! I'm Ron!' Or whatever!

I had wanted to scream - back then. My dream, my fantasy, for years had been to visit the Whitsunday's. My imagination had run riot: coral sand, seas and a sky to die for: yachts in remote bays. Not this! Not pedalloes and tennis courts, and twenty-a-side soccer matches.

I had wanted to scream and scream until I awoke from the nightmare.....

But the nightmare passed quickly - within three hundred yards of the pool area to be precise. Such a short distance, yet we're transported into the lush rainforest of the island's hilly interior [645 feet above sea level], and immediately we are lost in a wonderland.

We have proved once again that most people will not walk. They stick like limpets to the security of the overcrowded resorts - a mentality I don't understand, yet am eternally grateful for.

Within minutes we are alone in a shaded valley – alone, except for a colony of squawky, sleepy, combative fruit bats and thousands of hand-sized butterflies. There are so many of these ephemeral insects that by cupping your hands gently together, you can't help but enfold a living, multi-coloured magic.

It is impossible to describe the wonderment of nature at its very best, yet standing in that dappled sunshine, allowing a colourful cast of thousands to dance about you, is something which will live with us forever.

We tear ourselves away and continue our climb, all negativity banished. We walk, climb, descend, climb again for five miles in silent bliss - a silence broken only by the alarm calls of the hideous bush turkeys as the red kites silently circle and soar above; and by a gentle breeze which breathes through the leaves of the she-oaks and tall, dry grass.

We descend toward a remote coral beach. The wind fans upwards through the bush, adopting an eerie, 'Sh-sh-sh-sheeee.'

Our destination at last: Sandy Beach. It is a strange name for a beach consisting not of sand, but of billions of broken, blazing-white coral pieces, stretching in a perfect crescent for quarter of a mile or more.

A dazzling white, coral beach, kissed by the deep greens and greys of the native bush to one side, and caressed by a tranquil, turquoise sea on the other. A single, white yacht serves only to add the final touch to this perfect canvas.

We return, delighting in the exercise and silence.

Then, three hundred yards to go, and fifteen minutes until the ferry departs, the noise of people at play assails the senses once more. They are oblivious to what lies a few short minutes away.....

Another tortured scream brings me back to the present reality. Patsy is still standing on the bed, angst writ large across her face. The rello's have arrived too. They haven't had this much commotion in their house since God knows when. The bedroom is full of people, Agh's and Oowoo's.

The Oowoo is definitely coming from the fly screen patio door. Cousin John's sand fly story precipitated an immediate reaction from Patsy: A clashing and a locking of the door had followed. [Not that it would have helped matters anyway - the sand flies are so small they can get through the mesh screen.]

John eases open the screen door and releases the leg of the green tree frog. As if by magic, both frog and Patsy stop squawking. Silence reigns as our visitor hops away, leg in hand, and its backward, disgruntled look could almost have been human.

Good news! Next morning the frog is back, both legs intact and not harbouring any grudges.

Do you believe what you read in the newspapers?

Cape Hillsborough:

'So much to see and do at beautiful Cape Hillsborough National Park and Resort:'

'Now this might be a way to pep up your life….. So beautiful: So quiet!'

So the travel articles in a couple of newspapers said. But we don't believe newspaper reports any more. However, and unfortunately for us, we are in the hands of cousins who apparently do. It's either that, or their idea of reality and ours is somewhat different.

I certainly don't want the reader to run away with the idea that everything in Australia's garden is rosy - it's not. We have been to places which would have been better left unseen; places about which you struggle to find anything positive to say. Port Adelaide in South Australia jumps to mind immediately. That place was 'so ordinary,' as Aussies would put it that I'm left, even today, with an aversion to their Aussie Rules Footy Club doing well.

Now, added to the Aussie Doghouse, is Airlie Beach. At best you can describe it as 'tacky;' somewhere to leave as quickly as possible in favour of the reef. Then there's Bowen, the first European settlement in Northern Queensland. The local newspaper there tells us it is 'an up and coming place - and you must see its beaches.' Yeah! Right! Small, dirty and crowded.

But straight to number one in the Queensland Top Ten Horror Show is Cape Hillsborough. I don't know who wrote the piece in the papers, but it had to have been an estate agent in a pub having a laugh.

Caravans, tents and tiny wooden huts are thrown together higgledy-piggledy, crowded up against the low and dirty sand dunes. No privacy. No space. The huts - someone optimistically called them chalets - are ill-lit, bug-filled and leave you fearful of opening the ramshackle drawers; fearful of the night to come.

I can't help but be reminded of our first night on Fiji's Coral Coast, when the hotel security guard helpfully escorted us to our room. His "Don't worry! I'll be outside your window all night" at first felt quite reassuring - until you thought a little more deeply about it.

Our Cape Hillsborough accommodation came complete with its own ant army in the shower, and an unnerving battle to the death with a huge, wasp-like creature with evil eyes - a battle made necessary by the fact that none of the hungry geckos of various sizes and colours which adorned the walls and headboard would go anywhere near it.

It died.

Then the sun died. All at once, the still air fills with the sounds of axe on wood; the smoke of the camp fires and barbecues listlessly curl upward. Any light becomes confined to dwindling pools around individual encampments, the spluttering gas lanterns of the campers throwing their chasing and screaming children into ethereal relief. Like moths, the youngsters flit in and out of the darkness, ignoring the calls to bed. They aren't stupid; they'd much rather be outside and awake, than cooped up inside with God-knows-what lurking.

Our rello's head for bed; seemingly oblivious to the night. Patsy and I toss a coin. I can't decide who won or lost, but she gets to take the first watch, whilst I lie awake and try to think of a way out of our present predicament.

Eungella:

Broken River:

Eighty kilometres west of Mackay lies Eungella: [Pronounced Yungella].

We had followed the Pioneer Valley for as far as it went, then climbed the steep and winding road to the top of the Clarke Ranges. It was a long way to go, but infinitely preferable to hanging about in Hillsborough Hell.

Then we met Gertha, a stout German lady with a hare-lip, blazing eyes and an attitude all of her own. And all I'd asked for was some chocolate sprinkle on the top of my cappuccino.

"I vill not serve zee coffee with choc-o'-lat," came the reply from the surreal café owner.

"But....."

"You vill like my coffee, yah?"

My wife should have learned.....

"No! There eez no toilet here. Things don't verk here and zay doon't get vixed. Thees ees not zee suburbs."

"And what brings a nice German lady like you to a mountain top in Queensland, Gertha," I asked mischievously?

"I vish to be happy. You like my coffee, no? More?" she demands.

She stalks off in a huff, the long, flowing caftan-type thing she was wearing bristling in response to our, "No thanks."

We leave, cross-legged, in search of a private bush, and cross-eyed by the size of the bill.

Thus fortified, it was time for some serious bush walking. It began at the Broken River Encampment and was first class. The river itself, pure and untouched; steep ravine paths, darkened by huge palm trees and red cedar woods; a pair of satin bowerbirds; a huge turquoise Ulysses butterfly; skinks, large, slow moving; yellow and black monitor lizards; snakes.

Snakes! Plural! All poisonous: Three of them during the expedition: First, a six foot black snake, which slithered ungraciously off 'our' path. The start of the breeding season makes them crabby, as we found out later.

Next, a banded woma: Even the locals don't see these guys often. Ours was 'chunky' about the midriff - indicative of a fresh feed or a belly full of little womas. It was resting up in an abandoned burrow by some steps leading up to a crystalline waterfall. We agreed to ignore one another, even though its bite is not fatal.

The last, I choose to call Gertha. The poisonous brown does pack a fatal punch - especially this far from help - and it is as mean as a continental European coffee dispenser. I never saw it amongst the leaf litter - and now class myself as one of the luckiest people alive.

Lucky; because it was a juvenile: - Still old enough to send you to your Maker - but not if you're standing on its head. And I WAS standing on its head. Its tail recoiled in anger, coming up in a semi-circle at me and at about knee height. But its fangs are at the other end. Not that I knew which end was coming up at my bare knees in the heavy shade and in the split second that was available to me.

It jumped a half a mile and sideways. I jumped a full mile and straight up.

By the time I had landed, Gertha had slithered away, no doubt thinking baby skinks in the undergrowth were a better prospect than big, tastier blokes on the path.

A salutary experience: But not one that could possibly detract from the wonders of the Broken River wilderness.

A testing time on the Wheel of Fire:

Finch Hatton Gorge:

"Tea?" the young, unshaven teenager asked querulously.

"Or coffee," I compromised.

"Coffee?" He was doing a good impression of an inbred backwoodsman.

"You know - a brew?" I added to help him out a bit.

"Nah! Sorry! Could have done it, but the kettle blew up last week. Want a beer?"

His voice rose in eagerness at the word 'beer,' but it was 9.25 in the morning and I knew just then that we'd made a wrong move, stopping at this lonely roadhouse.

Still, in our defence, we had made an early start, travelled a long way through seemingly never-ending sugar cane fields and were nearing our destination, the Finch Hatton Gorge - the Wheel of Fire, to be precise: A Bush Walk for the insane!

We're not even there yet, but I can't help but feel we're being tested already. Yet, the lad must have recognized something in my face which said, 'No' to a beer for breakfast, as he asked optimistically, "I'll make you a brew if you want? But it'll have to be with hot water out of the tap."

He began scratching at his not-so-white vest and looked particularly blank as I politely declined, and, forcing back uncharitable thoughts, headed back outside. The harsh sunlight met me, burned my eyes after the gloom of the interior and, in the heat which was already oppressive, I began to sweat. I shaded my eyes and paused for a moment, to become adjusted to the conditions again. Our situation hit me. No tea. And we had misjudged the timing - badly. The Wheel of Fire awaits - something to look forward to, but in full sun and in the middle of the day? We must be crazy.

I look back into the roadhouse. The youngster is draining a tinny and waggles it in my direction. I guess he must think we're crazy too.

And we were both right. The bush walk was as hard as any we had ever done: Probably harder. No snakes, though - only a couple of medium-sized, sandy coloured goannas who looked at us panting and sweating humans labouring up the mountainside as a sub-species not worthy of a second glance.

We get to see a couple of the largest skinks we'd ever come across and they did their best to enliven our Himalayan-style trek. However, the arrival of the Aussie march fly certainly put us on our toes. Something akin to a horsefly, its bite had put one relative in hospital recently. And I do think there's something un-Australian about the March fly. For a start, it's September, not March, and the nasty blighters are not in a good mood. Maybe we are the first food they've seen in a while.

Still, the lung-bursting struggle up the Gorge of Fire brings its rewards - eventually. Near the top of the mountains, and as far as you can go in comparative safety [i.e. without climbing the impressive staircase of waterfalls], lies a large freshwater pool fed by one such cascade. The deep water is icy, but reviving.

We're lucky. It's still 'The Dry,' and today the waters gush, not thunder. Today it's a tranquil spot, not terrifying. Today the water eddies gently through the pool, unable to move the huge circular boulders which fill the ravine below.

We have time for reflection; time to let the heartbeat return to normal, the sweat to dry; time to pamper throbbing feet and legs in the healing waters. We delay for as long as possible - after all, such perfect isolation deserves time. And the return leg is not for the faint of heart either. It would be very easy to turn an ankle or overstrain the already protesting leg muscles.

At last, a final sip of water and a deep breath. We return safely, despite being battered by the relentless heat, near exhaustion and eventually, by no drinkable water.

Hard; without a doubt: An achievement; most certainly. But should you ask if we'd do it again, then the answer would be ……

[You never know, perhaps we'd wait in the roadhouse, maybe drink a beer or two until the kettle got fixed…..]

Journey 13
Tasmania

The Ferry

By now the avid reader will know that this particular travel writer doesn't like travelling - well, not in any aeroplane with fewer than four engines; something to do with not wanting to see the fear in the eyes of the driver. And now I'll let you into another secret: he doesn't like big ships either. Big ships mean big seas - mountainous things that can swallow up boats without trying. I know - I've read the Cruel Sea; seen the Perfect Storm - and my father's told me about what happened in the Second World War. Things were so bad for the capital ships on the Atlantic or Arctic Runs that he resorted to anything to remain aboard the coastal motor torpedo boats. He preferred to sit with a bucket between his knees, throwing up into it every few seconds, than to take his chances of disappearing without trace with the big boys.

Now, if someone told you "Take the ferry," what comes to mind? A little boat with character maybe: like the ones in Sydney Harbour that chug about the suburbs? Or maybe a native vessel out of Nadi in Fiji, surely nothing can be better - no more idyllic a way to spend a few hours - than watching the flying fish fly, and dolphins riding the bow waves of crystal clear water.

Dream on!

This ferry is a battler. Ten storeys high; double hulled, watertight, riveted windows that have been starred by years of misuse and driven spray. Today, it's driven hailstones out of a sky so low you can't see the top of the funnel. In the brochure, this experience is described as a 'mini-cruise' or something, but in reality, Samuel Johnson's words seem more apt when he compared travelling aboard ship to a jail - with the possibility of drowning.

The fog horn rents the air with its ferocity, but in a strange way, helps me pass the time. The American in the new, wide-brimmed, outback hat and ultra long, Driza-Bone is loud of manner - but can't compete:

Whoommm!
"I'm from....."
Whoommm!
"I've just got here from Georgia and....."
Whoommm!
".....taxman's waiting, so....."
Whoommm!
"I had to ask my agent," Whoommm! "Where's Australia?"

He was getting the hang, all too quickly, of how to continue to talk non-stop over the sound of the ship.

Now, you might think that this particular citizen of the world was lacking in his education. How can anyone not know where Australia is? After all, it is the size of Europe. It's easy! Believe me. Once, whilst in California, we'd thought about a side trip to the Rocky Mountains. We visited a travel agent, who'd never heard of them, but rang another office, the staff of whom came up with the simple answer. As John Denver sings about Rocky Mountain High, then they're "Probably up there near Denver somewhere."

I would have loved to have told my new companion this anecdote, but he never paused for breath.

With no alternative, I begin to think about resorting to drink. My Irish part would have approved and would probably have started singing. However, my Scottish Dissenter part would have thoroughly disapproved of that, and so my English Methodist part wins out by default. So I remain, suffering in silence, although secure in the knowledge that my English heritage would merely shrug its tolerant shoulders at his ignorance - should he ever get round to asking where Tasmania was.

Of course, he wouldn't be the first person in the world to ask that question - and struggle to have the answer explained to him. Back in the August of 1642, Anthony Van Dieman, the Governor General of the East Indies, sent Abel Tasman out on a 'Grand Expedition' to find the Southland. [Australia.] Four months later, Tasman's two vessels, the Heemskirch and the Zeehaen, had managed to miss the huge continent of Australia altogether [something which would appear impossible, when you look at a modern map and the route Tasman took] - but at least he did bump into the west coast of Tasmania. He promptly sent a boat load of military types ashore to hoist a flag, ingratiatingly calling it Van Dieman's Land - then left for home.

He left behind a green, yet rugged and mountainous island, about the size of Scotland or West Virginia, and where, under its temperate climate, huge forests had prospered untouched since time began.

It has taken us many years to get to Tasmania [due to lack of cash rather than a lack of maps,] but we do hope to stay a might longer than the founder of this jewel of a land.

Sniffing around old Hobart Town:

It was a strange day today, in that no-one we met and spoke to, was from Tasmania. There were two American men, two Russian sailors, a Puerto Rican woman and an English chap from Peterborough, who, as we chatted, admitted to being here in Hobart illegally for the last eleven years. We had met after he stopped my wife to advise her against walking alone along the kerb edge of a road and in an area which employs several hundred wharfees and sailors; they were always on the look-out for a 'good time gal.'

Patsy was only a hundred yards from Sullivan's Cove in the heart of the city, but had lost her bearings. There again, I suppose one shouldn't be surprised - either at my wife's infamous, and constant, lack of a sense of direction, or by the lack of a homogeneous population in Hobart. After all, at one stage, everyone was an immigrant.

Hard on the heels of Bass and Flinders, the explorers who visited Storm Bay and the site of Sullivan's Cove on 21st December, 1798, came the French - anxious to acquire an empire and put the English nose out of joint - and American whalers anxious for profit. To counter-act the attentions of these unwanted 'foreigners,' forty-nine settlers and Rum Corps men, plus twenty-one male and three female prisoners, were sent from the Australian mainland to occupy Tasmania.

That settlement failed, but, undeterred, two more ships were dispatched with a further 308 unfortunate souls aboard, who must have been asking themselves: "Why me?" Exposed to the ferocious biting of a million sand flies and the 132 degree temperatures amongst the sand dunes where they had decided to pitch camp, it wasn't long before both sad groups had banded together to set up home under the brooding bulk of Mount Wellington.

That impressive, towering peak, still snow-capped in the early spring, provides a suitable backdrop for Patsy's wrath. She was quick to catch onto the fact that it was me that had got her lost in the first place, and I have to plead guilty. Hobart, being such a small city, does pose problems of scale to a map reader. You expect to have to walk between locations, to seek out the historical sites: not so Sure, the homes of the locals now climb the hillsides surrounding the natural, deep water harbour, but you can still see the sights in this beautiful city, replete with its fine buildings of dressed stone, in a morning.

Sullivan's Cove leads to Constitution Dock, which leads in short order to Franklin Square. I pause here to try and conjure up once more, some connection to my ancestors. Franklin Square, from 1817, was used as a parade ground where the entire population of Hobart had to gather from time to time to be counted. Free settlers one day, convicts another.

My James Moresby, the lad from Yorkshire, ex-soldier and convicted thief, moved his family here in the January of 1808 after serving out his time on Norfolk Island. Although he settled at Clarence, some way outside the city, I like to think he would have lined up here with the rest of the free men to be counted. But perhaps not: Surely he wouldn't have wanted too, as he was claiming a land grant from the Governor for 50 descendants [in 1824] and James mustn't have been very good at arithmetic. I can only find evidence of a family of 14, so had he lined them up in front of a Governor who could count.....!

But back to the present day: Hobart, and its bustling, vibrant, Salamanca Place, with its open air bars and coffee houses, galleries, and art for all; the old village on Battery Point, all can be explored at leisure and on foot.

We saw the guy from Peterborough again - once in a chemist's shop, where he was dropping off a film. There, we learned that he was a 38 year old called Tom and worked in the Seamen's Mission.

The third time we met [I told you it was a small town] probably convinced him to abandon England forever. We'd just parked up the hire car and Patsy, walking away from it, stopped abruptly after a few yards: "I can smell rubber burning." With that, and on all fours, she began to smell at each tyre in turn; then the exhaust. Her concern was admirable - and catching. Soon, Cousin Margaret joined in. The only thing was that our car was blue - nothing like the red one they were sniffing at - and was parked on a different rank in the lot altogether.

The Ghost of Solomon Blay:

"Do you think I shall see Solomon Blay?"

These were the words uttered by one John King, when he was arrested for the murder of his common-law wife, Rebecca Hall, in 1858. They had been drinking at the Bulls Head in Hobart - Goulburn Street, to be exact - when they began to argue. He knocked her down - then shot her in the head with his pistol.

Of course, he did get to see Solomon Blay - the hangman in the penitentiary situated at the junction of Campbell and Brisbane Streets.

We were here to follow a Ghost Tour of the old gaol, known locally as 'the Tench,' and fortunately for us we had arrived early. So we had time to treat ourselves to a browse through the old trial records of the thirty-plus men, and one woman, who were hanged here in the bowels of this dark, dusty, musty and distinctly unpleasant, stone building.

Solomon Blay was an Englishman, a boatman from Oxford, who'd been transported for fiddling with the King's currency. Once in Hobart, he was given a choice: the labour gangs or become the hangman? Not much of a choice really.

He hung over thirty people in his fifty-year tenure of office - and never seemed to get any better at it. Many of his 'deserving?' victims hung for a long time before they expired. He also went in for mass hangings. His record: five at once - and these included the bushrangers, Black Pete, Wingey Stewart and William Ferns. With them through the drop was our previously mentioned John King, and one other, who unfortunately has to remain anonymous as I couldn't find his records.

But no matter, back to Solomon. He had the idea firmly fixed in his mind that he had to strap together the legs of all his customers. He did this as they stood on the trapdoor with the noose already around their necks, and in a multiple execution, he would intricately bind them together for their journey into the hereafter.

The Ghost Tour takes place at night and by torchlight. Okay, so maybe it is for effect, but only one word can describe it: eerie. The complex of tunnels - one of which has a stone floor which has been eroded by the feet of countless prisoners shuffling about waiting for their turn in the dock above - rooms, courts, cells and passages, all are cold and disquieting. And that's before the execution chambers are reached; one to be found directly above the other and connected by the trapdoor.

At every turn the guide reveals what apparitions have appeared and where: blue, hazy, spectral lights in the Hanging Judge's Courtroom; visitors being hit on the nose in passageways; shadowy figures hiding under the prisoner benches in the Chapel [third bench from the back on the left]; but in each and every case, the identity of the alleged ghosts wasn't known: Except one - Solomon Blay. It is he who regularly touches the ankles and lower legs of people visiting the upper death chamber. He is still tying together the legs of his victims.

There is no denying the unearthly quality of the whole place. Goose bumps rise all over the body; every distant noise raises the hackles and suspicions; the smell of vinegar, used to swill the gore out of the hangman's pit, assails the nostrils - but not until the guide introduces the idea to your consciousness.

It's all in the imagination, surely.

Then.....

Then, in the Execution Chamber, my new pen, with which I've been happily writing furious notes, just won't write any more. I scribble across the paper, then scribble violently, indenting five pages with pressure marks - but not a drop of ink. I curse, borrow another pen and continue.

"How many people did Solomon hang in here?" I ask.

"Thirty five."

"How many were hung altogether before hanging went out of fashion?"

"Well over 200, and most of them with this equipment you have in front of you."

I write the notes for myself: '35' '200+,' before returning the pen to its owner.

The tour ends and we return to the entrance hall, where I realize I need to make another note. I try my own pen again. On the same piece of paper, on the same place on the notepad, still indented by my scribbling, it writes first time. In the Death Chamber, nothing; yet now there is a free flow of ink. Not only that, but of the large notes I wrote for myself there - the '35' and the '200+' - there is now no trace.

I mention it to the guide; seemingly I'm the first person whose pen has refused to work at that location, but his nonchalant statement, "It's usually people's cameras that fail in there," gives me the shivers all over again. In fact, it happens so often, the novelty has worn off for him. But not for me; I think it's weird, and I would pose a question for you:

'Do you think I've just met Solomon Blay?'

Stop Press! American crap saves Hobart!

I have just sat at the window of my room on the 14th floor and watched a beautiful sunrise over the fishing fleet bobbing about in Sullivan's Cove. Beyond the vessels, there's a monument down on the shore dedicated to the Antarctic expeditions which have set sail from here, and, if I crane my neck a little, I can see the Russian Icebreaker waiting for its next cruise to cold places.

Directly in front of me, and across the bay, is Drought Point, a long, low headland which is practically devoid of vegetation; a strange phenomenon, when everywhere one is faced with so much forestation. There had to be a reason, and a story, behind that. And there was.

Back in 1804, Hobart consisted of a little gaggle of tents and huts, with casks stacked one upon the other along the docks. The population clung to life. For eighteen months they had been without bread, vegetables, tea, sugar and booze. It was a time of starvation and the early colonists, free or not, only survived by eating Botany Bay Greens - boiled seaweed.

But help was at hand from an unlikely source: the American whalers and sealers across the bay on Drought Point. The creatures they caught were hauled up onto the flesching decks, cut up, and the blubber rendered down for oil and such in huge, half-ton, iron try-pots. [There is one on display in the Tasmanian Museum and Art Gallery on Macquarie Street.]

How did that help the citizens of Hobart town? Well, they were allowed to eat the Americans' c.r.a.p. - that's the Cindery Residue from the American try-Pots. [Sorry, but I couldn't help myself.]

The downside was that, to keep the pots boiling, you needed wood. Lots of it: A full headland full. And so there it sits today, naked, in a world of trees and water.

Later, on one of those harbour cruises that everyone seems obliged to take, we meet Max, a larger-than-life New Englander who was following his 19 year old daughter around the world, "To make sure she was okay." [Her views are unknown, but she had told dad that she needed to go backpacking in the Tasmanian wilderness for her university course.] He believed her, of course, but just now he seemed more interested in the casino on Wrest Point and the whereabouts of a jazz bar.

Maybe his indifferent attitude to the wild bay on which we were sailing, and the unique history of the whalers and sealers and the untamed country that is Tasmania, would have been slightly different had he seen the morning papers:

A 7.9 metre long boat [i.e. larger than the one that we're sitting in] only yesterday and not far from here, crammed with Americans on a seal-watching trip, had been lifted out of the sea, spun round 180 degrees and dropped back down with a resounding crash. The culprit: a whale, who obviously had a sense of history and injustice. The tourists were reported as "Speechless at first" but the lawyer amongst them was soon demanding the trip be re-scheduled, "or else....."

A Policy of Apathy:

Does bureaucracy annoy you as much as it annoys me? Mind you, as I get older, I find I am becoming less and less tolerant - but maybe that's the same for every generation. I don't know. But what I do know is what happened today. If you had a First Fleet ancestor, like my James Moresby - someone who now has official acknowledgment [even his grave sports a Government-paid-for 'First Fleeter' plaque] you would be quite proud and pleased.

If you could, maybe you would spend a fortune and travel to the other side of the world to seek out the past, make it real, tangible.

If there was a painting of that now-respected old timer, no matter how cantankerous an old git he was in real life, [the records show he was] and the picture was in the possession of the Hobart Art Gallery, then maybe, just maybe, you would like to pay a visit and take a peek at it.

If you're a bureaucrat: "I'm sorry. It's in the archives and we're busy. You'll have to make an appointment."

"But I leave tomorrow."

"I'm sorry. Perhaps when you get home you'd be able to drop us a line."

And all delivered in that apathetic, 'I couldn't care less - go away,' voice.

Not that red tape is a phenomenon of the twenty-first century. In 1853 [twenty years after the death of James] Tasmania was granted its own constitution [Constitution Dock, in Sullivan's Cove, now marks the spot], and shortly afterwards the island ceased to be a penal colony.

It probably came then, as a bit of a surprise to the population of Hobart, when 64 old and infirm convicts in handcuffs and leg irons, 126 paupers and 79 lunatics, came ashore in the city centre. That was in 1877, after the infamous Port Arthur was closed for good. It is reported that the crowds watching this inglorious spectacle "Gaped and giggled" at the sight of the remnants of the British Transportation Policy. The bureaucrat's response: "They must serve out their sentence" - so it was 1886 before the stain of that particularly odious practice was over forever.

That was just three years before the death of one of my own particular Australian heroes - someone who just wanted a 'fair go' for the ordinary working man. His name was Peter Lalor, [Lalor being a derivation of our own Scottish name of Laidlaw] who had been born in 1827 in Ireland. His brother had been a hero of the Irish Resistance to British Rule.

Anyway, in the 1850s, Peter was a gold digger on the goldfields of Ballarat in Victoria, and became the spokesman for the ten thousand Diggers at Broken Hill who demanded, 'a fair go.' The outrage and unrest amongst the miners revolved around the red tape and bureaucracy of the camp officials, who just happened to think they were unaccountable in the issuing of high-priced licences, and the enforcement of their regulations at the point of a bayonet.

It all ended in tears, of course. In fifteen minutes, thirty miners were dead at the hands of government soldiers. Those in power play hard-ball to keep it. Lalor was wounded, hidden under a wood pile and later had to have his arm amputated. No-one handed him in to the authorities though, and he later went on to enter Parliament.

Because of the gold rush across the Bass Strait, it was said that by 1860, 'Hobart was left populated by people afflicted with apathy.' Maybe I just met one of their descendants in the art gallery.

Dennis Collins and me:

Today, Port Arthur, once described as Australia's Dachau and an emblem of hell on earth, stands as an enigma: green lawns; a blue ocean on which harbour cruises while away the time pleasantly; and a splattering of thirty or so old, stone buildings and wooden cottages with their 'English' gardens, all laid out for the enjoyment of the idling tourists.

But the sunshine and serenity can't mask the undercurrent of horror for long. Not long after Carnarvon Bay had been discovered by the ship Opossum, which had sought refuge from a storm, the first prisoners began to arrive. This was in 1830, the men being sent to build their camp on Mason Cove, a base from which they could harvest the untouched and colossal stands of timber in the area.

And so we meet Dennis Collins, an Irishman who had served in the Royal Navy during the French Wars of the early 1800s. His left leg had been smashed to a pulp by a loose canon which had been charging about the deck, and surprisingly, he survived the amputation without anesthetics, or any attempt at keeping the environment sterile by the surgeon, to end up in the Navy Hospital at Greenwich.

Here, things really started to go downhill for him. Being an awkward cuss, he soon got himself into trouble with the staff, was evicted to a life on the streets and denied his rightful pension. After exhausting all legal steps to try and get what was rightfully his, he tried to get attention for his cause by throwing a stone at the king, who was attending some race meeting or other.

He got attention all right - transported to Australia and ending up in the penal colony here at Port Arthur. He refused all work, even a request to sweep up the prison yard a couple of times a day. His refusal had consequences, which many of his contemporaries knew all about: 14 days' solitary confinement spent in total darkness; flogging of up to 100 lashes at a time; and leg fetters weighing up to 45 pounds which 'scraped the ankles to the bone.'

Eventually, he said that as he wasn't doing the king's work, he'd not eat the king's food. Within three months he was dead, buried on the Isle of the Dead out in the harbour - one of about 1200 prisoners who lie there without any cross or headstone to mark their passing.

After February, 1833, things got a whole lot worse with the arrival of a new commandant, Charles O'Hara Booth. He dealt with his recalcitrant charges by imprisoning them in solitary cells measuring seven feet by four feet, and in total darkness. Worst of all, absolute silence was kept.

Infractions of the rule were punished by a flogging with the 'Cat;' knotted 81 times and saturated in salt water before being allowed to dry out. In that condition, it "Cut flesh like a saw."

Even in church, the prisoners were not allowed to communicate with, nor even see, one another. A cough was treated as an attempt to pass a message - and therefore as an attempt to escape.

The prisoners may have gone into that silent, Separate Prison to have "Their minds reformed" - but plenty of the hooded and silent drones came out "Not as they went in." No wonder they built the mental hospital next to the solitary block.

Today, teenagers, full of life and high spirits, fill the individual, head high, lockable, pews without a thought for the past. They flick 'V' signs and shout, before taking their idea of havoc elsewhere. And that's fair enough; there's already enough of us feeling a black mood coming on about what happened here. Someone should kick over the traces and treat the barbarity of the place with contempt.

But despite the efforts of today's guardians to make Port Arthur acceptable and pleasing, somewhere for the tourist to have a good day out, the evil of the past hasn't gone away. On 28th April, 1996, the beautiful grounds, studded with the mature oaks and elms of a 19th century population desperate to be reminded of home, became the location of one of the worst, lone-gunman massacres of the 20th century. 35 dead; many more wounded. My own brother missed death here by minutes - if there hadn't been such a long queue for tea and meat pies.....! Instead, he spent long hours hiding from the gunman who shot at everyone he could find.

The new Garden Memorial certainly proves the enigma that is Port Arthur. See it and you will know what I mean. Yet Port Arthur is undeniably a worthwhile, must-do experience for every tourist, whether a student of history or not. Only remember, if you scratch the surface, that undercurrent of unease oozes through and grips your heart. By the end of the day, like Dennis Collins, you'll know when enough is enough.

A poem by Mary Gilmore dated 1918:

> I was the convict sent to hell
> To make the desert the living well
> I split the rock and fell the tree
> The nation was because of me.

Ugly Mug to Ugly Mood

There is a lot more to the Tasman Peninsula than Port Arthur. For instance, you can go see Ugly Mug, or even Doo F*ck All. But let me explain.

Pirates Bay is on the unprotected, seaward side of a narrow isthmus with the tidal, Eaglehawk Bay, an appendage of Norfolk Bay, on the other. Between the two, and measuring 120 of my paces, is the infamous Eaglehawk Neck, the only land bridge to freedom for anyone daring to escape from the penal colony of Port Arthur situated to the south.

Many had tried it: many had failed - although in 1830, an Irishman called Martin Cash, and two of his mates, braved the shark-filled waters off the Neck and swam to freedom. [Martin was re-arrested three years later, whilst visiting a lady friend in Hobart.]

In 1832, to stop the escapees, someone came up with the bright idea of placing dogs across Eaglehawk Neck. They were positioned close enough so as to be able to eat out of the same bowl, but chained so as not to be able to kill one another.

Enter Ugly Mug and his friends - other mastiffs with equally great names: Jowler: Tear 'em: Muzzle-'em. And these weren't your average hounds. They were described as: 'Black and grey, white and brindle, rough and smooth, lop-eared and crop-eared, gaunt and grim. Every four-footed, black-fanged, individual would take first prize in its own class for ugliness and ferocity.'

More dogs were added, to prevent the escaped prisoners from swimming further and further out to sea to avoid the dog line. Incredible as it seems now, these late arrivals got their own rafts out on the ocean.

Now, the historic area has been joyously restored, rejoicing in its past, in the fabulous Pirates Bay and most of all, in the incredible sunsets over Eaglehawk Bay.

Just along the coast, to the south, we reach Doo-Town, where practically every resident has cooperated by naming their homes with 'Doo' in the title: 'Sheil Do,' 'Much Adoo,' 'Doo Me,' 'Rum Doo,' - and my favourite: 'Doo F– All.'

The town - no, more a village - is a piece of harmless fun, heralding the fantastic coastal scenery around Tasman's Arch and the Devil's Kitchen - places where the huge seas of the Southern Ocean have smashed the cliffs into fantastic shapes, and where salt spray from the breakers is sent a hundred feet into the air.

There can be no better bush walking anywhere in Australia than here. The incessant booming of the terrifying ocean accompanies you through the fragrances of the bush in spring. Everywhere plants are blooming. There are whites and greens and yellows - but most of all there are the blues and purples of the poison pea, the kangaroo apple and the sun orchids. They bid you on your way from one fantastic, frightening look-out over the ocean to another.

And you can't leave the Eagleneck area without mentioning the Tessellated Pavement at the northern end of Pirates Bay. It is technically on the Forestier Peninsula, but what's a few hundred yards between friends. The worn-away cliffs have produced some very strange, flat, rock formations which protrude out into the ocean, allowing some great photographs as the dawn breaks.

But the lady we met that evening, over a glass of wine and a gentle roasting in front of a roaring wood fire, was only interested in the wild flowers. In fact there were two ladies, Susan and her mother, but so overwhelming was the daughter, that mum 'sort of' sat back, faded into the evening sofa and disappeared.

They were from Queensland, and Susan had driven all the way to the Tasman Peninsula to sketch the flowers, which she would later reproduce in water colours. She was 53, and had two sons, one of whom had left home and worked backstage with some rock and roll band.

By the time her third chardonnay had disappeared, we also knew she'd been to Western Australia to see the spring flowers there, but had been disappointed. She was also a student of history; "Well, it's a good bed time read: Sends you to sleep."

She certainly talked, became garrulous even, but after she described her ancestry as "Equal parts French, Swiss, Irish and Australian," I didn't take much more in. I know that's kind-of rude, but you weren't there and my mind had switched over to concentrating on her. From her looks, the 'part Australian,' must mean part Aborigine. The genes of her European forebears had obviously subdued her native ones, but there was still something in her facial expressions which hinted at least of some of her origins.

Of course, that sent my mind racing again. We know she must be a determined, strong character; brave even, to head off on such long trips with only an 80 year old mother for company, and in a car which would have been new off the production line when Herr Hitler pronounced it 'the people's car.'

But an Aborigine in Tasmania: - That takes some kind of balls!

When Governor Arthur, a pious man who'd fought with the 35th Regiment of Foot against Napoleon, arrived on Tasmania, a vicious war between whites and Aborigines had been going on for twenty years or so.

The war is thought to have been instigated by the white incomers, the first massacre of Aborigines being recorded on 3rd May, 1804. Later, dead Aborigines were used as food for the dogs and the women were sold to sealers as sex slaves. That's not to say the fight was all one-sided. The Aborigines set fire to shepherds' huts and killed the occupants as they were forced out into the open.

Arthur tried to separate the races. The Big River and Oyster Bay tribes would be moved forcibly to the north east corner of the island, but that attempt failed miserably. However, two years later, a policy of conciliation did work. The remaining 2,000 tribesmen were given presents of food and offered sanctuary. They accepted - and that was that for their race. By 1876, the last Tasmanian Aborigine was dead, her bones put on display for all to see. [They were removed in 1947.]

"I think I'll buy a water colour this time to give to my son....."

I came back into the present. Susan was still speaking and to my mind's eye, her native features were so pronounced, I don't know how I hadn't noticed in the first place.

"He's always saying how good my paintings are, but I'm never satisfied with them.....
I'll buy one. That one of the three lilies I saw. He'll like that, won't he mum?"

Mum said nothing and I guessed the rock and roller wouldn't be into flowers. It must be the other guy - and granny didn't seem too impressed.....

"Bed!" said mum, entering the conversation for the first time, and we went, reluctant to leave the fiery embers, but needing a respite from the rapid-fire talking at by her daughter.

"No! More wine!" snapped Susan, waving her glass airily in the direction of the distant bar tender.

Her mother sat back, to disappear into the couch once more - but we kept going. Do you know, I would swear I could feel her eyes burning into the middle of my back as we made our escape?

Next morning, enjoying a breakfast of fresh fruit, cereal and toast whilst taking in the incredible, panoramic views over Pirates Bay, Susan never spoke. Her mouth was set. She never looked up and studiously ignored our presence. Mum winked, and smiled out of the corner of her mouth from behind a hand, whilst supposedly covering a feigned cough.

Perhaps Susan was suffering from a chardonnay overdose. Or perhaps she was still annoyed with us, that we didn't stay up into the wee hours watching her drink. However, it's more likely that she had reached the chapter in her history book, the one about the Solution of the Aboriginal Problem in Tasmania.

Jeannies Duck.

Jeannie Murchison is from Stirling in Scotland, but just now her head's in the gutter and her ample rump is reaching for the heavens.

"Good morning, Jeannie," I say. "It's a grand day we have this morning."

"Yes. It's a real beaut isn't it," came the muffled Scottish tones. She may have forsaken Scotland for Tasmania fifteen years ago, but you can't mistake the accent.

I wonder what she's doing with a metal kitchen sieve poking down a storm drain, but she's concentrating so hard, I don't like to interrupt. And that silent concentration is so unlike Jeannie. From her normal, upright position behind the desk in the motel's reception area, she will talk forever, the conversation flitting this way and that as the next thought invades her brain.

"Did you hear about that woman who got eaten by a croc last night?" I eventually ask, peering over her shoulder.

"It was only a tourist," her voice echoed.

I couldn't contain myself any longer. "Just what are you doing?"

".....This poor duckling."

I kneeled alongside Jeannie and peered into the huge storm drain. Two fat backsides reach for the heavens. A long way down was a drop of evil-smelling water being churned up frantically by a duckling scooting around in circles and cheeping madly.

"They killed the croc to get her body back," I added, mesmerized by the ball of yellow feathers. It was kicking up a storm in an effort to survive.

"Ah! Poor croc! Fancy doing that to it," she replied, even before my echo had finished reverberating from below.

"Where's mummy duck?" I ask.

"On the swimming pool with the last of her brood."

"Sensible girl."

"She started with nine, you know," added a concerned Jeannie.

"That's where the tourist should have been: In the pool, not the creek."

"They'll all go the same way..... You think they'd learn wouldn't you?"

"It's too much to expect a duck....."

She turned her head, adjusted her metal framed glasses, and then held my eye as if to say 'stupid.' "Not the duck, dear: The bloody tourists!"

"The handle's too short, Jeannie," I said trying to redeem myself. I smile and nod toward the dripping sieve. "You'll never get it out....."

Obviously the duckling had had enough of us. It jumped onto a ledge above the outflow pipe and ran off, quacking, in the direction of the hotel pool.

"Okay!" Jeannie said with a sigh whilst knocking off the slime from the sieve. "I'd better go and start on the cakes."

"Shouldn't we get the ducks out of the pool and stick them back in the reserve over the road?"

"Nah! They're safer where they are. In fact, the tourists are more likely to want to swim in the reserve than walk about the pool area, now that the ducks are using it as a toilet."

I had two thoughts: One: was it incontinent ducks that drove the tourist lady to her death by croc? Two: Will Jeannie wash the sieve before cooking commences? Either way, we'll never know.

A Fanfare for Fray-sin-ay:

The Freycinet Peninsula, on Tasmania's east coast, is a truly spectacular location. It was discovered in 1802 and named after the First Officer of the ship which first passed this way, Louis de Freycinet. [Fray-sin-ay.] They may have been the first, but the range of mountains known as The Hazards, formed out of a pink granite which glows in the afternoon sun, are still casting their spell over everyone who sees them. They dominate the azure blue waters and virgin bush from which they rise, and spawn some of the finest beaches anywhere in the world. There is Honeymoon Bay, so named because it's only big enough for two; and Sleepy Bay, its pink gravely sand surrounded by red granite rocks, and where, despite its name, wild seas ravage its beauty.

Or how about the most delightful and secluded of beaches which lies only fifty yards from our wooden chalet, complete with roaring log fire and kangaroos by the door? The beach itself is long, deserted and spectacular, and has never been given an official name. Now it's known as Diesel's Beach, christened by the fortunate owner of our accommodation after his dog, Diesel. A strange name for a dog, but the four-legged critter earned his name because he has run almost non-stop up and down the sand ever since he moved in. He thinks it's his beach, and gets terribly depressed when confined to barracks, to prevent him being a nuisance to guests, like us. He doesn't like people, especially visitors, and especially when they're on his beach, and so he sits for hours staring out of the window of his master's lodge, no doubt harbouring thoughts of revenge. The beach is too nice to give to a dog, so I care not a jot about hurting the hound's feelings - but I do wonder about historians, who, in a hundred years time, will surely be pondering over the origin of the beach's name.

Then, of course, there is the reason that nearly everyone comes to Freycinet, braving the wooden hut hacked out of the bush and the subsequent wildlife invasions: Wineglass Bay - so named because some early explorer had a fertile imagination. I can't see a wineglass-shaped anything, but what the heck.....

In the early morning light, we walk the rough and difficult path which picks its way between Mount Amos and Mount Mayson. Ours are the only names in the ranger's book - an appropriate safeguard in case the weather turns bad or an accident occurs. This is not a place to treat lightly. The instructions at the Ranger Station are explicit: Take a litre of water per person; sturdy shoes are a must, as are waterproofs and jumpers..... And a whole lot more besides.

It is a long, difficult walk up between the mountain peaks, and an even longer and more difficult one down the other side, yet the early start is rewarded over and over again. Kangaroo tracks on the perfect beach; a blue tongued lizard; a pair of courting wrens; raucous, yellow-tailed black cockatoos; lizards warming themselves on the rocks; and penguins. Penguins!

Wineglass Bay may once have been given the accolade of being in the top ten of the world's beaches, and it is indeed stunning - white sand and turquoise water - but the sea is bitterly cold; hence the happy rock hoppers and blue-legged homo sapiens. Later, with much regret, we leave perfection behind and are faced with yet another difficult, long climb out.

By lunch time we begin to meet other visitors heading for Wineglass: Scots, Aussies, Italian's, Dutch, - the sure and certain [and unwelcome?] penalty for the success of the international publicity surrounding the freezing waters and perfect white sand of Wineglass. We are here because of it, that perfection, yet we don't want it spoiled.

Unreasonable jealousy rises; we don't want to share it, especially as there is something obviously wrong with some of the late arrivals.

It is hard going to get to and from the beach, dangerous even - especially if wet underfoot - and one chap is laudably carrying an army rucksack, full to overflowing, on his back, with yet another on his chest. He's not even sweating - but he's young and carrying everything the rangers ask. Next: a couple in flip-flops and bathers. Now, remember it's nearly a two-hour walk to the beach, through a bush full of bitey-stingy things. One of our companions urges them to think again, but they mumble something in German, and keep going.

Then comes a bunch of old folk carrying clip boards and reference books, sort of a mobile library. They are counting plants, only they can't talk because of hammering hearts, stressed-out lungs and glazed-over, staring eyes.

Finally, we emerge, unscathed, hardly happy at relinquishing our hold on the pristine beach beyond the mountains - but it's gone and that's that. With a good heart we set off to face our next daunting project: Aussie meat pies.

Gibbet Hill:

We left Swansea far behind, but not the little ditty that had permeated my brain to the exclusion of all else. It had been penned by a bushranger - just before they hung him:

'Me and me old dog Digger
We robbed the hills and downs
But it was here in the Swansea townships
They finally tracked me down.'

It was a pretty long road across country to Ross, and all the while the words worried away inside my head. I'm sure you know how it is.

Even our arrival in Ross, with its evident Scottish heritage and convict past, its coffee shops and boutiques and tourists, couldn't rid me of its spell. But then, as we move through orchards and wineries and rich pasture land toward our goal of Launceston - the third oldest city in Australia dating from 1804 - we come across Gibbet Hill.

The old execution site for bushrangers - in the days when they were strung up at the side of a road for all to see - looks pretty innocuous today; pretty much like any other hillside, covered as it is in gum trees and rocks, with dead wood a-plenty, and stock animals that cluster in whatever pockets of shade that are available.

But that haunting name broke the logjam, and the old grey matter was off and running once more. Back to the early 1600s and the Scottish Borders with England - in fact, to a time when the authorities had decided to rein in the illegal activities of the all - powerful Reiving Families, or 'Names.' For centuries, the border had gone its own way, answerable to neither London nor Edinburgh, and where banditry had been raised to an art form.

To break the families, the authorities employed a simple solution, which came to be known as 'Jeddert Justice' - or 'Hang 'em first and ask questions later.'

And here we are; at a place where a couple of hundred years later and on the other side of the world, the authorities were employing the same tactics against the bushrangers. In the Tasmania of the 19th century, many of these outlaws had begun their careers as kangaroo hunters, who then just stayed away from civilization. Their efforts certainly saved the early colony from starvation, and later they sold the kangaroo meat and the skins to the farmers - as well as helping themselves to a sheep here and there. Of course the 'roos got more and more scarce and they had to look for another source of income - robbery. These men, with their long, rat-like hair and thick beards, who covered their 'polecats' stench' with long, rough-made clothing, must have put the fear of God into the occupants of the remote farmsteads and travellers alike.

Still, the government had a solution. They formed posses of convicts – who would be rewarded with their freedom in exchange for the severed head of one of these 'sheep duffers,' or bushrangers.

I guess the rich Tamar and Macquarie river valleys were amongst the first to be cleared of 'undesirables', no doubt the local populace preferring to adorn their gentile countryside of today with steel templates and models of highwaymen and prisoner chain gangs, rather than the real thing.

I dare say we can't blame them.

Redundancy in old Jerusalem:

Ina runs a place near old Jerusalem in the Coal River valley. It is well off the A1 highway and therefore pretty remote. I say 'place' advisedly, as I can't really describe her business to anyone's satisfaction, least of all mine.

She was just putting out a tea/coffee sign as we drove past, and of course it drew us in. We hadn't seen anywhere to stop for an age, and although the old, corrugated-iron and wood building had seen better days, it did have that sign.

Ina was non-stop energy. Kettle on, she chatted as she rushed about her place, opening fresh sacks of potatoes: Southern Eyes, Pink Eyes, Bismarks; Dutch Cream. As she laid tables, a gentleman staggered in, delivering fresh, home-made, wood-oven cooked loaves: large cobs and long sticks: The room fills with a luscious aroma. The tables are left half done in favour of wrapping the bread into individual, white tissue parcels. The kettle boils and she's off. Tea, coffee, home-made scones and jams appear.

She makes everything herself from the raw materials that her husband grows in his huge garden at the back of their homestead. They sell the surplus. On cue, he appears, arms full of fresh-pulled beetroot, and informs us that the cabbages are ready too.

"It'll have to wait dear. We've got some nice people here. By the way, do you want some of our fresh picked raspberries?"

More customers arrive and we take the time to check out the shelves. They are full to overflowing with home-made tomato sauce, home-made jams of every description, home-made lavender products. The fridges are full of frozen fruits and vegetables, and cakes and pies, and..... Well, I could go on.

Ina is a Tasmanian by birth, but had spent her life following her husband's career through Western Australia and Victoria with the one-time Australian industrial giant, B.H.P. Now she has returned home, courtesy of her husband's generous redundancy package - and she's happy.

At seventy, I don't know how long she can keep up this frantic pace, but she seems to be thriving on it.

As we chat, more customers arrive; this time a husband and wife team from Wales. Courtesy of generous Foot and Mouth payments from the British Government, they are looking for a property on Tasmania [or Victoria], to re-settle and start afresh. Nearing sixty, I don't suppose it'll be an easy task, but the weakness of the Australian dollar, and a son in the business, should see them right.

Reluctantly, we take our leave, only later to renew our acquaintance with the generosity of B.H.P. When their steel-making operations wound down in Wollongong and Newcastle [both in New South Wales], Richard Booth and his wife said, "Thank you very much." She took the opportunity to give up teaching, and now both have sunk every cent they had into two holiday-let cottages and a second hand book shop.

Their humanity and friendliness certainly shone through the gloom of the dusty clutter of the book shop, where penny periodicals were stacked side-by-side with hardback, first editions. Boxes stood everywhere, some half empty, others full to overflowing. Some shelves were in urgent need of rescue from the punishing weight, whilst in other areas, the old wood stood bare: "White ants!"

"Yes," they are sure they do have the books we'd be interested in. "Only where.....?"

They didn't display as much energy as Ina had earlier, so, whilst we waited, a stroll through their wonderful 'English' garden seemed in order. Beyond the white painted picket fence lay roses and foxgloves and lavender, the sound of passing traffic being drowned out by the humming of bees. We were lost in silence and peace; lost in time and space, transported to our Shropshire home in summer.

Then, from a distant radio, a muted, angelic church choir confronts us with our present day reality. It's November 11th, not June or July, and it's Remembrance Day.

As it turned out, we couldn't be in a more appropriate place for our own silence.

Santa's little 'helper?'

Triabunna, on Prosser Bay, is a small fishing settlement on the east coast of Tasmania and was the location for the most surreal of experiences.

Rosie's Tea Room is simply full; full of Rosie and Rosie's things. She flounces around her cottage home in a tent-like, floral dress, swinging her ample hips and getting herself into a complete tizz as two car loads of tourists arrive at once on the street outside.

"Oh dear: Oh dear!" she lamented. "This always happens when he takes himself off fishing." For someone pushing seventy, she's certainly nimble on her feet and manages to disappear into her kitchen beyond the plastic-strip fly curtain before the bell on her front door stops tinkling.

We are already at one of the three tables available for her visitors wanting tea and home-made things. They are tucked away at the rear of her home, and to get to them you have to manoeuvre, with plenty of hip swerves, passed piles of old books and magazines [one entitled, 'Paris, 1938,' and written in French], second-hand clothing, crochet work, piles of pillows and bolsters, china nick-knacks; dangly, tinkly things which hang dustily from the yellowing, painted ceiling, large vases stuffed full of artificial flowers, and small jars overflowing with dried herbs and ointments.

The walls are not spared either. Clocks, paintings of Australiana, photo's of pioneers and other old folk in starched collars, and a single cuckoo clock that chips in rather too frequently.

In fact, it's all very unusual, bordering on the bizarre - a view which is substantiated when a porcelain plaque comes into view: 'Masturbation is not a crime.' Mmmh! That 'Vile and unusual practice,' may not be in the criminal code [unless carried out in public], but it certainly caused the 19th century Australian prison authorities plenty of worry. In fact, so concerned were they by the practice amongst the prisoners, they forced any inmate 'offender' to wear huge, leather mitts to – well, you get the idea.

Near 'that' sign is a print of a wallaby: this one is displaying his 'bits,' the size and configuration of which must have come from the imagination of an impressionist painter. Then the caption; written so small you have to strain your eyes to read it: "It might be small, but it's very greedy."

Now, I couldn't understand Rosie, or anyone, wanting that sort of stuff in her home, but then she waltzed past us, leaving the air behind her tainted with the smell of sherry. She hip-waggled her way to meet her new customers, but as she passed a Santa Claus hanging from his parachute at about head height, she pulled his todger. For that act of kindness, he began to sing, "Jingle bell, jingle bell, jingle bell rock....."

Ah well! It takes all sorts.

Rosie's place is now full to overflowing with people [there are six at the last count] and so we take our leave, edging past the new arrivals, whilst at the same time being ever so careful not to disturb the piles of merchandise. I, for one, am hoping that they'll enjoy the singing of Santa, who is belting out his tinny rhyme again......and again.

"Patsy! Come on! Leave him alone!"

Red Wine and Giant Squid:

Today's the day. I just know it is. It may be only 7 a.m., but the omens are working well. The storm of yesterday has blown itself out, the ocean is dead calm and in the spring sunlight I can see pods of dolphins frolicking just offshore.

But today, it's the whales – those wonderful leviathans of the deep, once persecuted to the point of extinction, and who have now adopted these deep offshore canyons as their home - that we have come to see.

The billboards and posters surround us - you know the sort of thing: huge whale tails lifted above the ocean's surface and set in stark relief against the pink glow of an early morning sky.

Today's the day, and I can't wait.

Excitement mounts, as fifty of the world's luckiest people creep by the boulder breakwater to exit the small harbour.

"There's a fur seal," points Seth, our guide for the day - a huge, deeply-tanned man, sporting a bright yellow Aussie 4-Ever baseball cap.

I look. I look hard. But I can't spot the seal. Still, today is 'Whale Day'.

We leave the breakwater behind and already the Japanese man is snoring, head thrown back, mouth gaping. The low chug of the idling engines suddenly gives way to a deep-throated roar. The stem of the catamaran settles and we're off. We slice into the first of the day's several thousand rollers; the swell is deceptively heavy, and we are rewarded by a burst of spray passing the windows: Exhilarating stuff.

Not everyone is of the same mind as me. The middle-aged French guy, the leader of a tour group who was so full of bravado on the pier head, vomits last night's red wine into his 'comfort' bag. [In the old days they were sick bags, and I never noted the change to cater for the sensitivities of the new century.] I poke another sea-sick pill into my mouth and give a thin-lipped smile of smug satisfaction. No-one relegates me to a seat at the bumpy back of the boat without a residue of resentment.

The rest of us learn about the tidal flows and the deep, deep canyons beneath our keel. It is the canyons that attract the whales, or rather the squid and stuff they eat, who also have taken a fancy to the waters hereabouts. But it's only male whales that are here; the water is too cold for the females and their calves.

We stop. And the rolling of the boat immediately gets worse; a lot worse. The captain is about to use his hydrophone to pick up whale-speak. We all walk the deck looking for the tell-tale signs we've been told about - like waterspouts. I say 'all' loosely. The Japanese bloke sleeps on. The French tour leader has been joined by his wife puking up; and the sour-faced English lady with the neck brace hasn't moved a muscle - not even to sip her fruit juice 'with added vitamins.'

I guess the sound of puking overrides the hydrophones, for after only two minutes we are off again, smashing through the ever increasing swell.

"Look out for the petrels," we're told. "They're a sure sign of whales being about, as they feed on what the whales miss." I wouldn't have a clue how to differentiate a petrel from a woodpecker, but there are sea birds everywhere you look. The initial excitement dies as soon as the fleet of tiny fishing boats is spotted. You have to look real hard; the boats are so small they are all but lost in the deep ocean troughs.

We're told of the technical workings of the hydrophone, but, time after time, nothing! Now, I'm no expert, but I know for a fact that David Attenborough never has these problems, and I remember him telling me [well, his T.V. audience] that whales can communicate with one another half way around the world.

Seth hasn't mentioned this, and I reckon that if he eventually manages to lock onto some whale-speak, then we could be in for a long cruise. I hope the French haven't worked this out for themselves yet, as by now, fifteen of them are doing their best to use up all the naughts and crosses bags. The more adventurous of us are playing 'Battleships' on theirs.

One of Seth's mates, a real big bloke with a scowl, tries to force his size sixteen hands into some little, white plastic, washing-up gloves. He advances on the French. Either he's going to tidy up or.....

We are told the reasons why the whales might not show up, although they 'usually' do. The record time for cruising without seeing a whale is one hour and fifty minutes. I manfully resist the temptation to check the watch, as the reasons for a no-show are listed: There could be killer whales in the vicinity - and they eat the other species, including the sperm whale - the ones we're after.

'That's okay,' I say to myself. I'd settle for the sight of a killer whale. I have no intention of going 'in there' with them.

"It could be yesterday's storm that's upset them," lied Seth. "It could have moved them to seek better water."

Yeah! Right! As if a sixty ton monster, with blood vessels you can swim through, cares a lot about three feet high waves.

Then, of course, "There's sex," Seth informs us.

That's more like it, although it fails to excite the Japanese or French contingents. I'm all for sex and I'd settle for a couple of cavorting whales. I could then ask Seth, "What are they doing?" But no such luck. The males could be away looking for a mate, before returning to their home waters and letting the little lady get on with it. Not very noble, but it sounds a likely explanation.

Then of course, there's us. Apart from their killer whale cousins and the giant sixty-foot long squid [nobody mentioned them before we got on the boat] the only predator the whales have is us.

I look about at our motley collection of folk from all over the world, and I'd take a bet on the fact that, between us, we could scour the seas for months without seeing a whale. Yet, it wasn't so long ago that people were out here in rowing boats, chancing death, and armed only with a knife tied on the end of a stick, in order to kill these monsters; monsters that could despatch even our modern craft today into eternity with a flick of the tail. But we, as a species, seem to be able to turn our hand to anything, so long as there's a profit in it.

I understand the Maoris of New Zealand gave up their traditional hunting of whales, which they saw as an omen of good luck, back in 1910, and I'm not sure if the Australian Aborigine ever bothered hunting them at all. But of course, in more 'civilized' societies, where good luck equals good money, we slaughter and slaughter.

I'm brought back to my present reality. "There's a yellow-eyed penguin," cries Seth.

I look and look and look, and see nothing. The English lady stares ahead, the French have collapsed, pale-faced, into their seats but continue to clutch at the arm rests, whilst the Japanese man sleeps on.

I have no idea why a yellow-eyed penguin is out here. He seems to be a long way from home. Perhaps he's as lost as the whales, and me.

I have travelled twelve thousand miles to fulfill one of my life's ambitions - to see the whales up close and personal - only for them to play a joke on me by taking off for the day. That offbeat humour allows me to share with you Phillip Adam's alternative words for the Aussie National Anthem:

> 'I love this ripper country
> of funnel webs and sharks,
> With blowies as big as eagles,
> Where your car gets booked by narks.
> Where your team gets trounced each Saturday,
> And the pub's ran out of beer,
> Where there's redbacks on the toilet seat
> And your nagged by Germaine Greer.'

A Strange Congregation of Ordinary Folk:

I am standing in the reception area of a pretty ordinary motel and looking at a brass plaque saying: 'In this spot in 1882, rest assured, nothing happened.'

That just about sums up our day - so I'm desperate for a story: The only thing for it is to delve into that section of my brain marked: 'I don't know what to do with these but.....' and include here the odds and ends of characters we've met who haven't yet managed to find a home.

*

The guy in the coffee shop looked pretty ordinary, except for the cup and saucer balanced on top of his head. He was pushing sixty, skinny as a rake and looked like he needed to scrub up a bit. As for his face, well, it was as melancholy as Jack Benny's was in his heyday.

"You trying to improve your posture, or just trying to get a refill?" I quip.

Delivered in a monotone voice came the reply; "It-is my-duty-to-act-stupid-in-order-to-make-my-fellow-man-happy."

I nodded - after all, it seemed a perfectly reasonable stance to take. But there again, it's 9.30 on a Saturday morning and we're the only people anywhere in town - apart from the Saturday girl behind the counter. She is young and looks uncertain; one nutter she can cope with, but two? She manages to produce a couple of stale bread rolls and then hunts about under the counter tops for something to fill them with. I hope it's refrigerated down there as it's over thirty degrees outside.

As she does so, cup-and-saucer man states in his wonderfully flat tones: "Isn't-it-wonderful-how-we-married-men-recognize-each-other?"

That earns him a hard look from my better-half - a look that is sufficiently damning to freeze his free refill.

*

For a while it was looking like Patsy and I were about to spend a long and uncomfortable night in our little hire car: Hotel after motel after bed and breakfast full, no answer or no thanks.

Then a little voice from behind the swivelly post card rack. "You can stay with me if you're stuck."

With a grateful "Sold to the lady in the pink hat," we accept her generous offer without hesitation. Anything had to be better than spending all night sitting upright in a lay-by outside the public toilets.

"The place is clean," she added, pushing her luck, and then proceeded to sell us her house over and over. For fifty bucks we'd see that it was "Nice out the back," and that there were "Nice views from upstairs."

Having been sold ages ago, I let the patter flow over me and concentrate on the owner of the little-mouse voice. She was probably in her early forties, overweight running to fat, with worry lines and a down-turned mouth indicative of some unpleasantness in her past.

I was right. I found out later she had separated from her husband seven years ago and he'd taken off with the two kids. One of the youngsters was now twenty two and "Doing his own thing," whilst the youngest, "Didn't come around much any more." "We're very close though." She had given up her nursing job, travelled alone to Europe, "As a dare to myself," but, faced by disaster in Greece, had dissolved in floods of tears and returned home without her bags. When she got to the bit about not having had a man in seven years, my fingers were just about broken by the clenching of my wife's fist.

Still; the night passed uneventfully - our host was out most of it wine tasting; leaving two complete strangers to do as they felt fit in her home.

I was left with the question of whether loneliness was affecting judgment here.

*

Johnno Haddad is larger than life. Of mixed Christian and Lebanese heritage, he owns and runs a clothing store in a small, one street, rural town. We were told, "Don't go in there and expect to come out without having bought anything. It won't happen!" Now there was a challenge that couldn't remain unanswered: But they were right. Johnno could sell sand to the Arabs, but there again.....

Anyway, he sold me a New Zealand rugby shirt - a shirt of the 'old enemy.' However, it was sixty bucks below retail and a real bargain. But even his moleskin trousers, oil-skin Driza-Bone coats, "Just like the man from Snowy River wore," 'ugly' rugby jerseys, hole-proof Explorer Sox, "As purchased by the Duke of Buccleuch, a very important person from Scotland," failed to part us from any more cash.

"No credit. No Layby's. No Appro [approval] Means, Cheap-Cheap-Cheap!" He talks non-stop. Sales patter interrupted by jokes. "Did you ever hear the one about the pom visiting the Lion Park? No? Well, this Aussie Lion Park offers entry for cars at ten bucks, pensioners for five bucks and poms on bikes free. One day this pom turns up on a bike and they let him go in with the lions."

"Go on then," I ask. "What's the punch line?"

"Well, the lions ignored the pom and ate his bike."

I felt that this story had some significance for me, like I'd just entered a lion park and met the chief lion. But Johnno was a perceptive salesman and saw no more cash was going to be forthcoming. Yet he was content to have made at least one sale. His honour was intact and he'd probably been trying to get rid of that jersey for years. He wrapped it carefully in brown paper, made a tidy package of it and tied it with string, complete with finger loop.

"Thank you so much for coming to my lovely little shop. You've made my day," he says, as he leads us to the door and the glare outside. He bows, shakes hands and thrusts a flyer in my direction: "Just in case any of your friends should ever pass this way."

Two minutes later, the waitress delivering the coffee to our table points at the brown paper bundle:

"You've been had at Haddad's then?"

*

Papataraya Anderson waits on tables in a small Returned Service Men's League Club. She works hard clearing tables and would be an easy person to overlook in the everyday hubbub of life; one of the many people who are there, but you don't always see them. And that's always a mistake.

For some reason we hit it off immediately. A smile, a word, an acknowledgment to a kindred spirit, I know not, but within seconds this kindly Maori-Scottish woman sits down with us for a chat amongst the residue of a massive fish supper.

Her children are living in London and have no intention of leaving the 'pub on every corner' lifestyle. She was illegitimate and the quest for her roots has led her into genealogy in a big way, ensnaring her as it had us. She knows her Maori heritage through the verbal tradition of her native family, but her genes have been diluted by two Brits. One was a Scotsman called Anderson, a whaler, who'd left his mark by bequeathing Papataraya with straight, light brown hair and green eyes. Number two was a soldier who'd deserted from the British Army in New Zealand between 1860 and 1865 during the Maori Wars. He'd changed sides and fought for the Maori Land Cause and is now a revered person within the continued life of her clan.

Papataraya Anderson exudes happiness, openness and warmth for her fellow human beings; a glaring testimony to the fact that everyone has a story that is worth listening to.

*

Ian McCloud is a good six feet tall and sports a black beard trimmed to within a couple of inches of his huge, round face. He has a bald head, is overweight and tattooed, and is accompanied by his mother who, at four feet ten inches, can dominate a whole room full of people.

We talk - two Ian's together: two opposites, both feeding off one another and enjoying it immensely. One is a retired cop, the other a retired Hell's Angel; both absorbed by the rugby match being played out in near total darkness. We're waiting for a dance to start in the local Girl Guide hall.

"Ooh!" he says, as the full back drops another high ball and is flattened. "How he doesn't get killed more often, I don't know."

Then, as I try to absorb that piece of home-spun philosophy, "I still miss my Harley," he says, with obvious regret. But no regrets about the loss of his pig-tail and the constraining of his once wild beard. He had worn both down to his waist and had exchanged them, and so the outward signs of his individuality, for a job working nights on a ward caring for the mentally ill, a day job gardening, and free board and lodgings back with his Mum. He'd loved the life of a Hell's Angel, but was as confused as I was, trying to understand how he could once have afforded to run a Harley and live without work on the open road, but now was in work, living at home, and could only afford a moped.

How does work and responsibility equate with cash shortfalls? Answers on a post card!

*

She grabbed my thumb and the trapped nerves of the carpel tunnel shot rivers of pain up into my brain.

"Aghhhhh!"

"Don't be such a wimp." She was forty, long haired, had mischievous eyes and was heavy chested. "Come here and I'll kiss it better."

A little voice chipped in a warning from several yards away. "That's not all she'll kiss better, given half a chance."

The pain was abating, but the brain still wasn't functioning properly.

"Come here," she continued, "And I'll give you a proper Aussie welcome."

I've heard of Maoris and Eskimos rubbing noses, of Westerners shaking hands and of Japanese bowing, but grabbing your backside, thrusting breasts in a revolving motion across one's chest and a lingering kiss full on the lips, was all new to me.

Ah! How these old Scottish customs have been adapted and improved in a new land.

Journey 14
The Northern Territory:

Alice Springs

The taxi driver didn't inspire a lot of confidence at first sight. He was six feet tall with three days growth of beard around a thin, weathered face rounded off by a goodly crop of straggly blonde hair. As we approached the rank from the airport terminal, he nonchalantly eased himself from the bonnet of his old and battered people carrier, took a last deep drag on his ciggy and flicked it away.

With some misgivings we entered his cab, to find the interior pretty much reflecting the owner: old and worn, but with a good heart. Certainly, once he knew we were first time visitors to the Territory, he was a mine of information and did everything possible to show off his city to advantage.

Alice Springs! Now there's a name to conjure with. Within three decades it has managed to transform itself from a dusty outpost, where the horses of the stock hands were tied up outside the pubs, to an indispensable tourist base.

Our driver pointed this way and that, whilst the hand left on the wheel did its best to keep us on the road. There was the weather station, the Flying Doctor, the reptile house, a dried-up river bed, the mall, etc., etc.

For the first time in a very long time, I feel like a tourist in Australia. Perhaps it's not surprising, for we have no real reason to be here, to undertake this journey, except to say, "Been there: Done that." And that makes me uncomfortable.

Yet, to the best of our knowledge, none of our forebears had settled in the Territory. No prospectors. No explorers. No drovers. No old and weary taxi-driving cousins several times removed. However, to prevent this chapter from becoming a total fraud, we can claim a rather loose family connection with this, the Red Centre of Australia.

And that was a tragedy forever in the making. A young man on drugs eventually gets himself sorted out after years of abuse and of putting his parents through a kind of hell that can only be imagined. Then, completely rehabilitated, he gets himself a job far away from his old life in Northern New South Wales - in Alice Springs - teaching English to the Aboriginal communities which dot the landscape hereabouts. Three weeks after he arrives, he's killed in a road accident.

The only other connection to the Northern Territory are a couple of WW2 Ack-Ack Gunners, who helped to defend Darwin when it was attacked by Japanese planes during the Second World War. Oh! – There is someone else as well; someone who made medical history up here: But more of him later.

Still, the connections to this vast, ancient land are not strong, and to be honest, it's difficult to get my tourist head around the first impressions of the Red Centre. I can try: Rugged: Beautiful. Extreme: Certainly, very, very different.

Like the majority of others arriving in Alice, we had travelled by air. For hours we'd crossed above greyish–green patchworks of 'farmed' land, studded with remote outposts of civilization. These properties were invariably clustered around bright green dots where artesian water had been brought to the surface, and were serviced by long, straight, dirt roads which seemed to head from nowhere to nowhere.

Even the dirt roads eventually succumbed to the serried, longitudinal rows of evenly spaced, one hundred feet high sand dunes which stretched out like vast, grey-yellow, then dirty red, waves across the face of the invisible ocean that is now the Simpson Desert.

Then the salt pans: They are unreal; eerie. Dead! But it is the waterways which fascinate. They wander to extinction in the desert heart of the continent. Here and there, the dying watercourses display a hint of blue in the form of shrinking, still pools, formed when the water can no longer penetrate the sandbanks. Soon it turns to mud, the mud cracks; the land dries.

There is a majesty to the land below - a majesty which gives rise to some unwelcome thoughts. Just what is it like down there? What unknown creatures come to drink that water? Could we survive? I don't expect so….. Although if the truth be known; we are hoping to experience just a little of that silent emptiness for ourselves.

In the meantime, our fellow tourists are happy, talkative and excited. The Aboriginal lady sitting next to me is informative and comfortable with her life in the modern world, preaching reconciliation between the races.

We arrive at our motel. It's cold. Zero degrees. The room smells of the sulphur-tainted water, but I couldn't care less. I'm tired, disorientated, and not even the group of Aboriginal men, swigging from bottles concealed in brown paper bags only yards from our bedroom window, can stop us embracing some much needed sleep.

The door is locked, we are buried under a pile of blankets and sleep beckons, as we wonder about what tomorrow will bring.

Five bucks short of Alice:

Alice Springs seems so much better today. The people are friendly and helpful and full of banter - even though I mistook a fellow guest for the cleaning lady.

It's warming up nicely too, 31 degrees, and after three days constant travelling, Alice does indeed come as a welcome relief. It is time for a day of well-earned rest and reflection.

The Outback Roadhouse had been something to behold: a low, corrugated- iron and mud brick building selling everything from aspirin to beer, cattle drench to tea towels. The locals - well, all four of them, with European roots - were clustered around the wall-mounted television in the bar, hootin' and a hollerin' at an Aussie Rules game - no doubt a bit of light relief from the ongoing cattle muster.

And that's a thing in itself: modern-day cattle mustering. No more charging about on horseback, taking weeks to gather in the herds which wander the million or so acres. Today, satellite technology switches off the water being pumped from the bore holes for the stock. And by switching off the water in sequence, the thirsty cattle are forced to move on to the next watering hole. Eventually the animals arrive, in prime condition, at a convenient loading point for the huge road trains. And that just happens to be next to the human watering hole we're in now - Mount Ebenezer Roadhouse.

I was fortunate to witness something of the muster, albeit from a distance. The muted lowing of the herd, the shouts and whistles of men on horseback, who were near lost in a huge dust swirl, and the rumble of hooves on metal loading ramps, carried to me on a warm, gentle breeze. Yet the distant mingling of muted sounds served only to emphasize the silence and stillness of the outback.

I drink it in, before eventually I have my attention drawn to some of the Aboriginal inhabitants of the Mount Ebenezer area who were now gathering outside the Roadhouse.

An old woman was lethargically making a fire in a primitive shelter, itself propped up against the rough hewn telegraph pole: Nearby sat an impressive looking elder, motionless in the shade of the barbecue area. He boasted a white beard and thick white eyebrows, whilst his greying hair was half-hidden under a pork pie hat. He sat in silence, impassive, enduring without movement the attention of the flies crawling across his dark and rugged features. He just looked so right, if you know what I mean.

He embodied the Territory - and I needed a photo. But I didn't dare ask him - it would have been like door-stepping royalty - and we had been warned as to the inadvisability of photographing the locals.

So, I turn my devious mind to the young black fella' - sort of an Aussie East End Barrow Boy, who was hawking some awful, if not original, Aboriginal paintings by the side of the road.

I approach.

He looks furtively over his shoulder: "No here! No see!"

I thought he was expecting trouble from the roadhouse owner.

"No see! Come! Come!"

We end up behind the outside toilet block, with only the unpleasant odour and a host of flies for company. I try to convince him I didn't need his infantile, still wet, painting of the crocodile or kangaroo [it could have been either] - just a photo of the elder.

A bit of negotiation; five bucks for an introduction:

I see the cash disappear in an instant - just as quickly as Jack the Lad. Over the fence and across the dog-filled yard he flew, leaving a lot of snarling, snapping and barking in his wake.

It took some time, but later it dawned on me that the guy wasn't frightened of being moved on by the roadhouse owner – he just didn't want any of his transactions witnessed by the elder. Of the 'why,' I can only guess.

Farewell to five dollars. Ah well! But it did seem a good idea at the time.

The Fruit of the Camel:

The air is dry enough to destroy the membranes in your nose; so your nose bleeds - frequently.

The sun is strong enough to burn exposed flesh and hurt the eyes with the glare from the red sand, red boulders and red mountains of the George Gill Range, which rise steeply out of the never-ending spinifex desert.

The daylight moon is smiling in the clear blue sky.

It is 9 a.m. It is 29 degrees. And it's spring.

And spring at Doughboy Creek, almost lost in the semi-arid vastness at the edge of the Simpson Desert, is in full swing. The desert oaks, blackened in last season's bush fires, are shooting once more. The sparse eucalyptus are a bright blue-grey colour at their base - but the trees are as nothing, compared to the yellows, blues, reds and whites of a desert in flower, little patches of colour struggling for recognition amongst the dry, all-pervading spinifex.

And pademelons: The yellow, tennis ball-sized fruit grow on long tendrils alongside the narrow roadway. The plant is not a native of Australia but of Afghanistan, introduced here when the camel replaced the horse as the most suitable method of transportation. The seeds came amongst the padding in the camels' saddles.

Much of the fruit is no longer at the side of the roadway, but is to be found on the actual carriageway, placed there courtesy of intelligent parrots, who need the fruit to be crushed so they can access the seeds. They push them out, then sit and wait.

We disturb two such turquoise-coloured sentinels, and they show their displeasure by squawking loudly and carrying on like a couple of naughty five year olds.

Not that we have seen many parrots. Feral cows, camels and brumbies [wild horses] - yes! - But native wildlife on the properties hereabouts - no, not much. [Just in passing, a property of less than 600,000 acres is seen as a 'hobby' farm.]

There could be many an explanation for so little visible wildlife. Perhaps it's the abundance of wedgies, [wedge-tailed eagles], the third largest bird of prey in the world. Or maybe it's the feral cats, which reputedly grow to sixty pounds in weight and are capable of taking down a young kangaroo.

That sounds like a pretty good yarn to me, but somehow, the apparent vast nothingness of the Territory makes everything seem possible.

The McIntyre Factor:

I listened intently to an old explorer telling a tale or two about his time in the desert heart of Australia. It was about July when he'd said to his mate: "What's eating you?"

"Nothin'," came the reply. "Why?"

"It's just you haven't spoken since February."

"Can't a bloke have a bit of peace and quiet, then?" he snapped back.

So, the old explorer thought, 'Well, that's okay,' and didn't speak again until October, when he couldn't take the silence any more. "Come on mate. What's wrong?" he asks. "You can tell me."

"You're always pickin' on me," he replied.

The story tickled my fancy, as it did to others privileged to listen in - all except for one bloke at the back. He said nothing - not a word, not a smile - and made no eye contact with anyone.

Ignore him.

But the old explorer's words struck a chord with me. For one thing above all else in the Territory, is the silence: It is the essence of the Outback.

Silence. The silence of an arid, flat-as-a-pancake landscape that stretches as far as forever. Few birds: Even fewer visible 'other things' that scuttle and slide about invisibly. You know they are there - somewhere.

And even when you're at some of the world's great places - like Ayers Rock [now Uluru] or the Olgas [now Kata Tjuta] - to witness the colour changes to the rock formations at sunrise and sunset; and where you are surrounded by hundreds of like-minded photographers all vying for the best spot; or are surrounded by the happy wine drinkers and boisterous barbecuers, there is always that underlying quality of silence which borders upon the religious.

Uluru is undoubtedly a very special place. Even in the glare of a full sun, when the tourists seek to haul themselves to the top by means of a chain anchored into its side, it still exerts an influence, something akin to the wonder and presence of the Garden Tomb in Jerusalem, the Tomb of the Unknown Soldier in Westminster Abbey, or any amount of other such significant places which can be found here and there throughout this world of ours.

Move away from the hordes and the silence closes in, allowing the creation tales of the Aboriginal peoples to take on a life of their own - tales of ancestors capable of changing from animal into human form at will, and who laid down the ethics for human behaviour.

It has been proved that the Anangu tribe have been here - around Uluru - for twenty-three thousand years believing their ancestors to have been the Mala - small wallabies which still inhabit this strange, silent world of wind and sand.

The guy at the back continues to inhabit his own strange, silent world. But ignore him.

The old-timer continues. This time he's telling of an Aboriginal man he had come across. Nothing unusual in that - except that this guy had a spear right through his leg.

The explorer says: "G'day mate! You want to be a bit careful there, or that shaft'll keep catching the other leg. Shall I cut it down a bit for you?"

But no! The Aboriginal man would have none of it: [a] the spear was too valuable; and [b]this was a traditional punishment for some misdemeanour and it was up to him to heal himself before he could be re-admitted to the tribe. So - no help; thank you all the same.

A stifled yawn from up the back:

'What's wrong with him?' I ask myself. 'He's obviously not into the spirituality of the place, nor the humour of the story teller. And he can't possibly have had three 4 a.m. starts on the trot, as we've had.' Our eyes meet; he glares and turns away. Ignore him.

Different parts of Uluru display evidence of the various legends attached to it. For instance: Lizard Man [Lungkata] still lies at the bottom of the monolith's western wall - still there where he fell after being smoked out of hiding by two hunters of the Anangu. Seemingly, they'd wounded an Emu and were tracking it for the kill when he nipped in and stole it. The hunters tracked the opportunist thief to a cave high up on Ayers Rock and smoked him out. Blinded by the smoke and heat, and in a fit of coughing, Lizard Man stumbled over the edge. When he hit the bottom, he turned to stone.

And he's still there - the Lungkata Stone, below the fire-stain marks high on the walls.

And different parts of the rock have other, secret significance for both men and women. Outsiders will never know the meaning, or indeed, all the stories, and I accept that whole heartedly. What I did find a little irritating was all the unexpected rules and regulations at every turn.

It was okay for people to climb Ayers Rock if they wanted to - but if you respected the request of the Aboriginal owners not to climb - to just walk around the base - then: 'Don't photograph here!' 'Keep to the path!' 'Don't..!' 'Don't..!' 'Don't..!' – Or the Rangers will get ya'.

And the fines are not small.

We move on to the Olga's, something like 32 dome-shaped, brilliant red hills not too far from Uluru. Wonderful photographic opportunities, but don't, don't, don't!

It may have been irritating, but it wasn't as bad as our moody companion. He followed in our wake up a steep-sided canyon, deep in shade: Then followed us back. And all the while a willy-wagtail hopped from rock to rock, keeping pace with us, preening its feathers and calling all the time, 'Tjintir-tjintir.'

Back to Ayers Rock in time for a spectacular sunset - an experience you don't want to end. But of course it did. The sun dies, the rock becomes black, its awe overtaken now by the heavens. The red planet, Mars, hangs low over our invisible red, scrub-covered plain. Both places are equally alien, yet spell-binding.

Later, my mood is destroyed. The free wine to toast the sunset had certainly had a marked effect on 'Old Moody' himself. He's loud. He's laughing. He's a McIntyre from Western Canada. He's God's gift to sail boat racing. He's…..

I spend my last hours before bed wondering over the price of Aboriginal stabbing spears.

'A cock in a frock on a rock:'

We have been walking on a beach today: Nothing unusual in that - only this one is over two thousand kilometres from the nearest coastline and is at least three hundred million years old. It dates from a time when central Australia was an inland sea; a time before the sun got to work.

We see the patterns of wavelets forever frozen in the red rocks; the casts of giant sea worms. And it's been hard-going to get to experience at least some of what this ancient land has to offer.

Yet we have gladly accepted the hardships along the way, to arrive at the remote and impressive King's Canyon, set as it is at the very edge of the George Gill mountain range. An eleven-and-a-half hour road trip; a night with an overflowing toilet; green algae dripping from the shower-head - but what the hell! This is the Northern Territory - don't whinge. Get on with it.

And to get to our beach has been an absolute joy for us. Three hundred yards - straight up the canyon wall, followed by a seven kilometre walk, all the while being burned to a crisp by the relentless sun which ignored countless sunscreen sloppings.

Water breaks are frequent, to give the flies a chance to demonstrate their contempt for the insect repellent we have plastered over ourselves. The water breaks are absolutely vital. Dead cows and camels - carcasses dried to the point of mummification and eaten from the inside outwards - are a great stimulus to share a drop of water or two with the local insect population.

We have enjoyed the climb, the exercise, the whole experience, after so many hours trapped in a vehicle. This was particularly so when we arrived at a gap in a rock face, instantly recognizable as the place immortalized in the film, 'Priscilla: Queen of the Desert.' This was the location where one of the transvestites delivered that great one-liner: "A cock in a frock on a rock."

Forgive me if I'm wrong here with the exact wording; I'm working from an old and tired memory bank.

Forty other 'explorers' had started the climb with us and within minutes I am left in awe of my fellow men. Thirty feet up the sheer cliff-face and the twenty-stoners are flagging. Still, fair-do's, they all keep going, showing a real outback spirit, to gain the prize of eventually squeezing through Priscilla's Gap into the Lost City - a host of red domes of rock which look remarkably like beehives.

We are immediately joined by an audience, a host of willy wagtails, at home in every nook and cranny. They are joined by other birds, notably fairy martins, which fly about the cliff faces above and below us.

In their own way the birds are at least a distraction - at worst, a danger - for it would be so easy to lose oneself amongst the rock domes, once home to the Luritja Aboriginal tribe. [I never did find the blue, 'This-way-idiot signs' we were told to look for. But I guess that's me all over.]

The Luritjas used to use their ancestor, the 'Willy Wagtail Woman', to keep an eye on outsiders - like the Uluru Lot [or us]. She would fly off, then report back to them up here in their domed, fortress-like homeland as to what was going on down on the plain by Ayers Rock.

Pushing aside all thoughts of the tales the willy wagtails would now be whispering - one certainty would be that of the now defunct McIntyre species, who, grogless once more, had become even more surly and ill-tempered before he'd taken his leave of us - we enter the Garden of Eden, an oasis set deep inside the mountain itself.

It was a long way down to the still waters at the bottom of the chasm, where we were left to wonder at the ancient cycad ferns, only one of over 600 plant species in the gorge. And all the while, the willy wagtails are with us, calling over and over. Eventually, they're helped out by the incredibly beautiful song of the crested bellbird.

The Garden of Eden is a true paradise for those who belong, and it certainly exerts a spirituality all of its own. It shouldn't be possible for it to exist within the harsh reality that surrounds us. But somehow, it does.

One reality hits home all too soon, as we lung-burst our way up and out of the cool gorge and emerge once more into the blazing, arid heat: it is hot! And getting hotter! The water we're carrying is getting less, and the less fit people are getting slower; but it's time to pick up the pace.

The guide tells us it is because the wagtails' report is due in - and if it's detrimental, then the Giant Devil Dingo could be summoned to chase us away. Personally, I think it's because our transport a-waits, and if we're much later, the driver is likely to call in a rescue chopper.

But what do I know. It could equally be the McIntyre factor coming into play, - so, just in case, I pick up the pace and try not to keep looking over my shoulder.

Darwin.

You can say a lot of things about the tropical city of Darwin. Historically, it is the capital of the Northern Territory, established on a large harbour in 1869. Back then, its gaol on Fanny Bay needed no walls, the isolation and inhospitable surroundings making captivity a more attractive proposition than the alternative of what lay beyond its boundaries. Psychologically, the city's destruction by 'Cyclone Tracy' at Christmas time in 1974 has had a lasting effect. One guy we met was nine years old at the time. He still views life as existing on the edge and lives accordingly. And he's not the only one.

So, get away from the guide books and glossy brochures and let us tell you quite simply that Darwin is brilliant. I can't put a finger on it, but the place has that certain special 'something' about it. Maybe it's that, 'life can end tomorrow' view; or maybe it's just the number of young folk about town, courtesy of the Armed Forces, who've moved into the Northern Territory en masse. The streets and bars and cafes may be full to overflowing with the young - but unlike in Britain, with its binge drinking and yob culture which are making town centres 'No-Go' areas, never once did we feel threatened in Darwin. Quite the reverse, we felt a part of the city.

Or maybe it's the outdoor cafes and bars, at night illuminated by hundreds of thousands of tiny lights strung through the trees which line the streets. Maybe it's the atmosphere generated by the throngs attending the night markets, where the niceties surrounding 'Green issues,' so ingrained in other states, are ignored. Here you can still buy sharks' teeth, crocodile skulls and kangaroo testicles [dried, and tied into the shape of a purse]. You name it, it's here.

And above all; the friendliest of people imaginable: Time seems to be of no consequence; a place where people have time for you.

Yes! We like Darwin very, very much, and that comes as a bit of a surprise, after the day we've had getting here. My mood had been in free-fall since a brush with an over-officious security officer at Alice Airport, a 'uniform' who seemed to think you're a pansy if you want to travel with mossie repellent in your pocket, a too-laid-back coach driver who didn't work to airport departure times making us late for the flight, and finally, a credit card which kept coming out of the machine saying "Refer to Bank."

So, stress levels on maximum - until Darwin exerted its magic: a special sunset over Darwin Harbour, the relaxation process completed with a couple of beers in a lush, tropical garden surrounded by the chorus of the Northern Territory at night.

The Big Stick Approach:

What does a kangaroo with one leg have in common with a bright green pigeon?

Answer! Neither took any notice of the stick!

Confused? Okay, so I've been a little obtuse, but the stick is of vital importance to people visiting the beaches in Aboriginal Arnhem Land.

On each beach we visit [and this one is Coral Bay], it stands some ten feet from the edge of the fabulously blue, Arafura Sea. With its gnarled digit pointing skywards, it is saying to the visitor, 'Don't go any closer: Salt Water Crocs!'

We know a twelve-footer has made his home in the bay, as we saw him yesterday. And overnight he's demonstrated his hunting ability - hence the corpse of the one-legged kangaroo being gently brushed by the tide.

And if that's not enough, throw in the patrolling hammerhead sharks, the Great Whites, the giant sting rays, and jellyfish that will kill you quicker than any of the above. So we resolve to obey the stick, before exchanging looks with the strange looking green pigeon perched on top of it. The bird ignores our laboured approach across the soft sand; maybe he knows he's not in danger, but his head keeps bobbing just the same.

We bob too - you know, just in case the croc is in the bush behind us. [They like it in there.] But any thoughts of danger are pushed to one side as we take in this part of the Coberg Peninsula in remote Aboriginal Arnhem Land.

It's a forty-five minute flight over Van Dieman's Gulf to get to this true wilderness - a flight in the care of a pilot who introduces himself, "Hi! I'm Steve!"

Then, somewhat disconcertingly, he adds, "You the Smalls? No? No worries, just climb in the back and we'll be off."

Not quite the formalities of British Airways, but there again our captain is dressed in a tee shirt [it looked like he'd just wiped the windscreen of his four-seater plane with it], shorts and a pair of thongs. [On his feet!] We share the plane with a lawn mower and a tray of tomatoes.

The flight takes us over the coastal fringes of the Territory. The waterways are muddy and sandy, and as they discharge into the Gulf, they affect the very sea itself. The area is no longer blue and inviting - more dirty yellow fading to turquoise, with mushroom shapes, blossoming beneath the surface, moved by invisible currents in a timeless turmoil.

It looks positively unhealthy.

Steve lands us like a veteran on a dusty, red runway cut out of the coastal scrub. No tarmac. Just dirt and wild buffalo poo which shoots up from the wheels, giving rise to thoughts of a propeller confrontation with a couple of tons of beef on the hoof.

We are handed over to Keith, a clean-cut, youthful looking thirty year old who greets us like long-lost relatives. And no wonder: guests are at a premium and the wilderness lodge has failed twice in the recent past, thanks to cyclones and its remoteness.

The lodge has a name derived from the Seven Aboriginal Seasons on the Coberg. Their seasonal changes are much more complex than the European idea of Northern Australia where it is either in the 'wet' or in the 'dry.' Instead, the Aboriginal peoples have seasons of lightning [November], thunder, rain, greening, wind, storms, fire and cloudless blue. The observant reader will have spotted that we seem to have eight spirits of Aboriginal origin, not seven - but who am I to argue?

I am pleased to establish that we are on cloudless blue time. The friendliness, the magic and utter tranquillity of Coral Bay - and a lunch consisting of prawns the size of your forearm, all combine to put on hold any dangers the wilderness might have in store for us.

The Philosophical Bushman:

"Croc!" The cry assailed our ears.

I hadn't seen the salty, but it seemed the sensible thing to do - leave the water. Quickly!

It was Jim who'd given the shout; who else but the ex-Australian Army veteran who paddled about the place in ragged shorts and cut-off wellies, the tops wrapped tightly in camouflage puttees.

We had been with Jim most of the day and our first expedition with him had established a sort of love - hate relationship. As a guide - and you need one on these uncharted walks through the open eucalypt forest to far flung beaches - there could be no equal. He knows his stuff: shrikes, whistling kites and other smaller birds of prey being 'bombed' by majestic, and territorial, sea eagles; reef sharks patrolling the tidal margins; even the very shy and rare quoll puts in a command performance for him. This cat-like creature, with striped coat to the rear end, remains unknown to many Australians, but is identified to us with relish.

Unfortunately, Jim is also a philosopher. Classically taught in another life and another place, he seems to live his life now in a perpetual dilemma. Immensely proud of his army service, he now tries to live out his philosophy of being at one with nature: harm nothing and no-one. One example from today's walk: we shared Jim on our trek with a French bloke whose father-in-law was a big game hunter in Africa. He poses Jim a problem: Should his relative kill a rogue elephant which destroyed three villages, or not?

No answer! Instead, a look of bewilderment descends across those piercing eyes of his: And stays there. That's the problem with philosophy; there are no answers - just a series of ever more complex questions. It's no wonder Jim is at home in this wilderness. Real life – Sorry - I can't say that. The Frenchman's life in Guadeloupe is as real as the African hunter's life - which is as real as Jim's - or yours or mine for that matter. So we'll try again.....

It's no wonder Jim is at home in this wilderness. The dilemmas facing ordinary people in a world far removed from this place would certainly be too much for him to cope with.

Jim stretched out his long legs and ate up the distance along the soft sand. It was as if he was making an effort to leave the unanswerable elephant questions far behind.

I later discovered that on his days off, he doesn't head for the bright lights and fleshpots of Darwin, or further a-field to his elderly parents' property outside Townsville. No! For rest and relaxation he goes bush, settles down by some crocodile wallow and stays there for days at a time. His friends at the wilderness lodge have had to go and look for him on a few occasions. "The days just seem to fade into one another," he explains.

And that is something we've already realized for ourselves in this land, a land which is still pretty much as God created it.

"Croc!"

I leave the limpid and inviting blue waters of the swimming pool to answer the call from the headland. A crocodile is in the bay below. It's not huge, but big enough to view without the aid of binoculars. A twelve footer or thereabouts - and probably, after what's left of the 'roo on the beach. Tough! The pack of dingoes got most of that carcass yesterday.

Dripping wet and towel-less, I am faced with my own dilemma: to the beach for a close-up look at Mister Croc, or the pool? The sun glitters on the pool, the blue melting into the brightly coloured tropical flowers that surround it. A soft breeze ruffles across the face of the bay, the incoming tide moving the predator closer and closer to the shore.

Pool or beach?

Decisions! Decisions!

It's enough to send you bush.

The White Aborigine:

I need you to meet an extraordinary young man: J.J. - mid twenties, bronzed, fair hair and blue eyes. He is now a professional guide to the watery and dangerous wonderland that surrounds our wilderness sanctuary.

The reason he's special is because he is one of only a handful of people with a European heritage to actually have been born in Aboriginal Arnhem Land - the product of a Swedish mission nurse and a journeyman engineer father.

And there's nothing that escapes J.J.'s attention: A swirl in the water, a shadow, the tip of a fin. His knowledge is not the knowledge gleaned from books or universities, but learned as being as much a part of the landscape as the Aboriginal people in the community where he was born and raised. He has taken their knowledge and the Aboriginal name they honoured him with.

He showed us so much that was beyond our ken: cruising reef sharks; lemon sharks; shy Irrawadi dolphins, who were determined to lose us in the reef systems; schools of milk fish; tarpon; flying fish; even the morwong or mother-in-law fish - so called because it tastes so bad that she is the only person you'd feed it to.

The list of species is near endless. Only the salt water crocs avoid us on our part of the ocean. Instead: trepang slugs, starfish, turtles, sting rays, manta rays; even the first lethal jellyfish of the season, - the Irrigangi.

That particularly monstrous jello was just off an un-named sandbar opposite the striking red cliffs of Gunners' Quoin, and its identification prompted one of the very few family history stories we have connecting us with the Northern Territory. I won't name the bloke, to save embarrassment, but he belonged to the Hogg's of Wollongong. He managed to make the medical journals as the only man [back then] to have ever survived an attack by the lethal jellyfish. Exhaustive tests on this unique guinea pig proved beyond doubt that what saved him was the vast amount of alcohol swilling about in his blood stream.

J.J. found the story so funny, he nearly died laughing. A missed backward step, and over the side he went. The water may be clear blue, warm and inviting, but no amount of the joshing and joking that followed could ever eliminate from my mind's-eye that look on his face as he emerged from the depths.

It only lasted a brief second, but I reckon I now know what sheer terror looks like.

A Croc at Bedtime:

I nearly stood on the damned thing!

For the first time since we'd arrived in Wilderness Arnhem Land, I was more intent on using my eyes to find the perfect location for the sunset over the Arafura Sea, than being aware of lurking dangers.

And that beach would do nicely. In a rush, I alighted from the land cruiser complete with its bull bars, huge Bowie knife strapped to the sun visor and a policeman's truncheon under the driver's seat [very Crocodile Dundee] to be immediately captivated by the huge, red ball sinking slowly toward the dark millpond of a barely moving ocean.

"Look out!" A shout from over there!

"Croc!" from somewhere else.

"Croc!" shouted my wife.

The warnings piled in, one on top of another.

"Where?" I ask, astonished.

Then I nearly stood on the damned thing!

"There!" everyone shouted in unison.

Between us, we must have scared the living daylights out of the poor wee thing. Six feet long, it was still young enough to be scared of its own shadow. It slithered into the ocean with a bad tempered flick of its tail, turned to let the wavelets wash over its gnarled back and eyed its spot on the beach.

I was getting into the swing of things now. "Shark!" I cried, pointing urgently at the water. My companions run – no-one wants to miss the expected confrontation between Australia's top two predators.

We subjected the ocean to intense scrutiny, only to find that the 'shark,' was a piece of seaweed turning with the tide. Everyone collapsed with laughter onto the sand whilst the crocodile hung about, no doubt trying to decide if its eviction was permanent.

The two whiskies early in the evening seem to have worked wonders on the small assembly; a 'devil may care' attitude pervades, taking over from common sense. But it didn't stop the champagne and beer flowing in celebration of life and the end of a perfect day. We trade tales of rainbow bee-eaters, jabaroos, micro-bats and a whole lot more of God's creatures.

The noise of our beach party gets louder, whilst the camera shutters click merrily away on automatic. A wild, heavily-horned buffalo, a feral pig, and several Timorese cows all shuffle and snuffle closer to see what the ruckus is. A roar of laughter startles them; they jump back, snorting and pulling faces, before moving off, obviously unimpressed.

Even our croc gives up all pretence of a night's kip on his beach and, with a forlorn look, submerges.

The Forsaken Settlement:

Remember all that has been written so far about the dangers of the sea? - The salties, the sharks, and all the rest, epitomized by the stick on the beach. Well.....

We're in the water, unwittingly re-enacting the invasion of British Marines, who waded ashore here on 27th October, 1838. Unlike us, they arrived armed to the teeth and carried out their 'opposed landing' manoeuvres under the bewildered gaze of some 400 Aboriginal tribesmen.

We are at the remote Victoria Settlement, plodging through the thigh-deep, dangerous waters because it's practically the only way for the modern-day visitor to get here. Plodging carries with it mixed emotions: excitement and trepidation in equal parts: Excitement at experiencing, for a few short hours, history in the raw. You can guess at the trepidation part.

The 400 Aborigines didn't fight the Brits on the beach - nor anywhere else, for that matter. In fact, as it worked out, apart from a flogging or two, followed by a night in a water-well for thieving naval stores, relationships between them were pretty good.

The tribe had occupied the area for about seven thousand years, and perhaps their laid-back approach to the influx of new faces was something to do with the fact that they'd never been totally cut off from the outside world. One such association was that with the Macassan Trepangers,* who had been visiting the place for hundreds of years and they were certainly happy enough to avoid the attentions of pirates by anchoring their ships and expensive cargoes under the protection of the British guns.

The British population at Victoria Settlement also numbered about 400 - mostly made up of sailors and marines, who went about expanding the Empire with a typical Protestant work ethic. Storehouses, docks, a church, and a hospital were built as well as quarters for the five officers who had brought their wives into the wilderness with them.

It is reported that one of these five ladies became very rich during the eleven year life of the settlement. I would hazard a guess that it wasn't for her expertise in needlework!

We make the shore unharmed, dry ourselves off, take a swig of precious water, and we're off on a long, hot, sweaty march through the eucalyptus forest. Eventually, we arrive at the graveyard of the fledgling colony. It is described in a 19th century letter home as 'A beautiful little spot,' but in reality, nothing can be further from the truth.

The letters to England made the settlement sound like Surrey, the harbour like Portsmouth - all in order to get more resources allocated to this outpost of civilization.

I look about at the scrub and the abandoned, vine-covered graves. Over forty people lie buried beneath our feet in this hot and humid wilderness. Never before had I come so close to understanding the true cost of Empire.

The first to die and be interred was an Aboriginal youth. Cause of death: T.B. And the arrival of that most feared disease must have shaken the colony to its roots.

Of course the Aborigine doesn't have a marked grave. In fact, only three of the forty plus graves on the site do, one of which remembers a Mrs Lambrick, who died with her baby during childbirth. She was in her mid-forties.

A sad story in a sad place:
However, the colony was needed for two reasons: firstly, to keep the French out of Northern Australia. And that was a bit of a joke. When two French ships did arrive, the shore batteries remained silent. Instead of a fight, they had a party, and when the French left they expressed the view that the Brits were crazy for wanting to stay in the place.

The second reason: the Dutch. They had sewn up the trade with the East Indies and were making huge profits. Of course, we British wanted in. By using the colony's port [Port Essington] and the new ocean charts, it was hoped that the Dutch monopoly could be circumvented.

Unfortunately, things didn't work out. When the population of the colony emerged from the protection afforded by the gun batteries, following a huge cyclone which hit during the night of 25th November, 1839, they found most of their good work undone. Basically, the cyclone knocked the stuffing out of them.

A break-down of military discipline followed: disease [particularly malaria], the stifling heat and, most of all, boredom, eventually brought the colony to its knees. Not even the successful 3,200 kilometre overland trek from Brisbane to Port Essington by the explorer, Ludwig Leichhardt, in 1844, could raise the spirits and the settlement was forsaken in 1849 - the third failure of the British to establish a permanent presence in the Northern Territory.

Now, there's nothing to remember the men and women who strove for a new life here - just the wild buffalo, cattle, deer, ponies, crumbling walls and three headstones.

Time to leave: On our return to the beach, we find the tide has turned. And that's bad news. Our boat is bobbing up and down in chest-high water. Worse! – It is now some one hundred yards from the shore.

The warning of the beach marker is burned indelibly into my consciousness - and I could have done without our guide reading from a colonist's diary just before we left. It describes this very beach:

'Alligators are numerous…… Shot a formidable beast ten feet long which devoured a favourite dog of mine…..and attacked the camp.'

Ah well! Where did I put that pioneering spirit?

* Fishermen from the Southern Celebes seeking turtle, dugong and trepang sea slugs, the latter being destined for the Chinese market, where they commanded good prices, based on the belief that they held magical powers.

Coming to terms with Life:

Now, I have no wish to be maudlin', but it's difficult not to be dragged down to something approaching despair when the company you are in, and the subject matter, is particularly mournful.

The bush walk to the ruins on Hospital Point turned out to be an unattractive one, beset as I was by the continuous attentions of the stinging and biting green ants. They are everywhere.

Not that the ants seem to be bothering our guide, a pretty twenty year old lass with legs like tree trunks. In fact, so muscle-bound are her limbs, that the soft sand is no more of a deterrent to her than the North African desert was to Rommel.

And she is garrulous, not miserable - that accolade goes to Jean, a middle-aged French guy, who is a particularly dough-faced individual and apparently close to tears half the time. He is supposed to have been in the French equivalent of the S.A.S. and is now involved in the close protection of government officials - but that makes me suspicious, as the couple of 22 S.A.S. men I've worked with wouldn't admit to being members of such an elite.

However, his wife, Martinne, has given us plenty of background information. He is currently working for the U.N. in Timor - sort of a 'holiday' posting after the Second Iraq War, where they had lost a lot of good friends in a car bombing. Seemingly Jean is suffering from some kind of stress - not sleeping, nightmares, etc.

It was nice of Martinne to tell us this - and I'm too much of a gentleman to say, "But I thought the French weren't in Iraq?"

It also seems a strange place to come for R and R. There are enough critters within a cricket ball's throw of our luxury camp that would kill you quicker than Saddam's mob.

My nightmares involve hand-sized spiders and unlit, midnight trips to the outside loo - but I reckon Jean's problems had a lot to do with Martinne, as her favourite phrase or saying was: "But it's not your fault, Jean."

Anyway, there we were on a sandy, low promontory in a tropical Garden of Eden with our young guide, who was busily opening seed-heads belonging to the ironbark tree, as I arrive, huffing and puffing. The berries are small and bright red, and settle in the palm of her hand:

"......just the right mixture of water and seed," she was saying, "And an Aboriginal woman can procure her own miscarriage with these. Get the mix wrong, and she dies."

She's off again, is our lass and I follow in her wake, hoping she washes her hands before lunch. Before long she starts grabbing green leaves off another ironbark.

"As a contraceptive, the woman could burn these and stand over the smoke, legs apart, to make her temporarily infertile."

I am just whispering to Jean that it's better to go to the chemist, when our leader continues, [I can tell she doesn't like interruptions, as she fixes me with a wintry smile]: "And I'd rather be a woman than a man. For you," again she looks at me, this time gleefully, "Take a sharp stone, make a hole in the penis near the base where the semen enters and leave the hole open. The semen escapes during intercourse. Want kids - then close the hole up with something."

I couldn't help it. Turning to my new French companion, I nudge him and say, "You'd be alright, Jean. If you had a little accident, Martinne would say, 'It's not your fault, Jean.' "

I am rewarded by his first smile of the week.

The rest of the walk was good. In fact, all you needed was the beat of far-away drums, to accompany the crashing in the tree canopy above us, to really believe you were in Africa.

But there are no drums here. Arnhem Land may be native-owned but the vast majority of Aborigines have opted for the chemist shops, pizzerias and the satellite televisions on offer in Darwin and elsewhere.

I for one can't blame them. I was never one to accept the Victorian noble savage idea, introduced by politicians to explain away the defeat of the British Army by the Zulus at Isandhlwana. Nor can I blame the indigenous people for rejecting their old tribal laws, when you can get a spear through the leg, be killed even, for being cheeky, not showing respect to your elders, or for eating the wrong food.

Just in case you think I'm getting on a high horse here, I should tell you that I took that information on Aboriginal law from the book, 'Gagudju Law,' by Bill Neidjie, who set down the traditions of his people before they were lost: And good on 'im!

We are in complete agreement, Bill and I. It is vitally important for the young to know of their roots. It is part of them for all time - gives them a starting point from which to grow.

For the record, I do my best to impart my thought-through, philosophical position to Jean - you know; something to act as a counterweight to Martinne's debilitating constancy. He struggles with the concept - or the English language - or both; so I simplify things for him:

"Jean, mate. Shit happens!"

Bill Neidgie:
"My children got to hang onto this story. It's important. I hang onto this story all my life. My father tell me this story. My children can't lose it."

Patsy and Ian Patterson, from their family history book, 'Of Caste and Clan:'
"All in all we are pleased with our family…… We are humbled by the travails of their lives, excited by their example and grateful for their stories."

Low Point:

Low Point in more ways than one! Three children have arrived. They wanted to go to Disney; instead, their parents and grandparents have brought them to be interactive with nature. That seems to include giving them a stick with which to poke anything that moves.

"Be careful with that spider, son," my wife chides one of them, who is trying to encourage a 'big 'un with hairy legs and fangs' into a plastic bag.

"It's okay," he answers. "It doesn't have enough venom to kill me and I want to take it indoors to show my granny."

Excellent idea!

It's all too much for the best guide around - Philosopher Jim. He's donned his ragged shorts, a shirt he nicked from the army and has gone bush until they leave. I doubt whether we'll see him again. Pity! - He's a good bloke.

So, it's a bush walk to Low Point without him; a low, red-rock headland dividing two stunning beaches. Eagles and sharks: Sharks and eagles.

And green ants.

Our leader brushes past one of their curled leaf nests - and they are out defending it. Only our leader is gone, striding out of range before the blighters can react. It's tail-end Charlie here who has to fend off the attention of dozens of the biting creatures. They are in my socks, down my shirt, under my hat.

Seemingly you can bite the rear ends off and get a lemony drink from them. Real bush tucker! No thanks! I'll have my drink from a can. For once, my idea of, 'I'll leave things from Mother Nature alone, and they'll leave me alone,' doesn't work.

High humidity with heat like a stove. Mosquitoes bite the bits the ants don't. I have so much anti-bug spray on, I should be able to nuke the jungle for a fifty yard radius. Only the Low Point mossies laugh at poison and take revenge for their less hardy cousins.

I wander off for a photo or two, only to find myself alone in a mangrove swamp close to a beach. It is rocky in places, ironstone worn away into strange configurations by the relentless heat and sea.

I look at the water's edge: A movement. Reef shark! It swerves away from a small, pitted rock.

Could it be? Surely not! I stand and watch and the rock doesn't move. It must have been my eyes, but I'm still not sure.

There is not much distance between the ocean and the precipice at the back of the beach, so I move behind a boulder - a big boulder - and peer out.

I know I've made a lot of the saltwater crocodiles in this section of our Northern Territory journey, but they are the number one predator and deserve respect. And these ambush experts are plentiful already, with numbers expected to increase unless the government withdraws their protected status.

Anyway, they have my attention. I continue to watch the rock.

The rock closes its eyes and sinks below the surface.

'Bugger this for a game of conkers,' I say to myself, and I'm off.

Just as well as it turned out, for at once, I realize the danger I had put myself in. The tide is running in behind me as fast as a steam train; perfect conditions for rocks with appetites.

I climb. I climb fast, to where the boulders are bigger. They force my pace to a crawl, yet it would take a bloody good croc to get me up here. Not so the snakes, of course, who like to bask in the spaces between the rocks which radiate the day's heat into the evening.

I make my way back toward the Wilderness Lodge – slowly, and testing every step. The sun is going and the backside's twitching, but I make it.

The thought of a relaxing swim fills my mind, but I've reckoned without the three young Tarzans, who are doing their lung-bursting, yodelling best, whilst swinging from the trees and 'bombing' the pool.

Kids or croc? Croc or kids?

The Whole World is Food and the Eater of Food.

It is not even dawn and we are woken by a commotion outside our shuttered fly-screen that serves as a window. We lie there, unwilling to move whilst it's still dark, yet trying to work out what is going on out there. It's not the wallaby, nor her baby – they are content to snuffle and scrat….. We wait.

Dawn comes quickly, to reveal an enormous amount of thrush-like, bottle green birds in the tree a mere six feet from our heads. The sky lightens and the reason for the rude awakening becomes clear. The innocuous looking tree with gnarled trunk and few leaves, which looked half dead on our way to bed, has burst into life with the steady overnight rain.

It's a sandpaper fig, now heavy with fruit and full of life.

Our headland home is alive with birds. They come and go, squabble, occasionally forcing each other to drop their berries for the earth-bound, but eager, wallabies. It took an age to tease the names out of the encyclopaedia on native birds. They may have different plumage, but they're all fig birds: male, female and juvenile.

Four hours later, and we are on a pristine beach by the ochre-coloured, wedge-shaped headland of Gunners' Quoin. The beach is unnamed, yet that's not surprising, as another seven hundred miles of unnamed headlands and beaches stretch out before us.

An unnamed beach - until now! It wasn't the customary sharks patrolling the shallows just a couple of yards from the sand that attracted us, but the smell of putrefaction. We follow our noses and it isn't long before we reach the source - a huge sea turtle, with its head and shoulders bitten clean off.

"Croc!" said the guide, crouching low. "And recent too….." He paused to sniff the air and read the marks on the sand: "Certainly within a couple of tides." Resuming his full height, he added, "It's the five metre guy. He'll be sitting out there right now watching us."

Our eyes become fixated on the ocean and remain so, despite assurances that we are too far from the water's edge to be in danger.

But the saltwater crocodile is a clever beast. It doesn't eat the whole carcass of its kill at once; it leaves some, knowing that dingoes will be attracted to it.

"Then it'll float in on the tide, conserving energy, hoping to ambush whatever is having a feed," he explains.

Within yards of the turtle is a pile of water buffalo bones, now devoid of any flesh and bleached white by the sun. A less recent victim of the fifteen footer.

"He got this one by the nose," our guide says, nudging the remnants of the skull with the toe of his boot. "Bit half the head right off. The beast bled to death right here. Recycling we call it."

"That's a novel way of putting it," I butt in.

"Can't use the 'death' word here for fear of putting visitors off." A statement thrown over his shoulder as he moves off.

Trouble was, I couldn't tell if he was joking or not.

Six crocodile-slither marks across the beach later, and a mystery: A beaten-up old galvanized aluminium row boat, or dorey - holed and abandoned.

"What we think happened here is that a fisherman [perhaps fishermen], met his end prematurely. Some unscrupulous ships' captains tow twenty or thirty of these small boats out to a reef and pay peanuts to youngsters in need of money to sit there and fish illegally for barramundi, dorey, or whatever. Accidents happen; a sudden storm perhaps. And because it's illegal, the disappearances don't get reported."

Nothing is said. What can you say? But we don't return via our newly-named 'Ambush Beach.' No! For us it's the hard walking through a mosquito-filled paper bark swamp, complete with crocodile wallows and herds of wild cattle.

We are told of the time when a group of bird watchers found themselves surrounded by two fighting salties to the front of them, and an inquisitive herd of buffalo pushing in from their rear. But, it's deemed safer this way rather than the beach, now that the tide is on the turn.

We also get to view the black red-tailed parrots, which were suddenly all about us, crashing through branches and indulging in a parrot-type brawl. Maybe numbering between forty and fifty, their raucous calls, intensely loud and aggressive, make us believe that they're encouraging one another to further boisterous, juvenile antics.

The reason: "They're drunk!"

[And that's not as stupid as it sounds, as I have seen starlings and sparrows in England feeding on the discarded dregs of home-brew kits, getting so tipsy they then fall off the neighbourhood garden fences and washing lines.]

Here, in the wilderness of the Northern Territory, it's an abundance of eucalyptus trees all coming into flower at the same time. Parrots head in from all over as the word goes out, "Party time!"

The flowers ferment in their gut and for the less scientifically-minded amongst us, the guide puts it succinctly. "They go a bit crazy."

Eventually, we emerge from the coastal scrub and onto a sandy beach lapped by the waters of a languid ocean. Only this time we have signs of civilization - the boat pier which services our encampment.

We pause, for despite our overwhelming desire to get our boots off, take a shower and eat, it has been known for eight foot long hammerheads to cruise in the area of the pier, just waiting to join in a feeding frenzy when the fishing charter returns to disgorge its contented passengers and the fish offal.

But not today: Instead, we have to make do with an array of small, brightly- coloured fish that bite at, and chase, one another. Two young black-tipped reef sharks put in an appearance. They dart in, swish their powerful tails; veer away. Then the highlight: From his backpack our guide produces several fish heads, which had obviously seen better days.

"Watch!" he commands.

The moment they hit the water, a moray eel slithers out from beneath his rock: But only half way. He's too nervous at the excitement being generated by his fellows, as they dart, flash, veer, tear and taste, the ecstasy forcing them to rise above the surface of the water in a violent thrashing.

Then it's over. In moments the fish lose interest, calm down, leaving the small flakes of flesh that are settling in the crevices to the razor-sharp teeth of the eel.

Too soon we have to leave. We are already late for dinner - something that will make the chef gnash his teeth and thrash about. But, of course, we needn't have worried. He never serves anything he's not completely satisfied with, so we have time for a whisky or two or three.

And above our heads, above the swirling ceiling fans, a fight to the death goes on: And on. Geckos cover the ceiling. I count fifteen [but they keep moving] of these voracious little hunters, who seem to have temporarily finished off the local mosquito and insect population and now seem intent on making supper out of each other. The larger, fat ones stalk the medium-sized ones, who in turn would just love to sink their teeth into the poor little guys.

Our red mullet, squid and barramundi duly arrive. We munch on, now oblivious to the battles for survival that go on all about us, whether it's in the bush, on the beach, in the sea or above our heads. Our need for food consumes all else.

But one thing is for sure: from what we have witnessed since before dawn, our deep-thinking philosopher friend in ragged shorts is right - The Whole World is Food and the Eater of Food.

Darwin: The Return.

It's only been a week in the wilderness, yet it feels strange to see traffic lights, well-tended grass verges, and people sitting outside pavement cafes enjoying a long lunch or lingering over coffee.

How Jim, the bushman; J.J. and friends; who live in the 'Out there' all the time, cope when they do eventually succumb to the delights of Darwin, I don't know.

Well, I do know - they can't cope. And to be honest, if I was of their mind-set, I would become a recluse too; give 'it' all away, exchange all the delights of a modern society, for a headland bush camp or the deck of a charter boat.

But I'm not a loner. I like people. I also like watching people, and now, within minutes of being returned to the city, we plunge into one of the lively café-cum-pubs.

I get chatting to a bloke emptying the litter bins. He's from Adelaide and couldn't get a start in life back home. So now he has a sixty thousand bucks a year job carting away the Council's rubbish - and the money is guaranteed for three years. It will be enough to give him his stake money to try again in South Australia.

He moves on - work to do in the thirty-eight degree temperatures. With the humidity at a sticky seventy per cent, I don't envy him one bit. I'm sweating profusely - and I'm sitting still. It is so humid that the clothes in your suitcase become damp in an instant, and you just know mildew trouble is brewing.

We take bushman Jim's advice: 'Do little or nothing between twelve and four' – but, of course, that option isn't open to anyone intent on making a buck. I sit and worry about my bin-man friend working the mall.

His view may be different, but for me there is no denying that Darwin is an exciting place; more so after darkness falls, when the streets are full of people, laughter, light, and the racket of thousands of rosella parrots settling into the tree-tops for another sultry night.

Goodbye Australia

There is a long wait for our plane. It needs a new 'bit', which unfortunately is somewhere a long way away in a country I have never even heard of. So we wait in the crowded airport lounge, and then later, by a rather nice hotel pool.

Time to reflect on yesterday's parting.....

It had been about eighty years since my immediate family first stood on the beach at Blacksmiths, the Great War behind them and a good future beckoning, at least for their children. The coal mines of Northumberland, T.B., hunger, unemployment, bad housing and an uncaring government gone but not forgotten – or forgiven.

My nostalgia is working overtime; it threatens to overwhelm me, as I stand up to the knees in the boiling surf. This – Blacksmiths - is a special place for us; no less so for many others. A few weeks ago, just where we are standing now, a young woman was swept away to her death. She was chosen; her two young children, standing beside her, left untouched by the ocean's frightening undertow. It pulls at our legs now; not wanting to release us - then is gone, re-grouping, to come again.

The young lady was unknown to us, as were our forebears, so perhaps my mood has been influenced by something else. Perhaps it is the plaintive drone of the single-engined aircraft overhead, belonging to Pelican Airways. Tomorrow that very 'plane will separate us from this, our adopted home. I know that my stomach will churn, eyes fill and throat catch as I look down at the ocean, at the inlets and homes far below. I never really want to leave. Perhaps I should follow the example of that ancestor of my wife's, the First Fleet Marine, who deserted rather than return to Europe. Perhaps this beautiful beach, the life-style embracing sun, sea and sand, have to be paid for by the occasional sacrifice. For us, it is only the constant pain of separation after encounters that are all too brief.

The little 'plane turns south towards the excitement of Sydney. But on the morrow, not for us the incredible harbour, the ferries, nor the bustle of the historic Rocks. No shopping on George Street, no lunch at the Fish Market. Instead, the worries of airport transfers, check-ins and a long, long journey to a cold northern Europe.

A cold homeland, but warmed by so much love from our kids, big and little, and with that thought my melancholy lifts. Did I say, "The life-style embracing sun, sea and sand?" The rain has been unrelenting recently, a mere inconvenience when compared to 'Up North', which appears to be drowning once again. Our beach is windswept, the two metre waves depositing mountains of kelp and dead fish about our ankles. My spirits soar as a chortling fisherman takes our photo; two Poms wrapped in jumpers and cagoules enjoying an Australian summer.

His light-hearted banter ringing in our ears, and all thoughts of desertion evaporating fast, we return to the couch in front of the cricket. It's pretty slow stuff, nothing much happening, so I skim the newspaper:

"Croc loses out:" screams the headline. "A forty year old woman fishing in dense mangroves some three hundred and fifty kilometres north east of Darwin was attacked by a crocodile yesterday. She tried to run but slipped and was grabbed by the leg. As the croc tried to flip her into the water she beat it about the head with a stick. She's now in hospital."

Don't you just love Australia! That fabulous; deceptive; virginous tart!

I can't wait to embrace her again.

But back to the present reality and the end of this traveller's epistle: Perhaps thousands of miles from home is a good place to end - just let the search for the fading footsteps of our exiled ain' folk, peter out in exhaustion, with no punch line, no witty quips, no penetrating insights. We just need to be home - a time to enjoy the security of the familiar..... For a while!

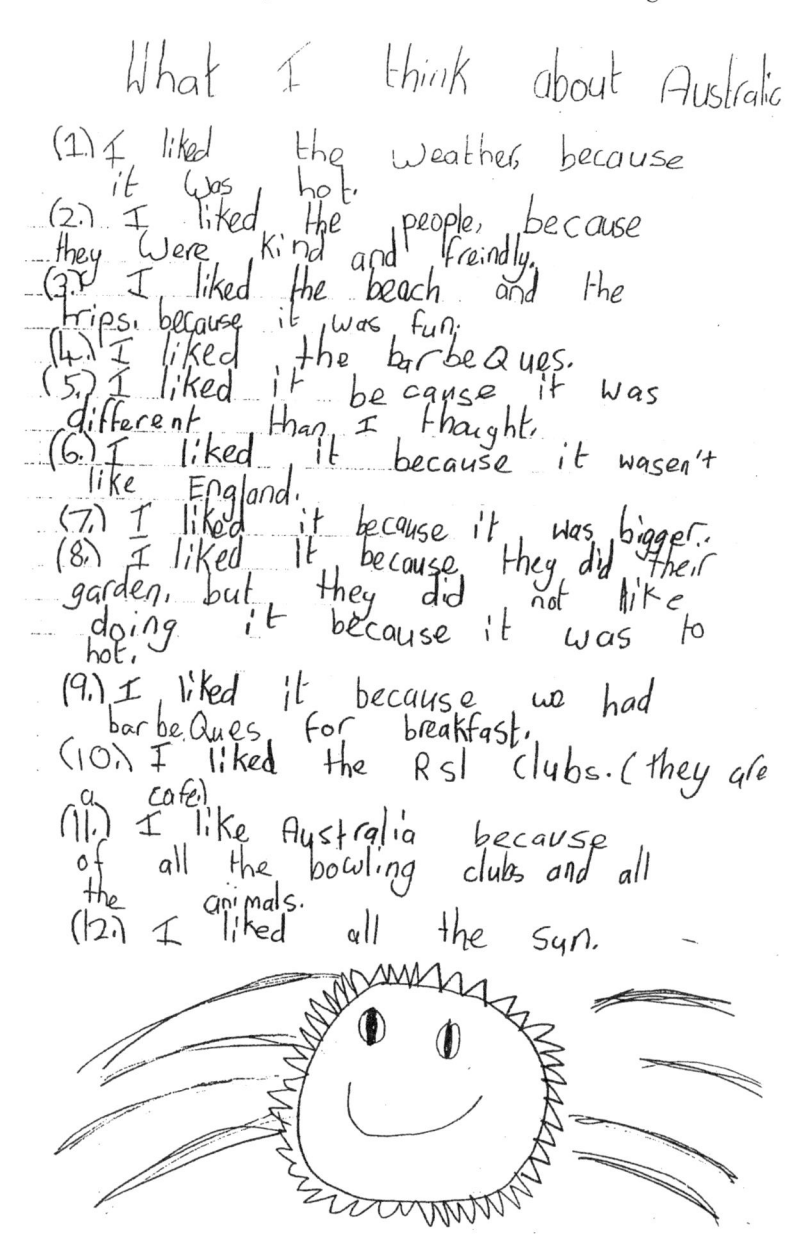

And maybe, just maybe, we've sown the seeds in the next generation!

What I think about Australia

(1.) I liked the weather, because it was hot.
(2.) I liked the people, because they were kind and freindly.
(3.) I liked the beach and the trips, because it was fun.
(4.) I liked the barbeQues.
(5.) I liked it because it was different than I thaught.
(6.) I liked it because it wasen't like England.
(7.) I liked it because it was bigger.
(8.) I liked it because they did their garden, but they did not like doing it because it was to hot.
(9.) I liked it because we had barbeQues for breakfast.
(10.) I liked the Rsl clubs. (they are a cafe.)
(11.) I like Australia because of all the bowling clubs and all the animals.
(12.) I liked all the sun.

Grandaughter Jessica's thoughts about Australia

John Reedhead, adventurer and his wife Sophia Heslop who with their firstborn, Sarah left for the goldfields of Victoria in 1857.

Memorial to James Morrisby, the Yorkshire lad and First Fleet convict who settled at Rokeby, Nr Clarence, Tasmania once he became a free man circa 1805-10.

Part of the Thompson family of Newcastle upon Tyne.

Isabella Johnson holding baby Margaret who died as an infant. Ned who left for Australia. Father William and son Cal who survived an 'inrush of water' in the coal mine where they worked. Cal emingrated to the USA.

Edward and Ramsay Thompson.

Photograph taken at Swansea, Nr Blacksmiths, NSW not long after their arrival.

The three Thompson brothers in later life, Ned, Bill and Ramsay.

The brothers had been appalled by the British Governments treatment of the miners in the north east following the First World War. They emigrated to Australia never to return.

Far right is Margaret Wilson, nee Johnson of Newcastle upon Tyne.
Her sister married into the Thompsons. Successive generations of both families have emigrated to Australia since 1920.

The Hogg family of Lucker Street on their arrival at the coke ovens at Wongawilli, near Wollongong, NSW. The horse was needed as transport into town.
From left: Mary Hogg, Mother Mary with baby Charlie, James 'Jimmy' Hogg on horse. His brother Tom tells the story of how they strained ticks from the milk through their teeth. Charlie served in the Far East with the Army during the Second World War before dying of cancer after his return.

Robert Hogg and his sister Peggy pictured in Newcastle upon Tyne. Peggy later died of Tuberculosis and never got to see Australia.

Thomas Watson Hogg and his wife Mary with daughter Mary after arriving in NSW.

Wongawilli Church

James Hogg, born 1920, Coniston, NSW.
Seen pictured outside Flinders Street Railway Station, Melbourne.
He served in the Middle East, Africa and Borneo during the Second World War.
James is the boy on horseback on previous page.

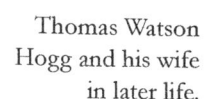

Thomas Watson Hogg and his wife in later life.

Robert Hogg in Australia together with his son Andrew around 1967.
The same Robert as photographed with his sister Peggy on previous page.

IAN & PATSY PATTERSON

Born in 1947 in Newcastle upon Tyne, Ian joined the police force in 1963 - something infinately preferable to the alternative - going down the local coal mine.

He rose to the rank of Detective Inspector and was awarded a scholarship to the University of Birmingham where he gained an Honours Degree in Theology.

Ian retired from the police after twenty five years service following an assault and now lives in a small village in rural Shropshire with his wife, Patsy. His two children and six grandchildren live in nearby Shrewsbury.

After his retirement Ian became embroiled in genealogical research, particularly in the field of Scottish Border Gypsies and that of his families who have emigrated to Australia, voluntarily or not, since 1788. This extensive travel and research throughout Australia, Scotland and elsewhere has formed the basis for further books.

Now available:

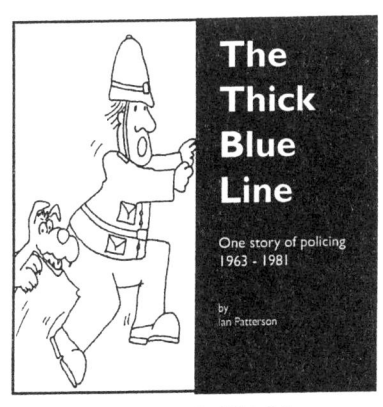

The Thick Blue Line

One story of policing 1963 - 1981

by
Ian Patterson

ISBN 0-9548793-2-5
www.getpublishing.co.uk